THE
SEA
REMEMBERS

This book is dedicated to Philippe Tailliez

THE SEA REMEMBERS

Shipwrecks and Archaeology

Edited by Peter Throckmorton

From Homer's Greece to the Rediscovery of the *Titanic*

BARNES
&NOBLE
B O O K S
NEW YORK

Contributors

General Editor
Peter Throckmorton
Adjunct Professor, Nova University
Oceanographic Center, Dania, Florida.

Willard Bascom
Professional oceanographer and
engineer. Deepwater archaeology
pioneer.

Mensun Bound
Director of Maritime Archaeological
Research Department (MARE), Oxford
University.

Emily Cain
Research and Co-ordinating Officer,
Hamilton-Scourge Project, Hamilton,
Ontario.

Margaret Crowther
Archaeological specialist, researcher
and writer.

Angela Evans
Archaeologist, Medieval and Late
Department, British Museum, London.

Anne G. Giesecke
Founder Historic Preservation Society,
movement for the protection of historic
shipwrecks.

Jeremy Green
Curator, Western Australian Maritime
Museum.

Victoria Jenssen
Conservator, Nautical Archaeology
Division, Parks Canada.

Michael Katzev
Vice-President of the Institute of Nautical
Archaeology of Texas. Director of the
Kyrenia Ship Project.

Parker Marean
Naval architect. Designer and specialist in
ship stability studies.

Colin Martin
Director, Scottish Institute of Maritime
Studies, University of St Andrews.

James Mavor
Emeritus Professor of Ocean Engineering,
Woods Hole Oceanographic Institute.
Designer of deepwater submersible *Alvin*.

J.S. Morrison
Former President Wolfson College,
Cambridge. Director of the Trireme Trust,
Cambridge.

A.J. Parker
Senior lecturer, Department of Classics
and Archaeology, University of Bristol.

Warren Riess
Assistant curator, Newport News
Maritime Museum.

Stephen Rogers
Marine biologist, researcher and writer.

Roger C. Smith
Assistant professor, Institute of Nautical
Archaeology, Texas A&M.

Sheli Smith
PhD Nautical Archaeology, University of
Pennsylvania.

David Switzer
Professor of History, Plymouth State
College, New Hampshire.

Shelley Wachsmann
Institute of Maritime Archaeology,
Caesarea, Israel.

Senior editor James Hughes
Art editor Paul Wilkinson
Cartographic editor Stephen Rogers
Editors Elizabeth Hubbard, Julia Gorton
Picture research Gillian Lythgoe,
Marie-Louise Collard
Editorial research and writing
Margaret Crowther, Stephen Rogers,
Zuza Vrbova
Production Philip Collyer,
Ninki Kinirons

Reconstructions Stephen Biesty,
Roger Finch
Maps Lovell Johns Ltd
Additional artwork Roy Flooks,
Hayward and Martin

Edited and designed by
Mitchell Beazley International Ltd,
Artists House, 14–15 Manette Street,
London W1V 5LB, England

Copyright © 1987 Mitchell Beazley
Publishers

This edition published by Barnes and
Noble Inc.,by arrangement with
Mitchell Beazley International Ltd. part of
Reed International Books Ltd.

1996 Barnes & Noble Books

Filmset by Hourds Typographica,
Stafford, England. Origination by
Gilchrist Bros Ltd, Leeds, England.
Printed in China

The author and the publishers will be
grateful for any information which will
assist them in keeping future editions
up to date. Although all reasonable care
has been taken in the preparation of this
book, neither the publishers nor the
author can accept any liability for any
consequences arising from the use
thereof or from the information
contained herein.

Library of Congress cataloging data
available upon request

ISBN 0 7607 0387 6

M 10 9 8 7 6 5 4 3 2 1

Contents

Editor's acknowledgments

It is impossible in a few words to describe all the influences that made it possible for me to become a nautical archaeologist and, finally, editor of this book. I am indebted to Bruce Norman of the BBC, who first suggested I should take on the job, to Paul Wilkinson the designer, and to James Hughes, who played a role far beyond the normal one of publisher's editor.

The reconstructions by Roger Finch and Stephen Biesty deserve a special mention. These are not just pretty pictures; practically every detail is drawn from archaeological evidence. In the case of the Yassi Ada ship, we have for the first time produced a technical analysis based on data from an archaeological excavation, prepared by an eminent naval architect, Parker Marean. Each of the drawings, which aim to combine technical accuracy with dynamism of viewpoint, is based on current knowledge. But we must always bear in mind that even marine experts disagree on fine points of detail.

On the scholarly side, I am indebted to the late Froelich Rainey, who taught me to glimpse some of the mystery and romance of Homer; and to the late great archaeologists Carl Blegen and Sir Mortimer Wheeler, who encouraged me to follow that star.

If the late Fr Gerard Groote had not put up with my incompetent learning efforts in salvage archaeology when I was very young, I should not have acquired the sustaining conviction that archaeologists have a duty to the past.

Harry Marr, whose grave in our family cemetery is visible as I write these lines, taught me the shipwright's trade so that I could later understand L. Francis Herreshoff's deep knowledge of the maritime past and how it related to the present in the design and contruction of ships.

If my late professors Margaret Mead and Clellan Ford had not encouraged me to follow my bent and be a maverick wanderer in the maritime world, I should never have gotten to a point where my ideas about underwater excavation made sense and received encouragement from Virginia Grace and the late Rodney Young.

Without the active inspiration of the late James Dugan, whose contribution to science in the sea has not been properly recognized, I would never have gone on in Turkey after 1958, and George Bass and I would not have gotten to Cape Gelidonya.

If Peter Stanford, founder of the South Street Seaport Museum, and Karl Kortum of the San Francisco Maritime Museum, had not inspired me, *Snow Squall, St Mary* and *Elissa* might never have happened. I am especially grateful for the facilities and cooperation extended to me by Dr Julian McCreary and the faculty and staff of Nova University Oceanographic Center. I am also very thankful for the help given me by my wife, Catherine Gates Throckmorton.

There are too many others to mention here. Their contributions in the following text speak for themselves. However, a very special word of thanks is due to George Bass, Cemal Pulak and Lars Einarsson, who have very kindly provided material from their work on, respectively, the Bronze Age wreck at Ulu Burun (p.33), the Ottoman wreck at Yassi Ada (p.91), and the 17th century Swedish warship *Kronan* (p.151).

Peter Throckmorton
Newcastle
Maine

An asterisk (*) indicates a reference in the chapter notes at the back of the book relating to the relevant passage in the text.

Foreword

I am glad to write a foreword to *The Sea Remembers* because it provides something for which I have been looking, and I believe will do the same for many readers interested in maritime archaeology.

My own interest came about in the most unlikely way, as chairman of a committee. In 1984, a young archaeologist called Mensun Bound, by origin a Falkland Islander with a passionate and absorbing interest in the sea, persuaded the University of Oxford to recognize the study of marine archaeology by setting up a committee under the name of Oxford University MARE – an acronym for Maritime Archaeological Research, and at the same time the Latin word for sea. Mensun Bound won fame in Italy as "archaeologist of the year" when he excavated what appears to be the first Etruscan wreck to be investigated, dating from the late 7th century BC, following that up with another "first", an Athenian wreck at Dattilo in the Lipari Islands of the 5th century BC, the Athenian century *par excellence* (see chapter 2).

I agreed to become chairman of MARE, and began slowly to get the hang of what was involved, finding particularly exciting the combination of history and archaeology with science and technology, plus the skills of diving. I also began to search for the organizing idea which provided the key to all this activity. Where was the focus of maritime archaeology to be found?

If only I had been able to read *The Sea Remembers* a year or two ago, I could have avoided several false trails on which I wasted time: the fascination of the world under the sea; the technological inventiveness which makes its exploration possible; the excitement of the search for buried treasure; the value and sometimes the beauty and craftsmanship of what is brought up. All these are part of the experience which attracts very different people to maritime archaeology, but they are not its central purpose.

In the end it was my own experience as an historian which led me to the answer that I found most satisfying. I came to see the importance of maritime archaeology as consisting in the recovery of a lost dimension of history: man's encounter with the sea and the role which this has played in the development of human civilization up to the early years of the 20th century.

The chapters which follow illustrate the richness of this dimension in a hundred different ways. For example, the spread of ideas, of religions, of technologies and the arts has again and again taken place by sea. An essential part of that intercourse was trade, for which the sea offered the quickest and safest means of transport.

The sea was as important for politics as for trade. The term "sea power" was coined by the Greeks (*thalassocratia*) to describe the power which enabled Athens, after defeating the Persian empire at sea, to create its own empire in Ionia and the Aegean. The key naval weapon in this takeover was the oared galley, the trireme, now recreated by Professor J.S. Morrison (see p.44).

Voyages of discovery transformed the world, from Vasco da Gama, Columbus, Magellan and Drake, to Captain Cook's exploration of the Pacific from New Zealand to Alaska. It was by sea that North America and Australia were peopled as well as discovered, and the great European emigration of the 19th century was carried overseas on shipboard.

I was delighted to find that Peter Throckmorton had come to much the same conclusion in his introductory chapter, where he writes of maritime archaeology as "the study of a vanished culture". This drew to an end at the close of the 19th century and the replacement of wooden ships with metal, and sail with steam, the end of a maritime tradition which, he reminds us, had lasted some 5,000 years.

Technological developments since the beginning of the 20th century have still further reduced our familiarity with and understanding of the sea. A new dimension of history, the atmosphere, has begun to replace it. Today we travel far more by air than by sea. It is not so much sea power as air power – rockets, ballistic missiles and mastery of the upper atmosphere – which constitutes military strength. The communication of news and ideas, now virtually instantaneous, passes through the air, over but not across the oceans.

There is no need for me to multiply examples. All you have to do is to turn the page and read on, enjoying as much as I have the first comprehensive account I have come across that describes what maritime archaeology has accomplished in little more than 30 years, written by men and women who have been actively engaged in it; an account that also mentions the riches which still remain to be discovered if those old enemies of archaeology, the looters and treasure hunters – the grave robbers of today – do not disperse them first.

The Rt. Hon. Lord Bullock, F.B.A.
St Catherine's College
Oxford

Diving into the past/Introduction

Underwater archaeology has been a hybrid orphan, ever since divers in the South of France began finding ancient shipwrecks just after World War II. For some time these were not even recognized as shipwrecks, being referred to as "fields of amphoras." But at least it was a beginning. Until that time, the vast storehouse of human material on the seabed had been exploited only by treasure hunters, salvage seekers, and local sponge divers.

Now, for the first time, it became possible to conceive of a new kind of treasure from the sea – treasure that would add significantly to the sum of human knowledge.

A brilliant early attempt at the scientific excavation of a shipwreck was carried out 30 years ago by Commandant Philippe Tailliez, working at the Titan wreck off the South of France. The excavation is not well known because Tailliez did not get the support from the archaeological community that he had counted on. Nevertheless, it is a landmark because it showed us all how to go about the job.

Underwater excavation, wrote Tailliez, was a "problem for sailors and divers rather than the archaeologist. How difficult to be all three at once!" Today it is considered simpler to train an archaeologist, photographer or draftsman to dive rather than to try and make archaeologists out of divers. Tailliez did not realize that excavation is the smallest part of most archaeology projects, whether they take place underwater or on land.

Archaeology and the aqualung

In June 1943, "a new and promising device, the result of years of struggle and dreams," was delivered to Commandant J.-Y. Cousteau at Bandol in the French Riviera. This was "an automatic compressed air diving lung conceived by Emile Gagnan and myself." Recording his reactions, Cousteau wrote: "No children ever opened a Christmas present with more excitement than ours when we unpacked the first 'aqualung'. If it worked, diving could be revolutionized."

The invention of the aqualung has indeed revolutionized not only diving, but our understanding of the sea itself, enabling non-specialist divers to explore the shallow edge of continental shelves to a depth of 200–300ft. Now a previously closed world has opened up, revealing much that has never been seen before. As an instrument of change, this simple device is equivalent in kind (though not in scale) to that of the Ford "Tin Lizzie", which provided universal cheap transportation, or the plastic boat (which made cheap yachting available to everybody).

However, for archaeology the immediate impact of the marvelous invention was negative. The aqualung became available to the general public in 1947, and in the next decade every known ancient wreck off the South of France and the Ligurian coast of Italy was destroyed. Tailliez' Titan wreck was the last known intact specimen at the time of its excavation in 1957.

The package that arrived for Cousteau has been the key to a whole new area of human discovery; but it has also opened a Pandora's box of disagreement between those interested in the preservation of sunken historical sites and those preoccupied by salvage and treasure. In the United States, even people of influence have attempted to defend treasure salvage as good old American enterprise. However, this attitude is perhaps beginning to change; even Mel Fisher, the grand old man of the American treasure scene, is now reputedly attempting to do good archaeology.

Even so, shipwrecks have been mindlessly destroyed by the hundreds in the Caribbean. Off the coast of Florida, the depredation of treasure hunters rivals the Mediterranean destruction of the decade after World War II. A similar situation is found off the coastlines of many of the newer nations in the region.

There are signs that this situation is

An Ancient Egyptian grain-carrying barge from a 4,000-year-old tomb painting (top left), illustrates the primeval ancestry of shipping in the Mediterranean, but the archaeological value of wrecksites was not fully understood before the work of Commandant Philippe Tailliez (above), whose meticulous excavation in the 1950s showed future maritime archaeologists the necessity of a scientific approach to field excavation. Tailliez took part in the earliest attempt at underwater excavation in 1952, when the French navy's Undersea Research Group, led by aqualung pioneer Commandant Jacques-Yves Cousteau, explored a Roman wrecksite at Le Grand Congloué, near Marseille. On that occasion, failure to map and record the finds in a systematic fashion greatly reduced the value of the operation. Tailliez's excavation (left) of the so-called Titan wreck, a 1st century BC Roman vessel found on the Titan reef off southern France, did not repeat these mistakes. Wrecksites, previously regarded as "fields of amphoras", could become windows into the past if scientifically surveyed and excavated (opposite).

changing, but even so it is probably true that, for every attempt at correct, methodical excavation in the Caribbean, dozens of shipwreck sites are being senselessly blown to pieces by irresponsible divers hungry for gold.

Maritime civilization

The invention of the aqualung followed by the growth of diving as a sport was instrumental in reawakening popular interest in the age-old relationship of mankind with the sea.

The maritime tradition goes back at least 5,000 years; its story is about the production of highly sophisticated wooden ships, built by incredibly skilful traditional craftsmen and then sailed by expert seamen.

This way of life was beginning to come to an end in the last half of the nineteenth century. Contemporary writers from Richard Henry Dana and Herman Melville to Joseph Conrad celebrated it, as well as engineers like W.H. White, who attempted 100 years ago to describe, in mathematical terms, the properties and functions of sailing ships.

By the first quarter of the 20th century, the age of the sailing ship was nearing its end. Among the writers who understood this was Alan Villiers, who in the 1920s sailed in a grain ship with his friend Walker from Australia to England, recording on film what they perceived to be the

end of an era. Of all the writers of that particular genre, Villiers perhaps best of all saw the demise of the great square-riggers as the end of one of the great heroic ages of mankind.

Sailing ships and the skills associated with them are largely responsible for our modern world. Yet the shipwrights' and seamen's trades have by convention always been mysterious and closed off to outsiders. Ignored and taken for granted in their heyday by the rest of the world, the castes were finally abolished by the arrival of steel and fiberglass and the advent of modern machinery.

Ancient traditions of building and sailing ships are still alive in corners of the world, but unfamiliar to all but a few concerned individuals. As late as the 1950s, ocean-going yachts were still built in the ancient maritime tradition, and the best were built in yards that had operated for generations.

With the advent of fiberglass construction after World War II, yachts became consumer goods, carefully designed vessels that could be "operated" by almost anyone. Navigation in the old sense became a lost art, replaced by modern electronics. For most modern yachtsmen, the old hard tradition of the sea is not even a memory. In the English language, ships have always been referred to as "she" – perhaps because the ship required love and attention and, unlike

most manufactured objects, had a personality. Today it is increasingly common to refer to ships as "it".

Many cargoes

The problem facing the new field of maritime archaeology is that it is in part the study of a vanished culture about which outsiders knew little, even at the time. Nevertheless, as probably the most sophisticated machine invented by mankind before this century, the ship is well worth study. Today, through the medium of maritime archaeology, it has become the destiny of the ships that did not arrive to tell the story of those that did.

However, maritime archaeology goes farther, for it is part of the general study of human civilization. The story of history from the sea is not only the study of the ships themselves, their performance, the effect of their development on exploration, trade and warfare, and their unification of a divided world. It also concerns the people involved, the ports of call, and what cargoes the vessels carried. Maritime archaeology is at least as concerned with what the ships contained as with their structure and capabilities.

Trade has probably generated more cultural change among humans than any other activity, and for at least 4,000 years a large part of the world's goods have traveled by sea. It has been estimated that until well after 1800, as much as 5 per

cent of all this material was lost to the sea.

Given this wealth of material on the seabed, it is not surprising that, apart from a handful of land sites such as the great tombs of Egypt, China and Mesopotamia, shipwrecks are often the richest archaeological sites to be found. Only in shipwrecks are we able to dissect and examine an entire cross section of life "frozen" intact in time, comparable to cities such as Pompeii or Thera, which have been overwhelmed by volcanic eruptions and thus preserved. There are few such cities, but thousands of ships. Each wrecksite represents a single moment in time, encapsulating not only the ship but also everything that went down with it – cargo, furniture, utensils, valuables, weapons, money and men.

Preservation and reconstruction

Archaeologists have become increasingly skilled at interpreting the evidence of wrecksites, beginning with the ships themselves. Europe began the 19th century as a collection of industrialized colonial nations and the history of shipbuilding is one of the best windows into that process.

But interest in ships of the past is not a modern phenomenon. As long ago as 1586, the English sovereign Elizabeth I encouraged a scheme to preserve *The Golden Hind*, Sir Francis Drake's flagship, in a purpose-built brick building at Dept-

ford. The sum of £220 was allocated for this project – a very substantial amount at the time. Unfortunately, the structure was never built; by 1662, *The Golden Hind* had rotted away after 80 years of neglect. A contemporary Turkish royal galley, stored on the shores of the Bosphorus under cover but with minimum care, has survived in good condition right up until the present day.

Since then, hundreds of "historical" ships have been preserved in over 40 countries around the world. One of the earliest of these projects involved the USS *Constitution*, one of the first frigates built for the American Navy, launched in 1797. This ship owed its preservation to a wave of popular sentiment, following Oliver Wendell Holmes's poem "Old Ironsides", when the Navy considered scrapping her.

The British, always more historically minded, kept Lord Nelson's flagship HMS *Victory* as the stationary flagship of the Portsmouth Naval Command until she was no longer seaworthy. In 1922 she was permanently dry-docked, and a civilian organization, the Society for Nautical Research, collaborated with the Navy in restoring the ship to her 1805 condition.

In the same spirit, Japan preserved the battleship *Mikasa* as a memorial to the battle of Tsushima in 1905, Chile preserved the *Huascar* as a naval relic of a victory over Peru, and Greece preserved the cruiser *Averoff* as a memorial of

victory over her neighbour Turkey.

These are by no means the only examples. However, it is important to remember that the preservation of these vessels was the result of a deliberate political decision. They were saved not because they were thought to be beautiful or valuable as representations of a dying tradition, but because they were historical monuments. The ship preservation movement began, not from a perception that the ships were valuable for themselves, but as political propaganda.

Constitution and *Victory* were both originally built of white oak, a material with a lifespan that varies considerably, depending on the cutting, storage and seasoning of the wood. During the Napoleonic wars, for instance, Britain's desperate need for ships meant that many were built outside from improperly seasoned wood that sometimes rotted even before completion of the vessel. On the other hand, wooden vessels built in Britain in the 1840s from carefully seasoned material remained sound till they were broken up 60 years later.

Today, only about 8 percent of the *Constitution*'s original structure remains, whereas *Victory* retains 20 percent of hers. The latter is being rebuilt in teak, which can last almost forever. The Americans, on the other hand, are using traditional white oak, live oak, and long leaf yellow pine (although modern

A vanishing world: 19th century shipping in Whitby Harbor.

features like epoxy laminations are beginning to be used in restoration).

What is the motive for preserving relics from the past, given that political propaganda is no longer of overriding importance? Originally, museums used to be collections of ancient art, and maritime museums were repositories of maritime collectables, while in the 19th century, showmen like P.T. Barnum extended the concept, making good money by exhibiting "curiosities" for cash admission.

The 1920s saw the initiation of projects like Colonial Williamsburg, which continues to thrive as a combination of archaeological project, museum complex, and recreation of the architecture and lifestyle of an 18th century town. Today, in both Europe and the USA, projects of this kind have changed from re-enactments of the past to attempts to understand it through recreation both of its structures, and of the lifestyle that went with them.

This new field, experimental archaeology, is the technique of authentically recreating a period so that we can actually experiment at living and working as our ancestors did. The work of experimental archaeologists has provided a whole new understanding of many aspects of ancient life. On the water, exact replicas of ancient vessels are created out of the information derived from undersea excavations and historical research.

These replicas offer new insights into the seaworthiness of ancient vessels. The most spectacular project of this kind is taking place at the time of writing: a full-scale replica of an ancient Greek trireme, designed by a specialist classical scholar in collaboration with a naval architect, and built for the Greek navy (see pp.44–49).

Field archaeology

Archaeology is more a tool of other disciplines than a discipline itself. Field archaeology is really just a set of techniques that can give insights not otherwise available, using the broken bits of the past as one uses a library. The information is there if you know how to extract it.

As the servant of many disciplines, archaeology may be found in some areas which would not automatically be associated with the subject. In the United States, the very recent discipline of historical archaeology investigates America's immediate post-Columbian European ancestors – a period for which full written records exist. Many conventional historians claim that there is little point in spending time and money digging up the recent past, when all we need to know is awaiting us in the libraries of the world.

No doubt this is true up to a point. But "wide-angle history" of the kind often taught in school and college seems so often to ignore the lives of ordinary men and women. What did they eat? How did they really live? What did they die of and how old were they when they died? How were the fields irrigated, the tools forged, the houses built? And how were the ships made and navigated?

Good field archaeology can answer these questions in a way that the archives never can, and pose questions that never arise in the archives. The most striking example perhaps is the work of Heinrich Schliemann at Mycenae between 1874 and 1876, which revealed a whole new civilization that classical scholars denied had ever existed.

The antiquities industry

The value of materials found in archaeological sites differs according to the values of the individuals who dig them up and deal with them after they are recovered. Tomb robbing is an ancient trade, usually carried out by poor farmers and peasants. However, apart from a handful of sensational exceptions, the great majority of archaeological sites on land produce material of little intrinsic value.

Nonetheless, objects ripped out of their archaeological context and sold on the commercial art market may be seen in most of today's great art museums, to the huge profit of dealers in cities such as New York, London, Zurich, Hong Kong and Amsterdam. The illicit trade in antiquities supports thousands, including

Famous ships were preserved as mementoes of a glorious past, long before the emergence of maritime archaeology. In the 16th century plans were made to build a structure to contain the *Golden Hind* (above), Sir Francis Drake's flagship, seen here in a recently completed ocean-going replica. In the United States, the *Constitution* (right) was saved from destruction through the propagandizing work of Oliver Wendell Holmes, whose "Old Ironsides" poem created a wave of popular enthusiasm. The British warship *Victory* (above right), Nelson's flagship at Trafalgar, has for many years been installed at a dry dock in Portsmouth, and remains a place of pilgrimage to this day.

some academics who prefer to turn a blind eye to the shady side of the business, and who are in effect the accomplices of the tomb robbers.

The antiquities industry is especially harmful because it drives a wedge between the archaeologists who are digging for knowledge and the establishments that should be supporting them. Big art museums seldom support the archaeologist working in the field because their exhibits are often produced by the antiquities market.

Most countries with deposits of saleable ancient art have developed archaeological services and passed legislation in order to protect their national heritage from the demands of collectors, including art museums. The less developed countries of the world are the ones that today contain most of the remains of the high civilizations of the past, while northern industrial countries, which were primitive when these civilizations were at their peak, can now afford to spend money on collecting art.

Modern archaeology

On the other hand, these same countries, France, Germany, and especially Britain, were all to play key roles in the development of the concepts and techniques of modern archaeology.

In Britain, a well-defined progression leads from the Dilettanti of the 18th century, personified by Lord Elgin and his amassing of sculptures from the Parthenon, to General Pitt-Rivers and to subsequent English archaeologists, who have opened windows into the past from Mohenjo Daro and Ur of the Chaldees to the decipherment of Linear B.

In France, Napoleon's invasion of Egypt brought the nation's most distinguished scholars to that country. They proved no less acquisitive than Lord Elgin and his successors. Yet today the name of Champollion, whose decipherment of the Rosetta stone gave the world the ability to read the literature of a high civilization, is much better remembered than the men who organized the systematic looting of shiploads of Egyptian art.

Fascination with a noble past characterized the growing industrial civilizations of the 19th century. Countries that owned the antiquities removed by the 19th century archaeologists tend to be less impressed by their activities. For the Greeks, Lord Elgin is a looter, and the return of the Elgin marbles is a major political issue. In Turkey, Schliemann is better remembered as the man who disappeared with the treasure of Troy rather than the visionary amateur archaeologist who rediscovered a civilization.

Scientific archaeology

Archaeologists today, dedicated as they are to turning the subject into a science, tend to forget that their direct ancestors were treasure hunters. But what is this "scientific" archaeology? It is simply the ability to apply techniques developed by the great excavators of the recent past, in combination with modern scientific processes, so as to extract the maximum of information from an archaeological site.

The method is the same, whether it takes place on land or under water. Excavation is usually the smallest part of the project, with 95 percent of the resources being devoted to conservation, study, analysis, and public presentation.

Purist archaeologists may underestimate the importance of the latter, feeling that they have done their job once they have published the scientific result of their labors. Others believe that they have a responsibility to explain to the public what they were doing and why. After all, the public does not generally read abstruse scientific journals.

The recent excavation of Wolstenholme Town, an early 17th century English settlement in Virginia, provides a good example of how "scientific" archaeology can be both scientific and popular. Located on the James River, the settlement was wiped out by Indians in 1622. Nothing much remained but the graves of some of those who had died, a pattern of post holes indicating a palisaded fort and buildings, some charcoal, broken pottery, and a couple of corroded steel helmets.

A treasure trove of everday objects: in their task of bringing the past to life, archaeologists often attach greater value to ordinary artifacts than to superficially spectacular finds. Objects recovered from the *Mary Rose* (far left), Henry VIII's ill-fated warship, include personal items such as musical instruments, a gaming board, a leatherbound book, coins, a comb and a leather shoe, from which archaeologists can reconstruct details of a long vanished way of life. A German stoneware vase (left) from the settlement of Wolstenholme, Virginia, totally destroyed in 1622 by hostile Indians, forms part of the almost miraculous reconstruction of the site achieved by Ivor Noel Hume.

No treasure here, no gold, no statues, nothing for the art historians, art museums or dealers. Yet in a brilliant excavation, Ivor Noel Hume of the Colonial Williamsburg Foundation was able to tell in detail the story of the little failed settlement and the people who died there. His book, *Martin's Hundred*, is as vivid as if it had been written by a good novelist with the assistance of a clairvoyant.

Having completed the excavation, Noel Hume was given the formidable task of creating a museum exhibit out of these vestigial remains. The result is an eerily evocative full-scale recreation of the site as it might have appeared soon after the burning, reconstructed solely from the material found and from well-documented analogies. And yet any visitor today, however unacquainted with the period, is transported back in time to March 1622, when the massacre occurred.

This kind of story is what modern archaeology exists to tell, whether on land or sea. Yet modern undersea archaeology is only an extension of archaeology's 100-year progress from treasure hunt to science. When archaeologists study ships and their contents – Etruscan pots, Greek statues, Spanish plate silver, or even luxury items from the doomed *Titanic* – they are trying to understand the genius of our own species. Part of that genius has created archaeology itself, and the desire to understand our common past.

Maritime archaeology today

Since World War II, ships have increasingly taken their rightful place in the world's inventory of artifacts worth understanding and preserving. It is beginning to be realized that the techniques of shipbuilding reflect important social changes in world history. For example, classical scholars today see the change in construction techniques that took place in the late Roman empire as reflecting the end of a slave economy and the beginning of a transition to a free trade system ruled by supply and demand rather than by imperial fiat.

Every well-planned shipwreck excavation, from George Bass's work on the late Bronze Age ships at Kaş and Cape Gelidonya to David Switzer's excavation of the 1788 privateer *Defence*, has provided not only an insight into the technical reality of the ships themselves but, more importantly, an understanding of the men in them and the societies from which they came. The same is true of reconstructions of 19th century vessels like *Elissa*, which stand at the end of mankind's long tradition of shipbuilding.

The story of our increasing ability to extract valid history from the sea is, then, one of growing cooperation between groups that have never had to cooperate before. Excavating a shipwreck, and understanding it, needs input from half a dozen professions and as many trades.

Conservators, for instance, need to be good organic chemists and have an understanding of marine microbiology, if they are to save from disintegration the delicate materials that the sea miraculously preserves. In order to study a ship, an archaeologist needs input from shipwrights and model makers as well as naval architects.

Most shipwrecks produce many categories of finds, each one demanding specialist study. As a result, scientific publication of a shipwreck takes years and the work of many specialists.

Good archaeology underwater could not happen until the archaeological establishment understood the potential of underwater sites, and the organization required to excavate them. The growing recognition of all this was well demonstrated in Sacramento, California in January of 1986, when the Society for Historical Archaeology held its general annual conference, in association with the 17th Conference on Underwater Archaeology. Perhaps 95 percent of all papers were by practicing professional archaeologists, and about one-third of all papers were on underwater archaeology. Things have changed mightily since George Bass gave the first report of a scientific excavation in the United States, in 1960.*

History from the Sea is the story of how all this has come about, told by some of the people who are making it happen.

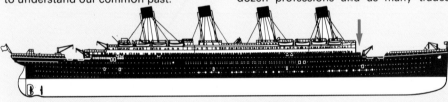

The sea preserves, but human ingenuity interprets and deciphers the enigmatic objects recovered from the seabed. The *Titanic* (above), sunk in 1912 and lying at a depth of more than 12,000ft, can now be studied thanks to the recently developed *Alvin* deepwater submersible. The photograph (left) shows how the portion marked on the ship (above) looks today. A brass badge (above), recovered from the 18th century East Indiaman *Batavia*, reveals the regiment of a Dutch soldier drowned in 1743.

The road to Gelidonya

Before Cousteau made diving a sport that could be practiced by amateurs, the sponge divers of the Aegean were the only men who had acquired an intimate knowledge of the Mediterranean littoral waters in the practice of their work. The amazing hoard of sculptures found off Antikythera at the beginning of this century, an event that prefigured the eventual emergence of maritime archaeology, was discovered and salvaged by sponge divers.

Sponge diving is a very old trade: Simi, the home port of the divers who found the Antikythera shipwreck, is supposed to have been founded by Glaucus, the legendary diver who accompanied the Argonauts in search of the Golden Fleece. Kointos of Smyrna, writing in the 5th century BC, referred to the Simiaki as the best sponge divers. Other lost ancient works about sponge diving include a comedy by Menander, and a play by Kroton called *The Diver*.

By 1868, when helmet diving gear reached the eastern Aegean, the naked diving of the traditional sponge diving islands had developed into a fine art. The best of the naked divers could go to over 200ft, with the aid of a carefully shaped stone sinker, a minute glass, and expert tenders who tended the line that brought the diver to the surface, even if anoxia, triggered by hyperventilation, caused the diver to pass out while underwater.

Surprisingly, Aegean naked divers had a good safety record. After the suppression of piracy in the 1830s, fleets of small diving boats from the eastern Aegean began working the rich sponge banks off Tunisia. By the time helmet diving arrived on the scene, the sponge diving of the naked divers was a big industry.

In 1868, one of the new gadgets was imported into Kalymnos. Twenty-four divers learned to use it; ten died that same year of the bends, an illness caused by the bloodstream's absorption of nitrogen gas under pressure. If a diver stays too deep too long, the absorbed gas will bubble in his blood like soda water when the pressure is released on the surface, causing agonizing pain which can be followed by paralysis or death.

This disease was not medically explained until 1878, when the great French physiologist Paul Bert published *La Pression Barometrique*, which laid the groundwork for the development of tables. These give times divers can remain at different depths, without ill effect.

By the time Captain Dimitrios Kondos and his men discovered the Antikythera shipwreck, Aegean sponge divers had learned to use the helmet diving gear with reasonable safety. It would be fair to estimate that in the boom years of sponge diving, between 1890 and 1910, Greek sponge divers put in about one million hours on the bottom per year.

As sponges were depleted in shallow water, the bravest and more adventurous began to specialize in deep diving, going to depths of well over 200ft. They found that they could keep the mortality down if dives were of very short duration at these depths. This meant employing up to 20 divers in a single crew, all of whom had to use the same helmet and pump.

By 1900, when Kondos made his great discovery, the system had developed as much as it ever would until plastics and politics killed the industry. The introduction of engines in the 1930s led to the change in diving boat types when rowers were replaced by engines which also powered the air compressor. The system remained the same. It remains so today, except that the Cousteau Gagnan regulator has replaced the 19th century copper helmet, and the modern wet suit canvas diving dress. The high pressure air compressors which are needed in order to fill diving tanks are too expensive and complicated to maintain in poor countries, so the last sponge divers still trudge along the bottom, leashed to the boat by the umbilical cord of the air hose.

"A heap of dead naked women . . ."

Accounts of the discovery at Antikythera are confusing, conflicting and inaccurate. However, we know that two sailing vessels, owned by the Lyndiakos brothers in Simi, put into the tiny harbor of Potamo on the north end of Antikythera island, to shelter from a southerly gale, probably in October of 1900. The expedition was returning from the Bengazi banks, and it was commanded by a captain from Simi called Dimitrios Kondos.

After three days the gale abated. Kondos decided to send the diving boat out around Cape Glifada a couple of miles to the east of Potamo harbor. The rocky north coast of Antikythera falls steep to a submarine sandy slope that begins at between 150-200ft, and slopes from there to the abyss. Just off a place called Pinakakia by the natives of the island, where the steep cliffs are streaked with red, Kondos put his first diver of the day over the side. His name was Elias Stadiatos, and he came from Simi. In five minutes Elias surfaced. When they twisted the copper helmet off, Kondos saw that he was scared out of his wits. Although most details of the Antikythera story differ in all the accounts, everyone agrees on what Elias babbled as he crouched, terrified, on the foredeck of the diving boat, raving about the nightmare vision he had seen 180ft below:

"A heap of dead naked women, rotting and syphilitic...horses...green corpses."

An experienced helmet diver (top), the Turkish sponge fisher Kiasim helped Peter Throckmorton to discover numerous wrecksites in the Aegean, carrying on the tradition of the Simi sponge divers of the Antikythera wreck. Helmet diving replaced the naked diver, but casualties from the bends were frequent. Simi today (above) continues as a place dedicated to the sea. Boats of age-old design are still built by means of traditional techniques.

Antikythera (above), the treacherous island at the gate of the Aegean where a vast trove of classical works of art was recovered at the beginning of this century. The wreck lay on the seabed at a depth of 180ft. Trained in the hard school of African sponge fishing, local divers from Simi took on a job beyond the capacity of any navy in the world at that time. The experience of the divers was an unrealized asset that could have contributed far more to the excavation if these men had been properly consulted by the archaeological authorities of the time. Divers like Kemal Arras (left), seen here recovering amphoras at Yassi Ada, made an invaluable contribution to Peter Throckmorton's discovery of dozens of wrecks in the Aegean, 50 years later.

Kondos pulled on the wet canvas and rubber suit that Elias had just vacated, and dropped over the side. He surfaced five minutes later with a corroded bronze arm attached to his lifeline.

Elias had found what was left of a great Roman argosy that had been freighted with bronze and marble sculpture. It appeared after more than 2,000 years as a concreted mound sticking up out of a sandy bottom, which lay at the foot of the steep cliff of Pinakakia.

Sources disagree as to what happened next. The official Greek version has Kondos finding the wreck in the spring, and, out of pure patriotism, taking the arm to the Greek Archaeological Service in the fall. In Simi, they say that Kondos and his men salvaged what they could before the weather changed that fall. There are rumors of many small bronzes sold in Alexandria between 1902 and 1910.

Although old waterfront rumors from a Greek island don't really prove anything, and at this distance it seems unlikely that any of the bronzes sold in Alexandria will ever be traced, there is another indicator which suggests that the wreck was indeed salvaged, either before Kondos found it, or, if he was the first to find it, by Kondos himself.

The lost anchors
Like all Mediterranean sponge divers, Kondos and his men had seen many ancient wrecks. The common ones appeared on the bottom as heaps of clay jars. Like the early French aqualung divers, the Greeks did not perceive these as other than "fields of amphoras". In the case of the Mahdia wreck, found seven years after Antikythera by another group of Greek sponge divers, a cargo of marble columns was described by the divers who found it as "cannons". It was not understood that the remnants of ships lay hidden, preserved in sand or mud, underneath these deposits.

What Greek sponge divers understood very well was that fields of amphoras or heaps of marble blocks, or stone "cannons" were liable to be associated with "bars of lead", flat copper bars, or bronze scrap.

The "bars of lead" were, in reality, ancient lead anchor stocks. The Antikythera ship was of the right size and period to have carried at least five lead stocked anchors, with stocks weighing 500-1,000lb each, like the ones we found in Taranto (see Ch. 3).

Although the wreck has been extensively salvaged and explored, no anchor has ever been found on the site, except for a small iron one which is undoubtedly modern. It seems certain, then, that the anchors on board when the ship struck the cliff must have been salvaged in modern times, presumably by Kondos, and melted into scrap. The absence of lead anchor stocks goes far to prove the rumors of the small statues sold in Alexan-

dria. When Kondos salvaged the wreck, under the supervision of the Greek Archaeological Service, only a couple of portable statues were recovered. When Cousteau made another salvage effort in 1976, a new, small bronze was found deep in the sand. Although the material from the wreck has never been adequately studied and published, it seems that possibly several dozen bases for small statues have been salvaged, and that there are many more small bases for statues from the wreck than there are salvaged bronzes to fit these bases.

Salvage at Antikythera
A rumor of the Antikythera statues came to the ears of an Athens University professor, A. Economou, who may have heard of them from the Lyndiakos brothers and Kondos. The matter was then

Black coral, made into ornaments by the Simi sponge fishers, is found at great depths off the African coast – an indication of the skill and endurance of the early divers.

brought before the minister of education, Spiridon Stais, who was shown the bronze arm discovered by Kondos as evidence. If the Greek navy could provide a ship capable of winching heavy objects off the seabed, Kondos offered to raise the remaining statues, on the condition that he and the Lyndiakos brothers were paid their full value.

Kondos and his divers, and the government that employed them, were not aware that they were undertaking the deepest salvage job in the history of diving up to that time. But divers from Simi and Kalymnos had been going to the 300ft theoretical limit of compressed air diving for years. Kondos and his divers wore watch fobs made from black coral that grows at great depths off Africa, where few men have been even today.

When the government expedition arrived off Cape Glifada on November 24, big swells from the north were breaking on the cliffs, but Kondos squinted at the

clouds and decided to risk a dive. The haul was impressive. It included a life-size bronze head of a bearded man; the bronze arm of a boxer, broken off at the shoulder; a corroded bronze sword, evidently part of a statue; two badly corroded marble statues of men, one life-size, both lacking heads; and a couple of boxes full of fragments of other bronze and marble statues, bronze bowls, clay dishes, and a sack full of broken pottery.

When the boat returned to Piraeus, pandemonium broke loose at the ministry. Stais had been right. Kondos had stumbled on the biggest hoard of ancient Greek bronzes found to that date. The first haul had included parts of at least 10 statues, picked from what Kondos claimed was a huge heap at the bottom.

The navy ministry now assigned a more maneuverable ship, the steam schooner *Syros*, to the task, and she arrived in San Nikolo, where the divers were still sheltered, on December 3. Economou stayed in Athens; the new man in charge was George Byzantinos, who was the director of antiquities.

The divers worked without interruption for five days before the weather broke, making two or three dives per man each day. Calm weather allowed the *Syros* to steam close to the cliff and pass the divers a line that could be attached to heavy objects on the bottom. These could then be raised by the ship's winches.

When the weather broke at the end of the week, the finds included the marble statue of a boy, a colossal marble bull, bronze parts of other statues, and bronze fittings, probably parts of furniture.

Back in Piraeus, the statues were put on public view, where they attracted crowds of visitors. This was the first major archaeological discovery made in Greece by Greeks, and it aroused very strong emotions. The wonderful wreck of Antikythera was full of Greek statues stolen by a foreign conqueror. Now it was being excavated without foreign help. It became a symbol of unity which the struggling young nation badly needed.

Hazards of the deep
At Antikythera, however, the divers were beginning to suffer from exhaustion; tempers frayed and enthusiasm waned as the work on the seabed became harder. Supervision of the project was put into the hands of an accountant in the archaeology department, a Mr Kritikos.

This appointment set a disastrous pattern characteristic of the archaeology of the day. In 1900 most archaeological excavations tended to be salvage jobs. The idea of a sunken ship as a slice of the past, preserved under the mud like an insect in amber, was far from the minds of the archaeologists of that time. They saw the Antikythera wreck as a marvelous treasure trove. Officials from the antiquities department made sure that nothing was stolen, but no one appears to have spoken with the divers. Had anyone done so, he might have learnt that the diver's weights had been cast from Roman anchor stocks, the compressor had been repaired with copper mined in Cyprus 3,500 years ago, and that the Aegean was full of ancient pottery.

In the event, the divers lived apart, carrying out as best 'they could the difficult salvage job for which they had been hired. Exhaustion was the worst problem. Kondos had six divers whom he worked two or three times a day in five-minute shifts, taking the time from when the diver hit the bottom. My own experience of diving, supported by a look at modern decompression tables, suggests that he was working his men at the extreme edge of safe diving, on a job that would have been rejected as impossible by any of the navies of the world.

Tests carried out by the United States navy's experimental diving unit show that a diver's reasoning ability deteriorates under pressure, possibly due to a buildup of excess carbon dioxide. Divers begin to be affected soon after 100ft and, as they descend to the limit of compressed air diving at 300ft, they get progressively "drunker". The Antikythera divers were working at depths of over 180ft, where the effect of narcosis is not unlike a couple of stiff whiskeys on an empty stomach. One feels fine, gets into the car, drives with great skill, and then complains of injustice when had up for drunken driving. Like drunks, divers are unwilling to admit that they were boiled out of their minds when on the bottom. But there is no doubt that the Antikythera divers were, on purely physiological grounds.

The effects of narcosis were further increased by the helmet diving gear, which acted as a trap for the diver's carbon dioxide-filled exhalations (the free diver's aqualung system carries away the exhaled air). Another hazard was the sand on the bottom, which floated up in clouds when the sponge divers tried to dig into it. It was as if the tomb of Tutankhamen had been excavated in five-minute shifts by drunken stevedores, working in semi-darkness, dressed in American football pads with coal scuttles on their heads.

At the end of January, the divers decided to strike for more money, and demanded that the government hire more divers. Stais and Economou went to Antikythera and pleaded with them. The next day was flat calm, and the divers finally agreed to go back to work after Economou personally guaranteed that they would be paid for the first statues as soon as they could be evaluated.

The "great boulders"

The wreck itself was covered by great stones which the divers could not move. Operations to maneuver them down the slope and into the abyss required judgment and skilful seamanship, but at last they were shifted. Now it became possible

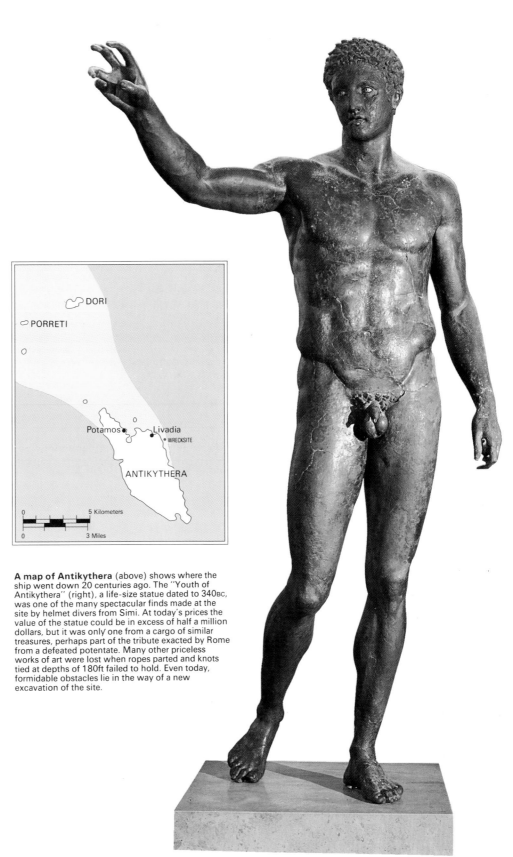

A map of Antikythera (above) shows where the ship went down 20 centuries ago. The "Youth of Antikythera" (right), a life-size statue dated to 340BC, was one of the many spectacular finds made at the site by helmet divers from Simi. At today's prices the value of the statue could be in excess of half a million dollars, but it was only one from a cargo of similar treasures, perhaps part of the tribute exacted by Rome from a defeated potentate. Many other priceless works of art were lost when ropes parted and knots tied at depths of 180ft failed to hold. Even today, formidable obstacles lie in the way of a new excavation of the site.

17

to raise the material that had lain under them. As a result, more than a dozen statues were rescued, and triumphantly brought to Piraeus.

At the risk of sinking the ship, Stais ordered the next great boulder to be brought to the surface. It was not a boulder after all. Through the clear water everyone saw that it was a huge statue of Hercules, with club and lionskin. The "great boulders" had been statues all along, so improbably big, so corroded and overgrown, that the depth-fuddled divers had failed to recognize them.

After a few dozen more marbles and fragments had been raised, numerous delicate objects came up intact; beautiful glass bowls, a gold brooch set with seed pearls and featuring Eros with a lyre, flat roof tiles, rough kitchen pottery. By the time the weather changed, the ship's deck was so full that the sailors had difficulty moving around. The divers were now completely worn out, and could no longer be persuaded to work until Easter, which fell at the beginning of April that year.

A week after work had recommenced, one of the divers died of the bends. As spring wore into summer, they were bothered by the northern wind called the *melteme*, and it became harder to work on the exposed side of Antikythera. Finds diminished, although every week there was at least one exciting discovery.

By the beginning of June all visible loose objects had been removed from the wreck. When the divers dug into the sand they continued to find objects, but little of value. They reported seeing other statues almost hidden under layers of sea growth, but could not be sure. In any case, the authorities had lost interest in the wreck after spectacular discoveries ceased, and so, at the end of the summer of 1901, the work was suspended.

Interpretation of the finds
In the following years, there was much controversy over the date and provenance of the ship. The material was stored in the National Museum in Athens, where it was examined piecemeal by dozens of experts. However, most of the material was never systematically studied.

The bronzes were identified as belonging to the 4th century BC. The corroded marble statues turned out to be later copies of classical originals. The domestic pottery suggested to one scholar that the ship had gone down in the first century before Christ. He was correct, but more than 60 years were to elapse before his thesis was proved.

Nearly a year after work had ceased, Valerio Stais, the nephew of Spiridon, noticed that a calcified lump of corroded bronze contained fragments that looked like clockwork. He identified it as either a clock or a navigational instrument, parts of which were marked with astronomical inscriptions in ancient Greek.

More experts were invited to investigate this curious instrument, and a long debate as to its use ensued. Whilst some claimed that it was a kind of astrolabe, others maintained (correctly) that the apparently complex mechanism suggested otherwise. The arguments did not stop there – to some, the artifact seemed out of place amongst a 1st century BC cargo of marble and bronze statues, and it was suggested that this was perhaps the remains of a medieval contraption which had found its way by chance onto the wreck site. Evidence for scientific instruments and mechanical objects dating from the same period in history has always been so scant that it was often assumed (and still is) that the Greeks had none.

In 1958, Dr Derek de Solla Price, English physicist and student of the history of science, made a detailed study of the four major pieces and several fragments that had survived. From the evidence he found of the style of inscription, the astronomical content, and the methods and materials of construction, he was able to conclude quite firmly that the instrument did indeed date from the 1st century BC. He was also able to make a tentative reconstruction of the instrument on paper, showing the probable configuration of dials and gears. However, his investigations at that stage were necessarily limited by the poor state of the fragments, incomplete as they were and spotted with calcareous deposits.

In 1971, Dr Price undertook another study of the instrument, this time using new techniques of X-ray investigation. From the radiographs, much more structural detail was immediately visible – it was even possible to calculate some of the gear ratios. From such intricate technical analysis, Dr Price was able to definitely identify the instrument as a calendrical Sun and Moon computing device. He argued convincingly that it was made in Rhodes, because the most complete inscription on the machine is part of a surviving astronomical calendar written by the astronomer Geminos, who lived in Rhodes during the 1st century BC. He deduced that the machine was made in about 87BC, according to the setting of the slip ring indicating the position of the stars. He also deduced that it was probably set for the last time shortly before the ship sank, and had been repaired several times during its working life.

The Antikythera "computer", with its complicated mechanism, is thus a relic of major historical importance, being the earliest extant example of the use of sophisticated gears and differentials (crucial to later technological progress). Moreover, the discovery of the instrument surely challenges the widely held view that the Greeks were scientifically backward. Other comparable "scientific" artifacts include only the Greco-Roman sundials – a few of bronze, the rest of rough-hewn marble – and the remarkable Tower of the Winds in Athens, built in the second quarter of the 1st century BC, and seen as a kind of planetarium of the classical world. In both spirit and scientific detail, it stands closely associated with the Antikythera fragments.

New studies of old material
The upheavals of World War II, together with administrative changes in the museum, caused the loss of some Antikythera material mentioned in earlier publications, but in 1958 there was still plenty in the storerooms, mostly uncatalogued. A group of specialists under

A contemporary photograph of the sponge fishers of Simi, taken in 1903, as they worked from their caique at the discovery site off Antikythera. Note the derrick used for lifting massive lumps from the seabed, and the smallness of the vessel. Sometimes the size of the objects threatened to capsize the boat. The achievement of the sponge fishers, considering the primitive conditions of the time and the fact that they were working at depths of 180ft, is astonishing. Not only were they unable to stay down for extended periods without risk of death or disablement through the bends; their judgment would also have been impaired, due to a buildup of excess carbon dioxide resulting in a kind of drunkenness.

Gladys Weinberg of the University of Missouri, for many years editor of *Archaeology* magazine, now began to examine this material. It consisted of pieces of glass, amphoras and dessicated ship's planking, shrunk to a fraction of its original size. From this "junk pile" of material, put aside since 1901 because it could not be compared with similar material from other dated sites, the group was able to produce valuable information. Such was the progress that had been made in archaeology over a period of less than 60 years.

Study of the amphoras by Virginia Grace revealed that five of the clay wine jars had probably been made between 70 and 80BC, and had come from Rhodes. Another group, from Kos, belonged to the same period. Two more from southern Italy suggested that the ship might have been engaged in the Rome-Aegean trade.

Kourouniotes, the scholar who in 1901 had dated the shipwreck to the 1st century BC on the evidence of the domestic pottery, was now vindicated after 60 years. A new study of the clay lamps, drinking cups, jugs and pitchers, made by Professor G. Roger Edwards of the University of Pennsylvania, also showed that the material came from the central part of the Asia Minor coast, and that the lamp was a type very common at Ephesus. None of the material, according to Edwards, came from mainland Greece. Examination of nine pottery plates, carried out by the Roman pottery expert Professor Henry Robinson, established that they too were from Asia Minor and belonged to the 1st century BC. The 11 glass bowls were from the same period and probably came from Alexandria, a center for the manufacture of luxury glass for the Roman market.

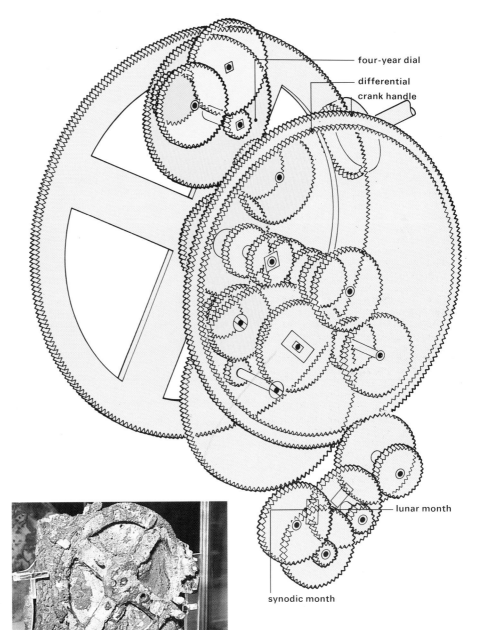

four-year dial

differential

crank handle

lunar month

synodic month

A mechanical marvel: X-rays of the Antikythera "computer" (left) reveal the secrets of the mysterious mechanism found at the wrecksite (above). Details of gear teeth, wheel circles and axes – hidden from the naked eye by obscuring layers of corrosion and marine accretion – are all clearly visible in this radiograph. With the extra information provided by these images, scientists were able to calculate the mathematical basis behind most of the gear train mechanism in the ancient Greek "computer".

A general plan of all the gearing (above) reveals a mechanism of astonishing complexity. Each gear wheel has a specific number of teeth so that it rotates at a prescribed rate within the gear train, representing a particular astronomical or calendrical cycle as it does so – perhaps the progression of a synodic month or a lunar year. There is even a differential turntable, evidence of considerable technological expertise, which is designed to allow greater flexibility in the gearing. The computer carries inscriptions, unfortunately incomplete, that apparently refer to planetary and zodiacal motions.

This historic artifact, certainly not a navigational instrument, as was once believed, must have been a rare object of great value like the rest of the Antikythera finds.

The ship and its structure

The remains of the ship's wood planks showed that they were fastened on top of each other by tenons neatly mortised into the planks. These had been covered below the waterline with a layer of lead sheets, like the Mahdia ship (found 1907), the Roman wine ship excavated at the Grand Congloué off Marseille by Captain Cousteau, and the Kyrenia ship (see p. 55). The Antikythera ship was copper-fastened and built shell first – the frames were put into the ship after the shell was built up, held solidly together by its tenons. When I finally managed to get into the National Museum's storerooms to study the wood, I estimated from the planking that the ship was quite big, about 300 tons, and probably decked – I found lead scupper pipes in the box that had contained the planking.

Carbon-14 analysis – a technique inconceivable to the researchers of 1900 – indicated that the tree forming the plank had absorbed its c-14 between 260 and 180 BC. "If large logs were used," the researcher wrote, "the particular sample which was dated may have come from the center of a log and would therefore have been earlier than the cutting of the tree by an amount equal to the age of the tree."

The Antikythera ship was planked with elm below the waterline. Ancient Greek ships seem to have used either Samos or Aleppo pine, whereas elm is commoner in central Italy. If the Antikythera ship had been built in Italy, she could have traded between the Aegean and Pozzuoli, near Naples, along the ancient sea road down the west coast of Italy to the Strait of Messina between Italy and Sicily. Many Roman ships sailed from the Antikythera channel to Methone, where they would wait for a favorable wind to take them up the coast to Corfu or Zakynthos. A run across the Adriatic took them to Brindisi, then Taranto, and finally down to Messina or around Sicily. The Antikythera ship's Tarantine jars could well have been picked up when the ship stopped at either Taranto or Brindisi some time before she was lost.

Sulla's loot?

The Roman general Sulla captured Athens in 86 BC. Three years later, in the spring of 83, he was at Ephesus, going on to Athens and finally returning to Brindisi in the summer. Sulla is notorious for having shipped back to Rome enormous quantities of classical treasures stripped from the cities of ancient Greece. Could the hoard of precious marbles at Antikythera be part of this loot?

A passage from Lucian, an Athenian writer of the 2nd century AD, claims that a ship sent off to Italy containing Sulla's trophies "sank off Malea with the loss of all its cargo." Antikythera lies off Malea, and Lucian was writing long after the event. The astronomer Geminos, the possible designer of the "computer", is

known to have been at Rhodes, not far away, at about the same time.

Alternatively, excavations in 1976 revealed coins from Pergamum dating to 88–86 BC, which suggests that the ship was carrying reparations exacted from that city after the Mithridatic war. The answers to many questions may yet be found in the hull of the Antikythera ship, 180ft below the surface and covered by about 3ft of muddy sand. The obstacles to working on the site are formidable, exposed as it is to the prevailing north winds of summer, and to the winter's dangerous northerly gales. The depth, too, allows "bounce" dives, but not the steady detailed work required for serious investigation rather than salvage.

From Antikythera to Bodrum

What can the story of what happened at Antikythera tell us today?

The problem was one that Tailliez put his finger on later; the enormous gap between the men who were actually doing the work (the divers) and the archaeologists who were supervising it. On land excavations, archaeologists could at least see what their hired laborers were digging up, and come to a mutual understanding of it.

A class of uneducated but capable diggers had appeared in Greek archaeology before Antikythera. Since the time of Schliemann, the rhythms of land digging in Greece had been dictated by the harvest, because the workers are recruited from villages near the sites. Seasonal work for archaeologists brings in welcome additional income. At Mycenae, to this day, you can meet men who boast that their great-grandfathers worked for Schliemann. The foremen ("pickmen") have skills acquired over many years. The relationship between a pickman and a young graduate student supervising the trench is similar to that between a sergeant and his young officer.

At Antikythera, the barrier of the sea prevented this relationship from developing. This situation was repeated constantly until George Bass became the first archaeologist to learn to dive, specifically so that he was able to conduct an underwater excavation.

At Antikythera, the vast resource of the sponge divers' knowledge was ignored. It continued to be ignored when, a few years later, divers working on a breakwater at Kyme, Euboea, stumbled on a heap of 15th century BC copper ingots from Cyprus. They salvaged the ingots and probably built the breakwater over the remnants of the ship. In 1907 the Mahdia wreck was salvaged using techniques no better than those at Antikythera.

The Bodrum Demeter

The discovery that precipitated the development of modern underwater archaeology occurred in 1953, off the coast of south Turkey, when a sponge

dragger found a bronze statue in his net. He dumped it on the beach at Bodrum, where it was seen by the famous scholar George Bean of Istanbul University. The statue was a 4th century BC original of the goddess Demeter.

In the early spring of 1958, I decided to make a film about sponge divers in south Turkey, as a result of which I met the photographer Mustafa Kapkin and Kemal Arras the sponge boat captain. Mustafa's friend, Hakki Gultekin of the Izmir museum, was enthusiastic about our film project. He was interested in the location of the Demeter statue. Could we interview

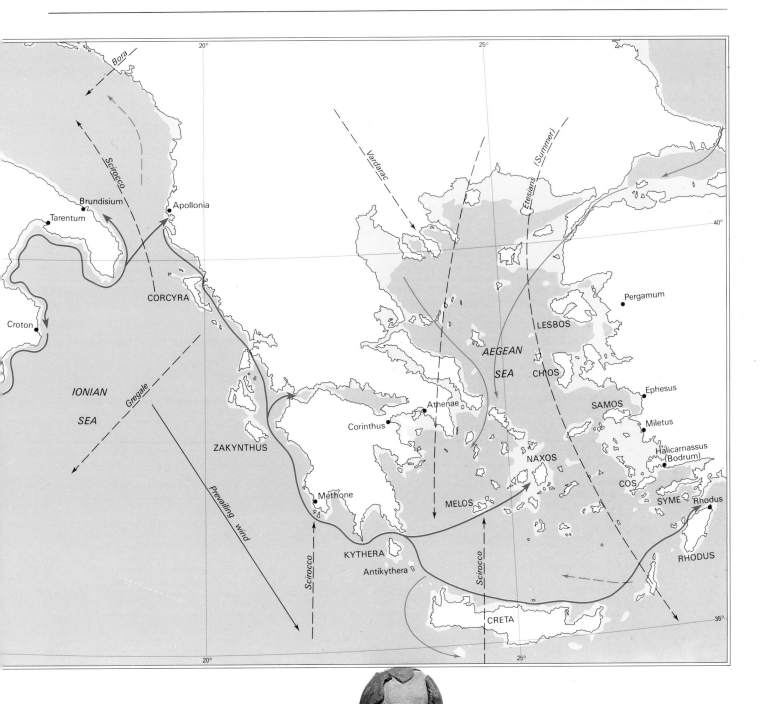

the sponge divers and find out where it had come from?

So, armed with a permit from the government, Mustafa and I arrived at the beautiful, primitive village of Bodrum, Kemal's home port, with its handsome crusader castle. It immediately became clear that the sponge divers knew about hundreds of ancient wreck locations and were perfectly willing to show them to us.

I knew some modern Greek, had a smattering of Arabic, and in a few weeks was communicating in Turkish with the help of a lot of drawings and hand wavings. Being a seaman helped, as did a

Ancient trade routes between Italy and the Aegean tended to hug the coast, with anchorages separated by a day's sailing. Once through the Antikythera channel the ships would make for their destinations in Greece, Asia Minor and the various groups of Greek islands, always bearing in mind the predominant northeasterly winds which even today can present problems to small craft. Pirates represented another hazard for mariners, and some archaeologists believe that the Antikythera ship may have been trying to shake off pursuit when she went down.

The Bodrum Demeter (left), a 4th century BC bronze statue recovered from the sea by a sponge fisher and left at the ancient town of Bodrum, formerly Halicarnassus, sparked off the creation of the museum.

knowledge of Latin and Italian. Sea terms are almost identical for all the ordinary sailors of the Mediterranean, whether the men are Greek or Arabs, Turkish, Italian or French. Although the Greeks and Turks are traditional enemies, the coastal fishermen of that time prided themselves on speaking "Roumja" (meaning literally, the language of Rome). If you spoke Roumja it meant you were an old hand.

I spent six months voyaging and diving with Captain Kemal and his men. In that time I documented perhaps 100 ancient shipwrecks and logged rumors of 100 others. One of the most exciting moments of my life came when I shoved my arm deep into the mud next to a heap of globular amphoras and felt the timbers of a ship that had lain there for 1,500 years, waiting to be excavated and understood.

This experience occurred at Yassi Ada, near Bodrum, an uninhabited waterless islet lying between the Turkish mainland and the nearest Greek islands of the Dodecanese. Its outlying reef had eviscerated scores of ships, creating a graveyard of lost ships where George Bass went on to do a series of textbook excavations (see pp. 84–91), and where a large percentage of competent underwater archaeologists working today received their training.

That summer I had my 30th birthday. I had finally decided on a career in a trade that didn't exist – maritime archaeology. A little later I was visited by Honor Frost, an English archaeological draftswoman who had worked with the famous excavator of Jericho, Kathleen Kenyon. Honor was a diver who had learnt the skill in the very early days in the South of France, and was familiar with the time when French divers had tried to make sense out of the discovery of dozens of ancient shipwrecks. By the end of the summer we were both convinced that, in Turkey, we might be able to avoid the mistake made in France.

I returned to New York that winter with photographs of what seemed to me the most fantastic collection of ancient shipwrecks that had ever been found and not looted. On the way I stopped off at Albenga on the Ligurian coast of Italy, where Professor Nino Lamboglia was excavating a Roman wreck. Lamboglia allowed me to dive from the research vessel *Daino*. I was surprised that the support vessel, with a crew of 100 men, was fielding six divers supervised by archaeologists who did not dive. In addition, the whole crew of divers was changed every six weeks.

I went on to meet Tailliez at Toulon. He felt that he had organized a good excavation, but that archaeologists had failed to take advantage of the opportunity. The advent of scuba diving had created an avalanche of looting and destruction, and there were no institutional mechanisms for dealing with it.

The great Cousteau had little respect for archaeologists, dismissing them as impractical pedants. Like the Greek Archae-

ological Service after Antikythera, the Italians and the French seemed to have learned nothing from the destruction of dozens of shipwrecks. Only Tailliez made sense to me, after Turkey.

An idea takes form
By the fall of 1958, then, I was convinced that it was possible to do scientific archaeology underwater, and that the seabed contained memories of maritime civilizations that had never been recorded. What historians had missed, the sea remembered. My reading, my experience in Italy and France, my summer in Turkey, combined with my time in shipyards and at sea, all these things had convinced me that there was a proper way to go about underwater excavation.

The most promising place to begin seemed to me to be Yassi Ada. The best

Honor Frost at work recording details of one of the wrecks found at Yassi Ada, 1958. Honor's experience as a diver working on wrecks off southern France, together with her ability as an archaeological draftsman, provided an invaluable contribution to the survey of dozens of wrecksites carried out during that summer.

preserved wreck there lay deep, on a slope that ran from 130ft at what seemed to be the bow of the wreck, to 150ft at the stern. It was an apparently undisturbed cargo of globular clay jars, with remnants of the hull preserved in the mud under the mound. The jars were Byzantine, of about the 7th century AD.

We would need plenty of divers (work at that depth can occupy only one hour or so a day), and therefore plenty of accommodation. Why not camp on the island of Yassi Ada itself? It would be much cheaper than working from a boat, and there would be space for all the equipment we would need. A barge moored over the wreck would be safe enough, since the wreck lay in the lee of the prevailing winds of summer. A local boat and crew could be hired cheaply to bring us water and supplies daily from Bodrum.

The wreck was big, with tons of cargo and tons of rotten hull structure. The wood looked fine when uncovered, but shriveled like burnt paper when it dried out. We would need a conservation lab somewhere ashore, where big tanks could be set up for chemical treatment.

Interesting experiments on conservation of material from the sea were then

going on in Stockholm, where plans were being made to raise the *Vasa*, an intact warship of 1628 (see p. 148). Other experiments were in progress in Denmark, after the discovery of a small fleet of 1,000-year-old Viking ships at Roskilde.

Bodrum: the making of the museum
In the late summer of 1958, it was becoming clear to me that a ship excavation required a permanent working base. In the few months we had worked at Bodrum, the necessity for such a base became increasingly evident after every new shipwreck discovery. At Yassi Ada alone there were wrecks piled upon wrecks at the top of the reef, ranging in date from the 5th century BC to the 1920s. Anything raised had to be carefully handled.

We had already discovered that clay amphoras that had spent the last 1,000 years underwater had to be washed in fresh water and dried slowly, thus allowing the water inside them to evaporate over a period of time. Otherwise they would shatter as they dried. There were thousands of amphoras on the globe amphora wreck alone. The pottery we were finding on the bottom was the spoor of ancient maritime man. Even where nothing remained but shattered fragments, the fragments had a story to tell. I already had a vision of a study collection, row on row, in the great vaults of the crusader castle. Each one would have to be drawn, analyzed, and perhaps keyed into a computer program.

The castle was the key. Yet its walls had gaps; the place was used as a cattle yard and public latrine every market day.

I was fascinated by the castle, originally constructed by the Turks on the site of the Dorian acropolis of Halicarnassus. It had been taken in 1402 by the Knights of St John of Jerusalem, who had reconstructed it with stone from the ruins of the Mausoleum – once one of the Seven Wonders of the ancient world.

The Knights were divided into national *langues* or divisions (literally, tongues), and the tower of the *langue* of England still stands. It bears the coats of arms of Henry IV of England, and the dukes of Clarence, Bedford, York and Gloucester. In 1522 it was taken by the Janissaries of Suleiman the Magnificent, the last Christian stronghold on the mainland of the Eastern Mediterranean.

It is undoubtedly inappropriate for a professional archaeologist to confess to psychic insights. Yet on my first visit to the castle I had the weird feeling that I had been there before.

My family includes several crusader ancestors who are buried in the church at Fladbury, Worcester. Sir John, the first of the family to be knighted, died in 1445. He was under-treasurer of England at the time of Henry IV. His grandson, Sir Robert, one of the privy council of Henry VII, died on a pilgrimage to the Holy Land in 1519. A defaced coat of arms that may

be his is built into a wall in Rhodes. May he not have been the bearer of the last injection of English gold to the Knights, in their final desperate attempt to hold onto a piece of Asia? Rhodes, a day's sail away from Bodrum, fell in 1522.

Sir Robert was "remarkable for his piety." Perhaps the last Grand Master of Rhodes, Villiers de l'Isle Adam, honored his efforts with a stone built into the wall at Rhodes, and sent him back to England for more money.

For whatever reason, Bodrum castle fascinated me with its layers of history. As the eleventh generation descendant of the man who may have raised the funds to build the last version of the castle, I was moved by its evocative ruin, and determined to see it restored.

Mustafa Kapkin, Hakki Gultekin and I got together, and Hakki persuaded the local governor to let us use the castle for a museum and laboratory. It was a great day when a volunteer crew of sponge divers, led by Captain Kemal, closed the gap in the castle wall with rough masonry, and the old watchman locked the ancient iron-studded gate.

Bodrum castle (above), built by the Turks on the site of the ancient Greek citadel of Halicarnassus; rebuilt by the Knights of St John of Jerusalem in 1402; and converted by the author into the first museum to be devoted to maritime archaeology.

A bronze statue of an African boy, dating to the Hellenistic period, is one of the museum's exhibits (left). The castle contains numerous treasures from one of the richest storehouses of maritime archaeology to be found anywhere in the world.

Sailors in the time of Troy

In recent years the sea has yielded spectacular treasures from the Bronze Age more than 3,000 years ago. Gold, silver, frankincense, glass, tin and copper ingots, tools and utensils, the personal possessions of long lost mariners – these are just some of the sensational discoveries made off a deserted headland in southern Turkey. Two excavations, 25 years apart, have produced finds hailed by some archaeologists as equal to Tutankhamun's tomb or Schliemann's "Treasury of Agamemnon".

When I was at Bodrum in the summer of 1958, Kemal the sponge boat captain and his divers showed me over 100 shipwreck sites in the region (see p. 22). They also mentioned many other wrecks that were too far away to visit in Kemal's little dive boat *Mandalinche*.

Among these wrecks, I was particularly interested in one that contained copper ingots, at a place far to the south called Cape Gelidonya (Cape of the Swallows).

I suspected that this might be very ancient, because the diver who told me about it recalled recovering a bronze knife from the wreck. Could this be the remains of a Bronze Age ship more than 3,000 years old? What if those copper ingots and that bronze knife were from a Mycenaean vessel, a sea trader of the time of Odysseus and the Trojan wars?

If we found a Bronze Age ship we would be like winners of the world's richest lottery.

The Cape of the Swallows
In 1959, through the film maker Stan Waterman, I managed to hitch a ride from an American yachtsman on a cruise in the Aegean, and from Kemal's description we were able to locate the wrecksite.

What we found did indeed turn out to be the remains of a Bronze Age ship, with a cargo of copper ingots from Cyprus, and many fascinating personal possessions belonging to the ill-fated crew. It lay in 90ft of water at the foot of a steep cliff on a desert island, where the current ran swift enough to snatch your mask off if you were not careful. This was Cape Gelidonya – the "Cape of the Swallows".

After two seasons in Bodrum, my mad project to start an underwater archaeology project in south Turkey had gone farther than I and my Turkish friends, Hakki Bey and Mustafa, could have dreamed. We had made friends with the sponge divers and the people of Bodrum. We had won the favor of the local authorities and the provincial governor, Bodrum's deputy to the Turkish parliament. We were beginning to get moral support from American and English archaeologists.

What we lacked was a permanently established institution that could back us financially and provide us with academic standing. From an archaeological point of view, the wrecks that Captain Kemal had shown me were the logistic equivalent of a buried city, to which were added the vast problems of conservation, along with the logistical problems of diving.

Land excavations in that part of the world needed little more than money to pay laborers and a storeroom workshop with a door that locked. We required tons of diving equipment; experts to train local people; boats, barges and a conservation lab; a space where all this equipment could be stored and worked on. The ratio of tinkering with equipment to actual diving is today about three to one; it was worse then, when underwater cameras were encased in housings that always leaked, and spare parts were thousands of miles away.

The final element that made it all possible was the interest and enthusiasm of Professor Rodney Young of the University of Pennsylvania Museum, who had been excavating at Gordium in Turkey for years and knew his way around the labyrinth of archaeological officialdom in that country better than any other American. He persuaded George Bass, one of his best graduate students, to take over the project, and set to work to introduce George and I to sources of funding and to solicit the Turks for a permit.

George and I devised a plan of action which, with modifications, has served as the research design for every successful scientific underwater excavation that has been done since.

We would be shore-based, and work from a boat moored over the site. We would need two boats, one as a diving platform, the other for trips to Antalya, the nearest large town, for supplies.

The crew would be a standard archaeological crew, i.e. director, associate director, photographer, surveyor, draftsman, conservator, logistics person, cook, and last but not least, the Turkish commissioner who would see to it that we stayed out of trouble with the local authorities and take charge of whatever we excavated, which was the property of the Turkish government.

In place of the traditional "pickmen" – local workers used for excavation – we would attempt to ensure that every member of the above crew was a diver, and we would need four or five extra divers, hopefully people that had usable skills: it would be too expensive and wasteful to take divers along if that was their only skill. We needed a chief diver who had worked with airlifts, the underwater vacuum cleaners used for moving sand and mud off the wreck.

Our policy was that everybody should be a diver, since diving is just a minor skill that can be learned by almost anybody who is reasonably young and healthy and does not suffer from medical problems. It is much easier to teach a skilled tradesman to dive than it is to expect unskilled

A sketch of Kemal the Turkish sponge boat captain with the author at a Bodrum café. Aegean sponge fishers like Kemal were familiar with the sites of hundreds of wrecks on the seabed in their area. Kemal had already shown us numerous wrecksites off Bodrum on the west coast of Turkey, and we had spent an exciting if uncomfortable season mapping and identifying them. However, it was his mention of bronze ingots at a place called Cape Gelidonya that we found especially interesting. It seemed more than possible that such objects indicated the presence of a wreck from the Bronze Age, the time of Odysseus and the city of Troy.

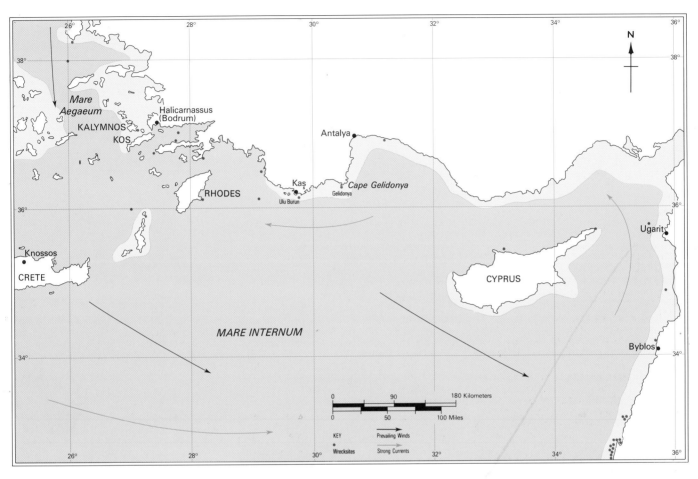

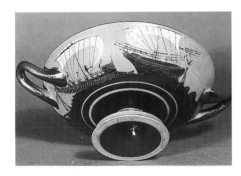

Bodrum is the Turkish name for ancient Halicarnassus, the birthplace of the "father of history", the 5th century BC writer Herodotus. It was also the city of Mausolus, the ruler whose magnificent tomb gave us the word "mausoleum", and gave the ancient world one of its Seven Wonders. Using the expert local knowledge of sponge fishers, we found a new world of ancient wrecksites on the seabed, and began to evolve new techniques for recovering, identifying, interpreting and preserving these precious fragments of the past.

Ships and the sea provided a rich theme for ancient Greek vase painters, whose patrons often owed their power to control and exploitation of the seaways. Oared galleys and sailed vessels, their hulls fitted together by mortises and tenons, were a prime means of transport.

Cape Gelidonya and its adjacent islands provided an inhospitable site for our excavation, with occasional rockfalls and daylong exposure to the sun. However, the deep bay was protected from all sides except the south, and would shelter us till the fall, Captain Kemal assured us.

people to practice a trade underwater when they have not learned this trade on the surface.

All this work required a considerable organization, not to mention the Turkish boat crews, which were commanded by Captain Kemal.

Although we were working on a shoestring, and considered our diving as just a common skill among many, we did not underestimate the dangers of working in 90ft of fast-flowing water. George consulted the US Navy on the best way to use their repetitive decompression tables. The Turkish divers, although they have a high incidence of bends, are fanatics about safety in other things: they are scrupulous about tending divers while they are down, and handling boats so that divers are not injured by them.

We set a high standard of safety at Cape Gelidonya: in the 26 years since the excavation, George Bass and I have supervised tens of thousands of hours of deep diving, and have never had a fatal accident or a permanently disabling case of bends.

The beach

George Bass and I, with the crew we had assembled, returned the next year, and after a struggle getting through customs, set sail from Bodrum for the camp site on the mainland that Mustafa and I had selected the year before. We had hired two boats, Kemal Arras's *Mandalinche* and a retired sponge dragger *Lutfi Jelil*.

Our first job was to set up a base camp on the only beach within miles that had a supply of fresh water, and was sheltered from the prevailing winds. The sponge divers called it Su Ada, "water island", and it was a godforsaken place, accessible only by sea. Its narrow beach would be underwater in a strong southerly wind, and a hard rainfall would cause rockfalls. Luckily, rain is rare before September in that part of the world, and southerly gales (the Turks call them *lodos*, the Greeks, Italians and Arabs *sirocco*) would not start until October. We hoped!

All our equipment had to be unloaded with the ship's block and tackle and ferried ashore with the launch. We had brought with us everything needed for a camp for nearly 20 people for a period of two months.

Our first requirement was fresh water. Everything we took out of the sea went into fresh water, which had to circulate in order to wash over 3,000 years of acquired chemicals from the delicate material. In addition to that, we needed water for cooking, drinking and washing. Twenty people use a lot of it!

We were anxious to get to work on the site, and above all worried that it might have been robbed in the year that had gone by since Mustafa and I had done the preliminary survey.

From cargo carrier, *Lutfi Jelil* now became our diving platform. On the first dive, Uncle Mehmet suited up in helmet

gear and led us to the site. We found, to our joy, that the wreck was intact, as I remembered it from a year before.

Our plan was simple enough: draw and mark everything, then start to raise material – but not before it was drawn! Photographs would be a help in making the drawings: black-and-whites would be shot every day, and developed that night. In the mornings the "officers" discussed what we would do next.

At Cape Gelidonya, as in all future excavations, we spent a lot more time discussing what we were going to do than actually doing it on the sea bottom. Before each diver went down, he or she was briefed on what to do.

One of the breakthroughs of the Cape Gelidonya expedition, seen through the hindsight of 25 years, was the underlying principle needed to develop what has become a new subscience – simply that an archaeological excavation must be directed by an archaeologist. The reason that there had been no successful excavations of this type before us was that no archaeologist before George Bass had bothered to learn how to command an expedition in the sea.

Frederick Dumas, Captain Kemal and I had become and remained divers because we were fascinated by diving and had an emotional attachment to it. George Bass learned diving because he was an archaeologist and there was material underwater that was worth excavating. George's dedication was, and remains, not to diving, not to any particular historical period (although he is a renowned specialist in the Aegean Bronze Age), but to archaeology itself.

The breakthrough at Gelidonya, then, was the idea that good technical archaeology could be done underwater.

George's attitude towards all technology could be paraphrased by a great shipwright joiner I once knew, who, when foreman at his local yard, said to his men that he wasn't there to tell good men how to do a job, just to see that it was properly done. There is no one right way to build a wooden vessel, although there are myriad wrong ways. The same applies to drawings underwater, or the multifarious other jobs that have to be done so that the archaeologist who must make meaning of an underwater excavation has usable raw material to hand.

The one principle that George got across in the first days of the expedition was that we were there to understand the site, not recover a lot of stuff. Until something on the bottom was understood in its relationship to everything else, it stayed on the bottom. Recovery could take place only when everything on the site was well recorded, in place. The sequence would be surveying, drawing, photography, and more drawing with the help of photography. Then excavation, followed by recovery of what had been drawn and excavated from the site, then more

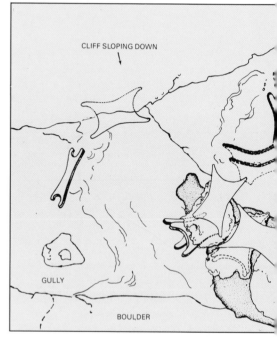

A **survey sketch plan** of the Cape Gelidonya wrecksite excavation area. Claude Duthuit and I made many photographic mosaics of the wrecksite, and Honor Frost drew up a series of plans on the drawing board. Comparison with the plan of the discoverer of the site, Mustafa, revealed that many of the ingots had already disappeared.

CLIFF SLOPING DOWN

GULLY

BOULDER

digging, more drawing and so on.

In his quiet way, George Bass impressed on all hands that he was not interested in things because they were pretty, or because they were rare, valuable or would look well in a museum showcase; but because they were there, and they said something if only one could understand what they were trying to tell us. At first, Dumas and I shook our heads when George would spend a whole dive hanging on to a rock, contemplating the site. We had been taught that when you hit the bottom you were supposed to do something down there.

Our first job, then, was to make a map of the site, which would be much more accurate than the sketch plan that Mustafa and I had made the year before. None of us had ever made an accurate plan of a shipwreck site before; we all had different and often conflicting theories on how to go about the job. I was in favor of photo mosaics, whereas Honor Frost, on the other hand, liked to sit on a rock and make drawings by eye and measurement.

Detailed drawings were part of the job, but they had to fit into an accurate master plan. George, remembering his basic surveying in archaeology courses, experi-

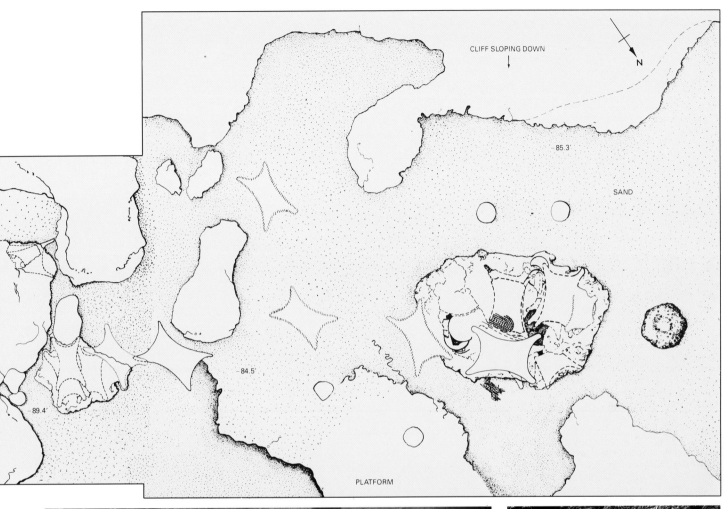

85.3'

SAND

CLIFF SLOPING DOWN

N

84.5'

89.4'

PLATFORM

Divers working at the wrecksite brought up numerous unidentifiable lumps and boulders that later yielded artifacts dating from 3,000 years ago; picks, hoes, axes, mirrors, chisels, a spade, as well as numerous cast bronze ingots of the so-called ox-hide type.

Beach camp at Cape Gelidonya. The cliffs rose sheer from a narrow strip of beach about 50 feet wide or less, exposed to a pitiless glare. Under the cliffs we found two springs where generations of voyagers had dug temporary basins in the sand to catch the fresh water seeping from the rock.

mented with leveling rods and string, and we sometimes got tangled up in it: not funny when one was 90ft down!

Once the top layer was drawn and photographed in place, we could begin to gather surface objects. We dived, then, with wicker shopping baskets and a slate, on which was written the numbers of the objects we were permitted to remove. Tiny objects went into plastic bags.

Raising lumps

The copper ingots that made up the main cargo weighed about 30lb (14kg) each and lay stacked into heaps where they had slid when the hull disintegrated. Each lump was covered by a thick layer of calcium carbonate concretion as hard as Portland cement.

The first job was to free the ingot lumps from the bottom. If we could get them loose, then they could be raised. Once ashore, they could be orientated to fit the master plan, and cleaned in place. It was obviously much easier to separate lumps under a tent flap ashore than to slave away in 90ft of water; although, if it had not been for danger of the bends, we would probably have preferred to work underwater, as it was hellishly hot on that Turkish beach.

We hit on a trick for separating the lumps from the bottom: a simple hydraulic auto jack. We dug holes in the bottom beside the lumps, inserted the jack, and presto! More often, though, we had to quarry the lumps out of the bottom, using a sledgehammer and stone mason chisels. The person who had to hold the chisel needed a lot of trust in the man wielding the hammer.

When we had planned the expedition, we had thought that the Turkish divers would be useful in the heavy work of separating the blocks of cargo from the bottom. However, in a current that was often so strong that mountaineers' pitons were required to hold us in place, the helmet divers could not stay in one place and swing a hammer.

Once cut free, jacked up, and lashed in a sling, the lumps could be lifted off the bottom and, with the help of a lifting balloon, moved so that *Lutfi Jelil*'s cargo hoist could be attached. They were then winched to the surface.

We discovered that the "cement" became rock hard and almost impossible to separate from any object if it was allowed to dry out. However, copper and bronze form a layer of nasty green corrosion between the metal and the cement of the concretion. If this is attacked while wet, it comes off easily.

Cleaning lumps became an obsession with some of us. The camp on the beach rang with the clink of hammer on chisel.

The hull lump

One area on the wrecksite contained much organic material. This lay between the great boulder that marked one end of the site, and the cliff down which the ship had slid when it sank. Under the heap of ingots that lay there we saw, peeping out from under a mass of hard concretion, traces of wood. These consisted of round and square-cut pieces: it seemed that we had found part of the actual structure of the ship itself.

Once we had uncovered just enough to get an idea of what was there, we were afraid to go on, because the wood was so delicate that it dissolved if a hand was waved over it.

There was also what appeared to be rope. One of the most moving experiences I have ever had underwater was when I saw that a knot had been tied in the rope. The knot was a bowline, well known to sailors. It dissolved before my eyes, but for a moment I felt in communion with the unknown sailor who had tied it more than 3,000 years ago. I knew then, 90ft down, under that savage rock, what Schliemann must have felt the day he lifted a gold mask at Mycenae, and saw a human face turn to dust before his eyes. That night, so the story goes, he sent a cable to the king of Greece announcing, ". . . today I gazed upon the face of Agamemnon."

I had no king to cable to, but I felt that I'd seen the handiwork of a sailor who might have known Odysseus. I'd learnt my bowlines from a man who had "sailed in strong" at the twilight of man's heroic adventure with sail. The man who taught the sailor who tied that bowline had lived in the bright dawn of it, a thousand generations before.

It was obvious that we would never be able to unlock the mysteries that the hull lump contained if we tried to excavate it on the sea bed. It would have to be separated from the bottom, without smashing it, wrapped up, and lifted to the surface, very, very gently. Raising the hull lump was a major project.

Before we moved anything, the delicate wood we had exposed had to be drawn and photographed. Honor Frost spent days making a careful drawing before we attempted to chip out the lump. Luckily, it came free easily. We built it a made-to-measure box, eased it in, and covered it with a sheet for the trip to the surface.

The last step in the excavation was to clear sand right to bedrock. The only tool that could do this was the airlift (although some kinds of dredges work well, we have subsequently discovered). This tool works as a giant vacuum cleaner. The principle is simple: you suspend a piece of pipe in the water more or less vertically. The pipe can range in size from 3in upwards. If you pump air to the bottom of the pipe, it rises in the pipe, creating a suction effect on its lower end, because of the difference in pressure: the water at the bottom is always under more pressure than water at the top.

Before we set out for Su Ada beach, we asked everyone who might know about airlifts – the US Navy, various submarine engineers – and got a lot of ambiguous answers which would have been useful if we were calculating fuel consumption against ability to move sand in quantity, as in, for instance, dredging a dock basin. For the sort of job we were doing, none of the answers made much sense.

Dumas was the only person on the crew who had worked with airlifts. On his advice, we provided ourselves with two sets of pipes, one 3in and one 6in, and we hoped that *Mandalinche*'s diving compressor could furnish enough air for them. We found that the machine worked well enough, except that the 3in version clogged because it was too small, and the small compressor on *Mandalinche* did not produce enough volume for the 6in. Although the device is very simple, making it work properly is not; skill in rigging it, and using the right material for the pipe is a very important factor.

The author lifting a copper "oxhide" ingot from the Cape Gelidonya wrecksite. It was once erroneously believed that such ingots were cast to resemble ox-hides, and that each was equal to the price of an ox in a kind of pre-monetary currency. In fact the protuberances are probably a kind of handle. In addition to ingots, the wrecksite yielded a mass of broken bronze tools, as well as pieces of 3,000-year-old timber from the hull and personal possessions of the crew.

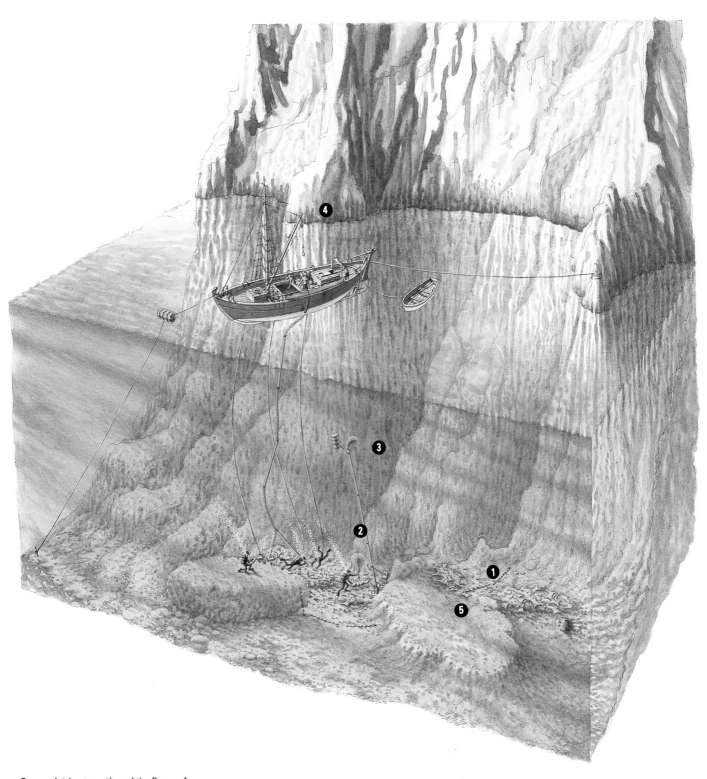

Our seabed excavation of the Bronze Age wrecksite, carried out at a depth of 80ft (24m), strangely resembled a conventional above-ground archaeological dig, with meter poles (1) scattered everywhere, and numbered plastic tags marking all visible objects. Marine archaeological equipment included lifting balloons (2), an airlift (3), and winches (4). In the middle of the wreck area was the "platform" (5), a rocky shelf covered with ingots, that we eventually got to the surface in one piece. It turned out to contain a cargo of Bronze-Age scrap – broken bronze tools and bits of ingots held together by limestone seagrowth. Ropes and part of a basket were found within a heap of ingots in this lump, and beneath it lay pieces of ship's timbers.

Significance of Cape Gelidonya

We finished cleaning up the site just as the first southerly gale of that fall brought great waves which washed us out of our tents. A heavy rain loosened rocks from the cliff above, sending huge pieces crashing down on our camp. We decided it was time to go.

Back in Bodrum, the salvaged materials were deposited in tanks expressly built by us inside the museum which Hakki Bey, Mustafa, Kemal and I had created from the ruins of the crusader castle (see p. 22).

As an adventure, the expedition was an achievement in its own right. Getting a variegated crew of Turkish villagers, British, American, French, and German divers, archaeologists and technicians to a remote beach in what was then a very primitive part of the world, along with the equipment needed for them to achieve their respective tasks, was an accomplishment. So was keeping them reasonably healthy (we all suffered more or less from malnutrition, without ill effect – I personally went from 207lbs at the start to 165 at the end). The diving program proved to be both safe and effective, involving as it did hundreds of hours of underwater work from a crew of divers of whom half at least were amateurs.

Doing the whole job for something like $25,000 of 1960 money was an achievement as well.

Yet there was nothing in the Cape Gelidonya field project that had not been done before, if one looked at its individual parts. The structure and organization of the project could have been done by anybody with the same kind of training that George Bass and I had both experienced, on expeditions and in the military. All the tools we used had already been invented elsewhere, and used better by others before our time.

Yet there was something unique about Gelidonya, something that had never happened before: it was the first time that such a project had been carried out under the direction of real archaeologists, as pure archaeology, with a crew to match. It proved, once and for all, that archaeology is only archaeology, wherever in the world it is carried out.

The historical significance of Cape Gelidonya, then, is that it demonstrated that problems raised by the need to dive to a reasonable depth, in a reasonably friendly sea, should not cause archaeology to become salvage.

Captain Kemal, Honor Frost, Joan Taylor, Hakki Gultekin and Rodney Young, with myself as the catalyst, had put together something that had not been managed before. Yet the whole adventure would have been meaningless, in the end, without the archaeologist George Bass, whose job it was to make meaningful a ton of corroding copper and bronze and the other things that we had raised from their ancient grave.

Bronze Age time capsule from 1200BC

George's final conclusions, worked out in collaboration with other scholars, were published long after the excitement of the discovery had died down, and the glossy magazines had announced our achievement of finding what was then the world's oldest shipwreck. From these corroded pieces of metal, together with fragmentary organic remains, he and his colleagues were able to trace out a fascinating and detailed story. This was published several years later, in *Transactions of the American Philosophical Society*. The following is a paraphrase.

At the close of the Bronze Age in the Eastern Mediterranean, c.1200BC, a merchantman of about 30–40ft (9–12m) was sailing toward Cape Gelidonya, the southernmost point of the Anatolian peninsula. Her last major port of call had been Cyprus, where the crew had loaded a ton of metal cargo.

Four-handled ("oxhide") copper ingots, each of them weighing about 45lb (20kg), were carefully wrapped in matting and stacked in neat piles fore and aft, and bronze "bun" ingots were stacked among them. Wicker baskets filled with bits and pieces of broken ingots and broken bronze tools – scrap metal for reworking – were placed wherever they would fit on the layer of brushwood that protected the thin planks of the hull.

Incidentally, the practice of protecting the hull with a "cushion" of brushwood continues to this day and was probably in use at the time of Odysseus – there is a passage in the *Odyssey* which appears to refer to this quite clearly.

Tin ingots (bronze is of course an alloy of tin and copper) may already have been on board, as well as scraps of lead and pieces of unworked crystal. Probably included among the items of trade, near the ship's bow, was a jar full of colored beads and a bracelet of adjustable size. The contents of the other jars were perishable, but they may have included spices.

The crew lived near the stern, with a single ship's lamp to light the area. Their meals, like those of Mediterranean sailors today, were supplemented with olives and, perhaps, fish which they caught themselves with lead-weighted lines. Storage jars probably held other food, and, of course, wine and water.

On board was a merchant, and his equipment enabled him to carry on trade in almost any Eastern Mediterranean port. His balance-pan weights, necessary for judging the price of metal in either scrap or finished form, were set to various standards that allowed him to deal with other merchants in Egypt, Syria, Palestine, Cyprus, Troy, the Hittite empire, Crete, and probably the Greek mainland. For official transactions he carried his personal seal, a cylinder which may have been an heirloom handed down from generation to generation. This seal was

500 years old when the ship went down.

The merchant or members of his crew also possessed five scarabs that may have served as religious talismans, seals, or even souvenirs. The presence of an astragal, a knucklebone token that Homer's heroes used to throw as dice are thrown today, may indicate that games of knucklebones were played on board. Alternatively, as the emblem of Mercury, god of merchants, it may have been used in order to discern the divine will in moments of doubt.

The final voyage

The ship was following the usual route from Syria and Cyprus to the Aegean, taking advantage of the westward current to make for the freshwater supply point of Phoenikous (modern Fenike). But first she had to pass Cape Gelidonya and its string of tiny islands, described by the classical writer Pliny as "extremely dangerous to mariners." Attempting to sail between the two large islands nearest the mainland, the ship ran onto jagged rocks and sank in nearly 90ft of water.

On board were found all of the elements necessary for bronze-making, including the earliest known industrial tin, and it is

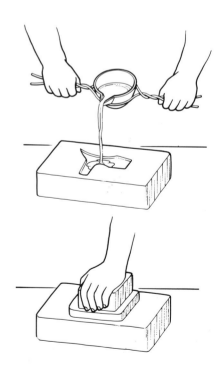

At the Cape Gelidonya wreck we found a tin ingot as well as numerous copper ones. The combination of these two metals, together with the presence of large quantities of broken bronze tools, suggests that the vessel may have been owned or chartered by a smith working his way up the coast, smelting tin and copper into bronze by means of this primitive but effective moldcast. The cargo would then have been the raw materials of a seaborne smith or tinker, perhaps exchanging new tools for old.

likely that the merchant not only traded in raw materials but also worked them himself. Metalworking tools were found in the "cabin" area, suggesting that hammering, sharpening and polishing activities took place on board. Furnaces for smelting could be quickly made of stone and clay at various stops along the route.

The nationality of the ship can be established with some certainty from the personal possessions of the merchant and crew. The merchant's own special cylinder seal is Syrian. The scarab amulets are almost certainly Syro-Palestinian imitations of Egyptian scarabs. The ship's lamp is also strictly Syro-Palestinian in form. The weights, though varied enough to allow the ship to trade in almost any Levantine port, are mostly Near Eastern. The basketry and matting also come mainly from the East.

So the evidence strongly suggests that the ship at Gelidonya was a Phoenician merchantman, sailing with a Syrian merchant from a Syro-Palestinian port. Dated to about 1200BC, it indicates that there was extensive Phoenician activity in the Mediterranean at a date much earlier than usually supposed. In the Bronze Age, they voyaged to Cyprus and Sardinia,

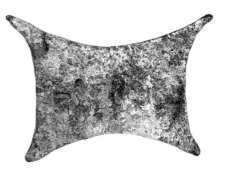

A bronze tripod from Cyprus (left) showing an ingot carrier, compared to an ingot found at Cape Gelidonya (above). Although these ingots frequently appear in ancient Egyptian wall paintings in association with the Keftiu (Cretan) people, they are in fact more closely associated with Syrian merchants, who carried on mining and smelting operations on the copper-bearing island of Cyprus.

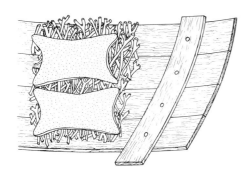

Wood preserved from the original wreck may have been part of the ceiling (inner lining) of the ship, according to George Bass, and seems to have been connected to a heavier strake. Over these ceiling strakes we found a large pile of cut sticks that may have served to protect the thin planks against the heavy metal cargo, lying beneath the ingots. This practice of cushioning cargoes with brushwood was still in use at the time of the excavation. Its presence elucidates a passage in the *Odyssey* 5,256, where Homer describes Odysseus as putting down a layer of brushwood in the ship he was building:

> He fenced in the whole with wattled bulwarks
> to keep it proof against the water, making the
> layer of brushwood thick.

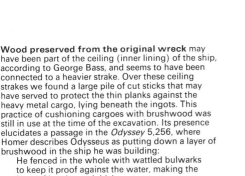

Personal possessions of the mariners recovered from the Bronze Age wrecksite reveal a strong Syro-Palestinian influence. The scarab amulets (top), good luck charms carried by crew members, appear to connect with sites in Palestine, Syria and Cyprus, although deriving from an Egyptian origin. The magnificent seal (above) probably belonged to the master of the ship and also has Syrian associations. The age of the seal is far greater than that of the rest of the ship, suggesting that it may have been a family heirloom conferring prestige and honor on its owner. The axes (left) formed part of the ship's cargo, possibly scrap metal awaiting re-use and recasting as the ship worked its way along the coast of Asia Minor from Cyprus. Archaeological evidence that Levantine mariners were active at this period (10th century BC) supports Homer's claim, long thought anachronistic, of "Phoenician traders" in the time of Odysseus.

where there were supplies of tin. Are these the Phoenicians whom Homer mentions in the *Odyssey*? It seems very likely.

After Gelidonya

Mention of Phoenician traders in the *Odyssey* has been used by scholars to prove that the work dates to the 8th rather than to the 11th or 12th century BC, as the romantics among us would prefer. Yet Bass has pointed out that "oxhide" ingots of the type found at Cape Gelidonya were manufactured from some time before 1400BC to some time after 1200BC. There may even have been a Cypriot-Phoenician monopoly in the trade during this period.

Ingot shipwrecks were discovered and salvaged by sponge divers before we excavated at Cape Gelidonya. Seventeen complete ingots from Kyme in Euboea, discovered in 1900, are earlier than the Gelidonya ones. From contemporary references we were able to explore the site, and found deep mud in the area described in the early reports. The rest of the ship may still be there, although it is probably under the breakwater.

In 1961, a year after Gelidonya, I was interviewing sponge divers at Kalymnos, and showing photos of ingots found on the site. A sponge dealer recognized the photo of a "bun" ingot, and claimed that an old captain he knew was using one for a door stop. Unfortunately, we found that the captain's widow had sold it for scrap years before. However, the last surviving member of the crew recalled the incident when it was recovered, and said that they had found a heap of ingots, both bun and oxhide, in the gulf of Alanya, south Turkey. He remembered that they had salvaged "over a ton" of copper, which was sold for scrap.

George Bass's crew searched the area with electronic equipment, but without result. We do not yet have detection devices that can find copper under mud. Someday we will, and these wrecks will then be found.

In 1975 we found what seemed to be a wreck from the Early Middle Helladic period of perhaps 2600BC, off the uninhabited island of Dhokos in the gulf of Hydra. Due to delays in obtaining official permits, and leaks to the press, skin divers got to the wreck first and robbed it. Something may yet be found there when the Underwater Archaeology Service in Greece becomes better organized.

The Treasures of Ulu Burun

In 1983, the present director of International Nautical Archaeology, Dr Don Frey, was giving slide talks in the sponge diving villages as a continuation of the education program Mustafa Kapkin and I had begun in 1958. He hit the jackpot. A diver claimed to have seen a heap of ingots at the bottom of a sheer cliff near Kaş, some miles south of Bodrum.

A team of archaeologists from both the INA and Bodrum Museum were sent

along to investigate the discovery. The wreck they found on the slope beneath the sheer cliff at Ulu Burun is undoubtedly the most spectacular ancient shipwreck ever discovered. Deep and dangerous, it begins at 140ft and ends somewhere beyond 170. A century and a half older than the Gelidonya wreck, it includes ivory, glass, copper ingots in hundreds, amphoras, stirrup jars, precious personal possessions from the crew, and timber from the ship itself.

The Ulu Burun wreck yielded 300–400 ingots, very many more than were found on the Gelidonya ship. These were mainly of the four-handled "oxhide" variety. Several fragments of four-handled tin ingots – the earliest known ingots of this metal – were also discovered, though these were in a very poor state of preservation, due perhaps to an electrolytic reaction with copper.

Studies of the Syro-Palestinian amphoras raised from the wreck have revealed traces of resin. These have now been shown to have contained terebinth. One amphora contained orpiment (yellow arsenic), a common pigment in Egypt in the 18th dynasty and later.

Two glass ingots, colored with cobalt – the earliest intact glass ingots known – were found lying loose under a thin cover of sand. Unworked ivory – both elephant and hippopotamus – was also discovered. Other finds included Cypriot export pottery stored within pithoi, Syrian pilgrim flasks, silver bracelets and a beautiful falcon-shaped gold pectoral, perhaps of Canaanite inspiration (although Bass

suggests that it could have been created at Ugarit). As at Cape Gelidonya, bronze tools, merchant weights and glass beads were also raised from the wreck.

Well-articulated timber remnants were found beneath the cargo. The ship seems to have been a mortise and tenon vessel, similar in construction to the Kyrenia ship of a thousand years later. Its nationality is difficult to ascertain, although the possible personal possessions are of Syro-Palestinian origin, and the merchant weights derive from the Near East.

Bass tentatively dates the wreck (mainly from the ceramics) to early in the 14th century BC – some 150 years older than the ship at Cape Gelidonya. He suggests that it provides further archaeological evidence of a coast-hugging sea route for the east-to-west transport of copper in the eastern Mediterranean throughout the Late Bronze Age. More specific details of the ship's route can only be the subject of conjecture. On the evidence of the cargo, both Cyprus and the Syro-Palestinian coast were visited before the ship sailed westward. It could have been destined for Rhodes, or the Asia Minor coast, or the Greek mainland, before being dashed against the promontory of Ulu Burun.

This wreck, even more than the one at Cape Gelidonya, undoubtedly supplements knowledge of the flow of goods, especially raw materials, depicted in Egyptian art – tomb paintings of the period show ships with pithoi on their decks, sailors with pilgrim flasks, and Syrians carrying amphoras, oxhide ingots, and even elephant ivory.

The Cape Gelidonya vessel and also the Ulu Burun ship, some 200 years older, may have closely resembled this depiction of a Syrian ship from the 15th century BC tomb of Kenamun, mayor of Thebes in Egypt. Egyptian artists' convention shows important personages – here the long-robed Syrian traders – as bigger than the other figures. One sees to the unloading of the cargo while the other presents merchandise for official weighing and inspection. Amphoras containing products such as wine and oil are unloaded by crew members, Shoreside booths offer goods for sale such as textiles, sandals and foodstuffs.

Finds from the Ulu Burun shipwreck, tentatively dated to the 14th century BC, by George Bass at a site not far from Cape Gelidonya. The ship carried a large cargo of raw goods: copper and tin ingots (above), glass ingots, unworked elephant and hippopotamus ivory, figs (or a fig product), amphoras containing terebinth and myrrh, orpiment (a pigment commonly used by Egyptian artists), and probably olive oil and wine. Manufactured cargo comprised

Cypriot fine wares (above), a gold chalice (top), silver jewelry of Canaanite type, a Mycenaean seal, haematite weights, bronze tools and weapons, stone artifacts, and beads of glass, faience and amber. Hull construction is similar to that of later Greco-Roman ships, Comparison of wrecksite objects with those from land sites suggests that the ship was sailing from east to west.

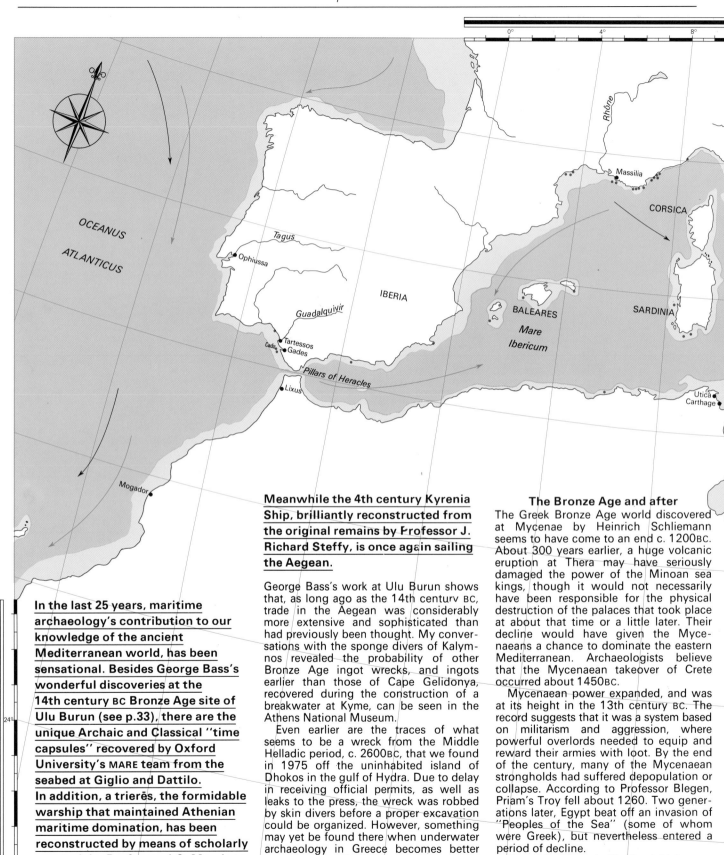

OCEANUS
ATLANTICUS

Tagus
Ophiussa

IBERIA

Guadalquivir

Cadiz Tartessos
Gades

Pillars of Heracles

Lixus

Mogador

Rhône

Massilia

CORSICA

BALEARES

Mare
Ibericum

SARDINIA

Utica
Carthage

In the last 25 years, maritime archaeology's contribution to our knowledge of the ancient Mediterranean world, has been sensational. Besides George Bass's wonderful discoveries at the 14th century BC Bronze Age site of Ulu Burun (see p.33), there are the unique Archaic and Classical "time capsules" recovered by Oxford University's MARE team from the seabed at Giglio and Dattilo.
In addition, a trierēs, the formidable warship that maintained Athenian maritime domination, has been reconstructed by means of scholarly research by Professor J.S. Morrison.

Meanwhile the 4th century Kyrenia Ship, brilliantly reconstructed from the original remains by Professor J. Richard Steffy, is once again sailing the Aegean.

George Bass's work at Ulu Burun shows that, as long ago as the 14th century BC, trade in the Aegean was considerably more extensive and sophisticated than had previously been thought. My conversations with the sponge divers of Kalymnos revealed the probability of other Bronze Age ingot wrecks, and ingots earlier than those of Cape Gelidonya, recovered during the construction of a breakwater at Kyme, can be seen in the Athens National Museum.

Even earlier are the traces of what seems to be a wreck from the Middle Helladic period, c. 2600BC, that we found in 1975 off the uninhabited island of Dhokos in the gulf of Hydra. Due to delay in receiving official permits, as well as leaks to the press, the wreck was robbed by skin divers before a proper excavation could be organized. However, something may yet be found there when underwater archaeology in Greece becomes better organized as a discipline.

The Bronze Age and after

The Greek Bronze Age world discovered at Mycenae by Heinrich Schliemann seems to have come to an end c. 1200BC. About 300 years earlier, a huge volcanic eruption at Thera may have seriously damaged the power of the Minoan sea kings, though it would not necessarily have been responsible for the physical destruction of the palaces that took place at about that time or a little later. Their decline would have given the Mycenaeans a chance to dominate the eastern Mediterranean. Archaeologists believe that the Mycenaean takeover of Crete occurred about 1450BC.

Mycenaean power expanded, and was at its height in the 13th century BC. The record suggests that it was a system based on militarism and aggression, where powerful overlords needed to equip and reward their armies with loot. By the end of the century, many of the Mycenaean strongholds had suffered depopulation or collapse. According to Professor Blegen, Priam's Troy fell about 1260. Two generations later, Egypt beat off an invasion of "Peoples of the Sea" (some of whom were Greek), but nevertheless entered a period of decline.

Events in this period in Greek history are

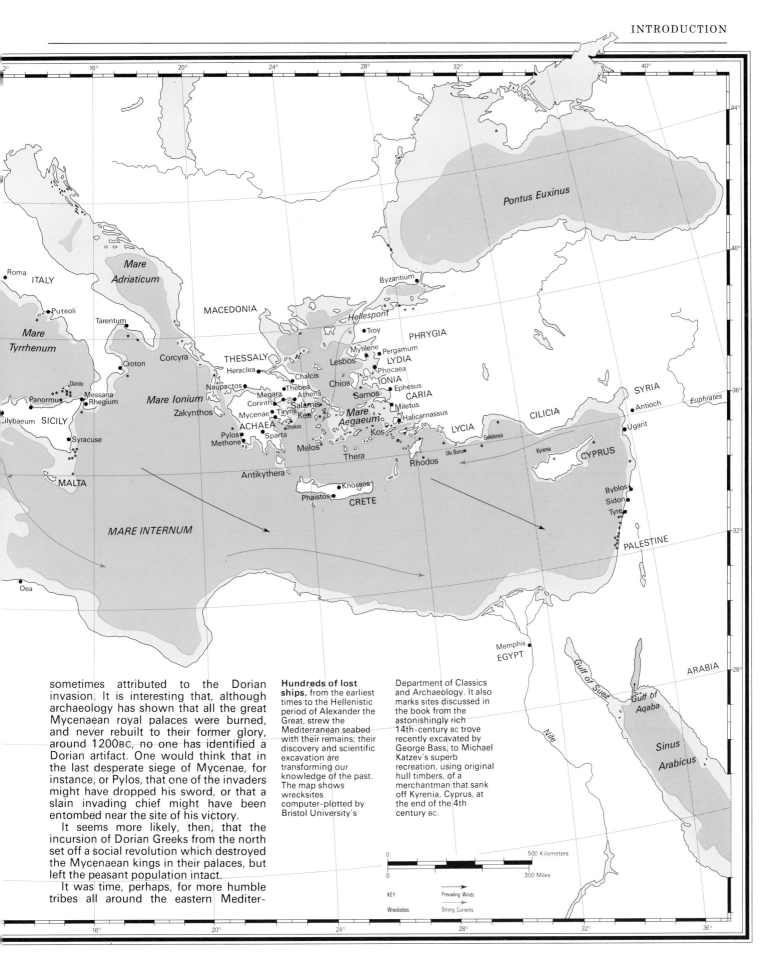

Roma
ITALY
Mare Adriaticum
Puteoli
Tarentum
Mare Tyrrhenum
Corcyra
MACEDONIA
THESSALY
Croton
Heraclea
Chalcis
Naupactos
Megara
Mare Ionium
Thebes
Athens
Zakynthos
Mycenae Tiryns
Dhokos
Kea
Salamis
ACHAEA
Pylos
Methone
Sparta
Melos
Thera
Antikythera
Knossos
Phaistos
CRETE

Lesbos
Chios
Mytilene
Pergamum
Phocaea
IONIA
Samos
Miletus
CARIA
Halicarnassus
Kos
LYCIA
Rhodos
Gelidonya
Ulu Burun

Byzantium
Hellespont
Troy
PHRYGIA
LYDIA

Mare Aegaeum

Pontus Euxinus

SYRIA
Antioch
Euphrates
CILICIA
Ugarit
Kyrenia
CYPRUS
Byblos
Sidon
Tyre
PALESTINE

MARE INTERNUM

Panormus
Messana
Rhegium
Dattilo
Lilybaeum SICILY
Syracuse
MALTA
Oea

Memphis
EGYPT

ARABIA

Gulf of Suez
Gulf of Aqaba
Nile
Sinus Arabicus

sometimes attributed to the Dorian invasion. It is interesting that, although archaeology has shown that all the great Mycenaean royal palaces were burned, and never rebuilt to their former glory, around 1200BC, no one has identified a Dorian artifact. One would think that in the last desperate siege of Mycenae, for instance, or Pylos, that one of the invaders might have dropped his sword, or that a slain invading chief might have been entombed near the site of his victory.

It seems more likely, then, that the incursion of Dorian Greeks from the north set off a social revolution which destroyed the Mycenaean kings in their palaces, but left the peasant population intact.

It was time, perhaps, for more humble tribes all around the eastern Mediter-

Hundreds of lost ships, from the earliest times to the Hellenistic period of Alexander the Great, strew the Mediterranean seabed with their remains; their discovery and scientific excavation are transforming our knowledge of the past. The map shows wrecksites computer-plotted by Bristol University's

Department of Classics and Archaeology. It also marks sites discussed in the book from the astonishingly rich 14th-century BC trove recently excavated by George Bass, to Michael Katzev's superb recreation, using original hull timbers, of a merchantman that sank off Kyrenia, Cyprus, at the end of the 4th century BC.

0   500 Kilometers
0   300 Miles

KEY   Prevailing Winds
Wrecksites   Strong Currents

35

ranean to rise and form their own little national states. The Assyrians came down "like the wolf from the fold" and destroyed the ancient state of Mitanni. The Hittites who had ruled Anatolia disintegrated as well.

If the invention of the "gleaming bronze" that adorned Homer's warriors had perhaps enabled the rule of the great royal houses of Mycenae, Tiryns, Pylos, Gla and many others, the discovery of iron perhaps spelled their downfall. Bronze was expensive and rare, and Cypriot-Canaanite traders like the men who owned the Gelidonya and Ulu Burun ships controlled the source. Iron was both cheap and common.

The discovery of iron was like the invention of gunpowder: both destroyed the dominance in battle of the panoplied knight, and gave common men a chance to rule themselves.

The hunger for land

In the aftermath of this period of confusion, landless Greek farmers, led by disgruntled aristocrats, went west (and also east) by the tens of thousands. The two major periods of colonization took place in the so-called Dark Ages (1100–900BC) and the Archaic period (750–550BC). Groups of colonists were often small, sometimes perhaps only a few dozen men, which explains how cities like Megara, Chalcis or Phocaea were able to found large numbers of colonies.

Reasonably good relations with numerically superior local populations had to be established if the new colonies were to survive. In some cases, commercial contacts had been made before colonies were set up; in others a rapport was established by combining religious beliefs or by intermarriage with the local population.

However, not all new foundations were free from trouble. In Sicily and southern Italy there were clashes with the Etruscans. South and east they came up against the Persians; in the Black Sea there was trouble with the Scythians. Everywhere, the other great maritime people of the early Mediterranean, the Phoenicians, were rivals in trade if not in arms. Nevertheless, by or before the 7th century BC, the Greeks dominated maritime trade in the Mediterranean, as they have done ever since.

Until very recently, no wrecks from either the Archaic or even the Classical periods of antiquity had been scientifically excavated. Now the work of the Oxford University MARE team, under the leadership of Mensun Bound, has thrown brilliant light on these hitherto dark areas (see pp. 42–43).

The Giglio wreck, dating to the late 7th century BC, is almost certainly that of an Etruscan ship, with a cargo that included mainly Etruscan, but also eastern Greek, Samian and Phoenician-Punic amphoras. Many of these held pitch, which has protected priceless material from looters and also bound together some of the pots. Much of the fineware pottery, as well as a magnificent bronze prestige helmet, came from Corinth, reflecting her commercial domination of the Mediterranean during the late Archaic period.

The other wreck being excavated by MARE, at Dattilo in the Lipari islands, comes from the 5th century BC. This is perhaps the most important century in antiquity, contributing more than any other to the foundation of Western civilization. Yet until now no wreck from this period has been found. The entire cargo so far examined consists of beautiful fine wares from Athens, indicating her dominance and ultimate takeover of the commercial and cultural scene from Corinth in the 5th century.

Ancient ships sail again

The chief naval weapon to enforce Athens' maritime supremacy during her period of greatness was the trierēs, which became the standard oared warship of the Classical period. This fearsome warship has now been reconstructed and relaunched in Professor Morrison's Trireme Trust, based at Cambridge, and has undergone tests at sea (see p.44).

Another seaworthy reconstruction features a wreck from the twilight of the Classical period, the Kyrenia ship. This Aegean coaster, superbly excavated and reconstructed a decade ago by Michael Katzev and his team, has now been rebuilt according to ancient methods, and has already made several voyages. *Kyrenia II* stands today as the best existing example of the sort of vessel that had to be conceived and built before modern maritime commerce could exist.

A possible Middle Helladic wreck, c. 2600BC, would certainly prove to be the oldest shipwreck ever discovered. It was identified in 1975 off Dhokos, near Hydra, by Peter Throckmorton, but the examination had to be discontinued.

An Aegean Atlantis

The legend of Atlantis, recorded in the 4th century BC by Plato from Egyptian sources*, has become widely accepted during the past 20 years as an historical myth based on the Minoan culture of the islands of the Aegean Sea.* Critical to the evidence of Atlantis's physical existence is a verified natural catastrophe that matches the final destruction of the fabled empire.

Plato's Egyptian informants spoke of an island nation called Atlantis, blessed with bountiful natural resources and possessing a flourishing maritime trade that supported art and architecture of a high standard. However, the people became "full of avarice and unrighteous power", received an unspecified punishment from Zeus, and, after attacking Europe and Africa, were defeated by the Athenians in a conflict that destroyed both combatants. Finally, Atlantis sank into the depths of the sea in a single day and night amid violent earthquakes and floods.

Atlantis and the Minoans
It has been known for more than a century that a huge eruption had taken place on the island of Thera in the Aegean, but only comparatively recently has it been established that an eruption occurred in the mid 15th century BC, and was followed some decades later by a second cataclysm, resulting in the collapse of the island into the sea. The episode coincides with the decline and then disappearance of the Minoans as an identifiable culture.

Who were the Minoans? Until 1900, when Sir Arthur Evans began his excavation of the great palace at Knossos, almost nothing was known about this unique Bronze Age civilization based on the island of Crete. Evans and his successors uncovered not only exquisite frescoes, vase paintings, jewelry and other works of art, but also huge and well constructed buildings. Everywhere were depictions of a graceful, sophisticated and opulent society where maritime concerns played a prominent part.

The period of the great palaces, beginning about 2000BC, saw a unique flowering of civilization for 500 years. Cretan influence extended over much of the Aegean, and colonies were established in many places, including the island of Thera, 70 miles (113km) away. Then, in about 1450BC, this marvelous culture collapsed. Thereafter, Mycenaean peoples dominated Crete, and the Minoan civilization vanished.

Before the stupendous eruption of the 15th century BC, in which billions of tons of volcanic products were blown out of the underlying magma chamber, Thera had been a round island about 12 miles (20km) in diameter. The collapse of the north-central part of the island followed the eruption, creating a steep-sided caldera. This bowl is 2,600 feet (800m) deep and has a volume of 4.8 cu miles (20 cu km), about three times that of Krakatoa – the Indonesian volcano whose massive eruption in 1883 is one of the greatest recorded in historical times.

The collapse of Thera is synchronous with an earthquake destruction pattern found not only in important sites on Crete itself, but also at settlements outside the island such as Trianda on Rhodes, Aghia Irini on Kea and Phylakopi on Melos. Studies of the correlation of earthquakes and vulcanism in the Aegean suggest that these earthquakes were related to and preceded the eruption of Thera.

A blanket of volcanic ash 100–160 feet (30–50m) thick covers most of Thera today, concealing extensive ancient ruins.

Thera and mythology
Plato's writings contain accounts of other catastrophes, such as the flood of Deucalion, which share a common thread of natural cataclysm and may be related to the Thera event. Some of these catastrophes have an astronomical character and could have described cosmic events of which the Thera eruption was the result. In both the biblical and Egyptian sources, a festival commemorating a great deluge, associated with the October/November zenith of the Pleiades, could be a remembrance of the Thera eruption.

Myths of Atlantis and other events that may have reference to the Thera eruption are an important part of the interdisciplinary study of the region. The mythology of the eastern Mediterranean is so rich and pervasive that it should not be ignored merely because it does not fit easily into the scientific methods of our time. On the other hand, blind acceptance

An elegant ewer (above) found at Akrotiri on Thera dates to 1600–1500BC. Its almost spherical form, with channel-shaped spout and emphasized eye, points to native Cycladic origins, whereas its painted decoration, with dolphins and wavy horizontal lines, suggests a Minoan influence.
A map shows the location of Thera (Santorini) and the probable extent of the rain of ash after the eruption (right). Core samples suggest a 250–320 mile span in the second half of the second millennium BC.

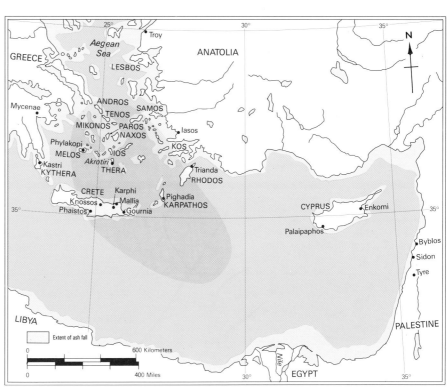

of ancient texts can be dangerous as well as wrong.

Nevertheless, the mythology that may have grown out of the Thera eruption causes us to focus on what may be profound and lasting effects, such as alterations in the psychology and religion of peoples. Rabbi Hirsch Cohen has observed that those who escaped destruction after a great natural catastrophe have an intensified need for belief in the survival of nature. He sees this as the motivation of the compassionate writer of *Genesis*, whose work may reflect some of the effects of the Thera eruption.* A post-eruption increase in the number of dedicated objects, noted by the archaeologist Platon, may reflect the same concerns.

It seems reasonable, then, to regard the eruption of Thera (also called Santorini from medieval times) as an interdisciplinary subject requiring the participation of scholars from many specialties. Yet most scholars have tried to study Thera without reference to Atlantis and other myths.

Interdisciplinary research theoretically brings together all kinds of knowledge and skills to bear on a problem. In practice, while contributing to new knowledge it also questions and sometimes demolishes long-held theories. In addition, it is inhibited by differences in the specialized languages of scholarship. For all these reasons, the question of whether Atlantis was a reality, and, if so, where and when it existed, is an inductive challenge for scholarship.

The Thera-Atlantis connection

Two decades ago, when I first took a serious interest in the discovery of Atlantis, few classical scholars doubted that Plato had invented the story. An exception was the classical archaeologist K. T. Frost. Frost identified the island of Atlantis with Minoan Crete, publishing his theories at first anonymously in *The Times* in 1909, and then at greater length under his own name in 1913.*

Frost saw Plato's story as fact, allowing for distortion and exaggeration, and itemized a number of similarities that favored such an identification: the geographical location; the political status of Knossos and the presence of other palace centers as possible "kingly states"; the importance in Crete of harbors, shipping and trade, and the extensive influence of the Minoans over that part of the Mediterranean; their peaceful disposition; and the evidence of bullfighting and sacrifice.

Thirty years later, Marinatos provided the link with the Thera eruption and the end of Minoan Crete, which in turn inspired the work of the Greek seismologist Angelos Galanopoulos. Luce and Platon also believed in the Cretan hypothesis of Atlantis.

Nevertheless, in 1969 the celebrated Cambridge classicist M. I. Finley, who doubted the devastating nature of the Thera eruption, and was convinced that

the Atlantis legend was altogether a Platonic invention, wrote in a review of my book *Voyage to Atlantis*:

> What is it that prompts scientists capable of precise and rigorous work in their own disciplines to career about in other fields of inquiry where they lack the knowledge, the tools of analysis, or even common sense?*

From my perspective of architecture, engineering and science, this deplorable "careering about" is a necessary part of successful research. Archaeology continues to be much in need of the creative aspects of these fields.

In 1965 I met Galanopoulos, who had recently written of the Thera-Atlantis connection and had added much detailed evidence to support it. Galanopoulos interprets Plato's story as a description of two islands. He equates the larger, or royal state, with Crete, and sees the smaller state as the metropolis and religious center located at pre-eruption Thera.

Plato portrays Atlantis as a round, densely populated volcanic island with an arrangement of internal harbors that in detail defy credibility. Taken more generally, the island had navigable inland waterways, was strategically located and suitable for comfortable living.

Galanopoulos and I decided at our first meeting that a geological examination of Thera, using undersea oceanographic equipment, could tell us Thera's pre-eruption shape and possibly confirm Plato's metropolis, at least in general terms. I arranged to organize the project from the Woods Hole Oceanographic Institution (where I was on the staff as an oceanographic engineer), and the result was two expeditions to Thera, one geological (1965) and the other archaeological (1967).

Woods Hole's 2,000-ton oceanographic research ship, *R.V. Chain*, was used on the first voyage, and in addition to myself and Galanopoulos, included geophysicists Rudy Zarudski and Hartley Hoskins, electrical engineer Harold Edgerton, Edward Loring (an American living on Thera), and geologist Floyd McCoy, then a graduate student at Columbia University. McCoy has continued to study the island for the past 20 years, contributing some of the most important evidence on the nature of the eruption.

After maneuvering the ship with its long strings of instruments into the deep caldera, we began to operate the seismic profiler (the most elaborate of the instrument systems). Thus we established a vertical profile of the layering of the Earth's crust, and the location of the volcanic vents. Using observations made by earlier geologists from the cliffs surrounding the caldera, we believed we could start to reconstruct the volcanological history of the island, and its shape before the Minoan eruption, to compare

with Plato's Atlantis. It has taken 18 years to find acceptable answers.

In addition to the seismic profiler, *R.V. Chain* also towed a magnetometer to measure the Earth's magnetic field. With this we were able to pinpoint the volcanic vents or plugs, identifying two within the caldera and three nearby to the south.

The deep-sea corer, an open-ended steel tube 30–50 feet (10–15m) in length, was useful in collecting samples of volcanic products at a distance from Thera, thus establishing the eruption's region of influence.

Scientific conclusions

My first project on returning home was to study the detailed reports of earlier geological surveys: one of 1948 by the Swedish ship *Albatross*, and the other of 1956–58 by the *Vema* of Columbia University's Lamont Geological Observatory. Thus I confirmed that a core containing volcanic ash, taken 62 miles (100km) southeast of Thera, had included organic material that could be dated to less than 5,000 years ago. It came from Thera, as was shown by measuring the optical refractive index of the glassy ash.

Before the cruise of the *R.V. Chain*, and some months after I had grasped the significance of these data, Dragoslav Ninkovitch and Bruce Heezen of Lamont Geophysical Observatory published a landmark paper called *Santorini Tephra*, which featured an analysis of the deep-

The geological stratigraphy of Thera is clearly exposed today (above). This has enabled a clear study of all the lavas produced at each stage of the volcanoes' activities. The late Bronze Age layers consist of large quantities of pink pumice and white ash, up to 200ft (60m) thick in places.

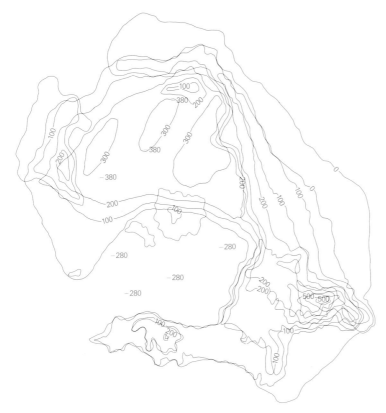

A spectacular view (above) looking northeast over the caldera from Thera today. In the background, on the right, the houses of Phira are just visible on the cliff top, with those of Oia on the far promontory. Opposite, the islets of Nea Kameni and Therasia beyond it represent remnants of Thera's outer limits before the eruption.

A contour map of post-eruption Thera (blue) superimposed onto one of pre-eruption Thera (red). Using seismic profilers and other instruments it is possible to reconstruct the original shape of the island, and thus to compare it with Plato's description of Atlantis.

sea cores containing volcanic ash from Thera.* The authors even speculated on the theory of Atlantis.

However, the geological answers we sought in 1966 were not finally published till 1984 with the work of Grant Heiken and Floyd McCoy.* They determined that before the Minoan eruption Thera had already had an internal bay in the south – a caldera formed perhaps 100,000 years ago in a previous eruption.

The northern part of Thera, which collapsed into the sea c.1450BC, then had three major volcanoes whose slopes met the internal bay in a plain at least 2.3 sq miles (6 sq km) in extent. This provided an inviting location for towns and farms, and a protected harbor for ships. Rivers probably flowed from the passes between the volcanoes to the bay.

While not precisely like Plato's fantastic description, this geological survey nevertheless proved that Thera was generally similar to, and suitable for, Plato's "metropolis". These results gratifyingly endorse the objective of *R.V. Chain*'s 1966 voyage: to find a geographical similarity between pre-eruption Thera and Atlantis.

The archaeology of Thera

The second phase of the Atlantis search, an archaeological excavation on Thera, began in May and June of 1967, when our team of Spyridon Marinatos, Emily Vermeule and myself discovered a Minoan town at Akrotiri on Thera.

We were of course not the first to excavate beneath Thera's ash: in 1867 the geologist Ferdinand Fouque discovered ancient buildings beneath the ash at Akrotiri, to be followed in 1870 by the archaeologists Mamet and Gorceix, who found frescoes, and by Zahn in 1900 who unearthed more houses.*

All previous excavators recognized that an ancient pre-Greek culture had been destroyed by the volcanic eruption, but their work preceded Evan's discovery of the palace of Knossos on Crete. As a result, their publications on the sophisticated artifacts and magnificent three-storied houses of Thera lay ignored, and the island remained a backwater until our discovery in 1967. Since 1973, the Thera excavations led by Christos Doumas have exposed a multitude of buildings and streets, storage jars, furniture, imported and domestic ceramics, and much else.*

By far the most historically important of the finds are the frescoes, and the majority of those now on display in Athens were discovered during that first season in 1967. One shows a detailed picture, 3,400 years old, of three towns, a fleet of 20 Minoan ships and small craft, a sea battle, and a coastal landing. The frescoes show that Minoan sailing vessels had booms, landing ramps on the stern, were paddled as well as rowed, carried a square sail with upper and lower yards, and decked over forward and aft. The rig is generally similar to contemporary Egyptian ships. The

larger vessels, estimated to be some 90 feet (28m) long (not counting the bowsprit), have curious roofed and decorated enclosures at the stern, probably to segregate an important person.*

The frescoes also confirm an issue previously in doubt, the existence of Minoan temples or sanctuary enclosures, thus justifying the temples of Plato's Atlantis. In addition, the dress and hairstyle of some of the people depicted suggest trade and maritime interaction with North Africa. Some frescoes show volcanic cliffs in the background, similar to today's landscape. We concluded that the entire island was heavily populated before the eruption, for we found ruins beneath the Minoan ash layer wherever it was accessible on the cliffs surrounding the island. All this indicates that Thera was a wealthy maritime center fitting Plato's description of Atlantis.

Thera and Crete

There has been some progress in correlating events on Thera with the long-known destruction of Minoan palaces on Crete. The first volcanic product to cover the Akrotiri buildings, to a depth of 16–23 feet (5–7m), was a frothy pink pumice from the volcanoes in the northeastern part of the island. Incidentally, the absence of personal possessions suggests that almost everyone had time to escape from the island before the eruption.

This was followed by a layer of fine white ash, 100–160 feet (30–50m) thick. The ash came from deep underground, erupting from the northern volcanoes and from underwater vents that had spread southwest into the southern, older caldera. Heiken and McCoy propose that the collapse of the island occurred at the same time as this final great eruption.*

Physicists W.S. Downey and D.H. Tarling have established that the pink pumice was contemporaneous with destruction levels in central Crete, whereas the later thick layer, which came 10–30 years later and marked the paroxysmal eruption, was contemporaneous with destruction in extreme eastern Crete.*

The massive destruction by fire of the Minoan palaces on Crete may have been due, according to I.G. Nixon, to a nuée ardente, a red hot jet of volcanic ash, that would have acted like a gigantic blowtorch directed at eastern Crete. This could have caused the extensive burning that cannot adequately be explained by earthquakes and tsunamis (giant waves).

Some investigators have assumed from the absence of major coastal damage that tsunamis could not have been a major force of destruction. However, my researches suggest that at Thera an initial oceanic seismic wave height of 330–660 feet (100–200m) was quite possible.

The maximum height of a tsunami varies greatly along a typical coastline and, given the steepness of most Greek islands, tsunami damage would normally

be confined to the shore. A highly energetic tsunami could have caused extensive damage on the North African coast without lasting effects in the Aegean.

In the case of tsunamis, mythology is a rich guide to possible historical records of catastrophic events. Examples are the flood of Deucalion in Attica and the drowning of Pharaoh's army in Egypt.

Since 1967 many scholars have made attempts to determine the exact absolute chronology of the Thera cataclysm. Vulcanism is responsible for distortions in the carbon-14 records, but the date is now generally accepted as between 1450 and 1350BC. If the events described in *Exodus*, dated between 1500 and 1200BC, can be shown to coincide with the Thera eruption, then a large body of Near Eastern mythology becomes more credible.

We cannot expect all the details of a legend to be consistent or historically verifiable, for they grow in the telling. There may be more than one Atlantis, and while Plato's story may have had the Minoans as its core, it is probably a composite of unrelated events recorded in ancient Egyptian archives through the ages, and worked into a cohesive story by Plato. But the fact that there is no single answer to the Atlantis riddle does not diminish the historical value of Plato's account. The evidence in support of an Aegean Atlantis lends credibility to that part which reflects the Aegean world, and justifies the search for additional historical meaning in other parts of the myth.*

The Minoan town of Akrotiri with a multitude of buildings and streets preserved beneath the pumice and ash layers, was revealed by excavation. One of the entrances (above) to the west of Complex Δ, one of the largest buildings to be discovered, was protected by a roofed "propylon" (porch) through which one could pass either into the building or into an open square backed by the West House (beyond). Dressed ashlar masonry was used to frame such doorways for strength and appearance.

A storeroom (above left) was found in the basement of a house (ground floor rooms and basements were usually reserved for storage). Rows of pithoi (storage jars) are set into benches for additional safety. Small conical rhytons (drinking cups) found were evidently used for scooping and measuring the contents of jars.
Highly decorative Cycladic pottery found at Akrotiri often featured birds (left), and sometimes rare ones, particularly on ewers. Such pottery would have been mainly for domestic use.

Part of a large frieze uncovered on a wall in the West House at Akrotiri (top) provides information on the architecture of buildings, peoples' attire, trade and maritime interaction in the Aegean and beyond, and a volcanic landscape that can still be seen today.
Minoan boats in the fresco (above) include large decorated sailing vessels with extended prows, booms, landing ramps, and square sails with upper and lower yarns. The roofed enclosure at the stern was evidently for persons of high status.

Archaic and Classical cargoes from the Tyrrhenian Sea

MARE, Oxford University's maritime archaeological research department directed by Mensun Bound, has recently come up with two fascinating wrecksite excavations from the Archaic and Classical periods of antiquity. They are the first major wrecks from either period to be investigated by archaeologists, and will enormously increase our knowledge of ancient maritime traffic and trade.

The pre-Classical wreck off the island of Giglio (600BC), excavated 1982-86, produced a wide range of products from many different locations. One of the most remarkable finds from the wreck was a pair of wooden calipers of Greek manufacture, that were excavated from a sealed context which had acted to protect them from worm parasites. These are the only calipers to have survived from antiquity. It seems more than likely that this precision instrument, which bears an extraordinary resemblance to modern calipers (see p.93), belonged to either the ship or the ship's carpenter.

The cargo included such bulk materials as copper and lead ingots, suggesting that Etruscan industrial activity at this time was flourishing as never before; but the fineware ceramics on board were predominantly from Corinth, and leave no doubt that this city state was the cultural and commercial center of the Archaic Mediterranean world.

By the Classical period, however, all this had changed; Athens with its maritime empire (see p. 44) was the new power in the zone. The Athenian achievement in the 5th century BC, the age of Pericles, is quite extraordinary, but it was made possible only by a strong economy. This, like that of Corinth in the century before, was based on an aggressive and thriving network of seaborne commerce.

The Giglio ship
The Archaic period of the ancient world (c.750-500BC) has for many years been one of the "black holes" of maritime archaeology. Now, a spectacular trove of items from a very recently excavated wreck, lying off the Tuscan island of Giglio and dating to c.600BC, promises to revolutionize our knowledge of this period. Exquisite ceramics from many different locations, musical instruments, pre-coinage currency, a wonderful helmet of outstanding artistic and technical merit, and even miraculously preserved wooden shipbuilding tools, make this one of the most exciting underwater finds of all time.

We still cannot be absolutely certain of the origin of the vessel, which dated to c.600BC, but all the indications so far point to it being of Etruscan manufacture. An abundance of copper and lead ingots from the wreck stressed the importance of the Etruscan metal deposits, which were

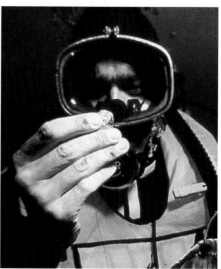

what attracted other nations to their shores and made them wealthy. The presence of musicians' pipes recalled the Etruscans' fondness for wind music, which was renowned in antiquity.

The pottery on board came from six or perhaps even seven distinct geographic locations around the Mediterranean. Corinthian wares dominated the collection, but there were also items from Sparta, Etruria, Samos, eastern Greece, and a Punic (western Phoenician) center of uncertain identity.

Other finds included lamps, tools, fishing gear, arrowheads, helmets, iron bars, copper nuggets, amber, gaming pieces, fragments of ornate inlaid furniture, a wooden plate, a writing plaque and an elaborately carved lid.

The amphoras – standard containers for the transport of commodities in ancient times – were of Etruscan, Samian, eastern Greek and Punic manufacture. They had held wine, pitch (which helped preserve the artifacts), olive oil and olives.

The painted fine wares found on board came from Asia Minor, the Peloponnese, and Corinth, and included craters (wine mixing bowls), oinochoe (jugs), lekythoi (narrow-necked oil vases), and shallow bowls. The cargo also yielded a batch of more than 20 aryballoi, elegant little round-bodied pots which were used in antiquity for holding valuable oils, perfumes and unguents.

A magnificent helmet, found on the site in the 1960s and now in Germany, had been made in Corinth from a single sheet of bronze. This helmet would have been a prestige object as well as a functional item of defense, indicating the importance of the owner.

Clearly the Giglio ship was not a tramp vessel dropping in at various ports in search of cargoes; rather she was a competitive vessel that was operating to an itinerary precisely worked out by a merchant, or merchant-captain, who was familiar with the markets. It also tells us that Greco-Etruscan trade and trading patterns were more sophisticated than had previously been thought.

The Dattilo wreck

In 1986, Oxford University MARE began work on the first major wreck from the Classical period to be investigated by archaeologists. Off the island of Panarea in the Aeolian archipelago, near a rock called Dattilo, a 5th century BC merchant ship went down carrying a cargo of Attic fine wares. The ship fetched up in a small area of seabed that is volcanically active.

By the 5th century BC the great ceramic trades of Corinth, clearly seen in the cargo of the Giglio wreck, had been eclipsed by the superior red clay wares of Athens. In comparison with the Giglio ship with its remarkably mixed cargo, the Dattilo wreck's cargo was homogeneous in nature. It consisted almost entirely of black painted cups, beakers, plates, jugs, bowls and lamps. It provides our first evidence for the largely bulk cargoes which thereafter became the norm.

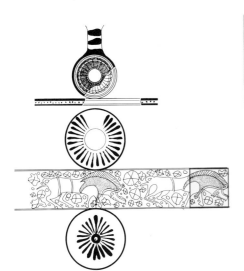

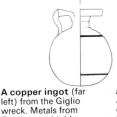

A copper ingot (far left) from the Giglio wreck. Metals from Etruria were highly prized by other Mediterranean cultures, so the Etruscans traded them for luxury goods.
A copper nugget (above left), displayed by an Oxford University MARE diver, was one of many found at the wrecksite. These were used as pre-coinage currency.
This superb Corinthian-made bronze helmet (left) was clearly destined for

a customer of high rank.
An aryballos (small oil or perfume pot) was found among the Giglio ship's cargo (above center). Made and painted in an Etruscan workshop, it imitates the animal friezes then popular in Corinth. Its full artistry and detail can better be appreciated in the drawing (above left), compiled from a series of tracings taken from the pot. The rather careless design on the bottom is probably the work of an apprentice.

A MARE diver holds one of the many skyphoi (drinking cups) (above) from the Dattilo wreck (5th century BC). This is the first wreck from the Golden Age of Pericles to be examined by archaeologists and it reflects the expanding maritime activity of Athens. Corinth was no longer the cultural and commercial center of the Mediterranean.
A patera (drinking cup) from the Dattilo wreck, still lodged in its concretion of volcanic material (left). The wreck lies in a volcanically live area, where the mud is still hot. The entire wreck is covered with a thin crust of volcanic and marine deposits.

An Athenian warship recreated

Naval supremacy was the foundation of Athens' success during her period of greatest glory in the 5th century BC. For half a century after the defeat of the Persian armada at Salamis, Athens controlled what amounted to a maritime empire in the Aegean, and the instrument of Athenian seapower was the oared galley called the trierēs. Today, after years of controversy, an accurate reconstruction of the trierēs has been built to sail the Aegean once again.

From the 7th to the 4th centuries BC, the Greeks were a people whose communications for trade, colonization, political expansion and warfare lay almost entirely across the sea. The cultural unity of ancient Greece was created by these sea-borne communications. To the exploitation of these and of the oared galleys in which they were primarily effected, Athens owed her economic and political hegemony in the 50 years after the defeat of the second Persian invasion in 480BC.

Athens at Sea

Writing at the peak of Athens' prosperity, an Athenian says of his countrymen:

> Because of their overseas possessions and the public offices they hold abroad, they learn to use the oar as second nature, both themselves and their attendants. In fact when a man is often at sea he must of necessity take the oar himself and his slave likewise, and learn the language of the sea. The majority are able to pull an oar when first they set foot aboard a warship, having had the preliminary training man and boy up to that moment.*

All Athenian citizens of a certain property rating were liable for service as trierarchs (captains of triereis), and for the expenditure which ensued. Aeschylus, the father of Greek tragedy, probably fought at Salamis; Sophocles, author of *Oedipus Rex*, commanded a naval squadron in the war against Sparta. The historian Thucydides also commanded an Athenian naval squadron.

The language of the sea, then, is naturally a constant element in Greek, and particularly in Athenian, literature. First, and always pre-eminently, Homer is full of seafaring; more can be learnt about the nature and handling of oared galleys from the Homeric poems, and in particular from the *Odyssey*, than from any other source. In the epic manner, the routines for setting out under oar and then raising mast and sail, and the reverse process for coming in

to a beach, are described minutely.* There is even a description of how Odysseus built a boat with the help of Calypso.* Homer's account of the mortise and tenon method of construction that was used by Odysseus is reflected in the wrecks of Mediterranean merchantmen found by marine archaeologists throughout antiquity (see p. 92).

In his tragedy *The Persians*, Aeschylus gives a vivid, detailed and probably accurate account of the battle of Salamis.* His contemporary Euripides describes in *Iphigeneia at Tauri*[*] how Orestes' oarsmen are hard put to it to get their beached pentecontor (50-oared ship) off a lee shore as their captain rescues his sister from the beach under a covering fire from archers in the stern. In the same author's *Helen*[*] there is an exciting account of how the disguised Menelaus succeeds in rescuing Helen from Egypt by hijacking a new royal Phoenician pentecontor.

Aristophanes was writing his comedies at Athens in the last quarter of the 5th century BC when the city was almost continuously at war. These plays give the strongest flavor of contemporary Athenian life with its constant relation to service in the fleet of 300–400 triereis. Athenian pride in this fleet is apparent when a citizen describes his country as being the place "where the fine triereis come from".*

Aristophanes also speaks of how the helmsman was trained, "first as oarsman, then as bow officer before being put in charge of the rudder oars".* He records the shout of the boatswain giving the time to the oarsmen ("*O opop, O opop*").* And he describes the frenzied scenes which followed a decision of the Assembly to launch a fleet of 300 triereis, each with a crew of 200 men:

> Athens would be full of the din of servicemen, of shouts for a trierarch, of pay distribution, of gilding of figure-heads, of the storehouse echoing, of measuring out rations, of waterskins, oar-loops and people bargaining for jars of garlic, olives, onions in nets, or trierarchic crowns, anchovies, flutegirls and black eyes.*

This vivid picture, achieving its effects by comic juxtaposition, contains the elements which later texts fill out. The trierarch's job was to see that his crew received some of their pay before sailing, to put his ship in good trim and draw the rations. "For this he was sometimes rewarded with a crown".* Crew members were responsible for personal equipment: cushions and the leather loops which held the oars to the tholepins, jars for water, nets of onions etc. Meanwhile, down at the dockyard in Piraeus, "the place would be full of the noise of oar planing, dowel hammering, oarports being fitted with leather sleeves, of pipes, boatswains, trills and whistles". The relative position and

the close packing of the oarsmen in a trierēs is memorably illustrated when he describes one of the oar crew of the state trierēs Paralos "making wind in the face of the thalamax [the oarsman sitting in the hold]".* The point is emphasized by the later author Xenophon when he asks the rhetorical question, "Do not those on board a trierēs avoid getting in each other's way only if they take their seats in order, swing forward in order, go aboard and go ashore in order?"* And another writer speaks of triereis as being "complicated mills".*

Ancient historians and the trierēs

In the histories of Herodotus, Thucydides and Xenophon there are many details of fleets, naval movements and engagements in the period from the 6th to the mid 4th century BC. The speeches of the 4th century Athenian statesman Demosthenes are also concerned with affairs of the trierarchy, stressing the importance of the maritime aspects of Greek, and in particular Athenian, history.

Thucydides underlines both the tactical and operational superiority which the Athenian triereis had achieved by the beginning of the Peloponnesian war in his account of the battle of Sybota in 432BC.* On that occasion the Corinthians, with a fleet of 150 ships, broke off an engagement in which they were winning when a second Athenian squadron, 20 strong, arrived on the scene.

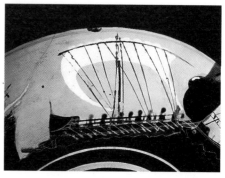

The three ship pictures painted on Attic black-figure vases are dated to the last half of the 6th century BC. The two opposite were in each case placed by the artist on the inside of a wine jar lip so that the ships would appear to be riding on the wine when the jar was full. The ship (bottom right) by the Antimenes painter (c.530–510BC), shows a triacontor, an oared galley with 15 oarsmen on each side at one level, while the ship (above right) by Exekias

(550–530BC), shows a pentecontor, an oared galley with 25 oarsmen on each side, also at one level. The ship above, painted on the outside of a cup by an unknown artist c.510BC, shows an oared galley with 25 oarsmen on each side, this time at two levels. The development of two levels of oars improved the ratio of oar-power to length (and hence weight) of hull, producing a galley of greater speed and maneuverability than the single level types.

The same point is made when, shortly afterwards, a small Athenian squadron made up of only 20 ships, based at Naupactus under Phormio, took on 47 Peloponnesian triereis at the entrance to the Gulf of Corinth:

The Peloponnesian ships formed as large a circle as they could, thus giving no opportunity for a breakthrough, with their bows outwards and their sterns inwards . . . The Athenians with their ships in single file moved round the Peloponnesians in a circle and hemmed them into a small space, constantly encircling them at very close quarters, and making them look out for an immediate attack. Phormio had given orders to his trierarchs not to attack until he gave the signal. He was expecting that the Peloponnesians would not keep formation, as infantry on land would, but that the ships would bump into each other and the smaller ships would be a cause of confusion . . . And he realized that the initiative was his to take when he wished, since his ships were the faster, and that that was the right moment for him to take it. As the breeze freshened, the ships which were already in a restricted space were beginning to fall into confusion from the simultaneous effect of the wind and of the smaller vessels, and ship was jostling ship and poles were being used to keep them apart. And the seamen were shouting and taking evasive action, and abusing each other, so that they were not listening out for the words of command or for the boatswains; and as the ill-trained oarsmen, being unable to get their oars out of water in the choppy sea, made the ships unresponsive to the helm, at that precise moment Phormio gave the signal, and the Athenians, moving in to attack with the ram, first sank one of the flagships, and then went on with the intention of putting the rest of the ships out of action as they fell in their path. The result was that in the confusion none of the ships turned to fight, but they fled . . .*

The Athenian tactical and operational edge over their rivals is again apparent in the next year when a Peloponnesian fleet 77 strong sought an engagement with Phormio's squadron of 20.* They drove nine ashore as they made their way back to Naupactus, hotly pursued by 20 very fast Peloponnesian ships. All, with one, possibly deliberate, exception reached the harbor and had time to turn and range themselves in line abreast with their bows facing seawards, ready for action if the enemy moved in against them.

When the Peloponnesian ships came up, the crews were singing the paean for the final attack. One Leucadian ship, far ahead of the others, was chasing the laggard Athenian ship. A merchantman was anchored offshore in deep water as merchantmen normally were, and the Athenian ship, reaching it first and swinging round it in a tight circle, rammed the Leucadian ship and holed her. This unexpected strike confused the pursuers; success had caused their formation to become ragged, so, with the intention of waiting for more of their ships to come up, some of the ships dug in their oars, stopping in their tracks and putting themselves at a disadvantage in view of the short distance between them and the enemy, who were in a posture to attack. Others, when they found themselves in strange waters, ran aground. When the Athenians saw what was happening they took heart and at a single command went over to the attack with a shout. Because of all the mistakes they had made already, and their state of confusion the Peloponnesians put up only a brief resistance, and then they turned.

Performance of the trierēs

In assessing the speed of the trierēs on passage, we have Xenophon's statement that the voyage from Byzantium to Heraclea on the south coast of the Black Sea, a distance of 129 sea miles, took a "long day" for a trierēs under oar.* Here one of the scribes who copied Xenophon's manuscript seems to have had some local knowledge – it was possible he worked in Byzantium, since he wrote, "A very long day". Certainly, the "long day" referred to

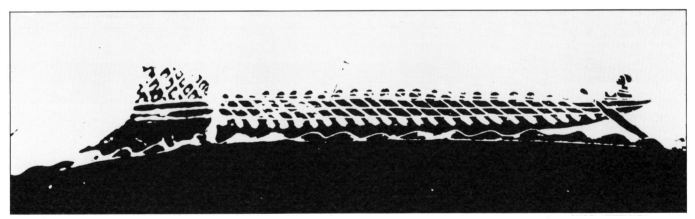

must be taken to mean anything from 16 to 18 hours with a break for the midday meal, if the average speed is not to be more than 8.5 knots.

The famous dash across the Aegean, made by the Athenian trierēs carrying reprieve for the men of Mytilene when the order to put them all to death had been countermanded, is of course exceptional:

> The crew made such haste that [they did not stop for meals] but pulled and ate at the same time, barley bread mixed with wine and olive oil, and [they did not stop to bivouac for the night but] some slept and others pulled turn and turn about.*

By good luck they had no contrary winds, and while the other ship (which carried the death sentence) did not make haste on such a disagreeable errand, the second hurried in the way described and arrived just in time to prevent the sentence being carried out. The distance was 184½ sea miles and the time taken was about 24 hours at sea, showing what a very fast oared vessel the trierēs was, when pulled by oarsmen with a high degree of dedication and skill.

By the middle of the 4th century BC such oarsmen were becoming scarce in Athens, as a speech written for a trierarch Apollodorus plainly shows:

> The fact was that in so far as I had manned the ship with good oarsmen in my keenness for a good reputation, so the rate of desertion in my ship was the highest in the fleet. In the case of the other trierarchs the oarsmen who served from the list [i.e. as conscripts] stayed with them, looking forward to their safe return home, whereas mine, full of confidence in themselves because they were good at pulling an oar, went off at the places where they were likely to be re-engaged at the highest rates of pay.*

The conditions of service during the 4th century for Athenian ships in the fleet of the second Athenian League were hardly satisfactory. Often, the general in command had no money to provide the crew with victuals, so it was up to the trierarch since, as Apollodorus says drily, "If they didn't eat they couldn't pull an oar".*

From these passages the reader may gain an idea of the kind of ship the Athenian trierēs was, both from the way she was. used at the peak of Athens' naval power and confidence, and the way she was used, and abused, in the days of Athens' naval weakness.

The ships

Although they occupy so prominent a place in the pages of 5th and 4th century Athenian writers, these oared galleys nevertheless present a somewhat con-fused image when we try to envisage the vividly described events in which they took part. The pentecontors (50-oared ships) and triacontors (30-oared ships), appear most attractively in 6th century vase paintings as simple "long ships" with 25 or 15 oarsmen a side in a single fore and aft file. There are a number of 6th century vases which show galleys with two files of oarsmen on each side at different levels. These are presumably still pentecontors and triacontors although the oars are never exactly 25 (12 + 13) or 15 (7 + 8) on the side shown. But the trierēs appearance and oar system is a much more difficult matter, in spite of the crucial part she played in Greek history for a century and a half, and the frequent references to her in the copious literature of that period.

It seems possible that the trierēs was the climax of a long period of development. First there are the simple oared galleys, seen in 6th century vase paintings depicting the ships described by Homer, and also those of the historical colonizers who spread throughout the Mediterranean, Adriatic and Black Sea coasts.

Then, when fleets began to be used in naval engagements, rather than merely as a means of transporting armed men to the scene of conflict, the keel projection in the bow came to be armed with a bronze sheath and was used as a ram. As a result the ratio of oar power to weight became an important consideration, and a second file of oarsmen, called the thalamian, was placed on each side of the ship in the hold or *thalamos* below and between the original file. The latter was known as the zygian because the oarsmen sat on the *zyga* or thwarts.

The trierēs is the next type of galley to appear; and it is a reasonable inference to suppose that this type represents a further step in the same line of development, this time with three files of oarsmen a side at different levels. The new third level, called the thranite, was located above and between the zygian.

This inference is supported by a number of reliefs and corroborated by two vase paintings. The Lenormant relief, dated to the end of the 5th century, shows the middle starboard section of an oared galley which can be reasonably interpreted as a ship with oars at three levels, the uppermost level of oars being pulled through an outrigger (a sort of false gunwale supported out from the ship's side). The relief is of course not labeled "trierēs", but at that date it could hardly be anything else.

There is a 17th century drawing in the British Museum showing a relief of a ship's prow on the same scale as the ship in the Lenormant relief, and presenting, often with mistakes, the same details. The depiction of this relief, which has now disappeared, may belong to the same monument as the Lenormant relief and must have existed in Rome at the time the drawing was made. A relief of a similar ship's stern on the same scale but not of the same marble as the Lenormant relief may be seen in the Abruzzo Museum at L'Aquila. Taken together, these can be interpreted as showing an oar system which is corroborated strongly by a vase in the Jatta collection in Ruvo.

Facts about the 4th century Athenian trierēs can be gleaned from two sources: the preserved foundations of the Zea shipsheds indicate a maximum ship's length of 118ft (37m) and breadth of 19ft (6m); and the inventories of contemporary naval dockyards show that the lengths of the oars were 13.2ft and 13.9ft (4m and 4.2m) while the number in each category – thranite, zygian and thalamian – were 62, 54 and 54. The difference in length is explained elsewhere* as the result of the narrowing of the hull at bow and stem so that, in any one unit of thranite, zygian and thalamian oars, all oars are of the same length. The difference in numbers between the levels is caused by the same narrowing, which affects the lower levels of oars to a greater extent than the uppermost level pulled through the outrigger.

The structure of the trierēs

Our knowledge of the ancient merchant ship, which sinks to the seabed and may be partially preserved by her cargo, has been enormously increased by marine archaeology. However the oared warship retained her buoyancy even when she was swamped. Accounts of ancient sea battles confirm that the trierēs, when holed in battle, remained on the surface; therefore control of the enemy's wrecked ships was a mark of victory.*

Nevertheless, the preserved timbers of contemporary merchant ships – the shell of timbers joined edge to edge by frequent

The bronze ram shown here (above) was found recently on the seabed off Athlit, near Haifa in Israel. It is too heavy to have belonged to a trireme, but is likely to have been lost by one of the larger oared warships which were built in the Phoenician cities of the Levant and in Cyprus in the 3rd and 2nd centuries BC. The timbers adhering to it display the features of the "shell" method of hull construction. By this method the hull was built up plank by plank, laid together edgewise and fastened by mortise and tenon joints at intervals of about 9in.

mortise and tenon fastenings – can serve as a guide to the method of hull construction used in the trierēs. Recent confirmation that this method was used for warships is apparent from the timbers adhering to a bronze ram found off Athlit in Israel. This ram is dated to the end of the 4th century, and from its weight is regarded as having belonged to one of the larger oared warships then in use in the eastern Mediterranean.

Our knowledge of the trierēs should be sufficient to enable us to form a fairly clear image of her. Her use is known from literature; her evolution shows that she is the culmination of a process of development. The aim was to achieve the best possible power/weight ratio in a ship designed for the quick turning and quick acceleration required by ramming tactics, and also for fast deployment over a wide area of operation. We see her as long and narrow, closely packed with her 170 oarsmen at three levels, of which the lower two pulled oars through oarports, the uppermost through an outrigger. The three oars in any one unit, consisting of one thranite, one zygian and one thalamian oar, were of the same length, and, it appears, were pulled with the same gearing.

Why, then, in the standard Liddell-Scott-Jones *Greek-English Lexicon* (new ed. 1940), does the entry which appears under *trierēs* read: "A trireme, i.e. prob. a galley with three men on each bench, each man rowing one oar, and three oars together passing through the *parexeiresia*"? Why do we find in the *Oxford Classical Dictionary* (2nd ed. 1970), "The long accepted view that the rowers sat in three superimposed banks is now generally rejected; it seems probable that, the rowing benches being slanted forward, the rowers sat three to a bench, each

rower pulling an individual oar (i.e. on the Venetian *alla sensile* system)?" Finally, why has the trierēs' oar system, which is central to the nature of the ship as a whole, been regarded (and is still regarded by some), as a problem "beyond all conjecture, like the song the sirens sang and the name Hercules bore when he dwelt among women", in the words of Sir Thomas Browne?

The riddle and the reconstruction

I must ask the reader's indulgence if the answer to these questions is given in a rather personal manner. In 1939, as a young classical scholar hoping to make an honest living as a teacher of ancient philosopy, I was preparing a lecture on the myth of Er in Plato's *Republic* when I came across the great man's description of the universe as "bound together with ropes like the undergirdings of triereis".*

Plainly the commentators did not know either why undergirdings were necessary in triereis or how, if they were necessary, they should be applied. Yet any 4th century Athenian, I reflected, would have had no difficulty in explaining what Plato meant by his simile. It did not need a philosopher or even a naval architect. But a little investigation soon showed me that to know why triereis had to be tied together with ropes required a knowledge also of what sort of ships they were and what they were designed to do; and this appeared to be a matter on which scholars and practical men had been at loggerheads for three centuries or more.

An ancient controversy

In the 16th century, scholars had noticed ancient monuments in Rome representing ships with oars at three levels, which they naturally took to be triereis. Queen

Elizabeth's Greek tutor, Sir Henry Savile, called them the "ancient portraytures remayning yet to be seene".

On the other hand, men like Lazar de Baif, the French King's ambassador in Venice, had seen Venetian galleys called *triremi* with three files of oarsmen on each side on one level, pulling separate oars *alla sensile* (the system described by Liddell-Scott-Jones and the *Oxford Classical Dictionary*). And later there were galleys, pulled *a scaloccio* by three, four, and five men to an oar, which were also called triremi, quadriremi, and quinqueremi. Naturally they assumed that these galleys were the direct descendants of the ancient Roman triremes and the Greek triereis. This view was supported by such people as Barras de la Penne, commander of Louis XIV's galleys, who declared that a ship with oars at three levels was a physical impossibility since the oars, being (he thought) of different lengths because of the different levels, could not be pulled together in time.

An apparently even stronger objection to the three-level system had been raised by Lazar de Baif: if a trierēs had three levels of oars, then a tetrerēs/quadrireme must have had four levels, and so on up to the monstrous tessaracontorēs of Ptolemy Philopator, which must have had 40 levels. Since this was a plainly absurd conclusion it followed, they thought, that the trierēs/triremis did not have three levels of oars but must have been like the Venetian *alla sensile* or *a scaloccio* galleys.

When I began looking at representations of ancient Greek ships in search of clues to the nature of the trierēs, I turned first, like everyone else, to the Lenormant relief. The trouble was that Dr W.W. Tarn, then the foremost British authority in the field and an eminent ancient historian,

A fragment of a relief depicting an oared warship (left), named after the French archaeologist Lenormant, was found in the Erechtheum on the Acropolis at Athens in the late 19th century. It is now in the Acropolis Museum. Its origin and the consequent date of about 400BC, means that it must represent the trireme. The German archaeologist Assmann recognized that the oarsmen represented were working their oars through an outrigger (see the superimposed diagram, left). An outrigger enabled the oars at the uppermost level to be of the same length as the oars at the other two (lower) levels (see also working model, above.) This disposed of the main objection to the three-level system, viz. that in requiring oars of differing lengths, it would be unworkable.

denied flatly that it represented a three-level ship at all. Then I came across a vase painting contemporary with the Lenormant relief in the Jatta collection in Ruvo, and found that the details it showed of the ship's stern exactly confirmed the proposed interpretation of the relief as a three-level ship.

Although the painting had been reproduced in A. Koester's *Das Antikes Seewesen* (1923), the nature of the ship had not been realized, probably for two reasons. In the first place the painting illustrated an incident in the story of the Argonauts, and the Bronze Age *Argo* could only be shown as a trierēs by anachronism. Secondly, the human figures were enormously exaggerated in size, thus putting the ship quite out of scale and making the details hard to recognize without comparison with the relief itself. However, such anachronism can be paralleled in many ancient ship pictures, and gross exaggeration of the figures is a hazard which the interpreter has to discount.

Taken together, the Lenormant relief and the Ruvo vase were certainly strong evidence for a three-level oar system. But the arguments against it still needed refutation, since it is because of these that the three-level oar system in the trierēs has been "generally rejected".

After the discovery of the relief in 1824, a number of writers had proposed three-level oar systems for the trierēs, some with and some without an outrigger, but in all cases the oars differed in length from level to level. In 1865 Napoleon III, who was writing a book about Julius Caesar, commissioned the distinguished naval architect Dupuy de Lôme, and an equally distinguished classical scholar, Auguste Jal, to design and build a Roman trireme on the lines currently favored. The hull was massively built and the oars were of differing lengths. Unfortunately, the ship was a disaster as she could not be pulled, and the practical men were triumphant. In fact, as we have seen, the oars of a 4th century trierēs did not differ in length according to the level at which they were pulled, and a model made in 1940 demonstrated this apparent paradox.

The second objection was weak in logic. The word trierēs/triremis could have signified, as the word trireme did later at Venice, a ship with three files of oarsmen a side, and the whole numerical series of warship names could have registered the number of files a side, not levels. A trierēs might nevertheless have had her oars at three levels even if that was not what the name meant; and the ships of larger denomination might never have had oars at more than three levels, although the number of files on each side of the ship might have increased by the *a scaloccio* system of more than one man to an oar.

In fact, although there are many representations of oared galleys from the period when ships of larger denomination than the trierēs were in use, there is no ancient picture of a warship with oars at more than three levels, If the Renaissance observers had taken from contemporary galleys and applied to ancient warships only the practice of naming them after the number of files on each side, they would have saved everybody a lot of bother.

Not only did the objections to the three-level system prove empty, but the proposed alternatives were, for the ancient trierēs, demonstrably untenable. The Venetian *alla sensile* trireme is ruled out as the historical successor of the Greek trierēs on two practical grounds: first, such a system is uneconomical of longitudinal space, and 170 oarsmen so arranged would not have fitted into any ship using the Zea shipsheds. Secondly, the *alla sensile* oars are almost twice as long as those attested for the trierēs. In any case, a historian of the 5th century AD remarks that the method of building triremes had been long forgotten by his time.

The *a scaloccio* system of the later Venetian galleys was also proposed in the Renaissance and again in the 19th century for the trierēs. But that proposal, which has much else against it, is killed dead by a text in Thucydides which shows clearly that in the last half of the 5th century BC each oarsman in a trierēs pulled his own oar. And the oars of an *a scaloccio* galley were a good deal longer than those of the *alla sensile* galley.

I put forward these arguments in 1941 in an article for *The Mariner's Mirror*.* Its reception was not encouraging, although it must be admitted that there were other

A reconstruction of the trireme (right). Notable in the stern is the signal staff (1) and the trierarch seated behind the steersman (2). The latter holds the tillers with which he is able to turn the twin steering oars. The leather sleeves fitted to the lower oarports are visible, also the crowding out of the lower two files of oarsmen by the narrowing of the hull so that they number 27 to the uppermost oarsmen's 31 a side. The brails (3), seen passing forward over the

yardarms, reach down through rings set on the front surface of the sails to the lower edge, enabling the sails to be brailed up in any shape. The bow officer is seen at his post on the foredeck (4). The ship carried a ram (5). The four archers and ten armed infantrymen normally carried on deck are not shown. The ship, shown here under oar *and* sail, normally used one or the other, not both at once.

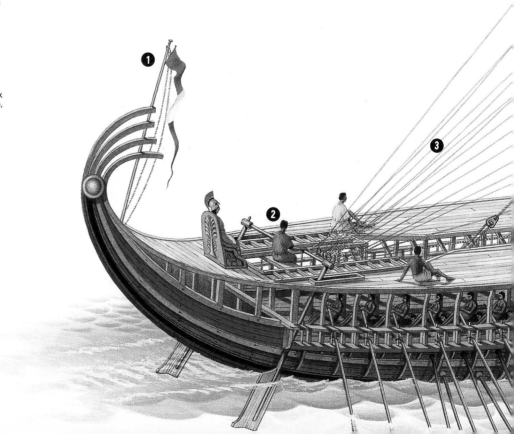

matters demanding the close attention of most people in Britain at that time. Dr Tarn, reviewing the article in the *Classical Review*, advised me to return to Greek philosophy. I took his advice as soon as possible, though I found time to answer Dr Tarn's review in the *Classical Quarterly* of 1947* and later to collaborate with R.T. Williams in *Greek Oared Ships*, where the arguments were repeated.

In 1981 I had retired and was working on a book about the later Greek oared warships with John Coates, formerly Chief Naval Architect at the Ministry of Defence. We concluded that no progress on this subject was possible until a reconstruction of the trierēs had been made, at least on paper, since the later ships were plainly developments of her although for different tactical purposes.

At this point I heard from the classical scholar Sir Charles Willink, whom I had known at Trinity, that money might be raised to build a replica of a trierēs. The suggestion came from Frank Welsh and Edwin Woolf, who together with Air Vice-Marshal Peter Turner, John Coates and myself formed the Trireme Trust in 1982.

In April 1983, we invited all the people we knew who might be interested, and might disagree with us, including a large party from Greece, to an Advisory Discussion at the National Maritime Museum, Greenwich. The record of the discussion, which has proved of great value to us, has been published.* The important sequel was the proposal made

to John Coates and Eric McKee, when they went out to Piraeus that September, that the Greek authorities should work together with the Trireme Trust to build the replica in Greece.

The Trust has been extraordinarily fortunate in finding that Greek archaeologists and the Greek authorities, in particular the Hellenic Navy, have shared our ambitions and are prepared to back our theories. For the Greeks of today the trierēs, reconstructed, can be a symbol and a reminder of the great days and achievements of the past. We have known the ancient Athenians as poets and dramatists, historians and philosophers. Now, in this recreated ship, we see them in a new and rather unexpected role, as the builders and exploiters of a technologically advanced naval weapon.

The Greek government has undertaken to bear the cost of the actual construction under the supervision of the Hellenic Navy and with the advice and frequent presence of the Trust's naval architect John Coates. The Trust, with much generous support from private individuals, a number of Cambridge colleges, the Classical Faculty at Cambridge, the BBC (which is making a film of the project), and a substantial bank loan, has been able to finance the research and development. This includes the experimental reconstruction of a tenth part of the ship, the Trial Piece, which was pulled on the Thames at Henley in July 1985 before being shipped out to Greece as a guide for

the boatbuilder, and for use in the training of the Hellenic Navy crew. Sea trials took place at the island of Poros in August 1987 with a Greek crew and a British crew.

The reconstruction is a serious and thoroughly researched example of experimental archaeology, which reflects the partnership of naval architecture with classical scholarship. As an experiment to test the design practically and to provide data of performance it is unique because it is based on no actual surviving remains.

The experiment is important for many reasons: the ship and her trials will help historians to fill a notorious deficiency in the accounts of naval engagements and the movement of fleets, and in our general concept of the nature and limitations of sea power in antiquity. But perhaps the most important achievement of all will be for the student of ancient literature, enabling him or her to recreate accurately the maritime events described.

Finally, as a postscript, there is the matter of "the undergirdings of triereis" from which, for me, the whole enterprise started. The trierēs, with the long narrow hull 115ft by 19ft (36m by 6m) and no structural deck, is in real danger of breaking her back in certain sea conditions, and needs a hogging truss. If the keel is thought of as the wooden part of a bow, the truss is the bowstring, doubled, and tightened by a Spanish windlass. This is undoubtedly the "undergirding". Quite how Plato thought of the universe as so undergirded is another matter.

Phoenician explorers

The Phoenicians, stemming from the Canaanites of the Bible, were not only the most enterprising traders and mariners of the ancient world; they also played a large part in developing the first alphabet. Tantalizing hints of ocean-going activities, probably connected with the search for new trading opportunities, have been recorded by other peoples. And yet, until archaeology began to uncover something of the Phoenicians, virtually nothing was known about this bold and skilful people except through the writings of classical Greek and Hebrew authors.

Literary sources suggest that the Phoenicians may have begun to move into the western Mediterranean in the late second millennium BC. The testimony of the Gelidonya and Ulu Burun wrecksites (p.22) certainly shows that their trading and bronze-smithing activities had extended beyond the Canaanite heartland by that date. It seems likely that the earliest western Mediterranean settlements arose as a result of a growing shortage of land, but these may also have been connected with the exploitation of mineral ores. Phoenician silverwork in particular is found all over the Mediterranean, and silver lodes were worked from early times in the south of the Iberian peninsula.

Phoenician Explorers

By the first millennium BC, the Phoenicians had spread far to the west. Carthage, the city of the legendary Queen Dido, was traditionally founded in 814BC, and it became the leader of the western Phoenician (Punic) colonies until its destruction by Rome in AD146. Situated close to modern Tunis, it came to control a territory extending far into the then fertile hinterland, and was said to be surrounded by a wall 20 miles (32km) in circumference. Archaeologists have uncovered an elaborate system of docks on the site.

Gadir or Gades (modern Cadiz), may have been founded even earlier, perhaps as early as 1100BC. The settlement was established on what was then a long thin island just off the Iberian coast. With these and other colonies or trading stations, the Phoenicians had become sealords of the whole Mediterranean by the 7th century BC, with centers all along the north coast of Africa from Lixus, in what is now Morocco, as far as Utica, in modern-day Tunisia, and even beyond the Straits of Gibraltar.

As befitted a people of commerce rather than of empire, these settlements tended to be autonomous trading posts rather than colonies, sometimes mere landing stages, usually one day's voyage apart. Phoenician cargo vessels were broad-beamed, with high bows and sterns and they had a single mast. Their shallow draught enabled them to find a safe anchorage in shelving coastal waters.

In addition to trade, the Phoenician colonists also practiced agriculture and husbandry, beekeeping, woodworking of all kinds, and masonry. They were also skilled in the making of textiles, which were dyed with the juice of the murex mollusc to produce much admired colors, from pinks to deepest purples.

Equally renowned were the goods made in ivory and semi-precious stones from east and west, including amber, and their wonderful metalwork.

Voyages of exploration

The Phoenician sailors would sometimes act as mercenaries. It seems that they were doing this when they undertook their spectacular first recorded exploratory voyage, reported in the 5th century BC by Herodotus, who heard the story in Egypt. The journey, said to have been undertaken about 600BC, was no less than the circumnavigation of Africa.

The Egyptian king Necho had apparently hired Phoenicians to venture around the continent after attempting to cut a canal from the Nile to the Red Sea. According to the story, the Phoenicians sailed down the Red Sea and out into the Indian Ocean, where, clinging to the coast as was their way, they took three years to complete the voyage around and up to the Pillars of Heracles (the classical name for the Phoenician god Melqart). Overwintering along the route and planting and reaping corn where they stayed, they at last sailed back through the Pillars already so familiar to them (now the Straits of Gibraltar) into the Mediterranean, and so returned to the Nile delta.

Herodotus did not doubt the story, but found one detail incredible – that the sun had been on their right (that is, to the north) as they rounded Africa. Yet it is this detail that makes the story of the voyage credible to us. Moreover, there is no doubt that the prevailing winds and currents made the voyage around Africa much easier from east to west than in the opposite direction. As yet, however, we know of no long-term outcome to this voyage, and no evidence of trading or settlement has yet come to light.

Discoveries to the west

At the time when this expedition around Africa was taking place, the balance of power was gradually shifting in the western Mediterranean. Carthage flourished, and was leader of the independent Phoenician colonies in the west. (In the 7th century BC the Phoenician heartland in the Levant became part of the Assyrian empire.) Trade flourished too, and the Phoenicians and Etruscans between them amicably controlled its course, happily

A map of the Mediterranean (above) shows Phoenician and Greek settlements and spheres of influence. According to legend, Levantine Phoenicians founded Carthage in 814BC. Biblical sources suggest that there was a Phoenician presence in the south of Spain in the time of King Solomon, and archaeological evidence suggests that the western settlement of Gadir (Cadiz) was founded as early as 1100BC. Cyprus and Sardinia already had some sort of Phoenician presence in the 9th century BC, and from Carthage influence radiated out around Africa with settlements dating from the 7th century BC. Phoenician trade flourished throughout the Mediterranean area by this time, often in harmony with the Greeks, whose expansion began in the 8th century BC. Greek influence was soon found in Punic art, and the Phoenicians had bases in the area of Greek dominance to the southeast. Even after the Greeks founded Massilia in 600BC, thereby strengthening their presence in the west, the Phoenicians were still powerful. They were founding new settlements into the 3rd century BC, with Nova Cartagena dating from 228BC.

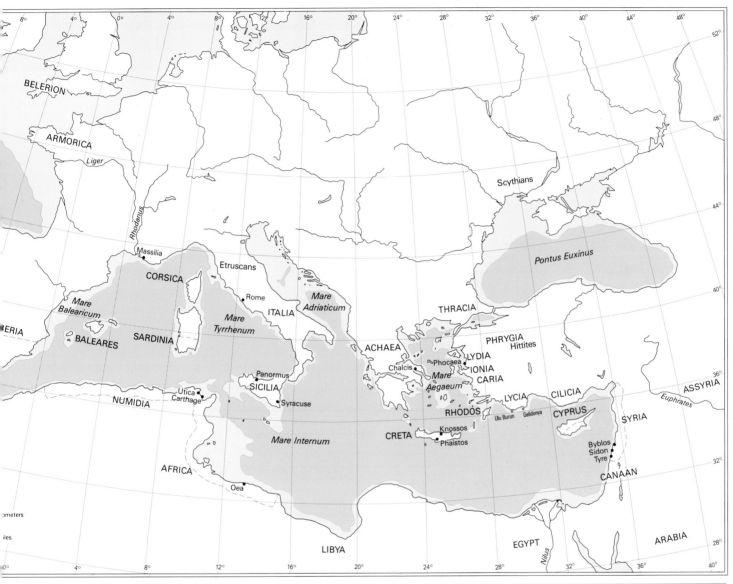

The tall vessel shown (right) being raised by marine archaeologist Mensun Bound and colleague Giuseppe Galfano is one of the more remarkable amphoras to have come from the sea in recent years. The amphora, lost off the coast of Marsala and of Punic origin, contained lime, which can be seen on Mensun Bound's fingers (above). Lime was a substance much used by the Phoenicians in tanning, agriculture, medicine and building. This particular lime had a high silica content and underwater it had taken on the properties of hydraulic cement. The lime was still in semi-fluid form when examined.

transporting Greek goods and selling them further west, and, it seems, transporting back the metal ores and other raw materials from which some of these goods were made. But Greek colonists were also moving westwards: in about 600BC, the Greeks founded the town of Massilia (modern Marseille), beside a Celto-Gallic settlement near the mouth of the River Rhône, in spite of Carthage's attempts to prevent this.

This was a heavy blow to Carthage for now the Greeks too had an important position in the west, with a town which was not only a strong sea port, but also a base from which they could control trade at the mouth of an important river, down which raw materials from the land of the Celts came to the Mediterranean.

This marked the beginning of the increasingly close alliance between the Carthaginians and Etruscans in opposing Greek expansion. With Etruscan assistance the Phoenicians kept the Greeks under control for more than a century and still enjoyed friendly relations which were good for trade. But while Rome was challenging the ally to the west, to the east Phoenicians were needed to aid the Persians in the wars against the Greeks, and here they found themselves involved in damaging defeats in 480BC.

The Phoenician position could have been severely weakened, but wisely they knew their own strength. They were craftsmen, traders and sailors; they knew the Mediterranean better than any of their contemporaries; and they controlled its western gateway, the Pillars of Heracles, with access to the oceans unknown to the Greeks. And they had a stronghold, Gadir, beyond these straits already, opposite the mouth of the river Guadalquivir, in the metal-rich Iberian peninsula.

Perhaps they were on the lookout for other sources of metal, especially the tin needed for the making of bronze. As the Bronze Age wrecks of Cape Gelidonya and Ulu Burun show, Phoenician vessels in the eastern Mediterranean region were carrying tin as well as copper ingots for bronze-smithing even before the beginning of the first millennium BC. Their colonies in the west would surely not have been slow to exploit the tin deposits of the Iberian peninsula.

The travels of Himilco

It was probably this hope that inspired the second great journey attributed to the Phoenicians – a journey in search of the sources of Celtic tin. About 450BC an expedition led by Himilco ventured far beyond the Pillars of Heracles and probably even reached the British Isles. The written sources from which we know of this journey came from much later in history from the Roman writer Avienus (4th century AD), who recorded in his *Ora Maritima* old Greek accounts of the voyage. It seems most likely that one source for this work was the writing of the

Greek historian Ephorus, from the mid 4th century BC, so that it is derived from a reasonably contemporary account.

According to this version, Himilco's sailors set out from Gadir and traveled around the Atlantic coast of Spain and Portugal right up to the ragged rocky coast of Brittany, the Oestrymnian promontory. Brittany was also a rich source of tin. But the Romans believed that Himilco went beyond this, across the Channel to the ancient tin mines of Cornwall. Avienus speaks not only of the insula Albionum (Britain) but of Hibernia (Ireland), where gold was to be found.

Certainly, it is possible that long before Himilco's time, Iberian influence had spread to Britain and to Ireland, and it was influence of a kind that suggests close Phoenician involvement: pottery and metal work from centuries before Himilco are markedly Cypro-Phoenician in style. The Phoenicians must at least have been middlemen, links in a chain which stretched far south of the British Isles. It seems highly plausible that even if they were not involved in operating all along the chain, sooner or later they would attempt to discover its extent for themselves, and that this was Himilco's adventure. The tales they spread of monsters and horrors lurking in the sea beyond the Pillars would be calculated to deter the Greeks from interfering in their long-established trade links.

Hanno's African expeditions

Of Hanno, king of Carthage's voyage down Africa's west coast some 25 years later, we have a transcribed version of the sailor's own account, originally recorded in the Temple of Baal Hammon (the Greek god Cronos, Roman Saturn) at Carthage.* The authenticity of the account has been questioned, however. This was an eventful journey which involved some 30,000 men and women, who traveled with their provisions in 60 pentecontors, sturdy 50-oared ships each of which probably carried its own long boat in which to row ashore.

The journey began uneventfully, as the huge fleet passed westward through the Pillars and along the northwest coast of Africa. Whether or not they were Phoenician towns at this point, several sites along the coast already had connections with Carthage; pottery thought to date from the 7th century BC has been found at Lixus and Mogador. Two days' voyage along the coast, the Phoenicians founded the town of Thymiaterion, high above a large plain; sailing on, they reached a wooded promontory (the sort of site they often made their own), where they dedicated a temple to the Phoenician god of the sea (Poseidon in Greek).

From this place, Soloeis, they sailed on for half a day until they came to a reed-covered lake not far inland, where elephants were feeding. Beyond this lake they founded six more cities along the

coast. Traveling on, they came to the River Lixos, where they became friendly with the Lixitae (probably the Berbers), nomadic shepherds whose flocks were pastured by the waters. There they remained for some time, and when they left they took some members of the Lixitae with them as interpreters on the rest of the voyage.

The Lixitae told the travelers about the inhospitable Ethiopians dwelling with wild beasts in land hemmed in by mountains in which "troglodytes of strange appearance dwell". The stories they brought back from this point onwards in their journey must indeed have amazed their hearers. They sailed along a desert shore (the Sahara?) for two whole days, founded a settlement on an island they called Cerne, sailed up river to a lake where they were stoned by savages, saw crocodiles and hippopotami, and encoun-

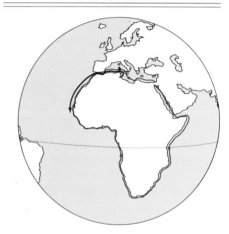

Phoenician explorations of the African coast are shown on a map of the globe (above). The journey undertaken c.600BC on behalf of Necho, king of Egypt, is marked in red. The circumnavigation of Africa, starting from the Red Sea, was said to have taken three years. The route of Hanno's fleet of 60 pentecontors around Africa's west coast is marked in blue. The journey took place c.425BC, beginning at Carthage and ending at the "Horn of the South", which has been identified as Sierra Leone or Gabon.

tered Ethiopians whose speech was unintelligible even to their guides. They came to an island with a salt-water lake which had a second island on it. There were forests in which flames leaped all night and from which came the terrifying sounds of flutes, cymbals, drums and babbling voices which soon put them to flight; they saw streams of lava pouring into the sea and land which was unapproachable because of the overpowering heat, more noctural flames, with one tall flame which seemed to reach the stars and which daylight revealed to be a high mountain – the Chariot of the Gods. Finally, past more lava flows, the "Horn of the South" was reached, and here, in a bay beside an island peopled with "women with shaggy bodies . . . called Gorillas", their supplies running out, they decided to bring their journey to an end.

Scholars disagree in identifying the places mentioned in the account of the voyage from the island of Cerne onwards. Cerne was probably an island off Senegal, but it is not certain which, and the Chariot of the Gods could be Cameroon mountain, which is more than 13,000ft (3,960m) high, though some think it was only the Kakulima (nearly 3,000ft/900m) in Guinea. Some think the journey ended at Sierra Leone, but others believe the evidence points to Gabon, beyond the vast Gulf of Guinea. By any account it was certainly an immense undertaking. And despite the assistance of the Lixitae, who seem themselves to have been knowledgeable about a surprisingly considerable extent of the African coast, Hanno's voyage was very different in nature from the following up of trade routes.

Phoenicians and Phocaeans*

Greece and Carthage had strong links over the centuries, as we know from the Greek influences that can be seen in Punic* art from the 7th century BC onwards. Despite Phoenician wariness when Massilia was first founded, archaeology has shown that there was constant cultural interchange between Massilia, the Phocaean city, and Carthage, except for a few short periods in their histories, when the struggles which took place over Mediterranean bases and sea routes and the alleged piracy of the Greeks in Phoenician-controlled waters caused rifts and led to shows of strength on the part of Carthage. At the beginning of the 5th century BC, before the journeys just described were undertaken, the Straits of Gibraltar were closed to the Greeks and thereafter they were kept under the control of the naval power radiating from Carthage, and at the beginning of the 4th century the teaching of Greek was prohibited. Yet on the whole the two centers of commercial power developed side by side and by the end of the 4th century Carthage again showed all the signs of strong cultural ties with the Greeks.

Pytheas discovers the Arctic north

During the period that followed, somewhere around 300BC, just after the death of Aristotle, the Greek Pytheas was born, under whose leadership the next great expedition by sea from the Mediterranean took place. This time Massilia was the beginning of the journey. According to Herodotus, at the time Massilia was founded, the Greeks (and not just the Phoenicians and Etruscans) regularly traveled beyond the Pillars of Heracles. He

Part of the harbor at Carthage is shown in the reconstruction above. Carthage was built on a promontory and the port played an important part in the life of the town. The artificial harbor was divided into two parts whose common entrance from the sea could be closed with iron chains. The rectangular fortified dock for merchant vessels was linked to a circular harbor, ringed with arsenals, which provided a dock for warships. It could hold 220 vessels ready to be drafted into the service of Carthage's allies. Several small canals running into the sea controlled the water level in the docks.

names the Greek sailor Kolaios and cites his voyage to Tartessos, source of silver* and tells of the friendship between the Phocaeans and the local king, Arganthonius. But by the time of Pytheas, Greek travel to the west was limited. And Pytheas was to explore much more distant territory than any of his predecessors. Like Marco Polo after him, he would be dismissed as a liar, so strange was the account he gave on his return.

Like Himilco, Pytheas was probably in search of tin, and also of silver and perhaps amber, prized by the Greeks. But the Greeks now had a more scientific bent, and the journey was probably undertaken in a pure spirit of enquiry too. Pytheas, like the Phoenicians, used Ursa Minor, the Bear, by which to navigate, and guided by it he traveled far to the north – some think even to Iceland, the Arctic Circle* itself. He was an excellent astronomer as well as geophysicist, taking accurate measurements of the sun-height at points on his voyage, and discovering the difference between Polaris (the Pole Star) and the celestial North Pole, as well as being the first to realize the connection between the moon and the tides. Furthermore he was shown "by the barbarians . . . the place where the sun goes to bed."

Massilia had Celtic roots and the goods which reached it via the Rhône came from the lands of the Celts. This may have helped tactically in a journey which, from the Iberian peninsula on, explored the Celtic coast and touched on Celtic lands. The Phocaean Greeks had several towns along the earlier part of the route, some of them with Celtish populations, at which Pytheas must have been assured a welcome. Oddly, perhaps, his first port of call beyond the Pillars was Gadir – but we have seen that there were close connections between Carthage and Massilia and perhaps Pytheas was able to exploit these.

From Gadir Pytheas crossed to the "mouth of the silver-rooted river" (the Guadalquivir) and then clung to the coast struggling against powerful tides to the southwest point of Portugal, around the craggy cliffs, north up the coast and on to the head of the Bay of Biscay and the western coast of the land of the Gauls. Here he correctly calculated that he was on the same latitude as Massilia.

Reports tell how he traveled on past the estuary site of another Celtic town, now Bordeaux, to the mouth of the Loire and the Celtic town of Cabilo (St Nazaire near Nantes), and after three days more reached Cape Kabaion (?Pointe du Raz at the Bay of Brest) and Uxiasme (Ile d'Ouessant). From here he sailed across the open sea to Balerion (Cornwall).

Having found the northern source of tin, Pytheas continued around the coast of Britain from the west, possibly also visiting Scandinavia. To the north the waves rose pillars high (as indeed they do at the tip of Scotland where the Atlantic Ocean meets the North Sea). Around the island of Thule, six days' sailing farther on, where, he said, for six months of the year the sun hardly set, his sailors encountered conditions in which land, sea and air were indistinguishable and where the sea was "congealed" – no wonder the Greeks branded him a liar!

The identity of Thule with Iceland is disputed – possibly it was only one of the Shetland Isles. By any reckoning this and the journey back down the eastern side of the British Isles was an extraordinary achievement for sailors who believed that the world came to an end beyond the narrow straits to the west of the blue Mediterranean seas. It was to be centuries more, after Carthage had been sacked by Rome and when Phoenician and Greek power were forgotten in the west, before Britain was visited again by Mediterranean people.

The voyage of Pytheas, the Phocaean Greek, to the Celtic tin lands c.240BC, is shown by a map (left). From Gadir onwards the voyage followed that attributed to Himilco, the Phoenician thought to have sailed to Cornwall c.450BC. In search of amber, as well as in a spirit of enquiry, Pytheas ventured on into unknown northern seas and perhaps discovered Iceland before returning to Massilia via Britain's east coast.

The tombstone carving (right) depicts a Phoenician trading ship of the 2nd or 1st century BC. Phoenician boats commonly had shallow keels and a convex stern. The larger trading ships had two banks of oars (as did the warships) and were defended by soldiers, whereas the smaller ships had only a single bank of oars with no room for military protection. Only the warships had masts. The round trading ships, with no sail, were similar to Greek coastal trading craft of the period.

The Kyrenia ship restored

Kyrenia, off the north coast of Cyprus, provides archaeologists with a name for the elderly Aegean merchantman that sank there 2,300 years ago. The discovery of the ship in 1967, followed by meticulous excavation, interpretation and reconstruction, has set a landmark for the scholarly study of shipwrecks. Much of the hull had survived, and it was the skilful reassembly of these timbers that eventually led to the construction of a full-scale, sailable replica of the ancient Aegean coaster. At last, on September 6 1986, the recreated _Kyrenia II_ set sail for Cyprus from Athens.

It was in 1967, almost 20 years earlier, that a small group of American archaeologists, led by the author, were invited by the Cyprus government to carry out underwater research off the coast of the island. Andreas Cariolou led them to the tombstone of a wreck that would become known as the Kyrenia ship – a mound of amphoras lying on the seabed at a depth of nearly 100ft (30m). Excavation and analysis began soon afterwards; layer by layer, the seabed sediments were airlifted away to reveal about 400 amphoras, crockery, millstones, iron ingots, ship's equipment, the remains of almost 10,000 almonds, and over 60 percent of the hull.

The consignment of freshly harvested almonds may have come from Cyprus and could be dated to 288BC plus or minus 90 years, but tests on the wooden timbers indicated that the trees used to build the Kyrenia ship had been felled a century earlier. So this was a rather elderly trading ship of the late classical period, built before Alexander the Great was born, and lost perhaps 20 years after his death.

Excavation and interpretation
Very little knowledge has come down to us from antiquity concerning the construction and design of Greek merchant vessels. Material remains surviving from the 4th century BC are few indeed, and there are not many significant representations of such ships in ancient art. The Kyrenia ship is, to date, the finest preserved ship of the late classical period of Greek civilization ever found. About 60 percent of her total area and more than 75 percent of her representative timbers have survived and have been recorded in very careful detail.

It took eight years for the team to raise, preserve and reassemble the ship. Five years went into raising the hull piece by piece, preserving it in PEG (polyethylene glycol), then mounting it for exhibition

inside the crusader castle at Kyrenia. The assembly of all the pieces, an extremely complex operation requiring patience and exact scientific knowledge, was carried out by Professor Richard Steffy, whose brilliant work eventually made possible the ship's full-scale replication in 1985.

At the time of her sinking, the team could establish that the Kyrenia ship had been an old and much repaired vessel. Her hull had been carefully patched on at least two occasions, and the entire area of planking had been covered with lead sheets to try to reduce damage by shipworm on the timbers – a method applied in many ancient ships, but in this case apparently not very successful.

An Aegean coaster's last voyage
The Kyrenia ship's cargo not only indicates her function as a tramp merchantman regularly working the Aegean coast, but also suggests the route she might have followed on her last journey.

Most of the amphoras were Rhodian wine jars probably taken on board at that island, as Rhodes was then a major wine producer for the classical world. Other amphoras were from Samos, suggesting to some researchers that this was the ship's port of origin on the last journey. A

collection of millstones came from Nisyros, another island along the way, and were stowed below, probably as ballast. The cargo of fresh almonds may have come from Cyprus. The disposition of the cargo on the seabed suggests that it included other perishable items, now lost.

Tableware and kitchen equipment found indicate that the crew consisted of four people, with four sets of plates, bowls, saucers, drinking cups and wooden spoons. Since most of the crockery was made in Rhodes, it is possible that this may have been the ship's home port.

The captain and crew lived in cramped conditions among all the cargo, which as we have seen almost certainly included perishable items such as bolts of cloth, stored apart from the mass of amphoras, ingots and millstones. Without this additional cargo, the vessel would have been stern-heavy.

Lead weights for fishing nets indicate an obvious food source for the crew; but the absence of a hearth on board, and the shortage of lighting equipment (just one oil lamp was found) indicate that the captain and crew cooked their meals and spent many of their nights on land, either at a convenient anchorage or at one of the ports en route.

The Kyrenia wrecksite (above) was carefully marked out, mapped and photographed before any raising was done. All the pieces were labeled, and the timbers removed, traced off, and quickly placed to soak in freshwater tanks.

Freshly harvested almonds from Cyprus (right and far right), dating to about 300BC were found among the cargo, which included items from several Aegean ports.

Remnants of food found in the wreck-site area included almonds, olives, pistachios, hazelnuts, lentils, garlic, sprigs of dried herbs, grapes and figs. The religious side of seaboard life was also in evidence: a large marble pedestal with basin for performing good-luck sacrifices was found.

Hardly any of the crew's personal possessions were found, which at first suggested the possibility that they had escaped with their belongings when the ship went down, possibly caught unawares by a sudden squall. However, subsequent examination of some chunks of concreted iron, located beneath the hull, revealed the presence of eight iron spearheads. Attached to several of these were traces of the lead sheath that had been placed around the ship's hull. So these were probably embedded in the ship's side when she sank which raises the possibility of a violent end.

If the ship had succumbed to an attack by pirates (whose swift-oared galleys could easily have been concealed in the numerous coves along the coast), all possessions would have been taken and the crew would have been sold as slaves. The vessel could then have been scuttled to conceal all traces of a crime punishable by death through crucifixion. Unfortunately, the part of the ship's lower planking where the pirates would have made their hole has been lost, so this hypothesis cannot be confirmed. Yet it remains a likely possibility.

The making of Kyrenia II

Richard Steffy's brilliant studies of the Kyrenia ship's lines and method of construction yielded a great mass of solid evidence, so much so that a full-scale replication of the vessel became a serious possibility. In November 1982 work began in earnest, following an approach from Harry E. Tzalas, president of the Hellenic Institute for the Preservation of Nautical Traditions. Manolis Psaros, descendant of a long line of shipbuilders, volunteered to build the replica at his shipyard in Perama, near Athens, using the "shell-first" construction technique practiced in antiquity.

We have seen in the Ulu Burun wreck (pp.32–33) that this method was used at least 3,400 years ago, and continued until the end of the Roman empire. By modern standards outrageously wasteful of wood and labor (although both were cheap in antiquity), this meant joining the entire shell of strakes edge to edge from the keel up to the cap rail, using closely spaced mortises and tenons locked with pegs – all before a single frame was adzed to fit inside that shell. It was a testimony to the open-mindedness of Psaros and his two builders that they attempted to construct a full-size ship in a method absolutely opposite to their "frame-first" tradition.

Our first aim was to replicate as closely as possible the original lines of the merchantman 46ft (14m) in length. But because her shipwrights had worked by eye alone, the 4th century hull was not symmetrical: it had 5 percent more wetted surface to port than it had to starboard. Although we decided for reasons of cost to build a symmetrical hull based on the lines of the better preserved port side, it is interesting that the finished replica still turned out to be slightly asymmetrical.

The Kyrenia ship's keel, as well as her planking, frames and interior scantlings had been made of Aleppo pine, a material no longer readily available in Greece, so we used the very similar *Pinus brutia*, acquired from Samos. In every other way, we were conscientiously faithful to the ancient hull: naturally curved timbers were used for the frames; tenons and tenon pegs were made of Turkey oak; and all the ship's nails were hand-forged from pure copper rod.

The curved "rocker" keel of the Kyrenia ship, measuring 31ft (9.3m) in length, had been hewn from a naturally curved tree whose heartwood followed that arc through its entirety. Duplicating this, though, proved a tough task, and it was not until the fourth attempt that a perfectly curved log of proper size could be cut down to our exact specifications.

The construction of the stem-post followed. The bow configuration of *Kyrenia II* had to be conjectural, since the forwardmost part of the original stem-post had not survived, so work was carried out based on ancient representations, sailing tests and common sense. A nearly vertical cutwater was dovetailed into the end of the stem-post and was reinforced by a substantial knee. Luckily, a portion of the aft end of the original keel had survived, giving us the initial angle of attachment of the stern-post. A major part of the stern-knee was found, permitting us to install a massive knee in *Kyrenia II*.

With these basic elements erected, the experiment in shell-first construction could begin. Rabbets were cut along the upper corners of the keel, and then the

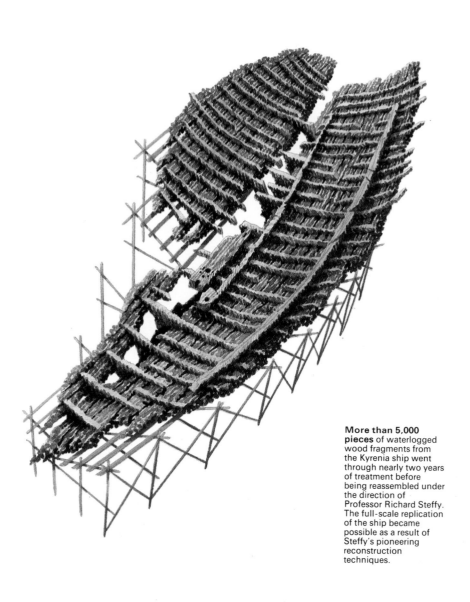

More than 5,000 pieces of waterlogged wood fragments from the Kyrenia ship went through nearly two years of treatment before being reassembled under the direction of Professor Richard Steffy. The full-scale replication of the ship became possible as a result of Steffy's pioneering reconstruction techniques.

The crew's utensils
(left) included tableware
for four people, with
plates, saucers, cups,
salt bowls and wooden
spoons. Most of the
crockery came from
Rhodes, which might
have been the ship's
home port. The absence
of a hearth on the boat
suggests that the crew
ate cooked meals on
shore.

**A precise
reconstruction**
(above) of the ship and
her cargo was
determined from the
remains and their
disposition on the
seabed. The vessel was
more than 40ft (13m) in
length, a shell-built
vessel with
edge-to-edge timbers,
fixed together by
mortises and tenons (1)
in the standard

technique of antiquity.
She had a single mast,
with a square sail and
brail rigging, and was
steered by means of dual
steering oars (3). When
loaded, she would have
had a very low
freeboard, and the cargo
was probably protected
from spray by a matting
fence (2). The location
of the domestic pottery
defined the crew's
cramped living quarters

fore and aft (they
probably spent many
nights ashore). On her
last voyage the ship was
carrying a bulky cargo,
including more than 400
amphoras. Tests showed
that she probably had
additional heavy cargo
in the bow, possibly
bales of cloth or other
perishable materials
which have disappeared
without trace.

builders used mallets and chisels to cut mortises into the keel, spacing them just 4-5in (about 12cm) apart, center to center. Next, the planks for the garboard and second strakes were fashioned. Because these strakes curved radically, their mortises had to be cut at ever-changing angles, all judged by eye. Oak tenons were sawn to nearly the same width and thickness as the mortise cuttings, and quick adze work lopped off the corners and tapered the ends before they were slid into the waiting mortises of the keel.

Then came the difficult task of setting the garboards and the adjoining second strakes. Positioning a mortised plank onto more than 50 tenons is not easy even for practiced craftsmen. Slowly, from one end to the other, a plank was fitted over each tenon, onto which pig fat had been dabbed, then gradually it was driven down into place until the seam was light-tight. This was done gingerly, since the chance of splitting a plank while hammering it home was high.

After several days in position, during which the wood settled, dried and shrank, the plank was again pounded down to tighten the seam. Then holes were drilled through the top and bottom portions of each tenon, and tapered pegs were driven home to lock the joints in place. After several days, the tenon pegs were restruck to be certain they were absolutely tight.

After emplacing only the first strakes, our builders were convinced that the ship could be completed shell-first. Their skill and confidence grew, as did their admiration for the precision joinery used by the ancients, who were in effect superbly skilled cabinet-makers. In July 1984 the construction crew was joined by master shipwright Michaelis Oikonomou, who became the sympathetic master builder of *Kyrenia II*. By February 1985 the shell of the vessel stood 12 strakes high, and four men were climbing around inside, wielding heavy equipment. Yet not a single frame had been inserted! More than 4,000 tenons and 8,000 pegged mortises were holding her rigid.

The Kyrenia ship had a system of framing that we now know was common in antiquity: floors alternating with half-frames, futtocks continuing the arms of the floors, and top timbers extending beyond the ends of the half-frames. Triangular chocks filled the cavity within the keel, garboard and second strakes. After only one month of work, all 23 floor timbers, plus five futtocks, and 25 pairs of half-frames were in place. Pure copper spikes, driven from outside the hull through drilled holes, held these members in position. After the nails had been driven home, their tips were bent, then clenched over to bite into the frame tops. The strength and tightness of these copper "staples" cannot be overstated.

Now 13 strakes high – as many as we had found – *Kyrenia II* floated into the sea for the first time on May 9 1985. Because

no evidence of calking had been found in the original ship, we had guessed that the ancients must have soaked new boats in the sea for several weeks before the seams closed up. Indeed, after two hours in the sea, *Kyrenia II* was totally awash; yet, when she was pumped out after only 24 hours, she remained high and dry apart from a few minor leaks. Within that short time, the wood had swelled enough to close the open seams.

The hull seemed very solid and sat evenly in the water. However, we decided to add a fourteenth strake to prevent the vessel shipping too much water in heavier seas. A cap rail completed the shell. A ship of this size, we believe, could have been constructed in antiquity by four men working over one building season.

It now remained to furnish the 25-ton capacity hull with decks, mast and rigging as best we could conjecture them. It was clear that the Kyrenia ship had been an open vessel still holding a belly full of cargo when she sank. In the stern, where the line of cargo had ended abruptly, there had been a bulkhead, tenoned in place, supporting the afterdeck. From this deck the helmsman-captain had steered and the crewmen had maneuvered the brail lines to the sail. We installed a covered hatch to the locker space underneath.

During the ship's original excavation, her "sail locker" had yielded nearly all the 176 lead brail rings that were found. These rings, sewn to the leeward side of a square sail in vertical rows, guided the brail lines that raised the lower skirt of the sail in the fashion of a modern Venetian blind. The locker had also contained spare parts for the rigging.

The excavation had not revealed substantial evidence of a bulkhead forward of the hold, but we all agreed that *Kyrenia II* needed a small deck at the bow from which to lower anchors and to handle the sail. Stanchions and railings like those shown in ancient vase paintings were built at the bow and stern decks for safety, and catwalks port and starboard enabled the crew to move about easily.

The pine mast step of the Kyrenia ship had been well preserved, and it was replicated exactly in *Kyrenia II*. No fragments of mast or yard were found, but we decided to follow Theophrastus' advice and made them of silver fir. Lacking evidence from the original vessel, we based most other primary features of *Kyrenia II* on interpretations of ships depicted in Greek art, on literary sources, and on the experience of our shipwrights and her new captain, Vassilis Vassiliades.

At sea at last
After hectic final preparations, launch day was a highly colorful affair, with Melina Mercouri and Susan Womer Katzev officiating. Our vessel was indeed something to behold: the ship's handsome golden hull had been adzed to the same smooth finish as her predecessor of 2,300

years before. Her lower hull had been coated with a mixture of soot, pine pitch and pig fat, giving the dramatic effect of Homer's "black-hulled" ships. The practical reason was to reduce weed growth, and it did. We painted "apotropaic" eyes – designed to avert evil – on both sides of the bow in a style seen on ships in Grecian vase paintings.

Kyrenia II was then shipped to the United States to participate in America's Fourth of July celebration. As our tiny, incongruous ship sailed past the Statue of Liberty, we could not help but compare our feelings with those of the original crewmen. They too would have seen a similar landmark, for the huge statue of Athena, with the sun glinting off her polished spear, was the first beacon that ancient sailors saw as they approached the metropolis of Athens.

After completing her sail up the Hudson River, *Kyrenia II* was shipped home to the Mediterranean and prepared for a second monumental voyage. On September 6 she departed Athens under sail, bound for Cyprus. Amid great celebration, she was greeted in Paphos on October 2 by more than 12,000 well-wishers. Since that time she has visited all the major ports on the southern coast of Cyprus.

More than 4,000 tenons and 8,000 pegged mortises were used to hold *Kyrenia II's* shell rigid. The photograph (above) shows a peg being driven through a tenon in the mortise of a plank, illustrating how the strake seams were secured in shell-first construction.

Kyrenia II (right), on route for Cyprus, September 1986, sails from Piraeus towards Cape Sounion. Materials and techniques used in the replica were all in accordance with ancient shipbuilding practice. The evil-averting eyes, painted on each side of the bow, recall a tradition seen in numerous contemporary vase paintings.

***Kyrenia II* (left) during sea trials.** Details of the foremost part of the ship and of the rigging had not survived, and were reconstructed according to ancient pictorial representations and common sense. When tested, the ship behaved well and her single sail could be finely controlled, enabling her to sail close to the wind.

Scarf joint (above) of the upper wale of the port side of *Kyrenia II*, showing tenons of the strake seam. The ship's two Z-scarfed wales (strong planks extending the entire length of the ship's side) added enormous girdling strength to the shell.

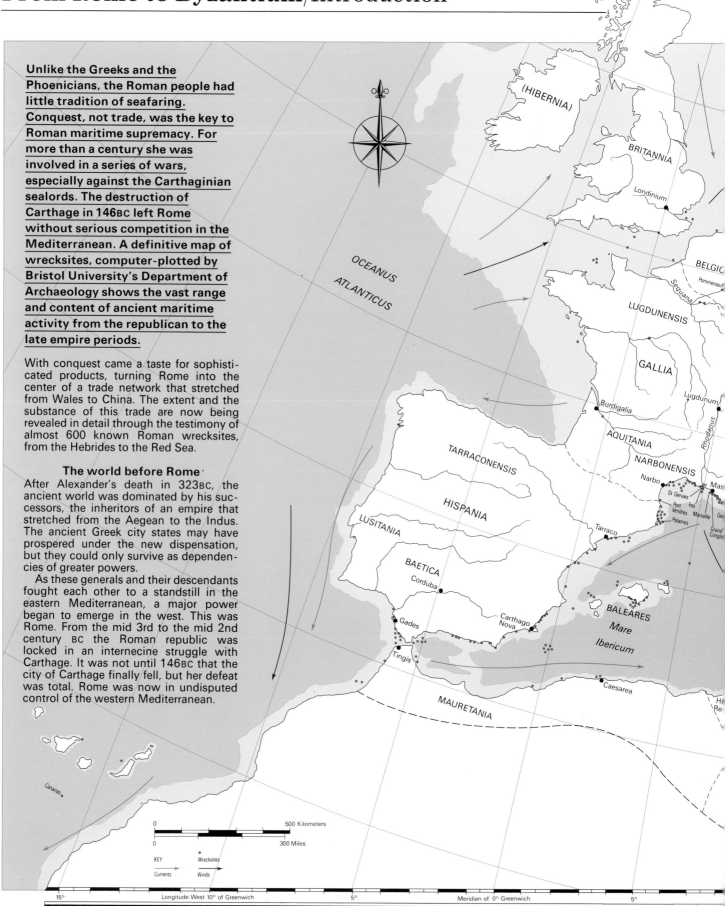

Unlike the Greeks and the Phoenicians, the Roman people had little tradition of seafaring. Conquest, not trade, was the key to Roman maritime supremacy. For more than a century she was involved in a series of wars, especially against the Carthaginian sealords. The destruction of Carthage in 146BC left Rome without serious competition in the Mediterranean. A definitive map of wrecksites, computer-plotted by Bristol University's Department of Archaeology shows the vast range and content of ancient maritime activity from the republican to the late empire periods.

With conquest came a taste for sophisti- cated products, turning Rome into the center of a trade network that stretched from Wales to China. The extent and the substance of this trade are now being revealed in detail through the testimony of almost 600 known Roman wrecksites, from the Hebrides to the Red Sea.

The world before Rome

After Alexander's death in 323BC, the ancient world was dominated by his suc- cessors, the inheritors of an empire that stretched from the Aegean to the Indus. The ancient Greek city states may have prospered under the new dispensation, but they could only survive as dependen- cies of greater powers.

As these generals and their descendants fought each other to a standstill in the eastern Mediterranean, a major power began to emerge in the west. This was Rome. From the mid 3rd to the mid 2nd century BC the Roman republic was locked in an internecine struggle with Carthage. It was not until 146BC that the city of Carthage finally fell, but her defeat was total. Rome was now in undisputed control of the western Mediterranean.

OCEANUS

ATLANTICUS

(HIBERNIA)

BRITANNIA

Londinium

BELGIC

Pommeroeul

Sequana

LUGDUNENSIS

GALLIA

Lugdunum

Burdigalia

Rhodanus

AQUITANIA

NARBONENSIS

TARRACONENSIS

Narbo

Mas

St Gervais

Port Fos

Vendres Marseille Gie

Palamos

Grand

Congle

HISPANIA

LUSITANIA

Tarraco

BAETICA

Corduba

BALEARES

Mare

Carthago

Nova

Ibericum

Gades

Tingis

Caesarea

Hi

Re

MAURETANIA

Canarias

0   500 Kilometers

0   300 Miles

KEY   Wrecksites

Currents   Winds

15°   Longitude West 10° of Greenwich   5°   Meridian of 0° Greenwich   5°

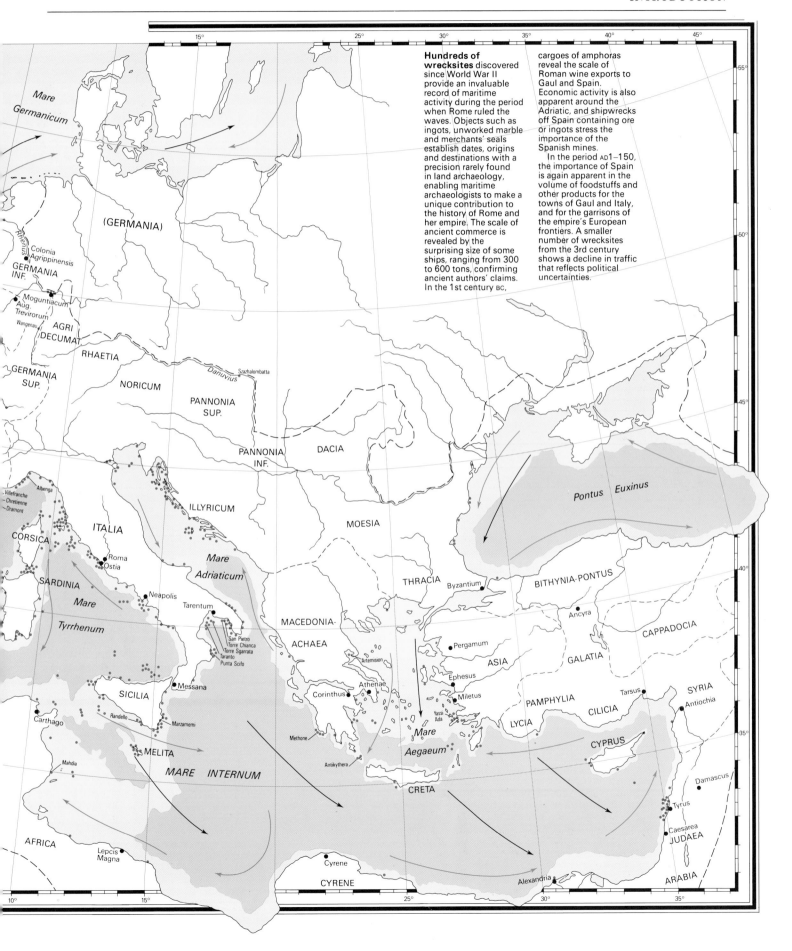

Hundreds of wrecksites discovered since World War II provide an invaluable record of maritime activity during the period when Rome ruled the waves. Objects such as ingots, unworked marble and merchants' seals establish dates, origins and destinations with a precision rarely found in land archaeology, enabling maritime archaeologists to make a unique contribution to the history of Rome and her empire. The scale of ancient commerce is revealed by the surprising size of some ships, ranging from 300 to 600 tons, confirming ancient authors' claims. In the 1st century BC, cargoes of amphoras reveal the scale of Roman wine exports to Gaul and Spain. Economic activity is also apparent around the Adriatic, and shipwrecks off Spain containing ore or ingots stress the importance of the Spanish mines.

In the period AD1–150, the importance of Spain is again apparent in the volume of foodstuffs and other products for the towns of Gaul and Italy, and for the garrisons of the empire's European frontiers. A smaller number of wrecksites from the 3rd century shows a decline in traffic that reflects political uncertainties.

Mare Germanicum

(GERMANIA)

Colonia Agrippinensis
GERMANIA INF.
Rhenus
Moguntiacum
Aug. Trevirorum
Wangenau
AGRI DECUMAT
GERMANIA SUP.
RHAETIA
NORICUM
Danuvius Szazhalombatta
PANNONIA SUP.
PANNONIA INF.
DACIA
ILLYRICUM
MOESIA
Villefranche
Chretienne
Dramont
Albenga
CORSICA
ITALIA
Roma
Ostia
SARDINIA
Mare Tyrrhenum
Neapolis
Mare Adriaticum
Tarentum
San Pietro
Torre Chianca
Torre Sgarrata
Taranto
Punta Scifo
THRACIA
Byzantium
Pontus Euxinus
BITHYNIA-PONTUS
Ancyra
CAPPADOCIA
Messana
SICILIA
MACEDONIA-
ACHAEA
Corinthus
Athenae
Artemision
Pergamum
Ephesus
Miletus
ASIA
GALATIA
PAMPHYLIA
LYCIA
CILICIA
Tarsus
SYRIA
Antiochia
CYPRUS
Carthago
Randello
Marzamemi
MELITA
Mahdia
MARE INTERNUM
Methone
Antikythera
Mare Aegaeum
Yassi Ada
CRETA
AFRICA
Lepcis Magna
Cyrene
CYRENE
Alexandria
Damascus
Tyrus
Caesarea
JUDAEA
ARABIA

The Punic (Carthaginian) wars had forced the military power of Rome to develop a naval arm as she extended her empire beyond the Italian mainland, beginning with the annexation of Sicily and Sardinia around 220BC, and Spain in 198–197BC. In the east, a governor was appointed for Macedonia in 146BC, with powers over Achaea (southern Greece). The province (or "sphere of action") of Africa was annexed in the same year, and that of Asia in the 120s.

This process continued to the end of the republican period, and in the 60s Julius Caesar's great rival Pompey added extensive tracts, including Pontus/Bithynia, Cilicia and Syria. It was the acquisition and administration of new territories that almost involuntarily turned Rome into a maritime power.

Seaborne trade
The archaeological evidence from the seabed has considerably altered and expanded our knowledge of the routes, volume, range and fluctuations of shipping activity during this period. Excavation reveals a preponderance of cargoes made up of amphoras – the all-purpose containers of antiquity (see p.64) – indicating the importance of foodstuffs and wine as export commodities. Wine exports from Italian vineyards correlate with Roman territorial expansion, especially in the later 2nd century BC as Rome was moving into Greece, Asia Minor and also North Africa.

The scale of the wine export trade is revealed by the Madrague de Giens wreck, found off Toulon and skilfully excavated under the direction of the French marine archaeologists André Tchernia and Patrice Pomey (see p.66). The cargo may have consisted of as many as 7,000 amphoras, with a total weight of 350 tons. Many of these bore shippers' marks indicating that they came from the famous Caecuban wine-growing region. The same wrecksite contained red coarse-ware pottery of the kind that archaeologists had formerly believed was made by Romanized Gauls. This find suggests that the coarseware pottery was in fact exported from Italy.

Wrecks from Spain reveal a lively trade not only in metals – predominantly copper, lead and tin – but also in foodstuffs. During the late republic and early years of the empire, Spanish trade appears to have flourished, dominating the western Mediterranean by the middle of the 1st century AD, as evidenced by numerous shipwrecks containing wine, fish sauce and olive oil, as well as fine pottery and glass. Locations of wrecks help to trace out two major routes from the Iberian peninsula: one went past the Balearic Islands, reaching Rome's port of Ostia and other Italian destinations, while the other hugged Spain's eastern coast and the French Riviera as far as the Rhône. Here portage and trans-shipment

carried the products on to the Rhine and as far as Britain.

However, Spain fell from favor in the 3rd century AD, and from then onwards the trade in wine and foodstuffs seems to have shifted to North Africa. Thus marine archaeology not only stresses the sheer size of seaborne trade during the Roman period; it also shows how this trade fluctuated in response to political and demographic events.

The Roman empire essentially achieved its final form under the emperor Hadrian in AD117. And what an empire it was, stretching from northern England to the Caspian Sea, from Germany to Morocco, from the Sea of Azov to the Upper Nile. Its capital on the River Tiber expanded to become a city of more than one million people, with an economy that drew on every corner of the then known world for its sustenance. In the words of Lionel Casson:

The Roman man in the street ate bread baked with wheat grown in North Africa or Egypt, and fish that had been caught and dried near Gibraltar. He cooked with North African oil in pots and pans of copper mined in Spain, ate off dishes fired in French kilns, drank wine from Spain or France, and if he spilled any of his dinner on his toga, had it cleaned with fuller's earth from the Aegean islands. The Roman of wealth dressed in garments of wool from Miletus or linen from Egypt; his wife wore silks from China, adorned herself with diamonds and pearls from India, and made up with cosmetics from South Arabia. He seasoned his food with Indian pepper and sweetened it with Athenian honey, had it served in dishes of Spanish silver on tables of African citrus wood, and washed it down with Sicilian wine poured from decanters of Syrian glass. He lived in a house whose walls were covered with colored marble veneer quarried in Asia Minor; his furniture was of Indian ebony or teak inlaid with African ivory, and his rooms were filled with statues imported from Greece. Staples and luxuries, from as near as France and as far as China, poured into the capital, enough of the one to feed a million people, and of the other to satisfy the extravagances of the political, social and economic rulers of the western world.

Trade in the Roman World
Throughout the Mediterranean, the old Greek and Hellenistic cities expanded under the Romans, and new ones were built. In Egypt, Alexandria rivaled Rome itself. In Asia, the impressive remnants of such places as Ephesus, Miletus, and Pergamum can still be seen. Newer cities of equal magnificence, like Lepcis Magna, sprouted at the edges of the North African desert, paid for by the grain trade to

The Byzantine world c. AD1050

Rome. Far to the north, the new foundation of London was eventually to become the sixth largest city in the Roman empire.

During this period of the *Pax Romana* it was much cheaper to send goods by sea or river than by land, so the cities on the Mediterranean or on major river routes flourished at the expense of landlocked towns. And the trade was in essentials; as we have seen, the evidence of the wrecksites suggests that cargoes consisted mainly of basic commodities rather than manufactured goods.

Another very important type of cargo consisted of building materials, the urban fabric of the empire, much of which stands to this day. Shiploads of marble and other materials have been found, revealing both the sheer size of the blocks and columns, and the places where the material was quarried. The remains of the

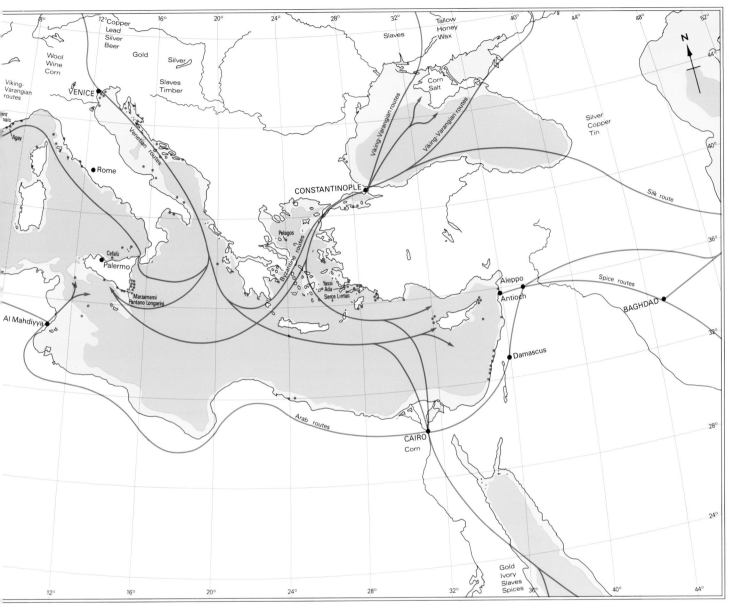

ships that made these cities of the Roman empire possible have been found all over the Mediterranean basin and no doubt there are more awaiting discovery.

The Roman predisposition for display can also be seen at the personal as well as at the civic level, with wrecksites yielding masses of finished, partially finished, and roughed-out marble coffin containers called sarcophagi (see p.73), again exported from favored quarries all around the Mediterranean.

The bones of the ships that made all this trade possible have turned up in Britain, Holland, Germany, and as far away as the Red Sea. Bulk carriers have been found in the Rhine, and archaeologists have discovered evidence, much of it not yet thoroughly studied, of Roman voyages to the Canary Islands in the west and India to the east.

The empire moves east

However, Rome could remain the capital of the world only for so long as the imperial armies were able to stave off the barbarian peoples crowded along the frontiers. This pressure continued, until by the 4th century AD the west was becoming untenable. In 476 the Western empire finally collapsed, but the center of the Roman empire had already shifted eastwards nearly two centuries before. Early in the 4th century, Constantine divided his territory and set up a second capital at Byzantium. The focus of classical civilization, following Constantine's new foundation, was now irrevocably fixed in the east, where it would remain for nearly one thousand years.

Centered on Byzantium, the new empire preserved the heritage of classical antiquity, developed its own magnificent culture, maintained vital mercantile and cultural links between Europe and Asia, and acted as a bastion of Christianity against the "barbarians" from the north and the rising power of Islam in the east. Not until 1453 was it finally overrun by a people from Central Asia, the Ottoman Turks. Wrecks from the earlier and later periods of this age throw brilliant light on a vitally important but largely neglected area of western history. The 7th century merchantman discovered at Yassi Ada, the subject of a textbook excavation by George Bass (see p.86), reveals fascinating affinities with present-day coastal trade around the Aegean, while the Serçe Limani wrecksite (the so-called "Glass Wreck", see p.88), dating to the 11th century, shows a fascinating combination of Islamic, Christian, and perhaps even Jewish commercial interests.

The amphora: jerrycan of antiquity

From the Bronze Age onwards, amphoras have been the all-purpose containers of antiquity carried by all Mediterranean ships – the ancient equivalent of mass-produced packaging. Containing wine, olive oil and other staples of life, their presence traces not only the ancient trade routes but also the immense and varied commercial activity that flourished in the Mediterranean for two millennia.

The Canaanites were, as we have seen, great traders, and traded products need containers. The Ulu Burun wreck carried such containers in the form of clay jars full of terebinth, along with her other cargo. Such jars have been found in many of the places where the Canaanite ancestors of the Phoenicians traded: a typical Canaanite clay jar was found in the tomb of a late Bronze Age Athenian lady in Athens, and Canaanite jars are seen in Egyptian tomb paintings.

Hundreds have been recovered from Bronze Age tombs in Palestine, and a warehouse full of them was discovered by Schaeffer in Ugarit, near the present day port of Latakia.

These clay jars are in a sense the remote ancestors of the ubiquitous five-gallon oil can, seen throughout the world today, particularly in less developed regions, where they contain the liquid products needed to maintain village economies: petrol, motor oil, olive or palm oil, linseed oil for making paint, and literally dozens of other items.

Amphoras and archaeologists
Clay jars have of course been used since the dawn of civilization, but the Canaanite jars had a difference: they were pointed on the bottom and they had handles, which adapted them for lashing onto an animal's back, and easy pouring; like the wooden barrels that replaced them, they nested together when stowed inside the hold of a ship.

Like the German genius who invented the jerrycan before World War II, the Canaanite inventor of the amphora took a common container, and turned it into one that worked better. The jerrycan vastly improved the mobility of Hitler's Panzer armies; the new model amphora gave those Canaanite traders an extra advantage in their sea trading ventures.

The Egyptians copied these jars, and so did the Bronze Age Greeks. The name itself is Greek (*amphiphoreus* or *amphoreus*); it first appears in the Linear B Syllabary, which was used by the Mycenaeans from 1450BC to write their early form of Greek. Homer tells us that Telemachus brought wine for King Nestor of Pylos in amphoras (*Odyssey* II, 290, 349, 379).

Before the advent of underwater archaeology, the amphora was largely neglected by archaeologists. However, the important exception was the German scholar Dressel, who analysed the many inscribed jars from Monte Testaccio ("potsherd mountain") in Rome. There, literally millions of broken jars, refuse from the docks, are still heaped in a manmade mountain, bearing everlasting witness to the Roman appetite for imported goods. Since then, similar mountains have been discovered at other important trading centers of antiquity, such as Mariut near modern Alexandria.

By the 5th century BC, Greek wine jars were becoming standardized to hold a little under seven gallons. Like modern containers, they were often stamped with the seal of the particular authority in the region in which they were made. On the wine-exporting islands of Rhodes, Kos, Samos and Thasos, and in Sinope in the Black Sea, this seems to be evidence of government-imposed quality control.

Although amphoras perhaps began to be replaced by skins or barrels for shipping liquids in bulk in late Roman times, versions of the ancient Canaanite amphoras compete to this day with the five-gallon tin can in Egypt and the Arabian Peninsula, in India, in modern Spain, Greece and much of the Moslem world. Columbus sailed with a large part of his stores contained in the medieval Spanish version of the amphora. Oddly enough, these "olive jars" had no handles.

It is probably reasonable to postulate that some 5 percent of all active trading vessels were lost each year in ancient times. For the whole span of Man's commercial adventures in the Mediterranean, until modern times, all Mediterranean ships carried amphoras. Trade routes of antiquity are permanently marked by this ubiquitous container.

Being made of clay, amphoras are almost imperishable. Parts of them survive in places where nothing else can, such as reefs where surf breaks for many months a year. After everything else is gone, these broken sherds indicate the presence of untold numbers of shipwrecks.

The ships' graveyard at Yassi Ada was full of amphoras, marking ships that didn't make it over the reef. They cover a time span of more than 2,000 years.

Until underwater archaeology became a reality, there was no way of getting an accurate estimate of the volume and pattern of ancient trade. Now, however, it seems increasingly probable that the amphora might well be the key to a new understanding of civilization in the ancient Mediterranean.

Amphora wrecksites
More and more amphora-carrying wrecks were found by divers as the sport of aqua-lung diving proliferated in the years after World War II. These range in date from the 6th century BC to the 7th century AD, but the majority came from the period of Rome's expansion (1st century BC to the 1st century AD), when the need to supply armies of occupation in the new spheres of conquest, or *provinciae*, was of paramount importance.

Properly examined, these wrecksites could have provided a wealth of new knowledge about the Roman world during its most dynamic period. Unfortunately, many were looted before their locations became known to the authorities, and so a priceless opportunity was lost forever.

Yet from the beginning there was a concerted effort to stop the process of looting and to develop techniques for excavating ancient shipwrecks. In 1950 the Italian government archaeologist Professor Nino Lamboglia followed up rumors of the existence of a great Roman

shipwreck off the little resort town of Albenga. A first attempt to excavate, using a clamshell dredge bucket, produced a number of smashed amphoras, pieces of Roman helmets and wood from the ship's hull structure. This took place in February of 1950.

After a week Lamboglia, to his credit, realized that there had to be a better way. He went on to organize a large effort at Albenga, supported by the Italian Navy, which continued for many years.

Lamboglia tried to get his divers to make maps underwater, set up teams of trained archaeologists systematically to record the recovered material, and saw to it that the salvaged material was preserved and published. He operated on George Bass's principle, that an archaeologist should be in charge of an archaeological excavation. But he failed to observe the corollary, that the archaeologist has to be a diver as well. Lamboglia's great mistake was that he forbade his young archae-

ologists to dive, and thus never learned what was really going on at the bottom.

Nevertheless, Lamboglia's work at Albenga gave the world its first look at a great Roman commercial cargo carrier of the 1st century BC. She had carried perhaps 10,000 amphoras, and might have displaced 450–500 tons.

Grand Congloué and Titan wrecksites

In 1952 Commandant J.-Y. Cousteau began the excavation of a Roman cargo carrier which had been found under the cliffs of the rocky island of Grand Congloué, off Marseille.

Cousteau and his divers worked on and off at the Grand Congloué for five years, and raised more than 200 tons of material. Unfortunately, the job was never properly supervised, although the archaeologist Fernand Benoit was nominally in charge. It has taken many years to sort out the questions arising from the excavation.

Some remain insoluble to this day. However, research has now shown beyond any doubt that two wrecks sank some 80 or 100 years apart at this same steep, rocky site near Marseille. The later wreck was a large ship, laden with at least three layers of Italian wine amphoras, probably of the late 2nd century BC. The earlier ship was smaller; her cargo included some 6,000 pieces of black-gloss pottery, about 50 amphoras of Rhodian and Knidian type from the south-eastern Aegean, as well as an important consignment of Italian wine, probably from Campania.

The same year saw the end of the Grand Congloué excavation and the beginning of Tailliez' project at Le Titan off Ile du Levant. Tailliez' work showed us all how to go about our underwater business. His excavation was the most systematic ever done on an ancient ship in the sea up to that time. Unfortunately, no young archaeologist appeared on Tailliez' door-

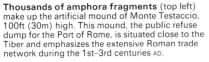

Thousands of amphora fragments (top left) make up the artificial mound of Monte Testaccio, 100ft (30m) high. This mound, the public refuse dump for the Port of Rome, is situated close to the Tiber and emphasizes the extensive Roman trade network during the 1st–3rd centuries AD.

The Albenga wreck in reconstruction (bottom left) shows how amphoras were stacked in a Roman commercial cargo carrier of the 1st century BC. The wreck, found off Liguria, was excavated in the 1950s to 1970s by Professor Nino Lamboglia.

The Titan wreck (bottom right) found off the Ile du Levant was one of the earliest underwater sites to be excavated. Amphora heaps are usually the first clues to the location of a wrecked ship.

Men unloading amphoras (above left) are part of a lively port scene depicted on a Roman stone carving. The port is probably Ostia where it is known that merchants and shipowners had offices for negotiating ship and cargo transactions. This is suggested by the three men in the roofed building on the right, one of whom is greeting a cargo handler who is disembarking from a ship.

Amphora stamps (above and top) provide us with vital information on the origin, manufacturer and date of production of the amphoras and their contents. From this, trade routes and cargoes for particular periods in history can be ascertained. The stamps are varied and easily distinguishable, like those from the wine exporting islands of Thasos (a) and Rhodes (b), and from Sinope (c) above.

step, and so the hull of the ship and the tons of material were never properly studied. Tailliez himself was posted away and had no time to organize the post-excavation work. Probably no one in France at that time understood the huge commitment of time and money required *after* the dig.

When discovered, the wreck was intact with her cargo of amphoras, which had settled on the bottom at a depth of 90ft (27m) without breaking. The shape of the cargo as it had been stacked in the hold was preserved even after the upper part of the hull had rotted away, thus forming the "tumulus" or mound, said to have originally measured 100ft × 40ft (30m × 12m). By the time Phillippe Tailliez began excavations, many of the amphoras had been stolen by divers.

Nevertheless, the excavation yielded much fascinating information, including the fact that some of the amphoras had contained pickled fish, and may well have been rations for Caesar's legions. There were certainly more than 1,000 amphoras, but we will never know exactly how many, because so much looting has taken place.

Madrague de Giens
In 1967, divers from the French Navy's diving school stumbled on the most spectacular amphora wreck since Albenga. It was conveniently situated near the French naval base at Toulon, at a place called Madrague de Giens.

That year was very significant for nautical archaeology in the Mediterranean and elsewhere. The University of Pennsylvania Museum's underwater archaeology section, under George Bass, was working intensively with major excavations at Yassi Ada in Turkey, Kyrenia in Cyprus, and Torre Sgaratta in Italy. More important, perhaps, preliminary reports on all the work that had been done by the Americans in the first half of the 1960s were coming into print in professional literature. Ole Crumlin-Pedersen's magnificent excavation at Roskilde was about to be published as well. In the fall of that year, the first truly international conference on underwater archaeology was held in Toronto, Canada.

The Madrague de Giens wreck lay in relatively shallow water, about 60ft (18m) as compared to 100ft (30m) at Kyrenia and an average of 150ft (46m) at Yassi Ada. She was a huge ship, on the scale of that at Albenga. Furthermore, she was untouched, and the wreck was far offshore and hard to find without sophisticated gear.

For the first time in France, a wreck of this importance got the attention it so richly deserved. It was excavated over a period of 11 seasons, and saved from looting through a laborious process of annual reburial and reopening – which took longer than the actual digging.

Patrice Pomey and André Tchernia, of the University of Aix-en-Provence, pulled together the mass of organizations and the financing that was needed for a Bass type excavation. These included the French navy, the local government, the university, the French national committee for scientific research, and others, all under the new institute of Mediterranean archaeology, with the cooperation of the *Direction des recherches archéologiques sous-marines* (underwater archaeology section formed by CNRS in the 1960s). Another key member of the team was Antoinette Hesnard, the third co-author of the interim report.

The job categories of the crew read like those for Cape Gelidonya.

At last, 20 years after Philippe Tailliez had written his sad article about the Titan wreck, the wheel had come around full circle, back to France.

Roman wine trade
Some amphoras recovered from the Madrague de Giens wreck proved to have contained wine from the south part of Latium, and were dated between 50–70BC. Clay stoppers still in place in some jars bore the seals of the vineyards that had bottled them. Subsequent research has revealed in fascinating detail the mechanics of this vast trade.

Wine of all kinds was of course made and drunk just about everywhere in ancient as in modern Italy. Furthermore, a well-tended vineyard stood for order over the wilder powers of nature, and occupied an aesthetic as well as a practical place in the layout of a landed estate. Thus the wealthier members of Roman society took an interest in wine-growing on their villas, developing a tradition in the production of fine wine that went back to the 3rd century BC.

Much of this fine wine was for private consumption, but a return on investment was also welcome. So, in the best wine-producing regions of Italy, what we should recognize as "labeled" wines, named after the region where they were made (Falernian, Caecuban, etc.), were carefully bottled in strong amphoras, lined with rosin (set hard) to make them wine-proof and stopped with a wide, thick cork. Labeled with the date and the type of wine inside, these amphoras could then be exported by road, or, better still, by water, to a suitable market.

An export trade had existed in the 6th century BC, when Etruscan wine was shipped to southern Italy and to the coastal areas of Gaul, but thereafter various local productions tended to eclipse the wine exports of central Italy. Then, in the early part of the 3rd century BC, the so-called Greco-Italic form of amphora was developed by potters in Etruria, Latium and Campania to bottle their vintages. This was derived from a common Greek type, but marks the first

stage in the emergence of a distinctive Roman wine export traffic. The earliest amphoras bear stamps of potters and scratched inscriptions of merchants in archaic Latin script, such as the amphora marked with the name L.AIMILIO, "for Lucius Aemilius", found in a wreck at Terrasini in western Sicily.

The First Punic War (264–241BC) may have caused some interruption in this wine traffic, but from the end of the 3rd century BC onwards, the wines of Italian producers are found throughout the Mediterranean region.

A notable example is from the Grand Congloué wreck, mentioned above. The later and larger wreck was laden with at least three layers of Italian wine amphoras, probably of the late 2nd century BC, many of them stamped by a potter belonging to the Sestius family of Cosa in Etruria.

The cargo of the earlier ship included some Greek wine jars, and a much more important consignment of Italian, probably Campanian, wine in Greco-Italic amphoras. Some of these were stamped TI.Q.IVVENTI, ("made by Tiberius and Quintus Iuventius"), and provide a dramatic demonstration of how wrecks can illustrate changes in commerce.

At Le Grand Congloué, the merchant who assembled the export cargo in Italy hedged his bets by including, along with the Campanian tableware and wine, some Greek wine; however, about 25 years later, at the wrecksite of La Chrétienne C, a mere handful of odd Greek jars were

A hard hat diver (above) examines remains from the wreck site of Yassi Ada during the early days of underwater exploration in the 1960s. A ships' graveyard, explored by Peter Throckmorton, contained wrecks covering a span of 2,000 years and included an enormous number of amphoras.

A Greco-Italic amphora found in 1975 at a depth of 130ft (40m) off the Cape of Béar, by a local fisherman, had on its neck a stamp bearing the name TR. LOISIOS. Although an isolated find the name Loisios was well known around 200BC; his amphoras, which have been found around the Mediterranean from Majorca to Carthage, Alexandria and Rhodes, were used for the export of Campanian wine.

The 1st century BC Madrague de Giens wreck, situated some 13 miles (20km) southeast of Toulon, was discovered in 1967 by French naval divers. The photograph (above) shows an overview of the wrecksite after initial excavation, with the amphoras already tagged and prepared for lifting to the surface.

The Madrague de Giens vessel (top) is photographed in a close-up view after the removal of most of the cargo. The exposed timbers which have been excellently preserved, are clearly visible, with a number of amphoras still *in situ* in the background.

found on board a ship laden only with Italian amphoras; and after the middle of the 2nd century Italian wine cargoes effectively had the central and western Mediterranean to themselves.

The amphoras of Ti. & Q. Iuventius are not particularly widespread, but the effect of the expanding trade in Italian wine can be seen well in the finds of amphoras marked TR.LOISIO. Trebios Loisios was a potter who worked either on Ischia or at Pompeii in the mid 2nd century BC. The map opposite shows how his amphoras carried Campanian wine not only to other parts of Italy but also to Rhodes and Egypt, capturing markets which had traditionally been supplied with Greek or Egyptian wines. From 166BC, inscriptions from the island of Delos record the presence of many Italian merchants, including men named Trebius from Campania, most likely related to the amphora-maker.

New containers for old wines

In the middle of the 2nd century, Italian amphora-makers turned to a new form of container, known to archaeologists as *Dressel Form 1*. In place of the pear-shaped body and thin walls of the Greco-Italic amphoras, these new ones were shaped rather like a chair-leg, and had a coarse, thick fabric. These were the robust, heavy-duty containers for the ensuing century, the great age of Roman wine exportation.

Three-quarters of all Mediterranean wrecks from the next century and a half were carrying a cargo of Italian wine. The actual quantity of wine which this represents can only be guessed at, but the millions of *Dressel 1* amphora fragments found at Toulouse in Gaul confirm that enormous quantities were involved.

The Etruscan amphoras of Sestius from the upper wreck on Le Grand Congloué are some of the earlier examples; from a half-century or so later (between 70 and 50BC) we have the amphoras of Publius Veveius Papus, lost in the great ship which sank at Madrague de Giens.

From this well-preserved and fully-excavated wreck have come thousands of amphoras made in the kilns of Veveius at Fondi, near Formia in southern Latium. Samples of the wine which some of these still contained (in much diluted and decomposed form) showed by chromatographic analysis a combination of tannins and other organic chemicals similar to that found in modern claret.

From ancient references we know the name of this wine: the esteemed *vinum Caecubum*, the Caecuban wine of Latium. This was no mouthwash, but a wine sought after by connoisseurs, carefully bottled and stored, and often kept for a considerable time to mature with age. The amphoras were stopped with a cork which was rammed down into the neck and secured in place with a plug of

mortar; this latter was fixed well down by being stamped, while still damp, with the mark of the person who was responsible for bottling the wine – a guarantee, like the modern brand on a cork.

The thousands of amphoras from the cargo have also shown that, while they are generally very similar, they in fact fall into three types, hard to distinguish without much practice. However, these tiny differences were evidently appreciated by the merchants who bottled the wine, for the variations in shape of the amphoras can be matched with the different marks on the mortar seals.

None of this could have been appreciated from finds of fragments on land; not only were the varieties of shape visible only when a large number of complete amphoras was studied, but also the very nature of the mortar seals applied over the cork means that they would normally be broken and thrown away when the wine was drunk, and so they are rarely found on land sites, and never in association with the amphora to which they belonged.

Fluctuations in the export trade

The exportation of wine from Italy reached its height in the first half of the 1st century BC, and thereafter declined, largely no doubt because of the civil wars which followed Caesar's death (44BC) and the proscription of many landed senators. After about 10BC the *Dressel 1* amphoras are no longer found, and, though Italian wine continued to be produced, the expansion of trade under the Augustan Peace increased the importance of new sources of supply.

The chief of these sources was Spain, especially the northeast (Hispania Tarraconensis) where a number of Roman senators had estates. During the 1st century BC (and, indeed, earlier still, but on a restricted scale) this region had built up a vigorous business supplying wine, not so much to far-away Italy, but rather to south-western Gaul and thereby to Brittany and even Britain.

The amphora generally used was a provincial derivative of the *Dressel 1* which archaeologists know as the *Pascual Form 1* amphora (after the Catalan Ricardo Pascual). During the reigns of Augustus and Tiberius another form of amphora was manufactured in Tarraconensis and was used for the export of wine: this was a thin, lightweight amphora derived ultimately from Greek models, known as *Dressel Form 2–4*. These began to supply wine even to places like Pompeii, which were centers of wine production in their own right. The *Dressel 2–4* amphoras resembled the local Italian products and were obviously intended to pass as containing wine of equivalent quality – but at a lower price!

These currents of trade are well illustrated by the finds of shipwrecked cargoes: the *Pascual 1* traffic is concen-

trated along the coast of Catalonia between Tarragona and Narbonne, while the Spanish *Dressel 2–4* cargoes are more widely spread, especially along the coast of Gaul and in the Tyrrhenian Sea on the routes to Campania and Rome.

A fascinating aspect of this trade which has only recently been discovered is the role of Campanian merchants. A number of wrecks from the 1st century BC and the 1st century AD have been found to contain, resting firmly in the hold, a dozen or so large jars, known as *dolia*. These jars, each equivalent to about 75 amphoras, were apparently for carrying wine in bulk.

This wine would be *vin ordinaire*, not the better quality wine bottled in amphoras (which were also found in these wrecks). Most of these jars bear a stamp which names a member of the family (or, as we might say, "house") of the Pirani, who were well known as citizens of the city of Minturnae (at the mouth of the Garigliano, between Formia and Naples).

In the Augustan period the amphoras which are found in the *dolium* wrecks are Campanian (of the *Dressel 2–4* form); the Piranus family were thus associated with the export of their regional wines, both choice and *ordinaire*.

However, in the later wrecks (dating from the middle part of the 1st century AD) the amphoras on board were made in northeastern Spain, and we can assume that the wine carried in the *dolia* was too.

A Greco-Italic wine amphora is brought to the surface by two divers from Oxford University's MARE team at Capo Boeo, Sicily. Careful identification of amphora forms, following a typology established by the 19th century German scholar Dressel, has enabled archaeologists to draw up a profile of trade patterns in the Mediterranean. classification on the surface.

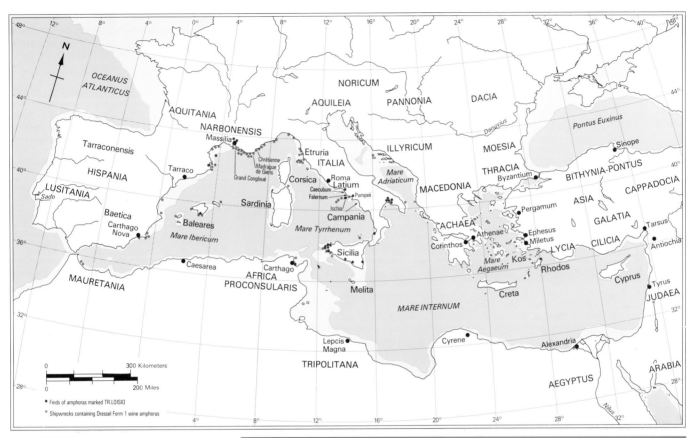

A variety of amphoras (left) from the Mediterranean region was first identified and classified by the scholar Dressel, whose typology is based mainly on amphoras found in Rome at Monte Testaccio and elsewhere.

Dressel Form 1, a very widespread type, succeeded the Greco-Italic amphora in the 2nd century BC. *Dressel Form 2–4* appeared at the start of Augustus' reign, after about 10BC. The map at top shows distribution of *Dressel* amphoras as revealed by wrecksites.

A *dolium* (above) found at a wreck off Ladispoli is examined by a diver. Such jars had the capacity of 75 amphoras and were used for transporting wine in bulk in the 1st century BC and the 1st century AD.

The map (top) shows location of wrecks carrying *Dressel 1* amphoras (c. 150–10BC), together with finds of Greco-Italic amphoras made in the early 2nd century BC pottery ot Trebios Loisios (see p.68).

69

The Pirani thus swam with the tide; they turned to dealing and importing rather than exporting when Spanish wine became popular, or more profitable. This glimpse of Roman commercial life has come about only through underwater discoveries.

Other amphora products

So far the amphora story has been told simply in terms of wine. Other liquids were of course carried in amphoras, notably olive oil (which, like wine, had been a valuable export from Republican Italy, but to Roman communities in the Mediterranean region rather than to the barbarian West).

Another important class of products which traveled long distances conveyed in amphoras was fish and fish products. The Romans inherited from the Greeks (and probably the Egyptians too) a taste for fish steeped in strong brine and for various sauces. The best-known, called *garum*, derived from fish. Such products served, of course, to augment the meager protein diet of the Mediterranean lands, where summer grazing can be scarce, but for Roman soldiers and others stationed in the frontier provinces (where meat was plentiful) they brought a tang of home and civilized life.

Salted tunny, mackerel, sardines and other fish were produced in most coastal regions of the Mediterranean, but, as with delicacies in any age, certain areas became specially renowned, and if their marketing measured up to their renown there would be a steady demand for the product. The most famous fish sauce, according to Latin authors, was the *garum sociorum* ("company sauce"), from Cartagena in southeast Spain.

Archaeological finds indicate that, whatever merchants may have claimed, most Roman fish sauce came not from Cartagena but from the south coast of Spain and the area of Cadiz. During the 1st century AD, the number of southern Spanish fish sauce cargoes lost en route to Rome or southern Gaul approaches even the Italian wine record of the Republican period. This trade had already begun in the 1st century BC, and an early example, but a dramatic and interesting one, is Tailliez' Titan wreck.

The original number of amphoras before looting is estimated at 1,200–1,700. So this was a medium-sized cargo, weighing about 120 tons; there may, of course, have been a further consignment of perishable goods, now disappeared. The amphoras were of two forms, both made on the southern coast of Spain (the province of Hispania Ulterior, or Baetica). Closed with a terracotta stopper, possibly placed over a cork, they contained pieces of tunny-fish (scales, bones, even heads and tails) and also the remains of shellfish. Some amphoras smelled of olive oil, according to the divers, so the fish may have been packed in oil, like modern

sardines. There were also amphoras (although it is not known exactly how many) which contained almonds.

This well-preserved wreck produced a rich assortment of shipboard supplies and equipment. There was a single *Dressel 1* wine amphora and a selection of glossy black Campanian tableware; these Italian supplies, together with the fact that the only two coins found were Roman issues, not from Spain, suggest that this ship's home port was in Italy. Other wrecks with cargoes from Baetica, however, have produced shipboard equipment indicating a Spanish vessel.

Exports from Africa

The Spanish provinces continued to be the chief supplier of many of the western empire's needs until nearly the end of the 2nd century AD. In the meantime the exports of other provinces, especially Africa Proconsularis (modern Tunisia), began to compete successfully; then, at the end of the century, many Spanish landowners lost their estates as a reprisal for opposing Septimius Severus, while Severus gave favors to Tripolitania, his home province. The result was that African exports seem to have seized and held the market for goods in amphoras during the uncertain years of the mid 3rd century, and then with increasing predominance from Diocletian (AD295–306) onwards.

The distribution of shipwrecks with cargoes of African amphoras also shows the increasing importance of the Danube frontier, which could be reached fairly easily through Aquileia, at the head of the Adriatic; exports from Spain are rarely found on this route, but finds of African amphoras have been reported from a number of wrecks.

Meanwhile, the nature of Roman trade was certainly changing: skins rather than amphoras may have been increasingly used for olive oil, since the latter are very rare in the 4th century. Thus, the evidence obtainable from wrecksites is more specialized. In addition, the cities (even Rome itself) came to depend for supplies largely on their surrounding areas, and less on long-distance imports. The picture of 4th-century Roman seaborne traffic provided by wrecks is thus both slighter than and different from that of earlier periods in antiquity.

Probably in the early years of the 4th century AD (though the date is not certainly fixed) a small trading ship was blown ashore and wrecked on the southern coast of Sicily, at Randello. Its cargo of amphoras numbered only a few hundred at the most, although there may have been other goods, now perished.

The amphoras originated from Lusitania (Portugal), most likely from the area at the mouth of the Sado river, and were filled with sardines, which had been preserved whole (doubtless they were preserved in

brine). Close examination of the actual amphoras showed that all except one had probably been made in one pottery, by a master potter with two or three skilled and several unskilled assistants.

In recent times the Sado area has been noted for the fine quality of its salt, due to special conditions found in the salt pans there. In the Roman period, the site exported a modest number of amphoras, and many of which would have contained fish products.

This part of Europe is, of course, particularly rich in fish; the sardine bones contained in the Randello amphoras show that the fish were caught off shore, using boats, throughout the summer, and this implies that both the fishermen and the processing factory were well established on a permanent basis.

This picture makes rather a piquant contrast with the small ship wrecked at Randello, from which no personal items or equipment other than some pottery survived. A handful of broken and bodged-up anchors remained on board when the ship drove ashore, presumably because they were not worth throwing into the sea. In contrast with the expanding economy of the late republic and the early empire, the implied picture in the 4th century is one where reduced spending power and centralizing authoritarianism rendered speculative trading an uncertain way of life.

A *garum* shop excavated in Pompeii in the 1960s (top) lends support to the evidence from underwater archaeology and literary references that *garum* was both a common trade product and a popular food commodity with the Romans. A sauce made from chopped up pieces of fish which were left to ferment in the sun, *garum* remains were found in five of the six *dolia* in the shop. The *dolia* had been carefully sealed with roof tiles to keep out the insects (above).

Peaceful conditions in the Mediterranean under the early emperors (late 1st century BC to 2nd century AD) are reflected in the distribution of shipwrecks found with amphora cargoes of fish sauce (*Garum*) from southern and southwestern Spain. In the 3rd and 4th centuries, when conditions were less favourable to commerce, and fewer cargoes were in transit, exports from Africa became important, especially towards the Danube frontier via the Adriatic.

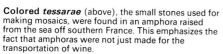

Colored *tessarae* (above), the small stones used for making mosaics, were found in an amphora raised from the sea off southern France. This emphasizes the fact that amphoras were not just made for the transportation of wine.

Fish vertebrae (above) were contained in a late Republican amphora raised during a survey of the ancient Punic harbor of Libybaeum at the western end of Sicily during the 1984 season of Oxford University's MARE survey.

A million tons of marble

The desire for immortality is a common trait among most of mankind: it seems as ingrained in us as the desire to have children, and perhaps it shares the same motivation. All through history, men with the power to command other men have used that power to build monuments to themselves. This tendency is clearly seen in the careers of Roman leaders, from the last days of the republic to the end of the empire.

The Roman senators of the second and first centuries BC were great collectors. As we have seen, they amassed cellars of fine wine, and on their own and their friends' estates they indulged their fancy for rare plants, exotic fish and song birds. Indoors, they acquired furniture, paintings and statuary – both old masters, reproductions, and newly created works.

At Rome, some of the most splendid collections and adornments were displayed for the public in porticoes and parks, or even built into public buildings. This was, for example, the fate of marble columns, which were used to decorate the stage building of theaters and to put a front on temples. The importation of "spoils" was thus firmly linked by Roman tradition with status (especially the prestige of a triumphant general) and wealth (rendered less objectionable by a concern for the public good). The Mahdia wreck of c. 100BC contained 70 columns (with bases and capitals) of Attic marble, in addition to a fine collection of works of art. Attic marble, historical sources tell us, was used by Lucius Licinius Crassus in a theater he erected in 105–103BC and the Mahdia ship must have been chartered on behalf of a Roman collector of the same kind. Obviously not only marble but also skilled craftsmen would be brought to Rome for special jobs such as carving and erecting the columns of a temple.

Julius Caesar was one of the greatest collectors, and the tradition was continued by his adoptive descendant, the first emperor. Augustus, not least in his reported claim to have found Rome brick and left it marble, clearly recognized the political importance of being seen to be magnificent – and munificent as well. In his reign, and that of Tiberius (AD14–37), the imperial house progressively acquired mines and quarries of the empire by all means at their disposal. They thus controlled the supply of the best and most famous stones, and could reserve them for their own use or display generosity by allowing others access to their stock.

In AD68 the Flavian dynasty took over from the Julio-Claudians with the veteran general Vespasian. Like his predecessors, Vespasian embarked on a pretentious

The typical Roman cargo ship is known to us both from depictions in wall paintings, mosaics and graffiti, and also from wrecksites. It was a broad round vessel with a high stern, the stern-post (2) being bent inwards and sometimes taking the form of a swan's neck. It was a sailing ship with two masts: one, amidships, carried a large square sail, sometimes with a triangular topsail set above; the other, stepped forward, was for the smaller sail known as the *artemon* (5). The ship had heavy timbers running along the sides, and steering oars (1).

The general design of merchantmen remained remarkably constant through the Roman period, demonstrating the continuity of the shipwright's traditional methods. However, there appear to have been at least two categories of cargo ship. Smaller ships, which could carry only 3,000 amphoras (or less), were able to make their way up the Tiber to unload at Rome. Larger ones, with a capacity of more than 300 tons, were able to carry about 10,000 amphoras, which had to be unloaded onto river barges at Portus. These carried several anchors (4), and the stocks are often inscribed with the names of gods, written in Greek or, less often, Latin. Astragals, objects similar to dice, also appear on lead anchor stocks, arranged in the "Venus", or lucky throw, position.

Most Roman wrecksites have yielded terracotta tiles from the galley roof (3), indicating the existence of cooking fires. Pots and tableware, including finewares presumably for the captain's use, are always found, along with storage jars for the crew's provisions. Terracotta oil lamps provided light.

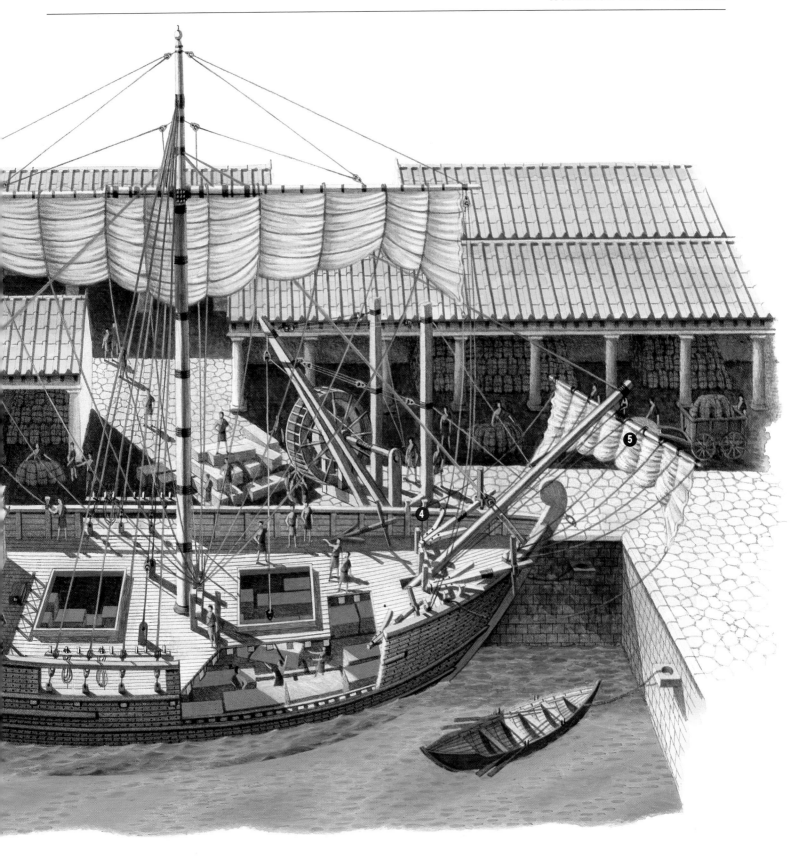

construction program, whose most spectacular surviving monument is the Roman Colosseum. All this cost a fortune, but Vespasian was a wizard at thinking up new taxes; his tax on public latrines is still remembered in Rome and Paris by the slang term for a public urinal; *vespasienne* in French, *vespasiani* in Italian.

Vespasian's son Titus died after a reign of little more than two years, but in the short period of his rule, he too built a number of massive monuments such as the Baths of Titus, a temple to the deified Vespasian, imperial palaces, and a huge temple to Jupiter with gold-plated doors and gilded roof tiles.

Trajan and after

Rome's next great builder was the emperor Trajan, who in the 19 years of his rule (AD98–117) expanded the empire to its farthest limits and embarked on a series of huge civil engineering projects, including bridges in Spain, harbor works in Asia Minor, aqueducts all over the empire, and a navigable canal from the Nile to the Red Sea. In addition he founded the great city of Timgad in North Africa.

Trajan's successor Hadrian was a scholar and philosopher who loved to travel, especially in Greek-speaking lands of the east. Towns, temples and libraries sprang up in his tracks, and many of these, for instance the celebrated temple in Athens, are still standing. Hadrian's villa at Tivoli spread over 160 acres and contained the largest art collection the world had ever seen. His most spectacular existing monument is perhaps the Pantheon in Rome, which was rebuilt by Apollodorus at Hadrian's command.

Antoninus Pius, who followed Hadrian, founded the so-called Antonine dynasty, and he and his successor Marcus Aurelius were both great builders. The death of the latter in AD180 marked the end of what Gibbon has described as one of the most glorious periods in the history of mankind.

From the inscriptions on marble blocks found in modern times, left unused in antiquity, it is clear that the emperors, especially Trajan and Hadrian in the first part of the second century, invested huge resources in the extraction and transportation of fine stone from distant sources without regard for actual needs. At Ostia, some blocks of marble which were positioned ready for use in building work in the late 4th century (but which in the event were not used) bore a quarry date of the early 2nd century.

During the 3rd century, the empire gradually lost its grip; but this did not stop rulers from continuing the tradition of grandiose monument building, which spread all over the Roman world. Diocletian for example (AD284–305) built a magnificent palace at Split, Yugoslavia, which still stands as a memorial to the ornate taste of the later Roman empire. The passion for monument building may be said to have continued right up to the

construction of the great church of St Sophia by the Byzantine emperor Justinian in AD527, more than 200 years after Constantine had moved the imperial capital to Constantinople (Byzantium).

St Sophia was of course dedicated to Christianity, the religion of the Byzantine emperors, and it differed from monuments of the Roman period in another important respect; it was largely built of local materials. Throughout the time of the Roman empire, marble facings and decorative carving in the round were favored, requiring the use of materials that had to be brought from elsewhere. The Byzantine architects preferred to use mosaics, or, when exotic materials were required, to salvage these from ancient monuments that had lost their meaning and importance. Byzantine imperial edicts ordained

Hellenistic works of art, including a dancing dwarf (above), were recovered from a 1st century BC wreck near Mahdia, Tunisia. However, the bulk of the cargo, most of which still lies on the seabed, consisted of architectural features such as marble capitals, bases and columns.

the destruction of many great pagan temples; others have survived because they were converted into Christian churches early on.

Testimony of the seabed

This vast trade in exotic building materials, continuing throughout the Roman period, supported quarrying operations in many parts of the empire. The most important types of stone used as blocks or columns were the gray or pink Nubian granites, the white marbles of Attica and Carrara, and certain colored marbles such as the so-called *Africano* from Teos or *giallo antico* from Simitthu (Chemtou in Algeria). Such stones provided large blocks without flaws, and were obviously carefully quarried and trimmed to make the best possible use of the resource.

The late 2nd century AD wreck at Camarina in Sicily had on board two columns, 20ft (6m) long, of *giallo antico*. Cutting a small sample from the weed-encrusted and discolored marble, and

finding the rich, honey-tinted stone inside, is an exciting experience, and gives an insight into the passion which these fine natural materials could arouse. There is now very little yellow marble left at Jebel Chemtou, mostly just gray and beige. At Iassos, where the red-and-white *Africano* was quarried, nothing remains at all – just a water-filled crater where the Roman quarrymen removed the entire marble deposit.

At Camarina, marble was not the only cargo on board: there was a consignment of cooking pottery from Africa Proconsularis, and an uncertain number of olive-oil amphoras from the same province, perhaps also cargo rather than ship's stores. The wreck has not been excavated, so the true nature of the ship and her possible home port are unknown, but it looks as if this was not a specialized freighter carrying stone in bulk but a relatively small ship which had picked up several consignments including a job lot or special order of a handful of columns.

Some of the most highly prized stones had to be quarried miles from any sea or river, often high in the mountains. Quarries which had immediate access to water offered the possibility of loading blocks directly into ships, which, especially for transport to Rome, brought significant savings in costs and might create a market for stones which would otherwise not attract attention.

Two such quarries were at Aliki on Thasos and on Proconnesus in the Sea of Marmara (so-called from the quarry island itself). Here the quarry floor was cut at sea level, so that blocks could be loaded straight aboard. The rather gray, dull marble from these quarries was not much sought after for building, but it became popular during the empire for smaller items such as sarcophagi, the coffins which were used for burial from the early 2nd century.

From Aswan, far up the Nile, came the red and gray granite that can be seen all over the Roman world. From the Greek island of Euboea, and also from Aphrodisias in Asia Minor, came a fine-grained marble very popular in Rome. Assos, also in Asia Minor, produced a gray granite called *Lapis Sarcophagus* (flesh-eating stone) from which the word sarcophagus comes. Interment in a coffin made of this material was guaranteed to reduce the occupant to bare bones within a short space of time.

Some years ago Peter Throckmorton found a cargo of four such coffins, made of Assos granite and dating to the 3rd century AD. They lay on the seabed off the small island of Sapientza, on the ancient sea road to Italy that led past what is now Methone in the southwest Peloponnese. Nothing of the ship survived.

Half a mile from this wrecksite we found columns made of granite from Aswan. Again, nothing remained of the ship, but the dimensions indicate not only

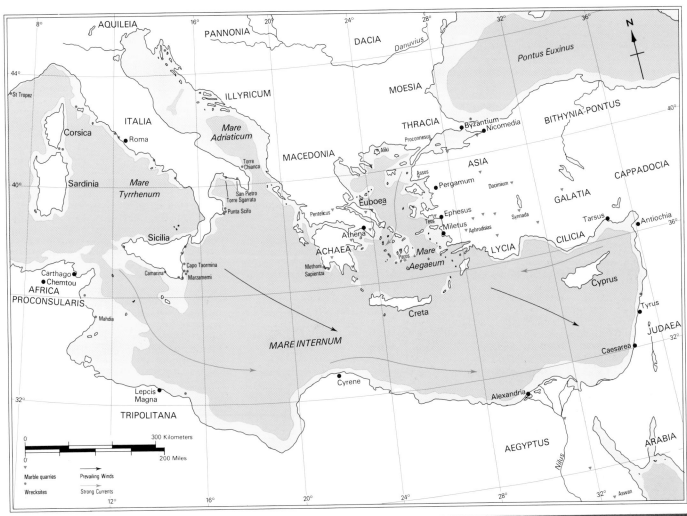

White, gray, pink and other colored marbles were quarried in many parts of the Roman Mediterranean (map, above) to embellish the empire's magnificent cities. Pink granite blocks from Aswan were found at Methone, Algerian *giallo antico* at Camarina, and Pentelic marble from Attica, including a piece weighing 40 tons, still lies in the sea off Marzamemi.

Two wrecks at Methone, half a mile apart, both carried marble cargoes on their last voyages. Four granite sarcophagi from Assos (right) were found off the island of Sapientza, and dated to the 3rd century AD. The second site yielded a number of massive columns (below), possibly once part of Herod the Great's huge colonnade at Caesarea.

that the columns were ancient, but also that when the ship went down they were being taken from their original location by later seafarers, possibly Venetians. The Venetian monument in the castle of Methone contains a column almost certainly from the wreck; and a careful plan of the site reveals that some columns were broken when they were shipped, suggesting that they had once stood as part of a colonnade.

We know that a huge colonnade, built by Herod the Great in the 1st century at Caesarea in Palestine, was standing until the Middle Ages, when it was torn down for building material. Caesarea was the terminus used by the Venetians for their pilgrim trade to the Holy Land. Since Methone was a Venetian way station in that trade, the columns may have been salvaged from Caesarea and were en route to Venice when the ship went down. St Marks in Venice has columns made of the same material.

Columns and blocks

As we have already seen, traces of the vast trade of the Roman empire lie on the sea bottom all over the Mediterranean. These include dozens of shiploads of building materials, nearly all of which lie on the sea roads towards Rome.

At Torre Chianca, Apulia, we surveyed a cargo of four monolithic marble columns 30 × 3ft (9 × 1m) in height, and weighing a total of 120 tons. Fragments of datable pottery in rocky crevices at the bottom suggest that the ship sank in the 3rd century. At Marzamemi, Sicily, Gerhard Kapitän surveyed a cargo of marble blocks weighing nearly 200 tons, also apparently dating from the 3rd century. A similar cargo, including marble blocks, has been discovered at St Tropez.

The very size and weight of some of the blocks thus transported and erected remains truly impressive. The greatest feats, of course, were to bring from Egypt and erect in Rome the massive obelisks of Nubian granite, tokens of the emperors' succession to the power and wealth of the pharaohs. The largest columns erected at Rome were 60ft (18m) tall and weighed 140 tons; still more impressive, since they had to be hauled up into place, are blocks such as the lintel block of the porch of Hadrian's Pantheon, a huge piece of Pentelic marble from Attica weighing some 120 tons. No block so large has yet been found under water, but even so a 40-ton block of Attic marble found in Gerhard Kapitän's 3rd century Marzamemi wreck in Sicily is awe-inspiring to dive on.

Story of the sarcophagi

Although sarcophagi were quarried from a multitude of sources around the empire, just three dominated the long-distance supply of Rome: Proconnesus, Mount Pentelicus in Attica, and Docimeum in the highlands of Phrygia. Probably these were quarries where there was a tradition of

carving sarcophagi for the Greek market before they became fashionable at Rome. Certainly neither Pentelic nor Phrygian marble was easy to ship, since in both cases a substantial overland haul was necessary to reach an inland waterway or the sea. Sarcophagi were carved to a finished state before export from Pentelicus and Docimeum, but at Proconnesus they were usually left unfinished, even though both there and on Thasos the rough-outs were shaped to a style popular at Rome but not used locally. These contrasting practices have both been illustrated by wreck cargoes.

When Peter and his team explored a wrecksite at San Pietro in Bevagna, Apulia, inspired by a 1935 article by John Ward-Perkins, he found 150 tons of blanks for still unworked sarcophagi. The wreck lay in only 10–20ft (3–6m) of water. There were 23 sarcophagi still at the site. Some had been left double by the Roman workmen; some had a lid (to fit a different sarcophagus) still attached. Some were rectangular, others were oval inside but rectangular externally, and some were oval in and out, with two projecting bosses on one side.

From these features, and from the amphoras found at the site, the wreck can be dated to the first half of the 3rd century AD. The bosses left on some of the roughed-out sarcophagi would be worked after their arrival in Rome or Ostia into snarling lion heads, and the front and side fields would be carved with Bacchic scenes; the oval shape is most likely meant to represent a *lenos* or wine vat, likewise associated with the Bacchic mysteries and the spirit of rebirth. The fine, crystalline white marble of the San Pietro sarcophagi has not been analysed scientifically, but it is most probably from Proconnesus (not Aphrodisias as at one time suggested).

In contrast, the Phrygian marble which made up most of the cargo of the early 3rd century wreck at Punta Scifo in Calabria included, as well as roughed-out blocks, some pieces which were half or fully finished. The Phrygian marble was of two kinds, a fine purple-and-white stone (*marmor Phrygium* proper, known in modern times as *pavonazzetto*) and plain white, a good stone for carving. There were six blocks (one white and five colored), which had been roughed out and gave no clue to their intended use, if in fact it was known.

There were also eight columns, of 12 and 20ft (3 and 6m) sizes, which had been dressed with a point, though a collar had been left at the base to assist handling and to allow for decoration if required. Five basins (with stands) in colored marble, on the other hand, were practically finished, as was the white marble group of Cupid and Psyche embracing. The mouldings on the base have still to be cut into the heavily shadowed motifs which were so characteristic of the

Docimean workshops and were popular in Rome at this period. Psyche's cloak and hair have not been fully carved, and Cupid's legs have been left thick in case they were broken in transit. It seems likely that craftsmen from Docimeum would have traveled to Rome to finish carving such pieces, and indeed they were probably resident there anyway as agents for their firm.

On board the Punta Scifo ship, besides Phrygian marble, there was also a small consignment of Proconnesian marble (two blocks and two plinths). This poses some questions about the route of the ship. If the Phrygian marble was transported northwestwards overland to Nicomedia on the coast, it could have been loaded on a freighter which then called at Proconnesus.

If, on the other hand, it traveled down the apparently easier route through the Maeander valley, it would have been loaded aboard a ship which also took on stone from Proconnesus, implying that the latter was offloaded from another ship. Evidence from wrecks with other types of

Dozens of unworked sarcophagus "blanks" were found at the 3rd century wrecksite off San Pietro (top). These would have been carved after delivery according to the customer's specifications. On a 3rd century sarcophagus from Acilia (above), the projecting hands were evidently cut from marble intended for a lion-head.

cargo shows that entrepôts were frequently used in the Roman world, and in this case, too, despite the inconvenience of transferring blocks of stone, it seems that the stone trade was sufficiently organized to make this sort of operation a routine one.

Ward-Perkins's article had been vague about the exact location of the San Pietro site, and by pure coincidence the search turned up a new sarcophagi wreck at a place called Torre Sgarrata.

This one lay half a mile offshore, in 20ft (6m) of water, and the cargo was almost completely covered by sand. An excavation carried out by the British School at Rome and the University of Pennsylvania Museum revealed 18 sarcophagi, 23 blocks, and one huge column. The estimated weight of the cargo was 160 tons. Surviving fragments of pottery were also from Asia Minor, and a coin of the emperor Commodus, minted in Lesbos, indicated a date some time after AD192. Of the remaining cargo, six of the blocks were of alabaster, probably from Egypt. The sarcophagi were filled with marble

sheeting typical of the kind used by the Romans to cover poured concrete walls.

At Torre Sgarrata, the heavy marble blocks had held down large fragments of the ship until they were covered with sand, and so preserved. The massive red pine planking had been cut, according to radiocarbon analysis, between 80 and 45BC. Signs of refastening and patching, crudely applied with iron nails (rather than the copper used in the original construction) bear out the view that the ship was very old when she sank.

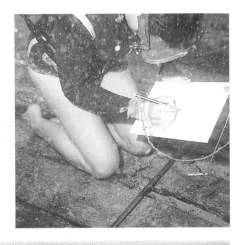

From these remains we deduced that she was either a big ship, perhaps as big as the Giens wreck (see p. 66), or she was exceptionally stoutly built for the trade. She must have been forced onto that evil lee shore in a southerly gale, and anchored when she saw or heard the breakers. Unlike the San Pietro ship or the vessel in which St Paul was wrecked (see p. 78), she did not survive till dawn so that the captain could see to run her ashore. Anchored where she was, the old hull must have opened up and sunk like a stone. Only a few men can have survived.

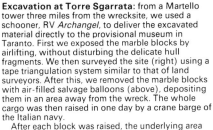

Excavation at Torre Sgarrata: from a Martello tower three miles from the wrecksite, we used a schooner, RV *Archangel*, to deliver the excavated material directly to the provisional museum in Taranto. First we exposed the marble blocks by airlifting, without disturbing the delicate hull fragments. We then surveyed the site (right) using a tape triangulation system similar to that of land surveyors. After this, we removed the marble blocks with air-filled salvage balloons (above), depositing them in an area away from the wreck. The whole cargo was then raised in one day by a crane barge of the Italian navy.

After each block was raised, the underlying area was carefully excavated and timbers were triangulated onto a master survey plan. Draftsmen worked barefoot (top right) to avoid damage to the fragile wood, and the timbers were raised in special lifting frames, tailor-made for each timber.

Shipwrecks and St Paul

Some time in the late first century AD, a ship's crew were desperately and vainly trying to prevent their vessel from smashing onto a reef. Nineteen hundred years later, the line of anchors that were cast overboard led marine archaeologists to the wrecksite, enabling them to recreate the ship's last hours in a scenario resembling that of St Paul's wreck on his way to Rome.

Seamen's anchors

In antiquity, anchors were made of wood, usually oak, with a stock or crosspiece of lead. The heavy lead stock made the upper end of the anchor lie on the bottom of the sea, so that the wooden flukes could dig into the sand or rock.

These lead anchor stocks have been found in the Mediterranean by the thousand, and a good deal has been written about them. Since they generally turn up as single finds by amateur divers, they are difficult to date exactly, although many are inscribed in Greek or Latin with the name of the owner of the ship, the ship itself, or the name of gods and goddesses, particularly Aphrodite. These inscriptions are often misspelled and sometimes the letters run backward, as if the writer had not gone very far in school, and so was not well educated.

Various writers, particularly Honor Frost, have shown how the lead stocks were cast in improvised sand molds on the beach, right around the hardwood shank. Sailors are traditionally superstitious, and Roman sailors were no exception. Sometimes they cast a winning throw of knucklebones in the lead as well. It seems fairly certain that the seamen who sailed the cargo ships around the Roman empire made their own anchors. Looking at the anchor stocks, it is not hard to imagine the small party of sailors squatting around their improvised furnace on a sandy beach, while the bosun and carpenter supervised pouring of lead into a sand mold, and the ship's boy held the big oak anchor upright in the sand while the stock was being cast.

Five Roman anchors

Some years ago at Campo Marino, near Taranto, I met Gaetano Sabonaro, one of the hundreds of professional aqualung divers in Italy who make a living by commercial spearfishing and by salvaging whatever of value they find on the bottom of the sea. In the course of his career, he had found and melted down hundreds of these anchor stocks, of all sizes from tiny ones for rowboats to ships' anchors. The previous year he had found five very large stocks in the sea. They were half a mile offshore, in a long line at a right angle to the coast. He recovered two, but the weather turned bad and nothing was done about the others.

I happened to hear about these anchor stocks because they were so big; 1,320 pounds (600kg) each. Gaetano's brother Gino had worked with me the year before at Taranto (see p. 76), when we had used big plastic balloons for moving heavy material around on the bottom. Gino suggested that he and I raise the anchors and split the proceeds with Gaetano. I refused, diplomatically, and the anchors remained on the bottom.

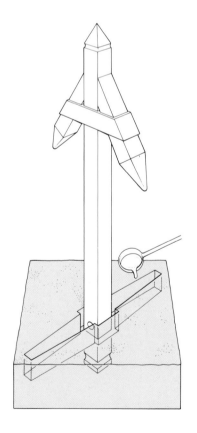

A casting of a Roman lead-stock anchor is shown (left). During the Roman period the lead stock developed in place of the stone one. It had a wooden shank and arms, and metal-tipped flukes. The shanks were grooved so that another anchor could be tied to them. The stocks were cast directly onto the shanks, which had a hole through the middle in which the molten lead set to form a strong bond.

A ship mosaic from Ostia near Rome (above) dates from the 2nd–3rd century AD. St Paul would have been traveling in a vessel like this when shipwrecked. These ships coasted back and forth throughout the Roman empire with cargoes of grain and wine, building materials, and marble and granite sarcophagi. They were constructed with mortise and oak tenon joints, huge main sail and small secondary.

Later that week, Dr Rainey, then director of the University of Pennsylvania Museum, came through Taranto. He and I proposed to the Italian authorities that the University Museum should purchase the three anchors at their scrap value as lead, and that they should receive one of the anchors in return for this.

I then made a deal with Gaetano, and we raised the anchors with plastic balloons. They lay on a very rocky bottom, a few hundred feet apart from each other. When we got the anchors ashore and weighed them, it seemed certain that they came from the same ship. All three were identical in design and weighed within a few pounds of each other.

Retracing the ship's route

The line of the three anchors, plotted on the chart, led to the southwest, the direction of the great seasonal gales that strike the coast of Apulia in the fall. The ship which had dropped the anchors must have been on the trade route from the east, leading from Methone, at the southwestern tip of the Peloponnese, up to Corfu or Zakynthos, then across the

Adriatic to Cape St Maria de Leuca. From Leuca, the Roman captain had to stay well out to sea to undertake the long run to the Straits of Messina.

If he were caught by an early southerly gale, he would be driven inevitably into the bay of Taranto. And once he saw the shore he had no choice but to anchor, in the hope of riding out the storm. His ship could not sail well enough to make headway to windward against the great seas kicked up by a gale that had blown across hundreds of miles of sea for several days.

Finding five identical anchors in a row suggested not only that they came from one ship, but also that the ship had not escaped being driven ashore. If so, then she would have gone onto the rocks somewhere very near the point where a line, drawn through the locations of the anchors plotted on the chart, hit the shore.

We searched the shore in the appropriate place, and found the remains of a Roman shipwreck on a reef just offshore. There were hundreds of amphora fragments, datable to the late 1st century AD. Two came from the Aegean – one from the island of Kos, another series from Rhodes.

Anchors and shipwrecks

For a graphic recreation of the ship's last hours we need not resort to imagination; a very similar shipwreck was experienced and described by St Paul in *Acts*. He was on his way from Caesarea to Rome as a prisoner under centurion's escort, there to be tried by Caesar, as was his right as a Roman citizen.

The party changed vessels at Myra in Lycia, boarding an Alexandrian grain ship on its way to Italy, but the ship made slow progress against constant headwinds. It was not till mid autumn that, following the coast of Crete, they reached the anchorage of Fair Havens, near Lasea. After mid September, the seas in those parts were considered dangerous, and thereafter traffic would be closed completely until March. Against Paul's advice, the ship's captain and owner put out to sea, aiming for a safe harbor where they could over-winter:

. . . But before very long a fierce wind, (a northeaster) called the Euroclydon, tore down from the landward side. It caught the ship and, as it was impos-

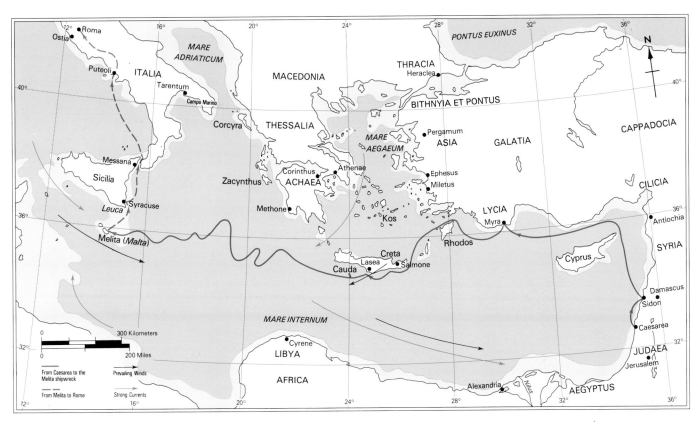

A map of the Roman empire in the 1st century AD shows the route taken by the vessel in which St Paul was shipwrecked. During the 1st century AD the Roman empire covered a vast area in which travel was unrestricted. Goods were regularly transported from port to port in ships which carried passengers as well. Paul made four missionary journeys in which he preached widely, from Jerusalem in the southeast right up to the west coast of Greece. On the journey in which the shipwreck occurred he was being taken to Rome as a prisoner. They had changed boats at Myra, boarding a grain ship from Egypt. They reached Crete in mid autumn, and the captain unwisely put to sea again, expecting to overwinter in a safe harbor before sailing on towards Rome in the spring.

sible to keep head to wind, we had to give way and run before it. We ran under the lee of a small island called Cauda, and with a struggle managed to get the ship's boat under control. When they had hoisted it aboard, they made use of tackle and undergirded the ship. Then . . . they lowered the mainsail and let her drive.

Next day, as we were making very heavy weather, they began to lighten the ship; and on the third day they jettisoned the ship's gear with their own hands. For days on end there was no sign of either sun or stars, a great storm was raging, and our last hopes of coming through alive began to fade . . .

The fourteenth night came and we were still drifting in the Sea of Adria. In the middle of the night the sailors felt land was getting nearer. They sounded and found 20 fathoms. Sounding again after a short interval they found 15 fathoms; and fearing that we might be cast ashore on a rugged coast they dropped four anchors from the stern and prayed for daylight to come. The sailors tried to abandon ship; they had

already lowered the ship's boat, pretending they were going to lay out anchors from the bows, when Paul said to the centurion and his soldiers, "Unless these men stay on board you can none of you come off safely." So the soldiers cut the ropes of the boat and let her drop away.

Shortly before daybreak Paul urged them all to take some food . . . There were on board 276 of us in all. When they had eaten as much as they wanted they lightened the ship by dumping the corn in the sea.

When day broke they could not recognize the land, but noticed a bay with a sandy beach, on which they planned, if possible, to run the ship ashore. So they slipped the anchors and let them go; at the same time they loosened the lashings of the steering-paddles, set the foresail to the wind, and let her drive to the beach. But they found themselves caught between cross-currents and ran the ship aground, so that the bow stuck fast and remained immovable, while the stern was being pounded to pieces by

the breakers . . . [The centurion] gave orders that those who could swim should jump overboard first and get to land; the rest were to follow, some on planks, some on parts of the ship. And thus it was that all came safely to land.

The Malta wreck has not been found, but this account rings true. Our five anchor wreck off the coast at Campo Marino suggests only one probable mistake. The text says that they cast four anchors out of the stern and slipped these anchors when they drove the ship on shore. It seems much more likely that they dropped the four anchors one after the other, and that they cast off the last anchor when it was time to drive the ship on shore. So long as the anchor warps did not chafe through, there was a good chance of saving the ship. With three anchors gone, holding to a fourth, and no reserve anchor to be dropped, then it was the best choice to drive ashore in daylight, sacrificing the ship to save the people.

This is very probably what happened, and so the line of anchors led us to the ship's final resting place.

The stone anchor with wooden flukes (above) is typical of the earliest anchors, which were stone weights pierced with holes. Sometimes they had only one hole, through which the line was threaded, but often they were triangular with three holes. The line would be passed through the top hole, and wooden stakes were driven through the pair of lower holes to act as flukes.

The lead anchor stock (top), with embossed knucklebones and dolphin, was found at Marsala. Such stocks had to be very heavy so as to prevent the rope becoming taut as the ship strained, thus pulling at the shank and dislodging the flukes. Anchor chains effect a horizontal pull on an anchor so that the flukes are driven in more firmly, so heavy stocks became unnecessary.

Another lead anchor stock (above) was found at the Titan reef wrecksite. This was also of great size, as can be seen from the relationship of the anchor to the diver.

The Galilee boat

Jesus lived and taught in the towns surrounding the shores of the Sea of Galilee (modern Kinneret), and many of his followers were fishermen and sailors. In fact, the New Testament is full of references to boats. The discovery in 1986 of a fishing boat in the Sea of Galilee, dating to this period, provides an exciting archaeological link between biblical times and the present.

Archaeology involves the study of artifacts left by man. Sometimes objects can be linked directly with a historical figure, such as Napoleon's guns found at Tantura (see p.202). Sometimes a specific moment in time is captured, as in the lava-covered ruins of Pompeii. And sometimes a historical era is evoked by the discovery of a particular artifact, as in the case of the ancient boat found in the Sea of Galilee.

It took Yuval and Moshe Lufan two months to find the boat. A two-year drought in Israel had lowered the water-level of the Sea of Galilee (called Kinneret in Hebrew). The brothers had grown up in Kibbutz Ginosar on the western shore of the lake, and had often scoured the beaches, not for shells, but for ancient coins and artifacts. When they came upon a number of coins, newly exposed on the drying banks, they began to consider the possibility of discovering something more unusual – an ancient boat perhaps.

Discovery of the boat
Although the Kinneret has a long nautical history, no ancient boats had ever been discovered there. This freshwater lake is relatively shallow and warm, factors which usually cause wooden wrecks to deteriorate rapidly.

However, the Lufans continued to search the shore until, in January 1986, they discerned an elongated oval outline in the mud several hundred meters south of their kibbutz. They consulted Mendel Nun, the recognized local expert on the history of the Kinneret region. The three men decided to notify the Israel Department of Antiquities of the discovery of a "boat – possibly ancient".

The Department's Inspector of Underwater Antiquities, Shelley Wachsmann, and his colleague, Kurt Raveh, were sent to investigate. Their preliminary probe determined that the Lufans had indeed discovered an ancient craft: mortise and tenon joints, known to have been used in Mediterranean shipbuilding from at least the second millennium BC to the end of the Roman period, were noted on the uppermost strake. Since iron nails connected the boat's frames to its strakes, it could not pre-date the Iron Age.

More evidence narrowed down the age of the vessel still further. A 1st century BC terracotta oil lamp was discovered in the mud which filled the boat, level with the top of the remaining stern. A clay cooking pot was found just outside the boat, dating from the 1st century BC to the 1st century AD.

Objects are likely to shift about underwater, and the pots could only give an approximate dating. Nonetheless, the archaeologists had an exciting new discovery. Not only was this the first ancient boat ever found in the famous lake, but it was possible that it dated from a fascinating period of history in the Galilee region.

An emergency excavation
It was hoped that a formal excavation and study of the boat could be made, but such projects require time and money. In the meantime the archaeologists decided to protect the find by camouflaging the site and delaying any announcement until the late winter rains caused the lake to cover the craft once again. However, such secrets are difficult to keep, and the press got wind of the story. The public's interest was aroused with tales of the discovery of "the boat of Jesus", and rumors of a lost World War I Turkish ship filled with gold coins. The Department of Antiquities decided on an emergency excavation.

A salvage dig was organized in three days. The objectives were to uncover the boat and its surrounding area; to study the craft *in situ*; and, if possible, to remove it for conservation. Professor J. Richard Steffy, of the Institute of Nautical Archaeology at Texas A&M University, agreed to study the hull's construction. His trip was quickly arranged through a cultural program organized by the United States

Information Service of the American Embassy in Israel. Many volunteer workers came from Kibbutz Ginosar, the nearby town of Migdal, and from all over the country. The Kinneret Authority co-operated by constructing a dam to prevent the lake waters from inundating the site.

The boat measured 27 × 7.6ft (8.2 × 2.3m) and lay perpendicular to the coast, with the prow facing the sea. The interior of the hull was excavated and all parts drawn and recorded. Though water-logged and fragile, the wood was in an excellent state of preservation. The craft had probably sunk and had been covered with clay deposits. This sealed the wood and the nails, protecting them from the ravages of oxygen and micro-organisms. The newly exposed wood was watered continually to prevent its decomposition.

The stem-post and the stern-post, along with other parts, were missing and appeared to have been removed in antiquity, possibly for re-use. A second row of mortise and tenon joints was discovered on a portion of the keel, beneath the present connection with the garboard strake. This indicated that the piece was being recycled and used for a second time. Northeast of the boat, the remains of two other ancient vessels were found.

These findings suggested to Professor Steffy that the site may have been an area of shipbuilding and repair in ancient times, and that wood had been in short supply. Although the boat was built primarily of cedar (strakes) and oak (frames and tenons), seven different types of wood, especially in the many repaired sections, were later identified by Dr Ella Werker of the Hebrew University.

From his preliminary examination,

A map of Israel, showing the Sea of Galilee (above).

A massive dike was built by the Kinneret Authority to protect the excavation site from flooding (above). Various remedies were proposed, including lowering the lake's level by pumping water into subsidiary reservoirs, but in the end it was decided to build a dike.

Professor Steffy deduced that the Kinneret boat was probably a fishing and transport vessel, abandoned at the end of a long working life, and subsequently used for "spare parts" for boats under construction. It was most likely sailed, but could have been rowed by a crew of four men. The techniques used in its construction indicate that it dated from the period covering the 1st century BC to the first century AD. Subsequent c-14 dating of wood samples confirmed a date of 70BC, give or take 90 years.

Removal and conservation

Once the preliminary examination of the boat was completed, Orna Cohen, the project's conservationist, devised a novel and successful plan for its removal and preservation. Fiberglass support frames were installed between the wooden ribs of the boat. The craft was then sprayed inside and out with polyurethane foam. Water from the lake was allowed to flood the excavation site, and the boat, buoyed by its synthetic cocoon, was floated up the coast to the Yigal Allon Museum at Kibbutz Ginosar. The entire excavation was completed inside 11 days and nights.

The boat was then lifted and placed in a special conservation pool. After removing the polyurethane covering, the pool was filled with water. The boat will remain here until the long-term chemical preservation process is begun.

Jesus and seafaring

Little is known about the ancient boats which sailed the Sea of Galilee. Apart from what nautical scholars will learn from a study of this craft, the discovery of a 2,000-year-old vessel near the ancient town of Migdal captivates many people.

Tarichae was the Greek name for Migdal; *Magdala* was the name that was used in the New Testament. Mary of Magdalene was one of its citizens.

During much of his ministry Jesus lived and taught along the shores of the Kinneret. Many of his followers and disciples were fishermen and sailors, and he spoke to them in metaphors which related to their experiences with the sea. Nothing connects any of these biblical figures directly to the Kinneret boat, of course, but it seems quite possible that it was used on this lake at about the same time.

An illustration of Jesus' awareness of his nautical surroundings appears in *Matthew* 16:2-3. In rebuking the Pharisees and Saducees he says:

When the sun is setting you say, "We are going to have fine weather, because the sky is red". And early in the morning you say, "It is going to

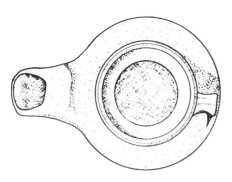

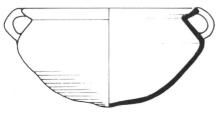

The terracotta oil lamp and clay cooking pot found during the preliminary excavation of the boat are illustrated in these line drawings (above). The lamp (top) was found in the mud which filled the Kinneret boat, level with the top of what was left of the stern. It dates from the 1st century BC. The cooking pot (above) was found upside down, next to the stem on the starboard side of the boat, and dates from somewhere between the 1st century BC and the 1st century AD. Although it was impossible to date the pots precisely, nevertheless their discovery did help to narrow down the age of the vessel.

Narrow white plastic tubing was pinned to the hull of the boat (above right) as part of the removal and conservation process. The purpose of this was to outline the planks for photographic records. Registration numbers, indicated by red markers, were given to each wooden part.

The boat, encased in its cocoon of polyurethane foam, "sails" the Sea of Galilee for the first time in 2,000 years (right). Water was pumped into the excavation pit and a steam shovel opened a channel to the lake. The boat then began its journey to the Yigal Allon Museum at Kibbutz Ginosar.

rain, because the sky is red and dark''. You can predict the weather by looking at the sky; but you cannot interpret the signs concerning these times!

Here Jesus is quoting sailing weather lore, which is of course today referred to thus, ''Red in the morning, sailors take warning; red at night, sailors delight.''

There are many other examples of Jesus' nautical knowledge. We find him crossing the Kinneret by boat on many occasions. Once he lands near Migdal; we find him preaching from boats, meeting disciples while they mend their nets, and appearing after the resurrection to the disciples while they are fishing.

The Kinneret boat, as we have already said, cannot be connected with any persons or events mentioned in the history books or new Testament. However, it has much to teach us about a type of boat in use on the Sea of Galilee during the period of Jesus' ministry, and therefore sheds light on relevant passages in the New Testament. It also has significance for Jewish history.

A Jewish battle

A few years later, during the Great Jewish Revolt of AD66-70, some battles between the Jews and the Romans took place in boats on the Kinneret. The most famous engagement was the battle of Migdal in AD67. The Jewish historian Josephus (*History of the Jewish War* XIII) describes how Titus captured Tarichae by entering it from the lake. Some of the Jewish rebels escaped from the town in boats. The next day the Romans constructed ''water craft'' and went after them. A bloody sea battle ensued, in which all the Jews were killed or captured. Describing the aftermath, Josephus wrote:

> During the days that followed a horrible stench hung over the region. The beaches were thick with wrecks and swollen bodies which, hot and steaming in the sun, made the air so foul that the calamity not only horrified the Jews but revolted even those who brought it about. Such was the outcome of the naval engagement. The dead, including those who perished in the town, totalled 6,700.

An arrowhead, possibly from that battle, although this cannot be corroborated, was found in the mud that was removed from the hull of the Kinneret boat. Yet the boat is our only tangible connection with this terrible battle, which amounted to a nautical Masada.

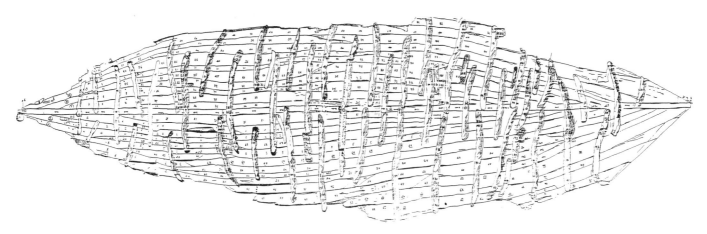

A line drawing of the remains of the Kinneret boat (above) was prepared by Hanni Efroni. The stem of the boat is on the left. The numbered individual pieces of wood can be made out.

The Kinneret boat lies in a specially constructed conservation pool (below) at the Yigal Allon Museum, Kibbutz Ginosar. The boat, resting on fiberglass frames, will remain here for a few years in order to prevent it from drying out.

A 1st century AD **mosaic** (below), found at nearby Migdal, depicts a boat with a painted stem and curving stern, a mast and sail, and three oars on the port side. Little was known about ancient lake craft prior to the discovery of the Kinneret boat.

Byzantine ships

The great mass of Byzantine history is little studied today, except perhaps in modern Greece. The events that transpired between Constantine's victory over Maxentius at the Milvian Bridge in AD312, and the Ottoman Turks' conquest, 1,141 years later, of the great city he founded, are a vast blur to most of us, full of strange names and stranger events.

Yet the battle of the Milvian Bridge in AD312 must certainly rank as one of the most crucial in history; for on that day Christianity, for the first time, ceased to be a religion punishable by death and started on the way to becoming the official religion of the West.

Constantine, now the emperor of the Roman world, attributed his victory to the divine intervention of the Christian god. He told Bishop Eusebius, years later, that before the battle he had seen a cross in the sky with the words "In this shalt thou conquer," and so it had happened.

For 12 years, Constantine fought a series of wars in order to preserve the crumbling empire. Finally, in AD324, he moved the capital to Byzantium, now renamed Constantinople. At his death in 337 he left behind a successful theocratic state, in which the squabblings of bishops and theologians were subordinated to the public interest.

Nevertheless, the Byzantine empire remained intensely religious. State sponsorship of the church did not reduce its missionary fervor. In the 5th century much of the Mediterranean was in the hands of Germanic northerners,' Goths and Vandals, who practiced a heretical version of Christianity. Under Justinian (527–65) these heretics were expelled and the lands returned to orthodoxy. As part of the political program, churches were manufactured in prefabricated sections and exported to the reclaimed provinces.

The Marzamemi "Church Wreck"

An astonishing example of such a prefabricated church is the so-called "Church Wreck" of Marzamemi, caught on a reef about a mile off the little fishing port of Marzamemi, Sicily. Any ship's captain who was not very familiar with the route would be unaware of the reef, which lies, at its highest point, a mere 10ft (3m) below the surface. In summertime a cool southerly current brings many kinds of fish to the relatively rich feeding ground. The fishermen of Marzamemi, too, like to moor their boats here.

It seems likely that for generations the Marzamemi fishermen were aware that on the underwater surface of the reef, and clearly visible through the shallow water (especially to anyone leaning over and looking for octopuses with a glass-bottomed bucket), was a great flat stone, dark green in color, and carved with a cross. Even though the stone has long since been removed, one can still meet people in bars or on the beach who say, "Do you know that there's a real church out there in the bay?"

In 1958, one of the old fishermen led the local archaeologist Luigi Bernabò-Brea and, later, an underwater specialist, Gerhard Kapitän, to the site. Kapitän subsequently directed operations which partly excavated the wreck and raised many of the more interesting pieces of stone; excavations to complete the project are now actively in preparation.

Finds of pottery and a few amphoras date the wreck to the reign of Justinian, and the stonework is of the same period. This was a time, as we have seen, when there was a revival of Byzantine power in the central Mediterranean, including the reconquest of Sicily in AD535 and the recovery of much of North Africa, and the building of churches was part of that political program. These "propaganda" churches included standardized, pre-cut pieces, such as the *ambo* or pulpit, the sanctuary screens and the capitals of the nave columns, which were quarried to pre-set designs and were then exported to the provinces.

Then, as we can see not only in the sunken church of Marzamemi but also in surviving actual churches in Cyrenaica and N. Italy, the local masons used limestone or some other convenient stone at hand to build the walls and main columns. Thus, at Marzamemi parts of the pulpit are of "*verde antico*" from Thessaly (N. Greece), while the sanctuary screens, etc., are of grey-white marble from Proconnesus (Marmara). Since the pre-carved pieces in the wreck never reached their destination (North Africa?), they have not been finished off, and the steps of the pulpit are too big to fit into a reconstruction of the whole construction. This poses a nice problem for the Syracuse museum authorities, who hope one day to be able to re-erect the basilica that never was in a maritime gallery.

Byzantines on the sea

Seapower was the single most important factor that kept the Byzantine empire alive against a host of invading peoples, and the most powerful class of galley in the Byzantine warfleet was the *dromon*. Traces of this effective naval weapon have been hard to find, but a 6th century wreck off the coast of Sicily at Cefalù may provide an example.

Here, in only 7ft (2m) of water, Gianfranco Purpura, while snorkelling in 1975, came across what at first he thought was a line of rocks. However, the rocks turned out to be overlying Byzantine amphoras and coarse pottery; this was not a seabed outcrop but the ballast of a ship.

Further exploration showed that there were timbers, probably cross-beams, within the ballast pile, and that the ship measured more than 110ft (35m), perhaps as much as 130ft (40m) in length, but was only 20ft (6m) in beam. A ship of this length, and with these proportions, must surely be a warship – perhaps even a *dromon*. The wreck has not been excavated to date, but it promises to yield exciting information in due course.

Ships and captains

The need to supply the city of Byzantium and the imperial armies with food meant that a large number of ships continued to be in regular use in the eastern Mediterranean through the fifth and sixth centuries, long after the decline of imperial power in the west. The organization of the *naukleroi*, who became responsible for this traffic, was rather different from that of the *navicularii*, who had carried goods to Rome during the previous five centuries. The *naukleroi* were more independent and generally responsible ship-owners and merchants, and they often traveled on their own ships. As such they were less amenable to control through honors and inducements or sanctions as the case might be.

Archaeology has given us the name of one such *naukleros*, inscribed on a steelyard and on an incense censer from the Yassi Ada ship. *Georgios Presbyteros Naukleros*, meaning "George the elder/senior sea captain", indicates the name and function of an individual who was

A phantom Byzantine church, long known to fishermen and partly excavated by Gerhard Kapitän, was found in the sea off Marzamemi, Sicily. Remains of the pulpit (above) fit into a reconstruction (right) after Kapitän. These prefabricated marble panels from the north Aegean were exported from Constantinople to a province (probably in North Africa) where church-building was part of the imperial government's reconquest program. Constantinople provided the tricky pieces, while the rest would be quarried and cut locally.

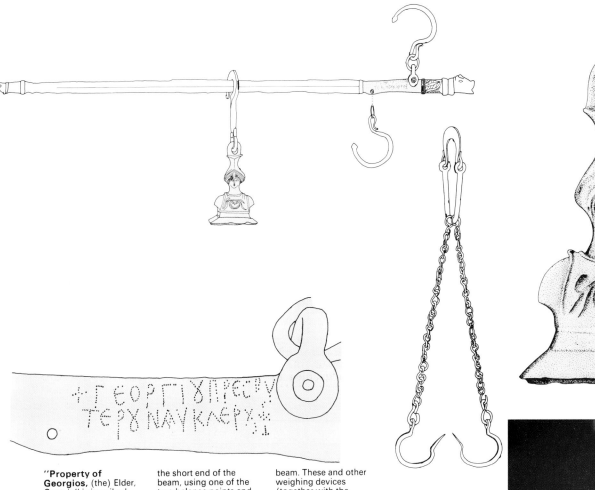

"**Property of Georgios,** (the) Elder, Captain" is inscribed (above) on the steelyard (top) and balance (above, right) from the Byzantine wreck at Yassi Ada, indicating that these skippers were in charge of both ship and cargo. The object to be weighed was hung from the short end of the beam, using one of the two balance points and the counterweight (top, right) of conventional design, representing the goddess Athena. This was moved along the beam until it balanced; the weight could be read off one of the two scales (heavy and light) on the beam. These and other weighing devices (together with the cook's equipment and various tools for use on board and ashore) show that the little vessel was a self-sufficient trader.

Discoveries of Turkish sponge divers at Yassi Ada (above) led archaeologists to initiate pioneering underwater excavations from 1961 onwards. Following up hints from sponge divers led to the discovery of the unique 14th century BC wreck at Ulu Burun (see p.33).

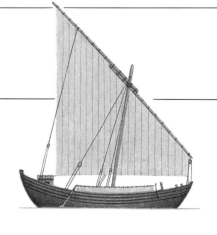

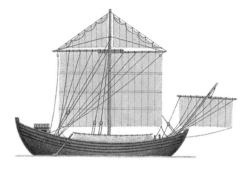

probably part owner of the little merchantman as well as its captain. The censer suggests that Georgios, like most Byzantines, was religious. A modern version of the censer's possible use comes from a practice witnessed by one of the authors of this article. At the Epiphany festival, the captain of a Greek coaster well known to Peter Throckmorton would swing an incense-filled censer while the village priest blessed the ship, making the Sign of the Cross with candle black on the overhead of the engine hatch (the area formerly occupied by the galley before the advent of engines). Georgios's censer was found in the galley area, but we will never know if the galley overhead of the Yassi Ada ship did in fact carry a blackened cross.

Georgios's ship, better known as the Yassi Ada ship, is one of three good examples of merchantmen from the 7th century. It was first shown to Peter Throckmorton by Captain Kemal and his men in 1958 (see p.22). The preliminary survey, carried out by Peter and Honor Frost, showed that here lay the bones of a fairly small vessel, with its anchors and amphora cargo still where they had landed when the hull had collapsed more then 1,300 years before. The stern area was full of tiles, probably from the galley. Most exciting of all, the sediment was thick enough to preserve significant parts of the hull.

George Bass began excavating the wreck in the summer of 1961. He conceived the excavation as an experimental proving ground for the ideas that he and Peter had developed at Cape Gelidonya. Fred Van Doorninck was in charge of studying hull remains, the galley and the anchors. Over four summers he and his crew, which averaged 16 people working from a camp on the island, accomplished 1,244 man-hours on the seabed, in 3,533 dives over 211 diving days, at a cost of about $100,000. The crew list for those years reads like a *Who's Who* of nautical archaeologists working today.*

This excavation saw the development of full-scale underwater techniques in the Eastern Mediterranean under the leadership of Bass and Van Doorninck. George Bass's definitive account of the shipwreck, which includes specialist contributions from 14 other individuals, was published in 1982.

After four years of work, the wrecksite was a scar on the bottom, vacuumed down to the bare rock. The salvaged material was deposited in Bodrum Castle, where it was labeled, conserved, numbered and given its correct location. As the years went by, Bass's group continued work also on a 4th century ship and then on a 16th century Ottoman ship in the same area which actually overlay part of Georgios's ship. Work on this is being directed by Cemal Pulak (see p.91). During all those years Bass orchestrated the interpretation of the remains.

The ship and her cargo

The ship sank in AD626 or soon after, in 100–130ft (32–39m) of water on the south side of Yassi Ada. Unlike the big vessels of the old Roman empire, which could carry hundreds of tons, she was a comparatively little ship, with a deck length of perhaps 60ft (18m), and able to carry slightly more than 50 tons of cargo. Although a simple and workaday craft, she was not unsophisticated. However, unlike the shell-first Roman argosies of the western empire, she was small and cheaply built. A reflection, perhaps, of the unstable age that produced her.

Her cargo comprised an estimated total of 900 Byzantine amphoras, mostly large globular jars, resin-pitched inside. None retained a stopper in place, though about 165 stoppers (many cut from old amphoras) were found in the wreck. Eighty of the amphoras bore scratched inscriptions on the shoulder, in Greek; these named contents, such as lentils or rice, or persons, Olympios and Georgios. The origin of the amphoras is not known: either the Black Sea or the eastern Aegean regions are possible.

Dr Fred Van Doorninck, who is presently professor at George Bass's Institute of Nautical Archaeology at Texas A&M, is now discovering fascinating new information from the duplicate amphoras left on the bottom when the excavation officially ended in 1964. Van Doorninck's recent studies show that the amphoras were not all of the same manufacture, and seem to have been made at different dates. Many have graffiti, of which there are many different varieties.

The contents of the amphoras are also something of a mystery. Sieving of silt contained within some of the globular amphoras has produced grape pips along with other plant remains, and it is thought that at any rate part of the cargo was wine, flavored with anise.

The fact that only 165 stoppers were found suggests that a good number of jars were empty before the ship sank. In the Greek islands today, winemaking is usually done by the tavern proprietor, who often buys the *musto*, or fresh pressed grape juice, from passing *kaikis*. A personal theory about Georgios's ship, and its final voyage, is that it may have been engaged in just such a distribution of the annual autumn grape pressing to the coastal villages, as still practiced by battered *kaikis* in the Aegean to this day.

Wine probably flowed no less freely on a Byzantine waterfront than on a modern one. The Yassi Ada ship could have filled in Thasos, and have been headed from north to south toward Halicarnassus (Bodrum), in order to discharge those last 200 amphoras. She must have been sailing almost before the strong southeast wind that prevails at that time of year, when she struck on the west reef a couple of hours' run from her destination.

Commercial gear included weights and

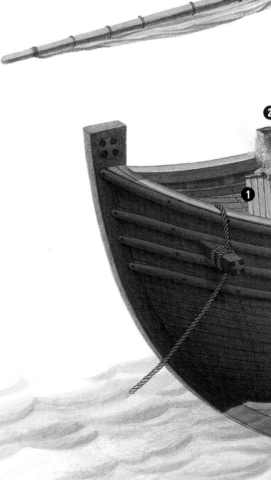

The Yassi Ada ship. This reconstruction drawing of Georgios' ship, as she might have appeared when she sailed, combines the hull reconstruction by Fred Van Doorninck and Richard Steffy with the practical experience of Roger Finch and Peter Throckmorton. Two sail plans are shown; lateen (upper left) and the conventional square rig (left), with mast locations and sail areas calculated by Parker Marean (see p.101). Van Doorninck favors the square, Steffy the lateen sail plan. We tend to agree with the latter, so the ship is shown as lateen in the main drawing. Archaeological evidence for the deck details includes location of the anchors (4) and reconstruction of the galley (1), accurately established by Van Doorninck during the excavation. The weather cloths (3), behind the figure in the illustration, are in accordance with ancient mosaics, and made like those on modern Greek coasters, as are the mooring bitts (2) and their decorations.

steelyards. Unusually for an ancient ship, some 70 coins, including 16 of gold, were in the wreck, though even so the sum represented is very small compared with the value of the ship and her cargo. A detailed study and model reconstruction have been made of the ship. She could have carried some 51 tons of cargo.

Excavation produced a lot of information about life on board. In the stern was a galley, a nicely designed and sensible affair as reconstructed by Van Doorninck. Here cooking took place on an iron grid above a tile-built hearth; smoke escaped through a hole appropriately positioned in the tiled deckhead above.

As well as pots and pans for cooking, eating and drinking, there was a big copper kettle, very like ones that can be seen today in Anatolian villages. The ship was also equipped with a comprehensive kit of iron tools, some eerily similar to those you can buy in Aegean village hardware stores today. Separately, there was a deposit of tools suitable for use on land, which the crew would have needed when they camped for the night in one of the sandy little coves along the coast. Kemal and his men had camped in just such a way when Peter Throckmorton cruised the coast with them at the time of the Yassi Ada discovery.

In short, the most striking thing about the Yassi Ada ship's outfit is its similarity to the little ships that still ply those waters.

Shipwrecks of the 7th century

Not far from Marzamemi, in the marsh of Pantano Longarini (once an inlet of the sea), a chance discovery yielded a large, quite well-preserved merchantman. The stern portion of the ship survived destruction by earth-moving machinery, and was recorded *in situ* by Peter Throckmorton and Gerhard Kapitän. We will go on to discuss (p.94) the important information yielded by this vessel regarding ancient shipbuilding techniques. The Pantano Longarini ship shows the beginning of the takeover from shell-first shipbuilding, practiced from the earliest times, to frame-first building.

The stern was of square counter, and the surviving timbers give the impression of a large vessel, confirmed by information from the workmen who discovered her and reckoned she was some 100ft long; they also reported seeing what must have been her name-board, carved with a Greek inscription. The date of the Pantano Longarini ship is uncertain: a few sherds of amphoras, and the similarity of the hull construction to the Yassi Ada wreck, suggest the early 7th century.

A quite different ship of the same period was excavated at Saint Gervais bay near Fos in southern France by Marie-Pierre Jézégou. This was a small ship – originally 50–60ft (15–18m) long – but slender and deep-footed. Her last cargo was pitch (carried in amphoras) and wheat.

Southwestern France has always been a noted producer of pine resin and pitch, and this part of the cargo of the Saint Gervais ship was very likely from the Narbonne region (the amphoras came from Byzacena originally, but were certainly reused). When the ship sank, evidently in an on-shore storm, the amphoras were broken, and the pitch they contained slopped out over the wheat, preserving it. This is a very rare example from the Mediterranean of what was a commonly transported commodity in antiquity.

The Saint Gervais wheat was probably rivet (*Triticum turgidum L.*), widely grown in much of the ancient world; the origin of the ship's cargo is unknown, though Italy, Africa or Spain are all possible, but it is likely that the wheat was being imported through the port of Fos to Arles or a neighboring town, since this area was not suitable for cereal growing.

The ship's timbers and her cargo thus tell us nothing definite about her original home port, but the few items belonging to the crew which were found show that she probably came from Greece or some other part of the eastern Mediterranean: two pitchers and a small dish, none of them of Gaulish type, bore scratched initials in Greek. Historical references anyway suggest that most traders dealing with the Frankish kingdom in southern Gaul at this period were in fact Jews or Syrians.

The Serçe Limani wreck

By 670, within half a century of the loss of the Yassi Ada ship, the eastern and southern shores of the Mediterranean had fallen into Moslem hands and traditional patterns of commerce had come to an end. Not until the 10th century are there again any definitely dated finds of shipwrecks, and these are of Saracen ships, quite likely combining business with piracy when they were lost off the French coast. This in fact marks a modest revival of traffic, as evidenced by wrecks, among them the "Glass Wreck" of Serçe Limani.

The Serçe Limani wreck belongs to what has been described as the golden age of Islamic seafaring. A unique documentary source known as the Geniza is available for this period, providing many first-hand insights into the commercial scene of the time, as seen through the eyes of Jewish merchants living in Cairo and other parts of the Islamic world. In this society, letters and other personal papers that included, or were even thought to include, the name of God, were deemed too holy to be destroyed.

Such papers were hidden away in a room in Cairo, the Geniza, which was not opened until modern times. The documents are hard to read or interpret, but contain many references to seafaring and long-distance trade. They show that the trading community was based on families; younger brothers or cousins stationed in distant ports reported on prices and availability of goods, and saw to the loading and unloading. Other members of the

family often traveled with the goods to check on pilfering and so on.

Much of the merchandise was of low bulk and high value, especially fine cloth; more than half of the commodities traded in the Mediterranean region were imported from India and the Far East, emphasizing the oriental perspective of the Islamic world. Seafaring was of great economic importance, since availability of goods determined market prices.

The ships mentioned were sailing vessels, usually lateen-rigged and of modest size. A ship would normally be owned by a single proprietor, a merchant, but a cargo would probably be made up of the goods of several merchants; despatches were normally divided between sailings to minimize the risk of loss. Sailing hardly ever took place in winter.

There are a number of references in the Geniza documents to the loss of ships, whether in storms or, especially, in rough water close to the coast when leaving or entering ports, particularly Alexandria. The agents who traveled with valuable consignments augmented the number of people on board, including not only the crew but also passengers.

The Geniza letters betray a well-founded fear of death at sea; as when we read of one episode when some travelers spent 35 days stranded by storms on an unidentified island between Tunisia and Sicily. But goods could be salvaged from sunken ships; for example we hear of some iron raised from a wreck near Bab

A galley was identified in the stern of the Byzantine ship at Yassi Ada, following underwater recording by divers and subsequent model-building by Richard Steffy and Fred Van Doorninck. Here meals were prepared on a tile-built hearth, and smoke escaped through a hole in the deckhead above.

al-Mandeb. Losses from bad weather or other accidents, and from enemy or pirate action, could be heavy. In one year, out of 14 ships known to have set sail from al-Mahdiyya (in Tunisia) no more than 7 arrived safely at Alexandria.

As well as the decked sea-going merchant ships, the Geniza documents also mention open vessels (called *qarib*) which sometimes sailed alone (with a cargo) but often accompanied a larger ship. Where they sailed together, there were obviously many ways in which the smaller vessel could assist the larger, but perhaps a particularly important one was to provide defense in a fight.

A curious but exciting discovery at a wrecksite off Agay (France) was that of a mid-10th century Arab ship, 65–80ft (20–25m) in length, which sank accompanied to the bottom by a boat 27–33ft (8–10m) long. The boat contained the skeleton of a man, aged about 35, with a sword and a cutlass sheath. Maybe this boat was a *qarib*; but what its role had been in the moments before it went to the bottom, one can only guess.

The excavation at Serçe Limani

The world of the Geniza, then, is reflected in the Serçe Limani wreck. This dramatic discovery took place in the landlocked bay of Serçe Limani ("Sparrow Harbor"), Turkey, at a depth of 100ft (32m). Divers led by George Bass and Fred Van Doorninck were feeling in the sand and silt covering what appeared to be a wreck

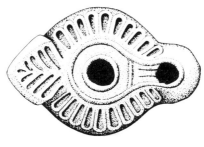
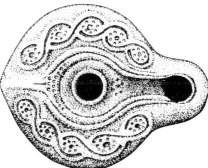

Two of the 24 oil lamps (above) found among the equipment of the Yassi Ada ship. Like the pottery and the copper coins found on board, the lamps are from the Black Sea, Constantinople and the northern Aegean regions.

A bronze sword hilt (above) from the Serçe Limani wreck, decorated with a bird in Indian style, emphasizes the far-flung extent of trade in the medieval Islamic world.

The Serçe Limani wreck yielded vast quantities of glass. This included more than 80 Islamic items (above, left) consisting of bottles, jars and bowls. The great bottle held by Cemal Pulak (above, center) perhaps the largest glass vessel to survive from antiquity, could only be restored thanks to careful sorting of the million fragments found on the site by the whole team for nearly a year (above, right). These were found at the bow and stern, where they were stored under the personal care of the merchants' agents. Such arrangements were typical of the commerce described in contemporary documents. The ship also contained more than 3 tons of broken glass and raw "cullet" (waste to be melted down for re-use). Analysis shows that the glass originated in several parts of Turkey and Persia, and it may have been taken on at more than one port.

site, when their hands came out of the sand cut and bleeding. Underneath lay a mass of broken glass! The excavations which took place later (in 1977–79) revealed, not only a spectacular cargo of glass, but also insights into the early 11th century Mediterranean world.

There were about three tons of glass on board; it was nearly all broken, and the excavators could show, from the findspots on the site, that it had been smashed before being loaded on board – almost as if some worker had been given the task of tamping down a mass of pieces to fit them tightly into the cargo space. The glass includes not only pieces of complete vessels (more than 100 have been laboriously reconstructed), but also cullet (raw glass) and deformed pieces and odd offcuts, evidently factory waste. The cargo thus represents a load of "scrap" glass on its way to some harbor town where it could be sold for making bottles or tableware.

The range of colors, shapes and decorative patterns found provides a fascinating collection of workshop material to set alongside well-known products of Islamic glassmakers, such as mosque lamps.

Other cargo was found. There were some Islamic glazed pottery bowls, just the sort of small consignment which we read of in the Geniza letters. There were also amphoras, of a known Byzantine form, bearing scratched inscriptions in Greek; they were lined with pitch and are thought to have contained wine. It could well be that there was more cargo, of a perishable nature, for study of the ship's hull indicates that she could have carried about 27 tons (or more if loaded down).

This was quite a small ship, 48ft (14.5m) on the waterline, of very rounded form. The hull was assembled by nailing planks to frames without any attachment between one plank and another, though it seems that even so the lines were not completely lofted in advance, but that the shipwright set up guide-planks to get the form of the frames right. Whether the shipwright was a Moslem or a Christian, the ship had been equipped at a Moslem port, for one of the iron anchors on board was stamped with Arabic letters.

What, then, of the merchants, the captain and the crew? There were living quarters in the bows, with fire-blackened pots, unbroken glass vessels, glass weights and wooden combs. Another living area was located in the hold.*

Weapons found on board included iron swords, an axe, four lances, and at least two dozen iron javelins; these last could have been for trade rather than for defence. Someone had lost a purse or bag containing a gold pendant and five silver rings. Presumably one of these living areas was the crew's, the other that of the merchants and/or passengers. They were evidently prepared to defend themselves if they ran across a hostile ship.

Who were the people on board, and what enemies might they fear? This was a period (c. AD1024, the date of a weight found in the wreck) when warfare between Moslems and Christians (under one flag or another) was frequent. That some of the Serçe Limani ship's equipment was of Moslem origin we have noted already; so, too, were the weights and the glass vessels found in the forward "mess", and on board somewhere was a bucket with an Arabic inscription.

However, there were also (Christian) Byzantine coins and seals, cooking-pots with Greek graffiti, bones from two pigs (which could not have been eaten by Moslems or Jews), and Christian symbols on some of the net-weights. Analysis of some of the lead objects and of the lead contained in the glass fragments suggests that they came from a number of original sources in Anatolia and Persia, and that the manufactured goods could have been taken on board at several ports.

Thus, although further study of the finds from the wreck may bring better insights, the precise mixture of people and religions on board remains enigmatic. However, from the nature of the cargo consignments, the apparent presence of agents travelling with goods, and the relatively small size of the ship (equipped, however, with adequate supplies for an off-shore voyage), we can fairly match the picture provided by the wreck with that offered by the Cairo Geniza documents.

The later years

In the succeeding centuries, shipwreck finds are scarce. One reason is that skins (referred to in the Geniza) and barrels took the place formerly held by amphoras in shipborne commerce, and so wrecks are less easily found. It also seems probable that long-distance traffic on the scale of the Greek, Roman and early Byzantine periods never really revived.

The loss of Anatolia to the Seljuk Turks in AD1071 was the beginning of the end for the Byzantine empire. Less than 20 years earlier, the final schism between eastern and western churches had opened the way for the Crusaders' onslaught on the city, which finally took place in 1204. From then till the Ottoman Turks' *coup de grace* in 1453, Constantinople survived as a shadow of its former self.

In the millennium of its existence, the empire had developed into a new kind of civilization. At a time when Rome had become a provincial town and illiterate barbarians were burning libraries all over the west, until almost nothing remained of the great literary works of ancient civilization except what survived in a few fortified monasteries, the school children of Constantinople were studying Homer in the original, as their ancestors had 1,000 years before them.

Nevertheless, trade of a sort went on. In the 12th century, table ceramics continue to be fairly well represented in the underwater record. Potteries which successfully produced attractive glazed wares were evidently able to market them at a distance, at least in certain periods. One wreck with such goods on board was partially excavated by Peter Throckmorton at Pelagos Nisos in the Sporades islands.

This was the wreck of a ship at least 80 by 27ft (25 by 8m), and of a typical eastern Mediterranean construction. The cargo consisted mainly of amphoras, plates and dishes, totalling more than 1,500 items. The majority of the articles were elegantly decorated, using the *sgraffito* technique of incising the design on the top layer of glaze. Decorative themes show the influence of Islam with geometrical patterns and Kufic (early Arabic) lettering, as well as birds, animals and floral patterns. The decorative techniques date the wreck to the mid 12th century.

The fall of the great city to Roger De Flor's Catalan Crusaders in 1204 not only prefigured Constantinople's final end; it also resulted in thousands of looted books becoming available in Italy. In 1453, when the last Paleologus, the 107th emperor of the East, died at the barricades on what is still called Black Tuesday by modern Greeks, the torch of Christian Civilization was ready to pass to the west. If the city had survived for another 200 years, the forces that explored and conquered the New World might have gone eastabout, rather than westabout, and our lives might have been entirely different.

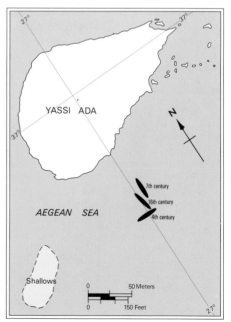

Three wrecks from Yassi Ada (above) provide windows through which we can glimpse three different periods of the past. Ships claimed by the reef include a 4th century AD vessel of the Roman period, the 7th century Byzantine merchantman once captained by Georgios the Elder, and an Ottoman wreck from the late 16th century now being excavated (see opposite).

Sgraffito **ware** (top) from the Pelagos Nisos wreck (above). The ship, which weighed 100 tons or more, sank in the mid 12th century with more than 1,200 pieces of brightly colored pottery in her cargo. Although long-distance trade was less intense in the Medieval period than under the Roman empire, some products, including glazed pottery such as this, could command a market remote from their place of manufacture.

Yassi Ada wrecked not only ancient and Byzantine ships, but also their Ottoman successors. While Bass's team were excavating a 4th century AD ship, they found the remains of a later vessel, which was excavated in 1983 by Cemal Pulak and an all-Turkish team (top). Pottery (above right) indicated its origin and gave a probable late 16th century date, supported by silver coins (top left) minted in Seville 1566–89. Cannon balls (above left) suggest this sturdy but cheaply built vessel was either a warship or a supply vessel, and may have been connected with the battle of Lepanto (1571). Pulak is now reconstructing the ship.

We have seen earlier how Homer and St Paul, separated by many hundreds of years, were both concerned with maritime matters, and we have also seen how these have been reinterpreted in the light of comparatively recent underwater discoveries. Archaeology has also proved decisive in discovering how the ships themselves came to be constructed.

Herodotus (5th century BC) wrote a passage about Egyptian ships which was not well understood until actual Egyptian ships were discovered and studied. This passage has recently been retranslated by Lionel Casson:

From this acacia tree they cut planks 3 feet long, which they put together like courses of brick, building up the hull as follows: they join these 3 foot lengths together with long close set dowels; when they have built up a hull in this fashion (out of the planks), they stretch crossbeams over them. They use no ribs, and calk seams from the inside, using papyrus fibers.

The 5th dynasty mastaba tomb of Ti illustrates this. But it was not until two 12th dynasty boats were discovered in 1893 at Dahasure that this could be studied.

Shell-first construction
In the 1930s, James Hornell, the great British student of primitive watercraft, studied the modern rivercraft of Egypt and discovered that the philosophy of their construction was precisely that of the Dahasure boats, with adaptations for modern materials. It might be said that these boats, both ancient and modern, were made as Herodotus had described: shell first, or in the words of a modern builder, inside out.

The idea of building a boat shell first is strange to individuals familiar with the European shipbuilding tradition, where the practice is precisely the opposite: that is, the frame or structure is erected first and the planks are then hung on it.

The idea of building a strong outer shell, with planks attached to each other and framing put in as an afterthought is still, however, standard practice in Arabia and the Indian subcontinent, as well as in Southeast Asia and China. Scandinavian lapstrake building follows the same shell-first philosophy, but is a separate tradition.

The earliest example of a shell-first ship in the west is the great river barge buried as part of King Cheops funeral array in about 2500BC, just south of the great pyramid of Giza. The ship is 140ft (43m) long, and the techniques used in her construction must have taken a long time to develop. She appears to have been assembled first by attaching the planks to each other with pegs: the planks were then lashed together with rope through slots cut into the planking on the inside: the ropes that connected the slots passed over battens which in turn covered the inside of the seams.

It is my belief that the pegs were used to hold the structure in one piece until it could be lashed together and framing put in to keep it rigid. Once the structure had actually been assembled the pegs had little function.

The mortise and tenon technique
By the time the Dahasure boats were built, the lashing technique seems to have become obsolete: instead, boats were held together with interlocking mortise and tenon joints. This technique, the monocoque hull, was applied throughout the Mediterranean until at last it became obsolete at the end of the Roman empire. The last examples of its use, as a technique for setting up a hull in a fair shape and keeping it there until it could be framed out, are seen in the Pantano Longarini and Yassi Ada ships, from the early years of the Byzantine empire.

The shell-first construction philosophy prevailed in the Mediterranean for some three and a half millennia, until it was superseded by the frame-first techniques. There seems to be a standard technique, as illustrated, which prevailed from at least the 14th century BC Kas ship to the Torre Sgarrata ship which was built a millennium and a half later.

There are fascinating exceptions, such as the 6th century Etruscan ship Bon Porte 1, in which round pegs replaced the conventional tenons, and oblique pegs replaced the treenails which kept the planks from separating. Yet the philosophy of shell-first construction remains the same.

Advantages of shell-first construction
It has been surmised that this type of construction was practiced in Egypt because of the lack of good long ship timber in that part of the world – the pegging or tenoning technique made it possible to use available timber such as the acacia wood mentioned by Herodotus. Yet the Cheops ship is made of Aleppo pine, the Antikythera ship is planked in part with elm, and the Torre Sgarrata ship is made of red pine, meticulously mortised and tenoned together in long lengths.

There must have been another reason for the incredible longevity of a system that consumed labor at five to ten times the rate required for a frame-first construction, as the shipwrights who built the Kyrenia ship replica discovered.

Recent research has shown that frame-first construction existed simultaneously with the standard Roman shell-first tenoned construction, at the end of the

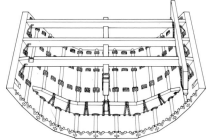

Ancient Egyptian boatbuilding, seen in its earliest known form in a cross-section of the c.2500BC Cheops ship (right), followed the shell-first system: the hull was put up first and internal strengthening structures were added later. The superb Cheops ship, which was found in 1952 in an almost airtight chamber south of the pyramid of Cheops, has strakes joined by pegs and then lashed together. In the Dahasure boat (above), found near the pyramid of Sesostris III (1878–42BC), the planks are edge-joined with interlocking mortises and tenons. The shell-first method endured in the Mediterranean for more than three millennia.

The shell-first technique (below), as seen at the peak of its development by Mediterranean shipwrights of the 2nd century AD. After setting up the keel, the stem post and the stern post, a batten was used to lay out the ship's curves. Only when the outer shell had been completed were the frames and floors shaped and then fastened into place. (Drawing after J.-Y. Gassend).

A pair of wooden calipers (below right), recovered from a 7th century BC wreck at Giglio Island, off Italy, was amazingly well preserved in pitch that had spilled from broken amphoras. This carpenter's tool would have been useful, among other things, as a gauge for the mortises and tenons that were cut at close and regular intervals in the planking of ancient ships. Its resemblance to modern calipers is quite striking.

Plank tenoning (below) typical of antiquity used numerous tenons inserted in mortises and blocked by pegs. On the 7th century Yassi Ada ship (bottom), tenons had become vestigial and were used only to keep planking in place and to shape the hull before the floor frames were installed. (Drawings after F. Van Doorninck).

Ancient Egyptian shipwrights, depicted in the Fifth Dynasty tomb of Ti from the 3rd millennium BC, are shown at work with adzes and wooden-handled chisels (right).

empire. In any case we know that the technicians of the Classical World were very competent indeed. It has been argued that the transition from shell-first to frame-first, as seen at Pantano Longarini and Yassi Ada, marks the change from the slave economy of classical times to something resembling a free market economy, with both labor and materials becoming more expensive. It has also been argued that the shell-first technique evolved because it was the only method of creating a fair shape that the shipwrights knew – a shell that could be carefully erected by eye and measurement as it went along. This would explain the tenons in the Yassi Ada and Pantano Longarini ships, which, like the pegs of the Cheops ship, seem to have been used only to set the below-the-waterline part of the hull into shape, before framing it up.

The characteristic lapstrake build of Viking ships was one of the many solutions to the problem of getting a fair shape: the Vikings shaped their ships on the fair curves of long planks which were lashed or clenched together before the frames went in: primitive small ships in Norway in the 19th century were set up just as the Yassi Ada and Pantano ships were, that is by setting up the hull shell first (but with lapped strakes) up to the waterline, then framing and planking above it as in a frame-first construction.

As we find more ancient ships, and as more and more archaeologists begin to study them seriously, another theory has emerged which, in my opinion, neatly explains the long survival of the mortise and tenon technique.

Ships built to last

It seems that many of the ancient ships that have been carefully excavated were very old when they went down, the Kyrenia ship and Torre Sgarrata among them. The tenon method, although expensive compared with frame-first construction, seems to have made ships last a long time. This would have compensated for the high labor cost of constructing such a ship, and ensured that tenon-built ships predominated in ancient times.

Any competent marine surveyor will tell you that in a wooden vessel, frames rot first, and usually from top to bottom. The area most prone to rot in a wooden vessel is under the edges of the deck: if water penetrates, it will affect the upper ends of the frames. Planking, especially below the waterline, is not so prone to rot.

A wooden hull is like an eggshell: it gains much of its strength from the compression of the calking, keeping the whole structure in tension. In the case of the tenon-first Roman ship, the compression came from the swelling of the accurately planed planks, which ensured a watertight fit when the ship was launched. The tenons, fastened securely in place by their treenails, held the planking tightly joined. In these ships, rotten frames did not con-

demn the ship, as the watertight integrity of the hull did not depend on them. The frame-first ship depends on her frames in order to hold the planking in place. If the frames are rotten, the calking will not stay in place and the ship will leak. In extreme cases, planks have been known to drop right off frame-first ships, because when spewn calking destroys the tension that is so important to the eggshell of the construction, the frame-first ship works like a basket, causing metal fastenings to break and planks to split.

In working around shipyards whilst a marine surveyor, I have often come upon some lovely old lady of a yacht, kept alive in her last days by a fiberglass coating on the outside of the hull. Such vessels are usually doomed, because the new fiberglass cannot flex with the old hull, and consequently the encapsulated old wood will rot even faster.

The Roman shipwright had no such problem; if a tenoned hull got leaky, he simply built another shell of planks outside the leaky one. Such a ship has been found, at the Ile de Levant in the south of France (known as the Titan wreck – see p.65).

From shell-first to frame-first

Although there are more than a dozen tenon-built vessels which prove that this was a standardized technique, and we know that there was a gradual transition from shell-first to frame-first, as exemplified by the Yassi Ada and Pantano Longarini ships, there is a gap, which is only partly filled by two eastern Mediterranean shipwrecks. One of these vessels was the Glass wreck at Serçe Limani, which was thoroughly excavated by George Bass and his group in the late 1970s.

She was an Arab vessel, with a trading cargo of bulk glass, lost on the coast of Turkey on her way north, perhaps from Alexandria. Similar in size and shape to the Byzantine ship at Yassi Ada, she was built around AD1000, and was definitely of frame-first construction, without tenons in the structure.

With Dr Harry Kritsas of the Greek Archaeological Service, I surveyed and partially excavated a Byzantine vessel built about a century later. She was bound from Constantinople, perhaps, with a cargo of beautiful Sgraffito-ware plates among other things, and was lost at Pelago Nisos in the Sporades.

We excavated a small test trench which revealed part of the hull: compared to more ancient vessels, her planking was thin, not tenoned together, and was fastened to heavy frames with small iron nails. She appears to have been refastened many times, and to have been a frame-first vessel. In short, the ship's planking seems to have served mainly to keep the water out rather than as a main structural member.

Somewhere in the 350-year time span between these four ships, something

happened that rendered tenons obsolete once and for all. Both of those later vessels, one Byzantine, one Arab, were essentially modern ships – the direct ancestors of vessels being built in the Mediterranean today.

Birth of the modern shipbuilding industry

By AD1000, for the first time in history, shipbuilding was beginning to turn into a modern industrial process. Ancient ships could only be built one at a time with a fair shape obtained by setting up the shell by eye and simple measurements. Frame-first ships required that the shipwright knew how to predict the eventual shape of a ship and set up frames which had been pre-fabricated. In order to do this he had to know how to draw out the full-sized frames on a level floor, or set up patterns used to bend battens from bow to stern, from which in turn patterns could be made to allow fabrication of frames.

Whatever the system, it must have been a primitive form of what we now know as lofting, the process by which all the elements in a ship can be drawn out full scale on a floor. The loft floor is used to predict the shapes of the timbers that go into the ship so that they can be pre-fabricated before fitting – a huge saving in time and effort.

Although it is impossible to accurately estimate the ratio of labor cost versus cost of material in ancient times, the ratio

Bottom of the Byzantine Pantano Longarini ship after the transom timbers had been removed (above), revealing the waterline wales (timbers extending along the whole length of the ship's sides). Inside the wales are remnants of bottom planking, which was tenoned.

seems to have remained fairly constant in recent times in most countries. About half the cost of construction is materials, and half labor, with the ratio varying according to the type of vessel and how complicated she is. It is generally agreed that one third of the cost of a large yacht is machinery, another third the hull, and the final third everything else, from sails to coffee cups. In a vessel like the Yassi Ada ship, one might assume that some 70 percent of the money invested went into the construction of the hull, and that a minimum of 30 percent of that was the cost of labor. So vessels like the Serçe Limani and Pelagos ships cost less than half as much as a typical tenon ship of the same size.

Dick Steffy, who reconstructed the bones of both the Serçe Limani and Kyrenia ships, has said:

> The Kyrenia shipwright had to keep a complex design in his head and there was no way of communicating it to other shipwrights. It was a process that had to be memorized through a long period of apprenticeship . . . The Serçe Limani shipwright now measured everything he did with a standardized ruler (23.4cm long, or roughly a hand span) . . . (designs) could be communicated and written down.

The shipbuilding and seafaring trades have always been conservative: traditions are important and are carefully main-

Molds laid out on a screive board at a modern Greek boatyard (above). Taken from sections of a half-model of the projected boat, these molds are enlarged to full size and laid out on a screive board. Battens make it possible for the designer to obtain fair lines to a 1:1 scale, which can then be transferred to shapes of frames. This invention made the use of tenons unnecessary.

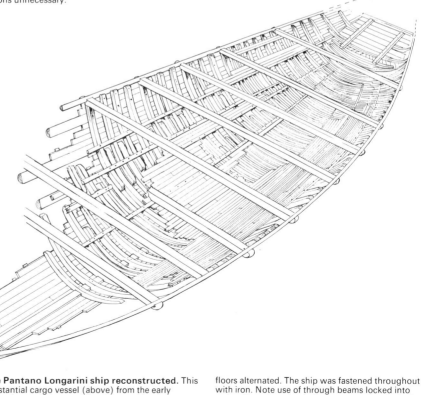

The Pantano Longarini ship reconstructed. This substantial cargo vessel (above) from the early Byzantine period exemplifies the transition from shell-first to frame-first techniques of shipbuilding construction. This is still in the Roman tradition, but has begun to take on medieval or modern characteristics. The ship was very heavily framed with grown timbers roughly adzed to fit into place. However, as in modern construction, frames and floors alternated. The ship was fastened throughout with iron. Note use of through beams locked into wales. Brunel used a similar concept when he built the first longitudinally framed ship, the *Great Britain* in 1843.

95

tained, sometimes for millennia, as we have seen in the history of the shell-first tenoned ship. The ancient world was remarkably self-contained: although the Romans traded with India, this trade was conducted over land until about AD47, when a Greek navigator called Hippalus discovered how to use the Indian Ocean's trade winds in order to sail to India and back. It is, perhaps, no coincidence that we begin to see the end of the tenon tradition in the years that followed.

Later developments
By the time that Constantine moved the Roman empire to Byzantium, the Mediterranean was being assaulted on all sides by primitive peoples. The Italian peninsula became a Germanic fiefdom, and great tribal movements, beginning with the Mongols, began to flow into what is now Eastern Europe and Asia Minor, followed by Turkish-speaking tribesmen, Seljuks and then Ottomans. Under the green banners of Islam, peoples from the Arabian peninsula occupied the southern littoral of the Mediterranean and large parts of Spain.

The Byzantine empire was the bulwark that held off all these invasions, and Constantinople, as Rome had been a millennium before, was the center of the civilized world.

The Venetians, safe from invasion in their Adriatic stronghold, created a maritime empire, which was in a sense a kind of buffer zone between the Arab Levant and the Byzantines.

By the 11th century, Viking Bersakers in their shallow-draft longboats had begun to fight their way down the Danube, through tribes of hostile Pechenegs, to Byzantium, where they found employment in the empire's version of the Foreign Legion, the Varengian guard.

By the 12th century AD, armies of Crusaders from the North were setting out to recapture the Holy places of the Bible from the Arabs. One obvious path to the Holy Land led through Venice – and the Venetians were happy to hire out their merchant fleet as troop transporters.

The Venetians, like the Genoese, mass-produced the ships they needed using the frame-first system. For a long time, their trading fleets were great rowing galleys that could fight off Arab corsairs, but round ships were needed too: a big galley with a couple of hundred oarsmen was obviously an inefficient and expensive cargo carrier.

Until the invention of the cannon, it was easy for a galley to capture a round ship, but the round ship as a fighting platform eventually put the galleys out of business.

The Ottoman Turks captured the great city of Constantinople in 1453. The secret of their success was sophisticated gunnery. The loss of Constantinople put an end to the commercial empires of Venice and Genoa, and so imaginative seamen began to look for new commercial opportunities. One of these seamen was Christopher Columbus.

The frenzied maritime activity of the late Middle Ages had led to the adaptation of a whole set of new ideas about how to construct and sail ships. Rudders replaced steering oars and the lateen sails so popular with the Arabs began to supplement the simple square sails so typical of the ancient ships. As simple round ships turned into larger and larger gun platforms, improvements in rigs became necessary, as sails above a certain size were too hard to handle and thus rigs had to be divided.

By the time that Columbus sailed for the New World, the frame-first system of shipbuilding in the Mediterranean had reached the same level of standardization that the tenon system had reached at the time of Christ, and was well on its way to invading Northern Europe.

Developments in the north
The lapstrake tradition of the north is as ubiquitous as the tenon tradition of the south. It begins with the Hjørtspring boat, a 3rd/2nd century BC log canoe, built up with lapstrake planking. Due to the habit of Viking chieftains of using their longships as tombs, we have a whole series of surviving Viking warships.

The tradition is still alive in Scandinavia, in the form of several varieties of small craft that are still ubiquitous. The Church boats of the Dahlen Lakes, for instance, are directly descended from longships of the Vikings.

Merchant ships were built in the same manner. The Bayeux Tapestry shows William invading England in what are obviously lapstrake vessels, similar to the cog which has been excavated and is being preserved in Bremen.

The *Henry Grace à Dieu*, built in the 1400s, was constructed of several layers of lapstrake planking. By 1510, when the *Mary Rose* was built, English shipwrights were using the frame-first systems developed in the Mediterranean.

By the middle of the 16th century, the frame-first system which we see in its infancy at Serçe Limani had become the standard throughout Europe. It moved to North America with the earliest settlers.

Shipbuilding in North America
For the Americans of the New England colonies, with the sea in their front yards and the seemingly endless forest stretching behind, shipbuilding and ship managing were, for two centuries, the way to fame and fortune. By 1776, one third of all British ships were being built in the colonies – mainly in North America. Eighty years later, the United States led the world in shipping tonnage. Yet the basic rules of construction had changed very little even a lifetime afterwards, when the end of big wooden ship construction came with the building of wooden steamers by the shipping board in World War I.

A Scandinavian church boat (opposite above), directly descended from Viking craft, is one of many still used to bring worshippers to church in the more remote regions of the country.

Ships of the new English navy in 1520 (above), gathered at Dover to escort Henry VIII to France for his Cloth of Gold meeting with the French king Francis I. The four-master leaving the harbor may be the *Henry Grace à Dieu*, and the other four-master may be the *Sovereign*. The three-masters are probably the *Mary Rose*, the *Gabriel Royal*, and the *Katherine Forteleza*. The scene is probably not an actual representation of the event, but rather the artist's depiction of England's most prestigious naval vessels of the time.

Venetian galleys at Lepanto (1571) (above), when the Turkish fleet of more than 280 vessels was defeated by the combined forces of Venice, Spain and the Papal States, numbering about 211 ships. The role played by the Venetian oared warships is emphasized in this contemporary painting.

The cog seal of Stralsund, 1329, and the seal of the Admiral of France, Louis de Borbon, 1463–86, indicate the evolution of the ship in medieval times (above). The former shows the first use of the outboard rudder rather than the steering oar; the latter depicts a three-master ship, but with square sails on each of the masts.

The vast quantity of timber in North America meant that there was little need to change existing methods of building in order to conserve material. The Californian trade in the early 1850s was so lucrative that a pure profit was expected after only three or four voyages.

Since both labor and timber were cheap, good ships were built to last for a span of 15 years. The same basic design was used for many years. In 1890, the builder of the last full-rigged American wooden ships used as his reference a work written more than 60 years earlier, Lauchlan McKay's *Practical Ship-builder*.

The final flowering

It is widely believed, especially in the USA, that wooden shipbuilding reached its highest point in North America with the great clippers and down-easters, and in the smaller traditional craft developed there.

However, techniques used in the United States were primitive compared to those developed in England. Ships built in that last flowering of craftsmanship, before engineering overwhelmed tradition, were among man's greatest achievements.

The last chapter of McKay's 1839 treatise on ship construction concerns steamers, and contains a strong plea for technical improvement. He contrasts America's "backwardness" with the British government's "[vigor]" in encouraging improvements . . ." He does not appear to have understood that in England the Industrial Revolution was already more than half a century old.

By the last quarter of the 18th century England was well on the way to becoming an industrial society. The production of wrought iron had risen from 68,000 tons in 1788 to 250,000 tons by 1806. Fifty years later, world production of wrought iron was about six million tons annually, and Great Britain produced half of this.

In contrast to North America, England's supply of wood was limited. Britain had been combing the world for ship timbers ever since the mid-18th century. The demands of the Napoleonic wars had ravaged the forests of Europe by 1815, but even before that time the forests of England were seriously depleted. A survey of 1783 shows that a reserve of no more than 50,000 loads of oak remained in the royal forests. This was only enough to build thirteen 74-gun ships, the smallest ships of the line, known as third rates.

Traditional builders were slow to turn to the use of iron. The first seagoing iron ship was not produced till 1821, 35 years after the first successful iron vessel, a canal barge, had been constructed. The Royal Navy was conservative and opposed to all but minor technical changes. Forged iron knees were used in a ship built by Henry Dundas in 1781. Ten years later the distinguished naval constructor Robert Seppings officially proposed the use of iron knees in warships, only to be turned down on the grounds that iron knees would increase the damaging effect of cannon shot on a vessel.

After the American Revolution, the United States was no longer an unlimited source of timber. Yellow pine, imported from Georgia during the Napoleonic wars, became more scarce, due to trade restrictions following the war of 1812.

Britain now turned to West Africa for iroko and upepwe, described as "African oak", and Indian teak may have come into use as early as 1750. The Bombay naval dockyard was producing teak frigates before the end of the French war and beyond: *Foudroyant*, a frigate of 1817, still survives, moored off Portsmouth.

Later, Burma produced shiploads of beautiful teak when it came under the colonial aegis, and the wood was used lavishly in mid-19th century ships.

The New England shipwright, Lauchlan McKay's brother Donald went bankrupt in 1869 with the building of his last ship, *Glory of the Seas*. It is significant that his last ship was built on the same principles as his first, whereas the contemporary *Cutty Sark (1869)* was one of the most modern sailing vessels of her time.

From wood to iron

In McKay's lifetime, the age-old trade of shipbuilding had been transformed by England's booming Industrial Revolution into a very different sort of profession, where ships were designed by engineers, and mast shipwrights gradually lost their status. *Cutty Sark* and her contemporaries mark the final flowering of traditional craftsmanship and the primacy of the master shipwright in England. If the building of seagoing sailing ships is an art form, then the British tea-clipper builders of a century ago were the ones who made maximum use of the materials available at the time, producing tea clippers that were real works of art. This continued until 1869, when the Suez Canal put an end to their usefulness.

This is not to belittle McKay's *Glory of the Seas* and all the wonderful down-easters built after her. They were made as well as possible with the materials at hand in the old tradition.

The British builders went a giant step further and combined the tradition with the Industrial Revolution, creating vessels that compared with American ships as a celadon bowl compares with a clay one. Mid-19th century English hulls were, quite simply, the strongest and longest-lasting wooden vessels ever built since the age of the tenoned ships.

Three of the iron-framed teak-planked ships of this final flowering still survive. They are the *Cutty Sark*, lovingly restored in her dock at Greenwich, the *Carrick* at Glasgow, and the iron frame of the *Ambassador*, beached in the Straits of Magellan. Two ships, both in the Falkland Islands, survive to illustrate the development of composite construction in England: the *Vicar of Bray* and *Jhelum*.

The *Jhelum* and the *Vicar of Bray*

Both *Jhelum* and *Vicar of Bray* show the utilization of wood and iron technology in an advanced form. These two small ships are more sophisticated in their construction than any other wooden merchant ships surviving from the 19th century. By the first half of the 19th century, when both ships were built, the construction of conventional wooden vessels was pretty well standardized. This is not the case with either *Jhelum* or *Vicar of Bray*, which are both experimental in the different ways that iron and wood are used in their construction.

Built in 1849 at Liverpool as an East India packet, *Jhelum* has been at the end of a jetty in Port Stanley since 1870, where she arrived "in a sinking condition" after rounding the Horn. Her crew had refused to sail any further in her. Condemned as a constructive total loss, she was sold where she lay as a hulk, and was scuttled at the end of the jetty. Circumstances made it cheaper to write her off than to repair her.

She has iron rather than wooden hanging knees. Most of the timber is tropical hardwood, probably iroko and teak. The quality of the construction is high. Where it is not marred by weathering, the carpenter's work is beautiful: the joints still fit, anything that is going to strike the eye is pleasingly beaded. Even more interesting, however, is the extreme sophistication of her construction.

The East India trader *Jhelum* (top), and the *Vicar of Bray* (above), two of the many wrecks to be seen in the Falklands, illustrate how the Industrial Revolution and colonial expansion were changing the shipwright's art in the mid 19th century.

Jhelum's poop has survived almost intact, because at some time a tin roof was put over it and it was used as a carpenter's shop. The partitions once delineating the cabins have been removed, but the four great stern windows in the after end of the cabin are still in place, although without their frames and glass. The upper level under the poop deck itself has iron lodging knees between the extreme stern and the break of the poop. The main deck, too, has iron knees. Deck beams on both decks are supported by iron stanchions amidships. Elsewhere, the knees are of oak.

The *Vicar of Bray* was built at Whitehaven eight years earlier than *Jhelum,* but was no less sophisticated a vessel. Named after the character in the traditional song, who shifted before every political wind, she was pronounced in terms of the general quality of her workmanship "as good as can be made" by a Lloyds surveyor. Keel, stem and stern post were built of "African oak" (iroko). The floors and futtocks were English oak, the lowermost planking American elm.

The layout of the *Vicar*'s ironwork is similar to *Jhelum*'s, in that the iron dagger knees run aft from amidships and forward from its fore end. But in the midship section *Vicar* has an "X" structure of iron hanging knees. The superiority of the *Vicar*'s construction is demonstrated by the fact that she has held together better than the *Jhelum.* The first composite ship may have been built as long ago as 1839,

Donald McKay's East Boston shipyard (above) where 32 vessels, many of them clippers, were built between 1850 and 1869. Materials and construction techniques in American shipyards of the time were almost identical to those used a century before.

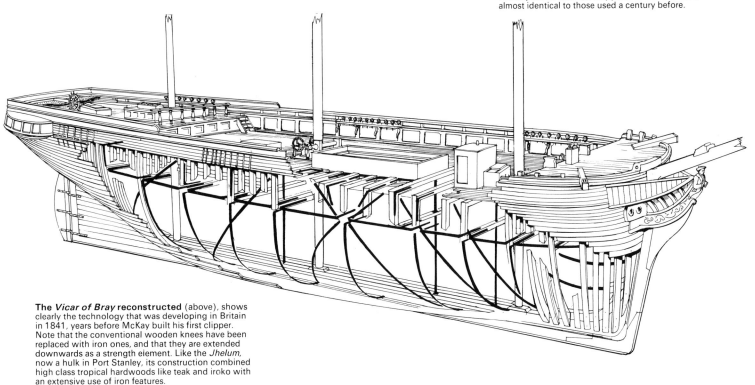

The *Vicar of Bray* **reconstructed** (above), shows clearly the technology that was developing in Britain in 1841, years before McKay built his first clipper. Note that the conventional wooden knees have been replaced with iron ones, and that they are extended downwards as a strength element. Like the *Jhelum,* now a hulk in Port Stanley, its construction combined high class tropical hardwoods like teak and iroko with an extensive use of iron features.

but it was not until 1862 that Lloyds gave their consent for composite classification, after many years of experimentation and campaigning by shipwright Alexander Steven. The last to have been built in England dates from 1879, although the Dutch continued to build composite vessels until nearly the end of the century.

The *Ambassador*

The earliest composite ship that can still be studied is the wreck of the clipper ship *Ambassador*, now lying to the east of Punta Arenas, Chile. Built of teak planking on an iron frame, she must have looked like an all-wooden vessel when afloat. The same is true of the *Cutty Sark,* if one boards her today. Although more than half her structure is iron, *Cutty Sark* strikes the eye as a wooden vessel.

It is not generally realized that these composite clippers hardly ever wore out. They disappeared because the trades for which they had been constructed came to an end. Then, passing into other hands, they might be cut down to barges, or put into unsuitable trades so that vessels designed to carry tea foundered at sea with cargoes of coal.

Moments when one realizes that one is looking at something unique occur very rarely. The experience came to me in the 1950s, when I was delivering a boat to Noumea, New Caledonia, in the Pacific. There, sunk alongside an abandoned dock was a composite clipper! I never knew her name. Half sunk, in tropical waters, with everything imaginable straining at the structure, she sat there, intact.

Tropical waters are so destructive that steel ships disappear in 10–15 years. Also at Noumea were several vessels from World War II, including a troopship and some landing ships. The steel structures of these vessels had corroded to lace. Yet here was a forged iron, teak, greenheart and rock-elm ship, more or less intact where she had been for the last 20 years. She was probably 60 years old when she arrived there, long before the steel vessels had been built.

Nineteenth-century British ships of this type were built to last forever. The World War II landing ships wasting away on the reef were built for a specific purpose and were designed to be expendable.

It seems clear, then, from study of the Falkland Islands ships, that American vessels of the 19th century were obsolete before they were even built, and the lessons learned by the builders of *Jhelum* and *Vicar of Bray* were ignored.

These great men realized, very early on, that oak and pine were poor shipbuilding materials, except in very specific applications. They searched the whole world for materials that were permanent and foolproof, and they found them. Today, these materials are ignored. The demise of wooden shipbuilding may well be a direct result of the inferiority of the wooden materials used today.

Tea clippers like the *Ambassador* (left), seen here as a wreck in the Straits of Magellan, were often composite, that is, built with teak planking in iron frames, although the first modern metal ship's structure, the *Great Britain*, had been built a generation before. Among the design innovations were double bottoms and longitudinal framing.

The *Great Britain*, Isambard Kingdom Brunel's magnificent metal construction of 1843, powered by a steam-driven screw propeller, is shown (above) undergoing reconstruction at Bristol after her rescue from the Falklands, and in a contemporary painting (top). She has been called the first modern ship, the great-grandmother of *all* today's ocean-going shipping.

Ship stability, ancient and modern

Modern techniques of naval architectural analysis, developed over centuries as sailed warships and merchant vessels evolved, can also be applied to ancient ships. Information from the Byzantine coaster lost at Yassi Ada (see p.86), when put through the computer, has yielded new interpretations of the archaeologists' findings and new lines of research.

It was with considerable curiosity that we decided to apply today's naval architectural tools and data to the analysis of the 7th century Yassi Ada ship, so skilfully excavated by George Bass. What sort of a ship was she to sail? How was she loaded? What was her stability (safety characteristics)? The approach was to consider the published design and construction data as if this was a proposed new construction. However, we knew that this basic type of vessel had evolved over more than 1,000 years, so she was presumably well suited to her 7th century activities and was a successful ship.

The key to thorough and meaningful naval architecture lies in the establishment of a vessel's weight and the centroid (center of gravity) of all this weight. The most accurate method of determining the weight and center of gravity of the vessel, together with all its equipment and cargo, is by brute force and tedious calculation – piece by piece.

The difficulty of putting together the shape of a vessel from fragmentary pieces of excavated wood, often deformed and degraded, is obvious. However, it can be done by skill, perseverance and an intuitive grasp of the original shipwright's intentions, as Professor Richard Steffy has proved with his scale models of both the Kyrenia and the Yassi Ada ships. The Kyrenia model was used, as we have seen (p.57), to construct a full-scale replica.

Weight, wetted surface and sail area

From the data published on Yassi Ada, we could estimate the weight and center of gravity of the hull outfit; anchors, ropes, mooring lines, bitts, etc.; and the simple furnishings and galley equipment. Then we considered the weight of the probable number of the crew and their personal effects, stores and provisions, reported weight of the ballast, and the weight of the cargo of amphoras and their contents:

Item	Weight (long tons)	Vertical cent. of gravity (ft above keel)
Structure	29.6	5.8
Furniture	0.2	8.0
Hull outfit	2.1	9.3
Rigging (*see below*)	?	?
Misc.	0.3	6.6
Ballast (reported)	0.6	2.6
Crew and effects	0.5	9.0
Stores	0.3	5.5
Amphoras (reported)	8.04	4.43
Amphora contents	27.15	4.43

From the sketched sail plans we estimated a weight of 2.7 long tons with a center of gravity 41.6ft above the keel for spars and rigging.

With minor adjustments of longitudinal centers of gravity, and using the 0.6 long tons of ballast rock found in the excavation as trimming ballast, we were able to arrive at a Light Ship weight of 34.9 long tons, with vertical center 8.7ft above the keel, and longitudinal center 3.5ft aft of the midships.

Our first attempt at determining the flotation waterline and the initial stability for the light ship indicated the surprising result that the ship would not float upright without additional ballast.

Our calculations indicated that the vessel's "large angle" stability, or righting arm at large heel, improved dramatically with load, but was still not really powerful enough to sail. We concluded that the vessel, at least when sailing light, must have had more ballast of about 10 long tons to sail even short distances.

Checking with the principal excavator, we established that the ballast rock could not have been discarded unknowingly. However, the site seemed to contain an unusual amount of sand. Could this have been used as ballast? The linguistic evidence was suggestive: the Latin word for ballast is *saburra*, which literally means sand. Perhaps the sand acted both as ballast and as a convenient medium into which the first rank of amphoras could be securely stacked.

This raised a further question: was the Yassi Ada ship a container ship or a tank vessel? The former would trade amphoras and their contents; the latter would trade contents but keep containers. Excavation of the wreck indicated only three sizes/types of amphora on board. If the majority of amphoras appear of the same age and manufacture, with perhaps the odd replacement for loss or breakage, then we may be looking at a tank vessel rather than a container ship.

Conclusions

We re-calculated the initial and large heel stability of the vessel, both when sailing "empty", with a hold containing 8.04 long tons of empty amphoras set in a bed of 10 long tons of sand; and fully loaded with 27.15 tons (net contents) of cargo. These two loading conditions were also compared to sail stability parameters to test sail carrying power and safety.

We found that the full load condition with a 1,750 sq ft sail area provided ample safety under sail. However, the initial stability, and consequently the power to carry sail, still appeared to be less than would be expected. In the "no cargo" condition, we found insufficient sail stability to carry sail, plus inadequate resistance to sudden squalls and gusts. The combination of results leads us to consider whether the vessel actually had 6–12in more beam than that of the model.

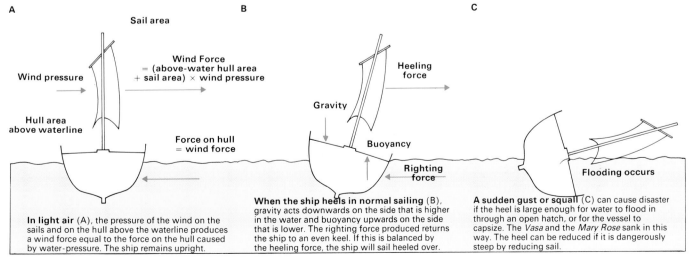

A

Sail area

Wind pressure

Wind Force = (above-water hull area + sail area) × wind pressure

Hull area above waterline

Force on hull = wind force

In light air (A), the pressure of the wind on the sails and on the hull above the waterline produces a wind force equal to the force on the hull caused by water-pressure. The ship remains upright.

B

Heeling force

Gravity

Buoyancy

Righting force

When the ship heels in normal sailing (B), gravity acts downwards on the side that is higher in the water and buoyancy upwards on the side that is lower. The righting force produced returns the ship to an even keel. If this is balanced by the heeling force, the ship will sail heeled over.

C

Flooding occurs

A sudden gust or squall (C) can cause disaster if the heel is large enough for water to flood in through an open hatch, or for the vessel to capsize. The *Vasa* and the *Mary Rose* sank in this way. The heel can be reduced if it is dangerously steep by reducing sail.

Archaeology and conservation

Fully preserved after a 330-year burial in Stockholm's harbor, the flagship *Vasa* towers breathtakingly over the museum visitor in the environmentally controlled building. The sight of her on her keel inspires reveries equaled perhaps only by reading *Mutiny on the Bounty*. Only the lofty masts and sails and perhaps crew in pantaloons are lacking.

Around the world, other museum goers may muse over evocative exhibits of nautical items found in the sea: a barnacle-encrusted bottle still containing potable brandy, a Tudor period velvet barber-surgeon's cap, a leather shoe once deformed by wear, a Bronze Age Greek copper ingot, or a once prized 18th-century boxwood navigational instrument. To further heighten interest, the items are presented with related finds in the context of a shipwreck which tells its own story.

That the public can enjoy such a spectacle is due not only to the archaeological team that located and retrieved the items, but also to the seabed that miraculously preserved the site and to the group of conservators who contrived, against the laws of nature, to bring the wet, often degraded, finds to a dry and, with luck, an undamaged state.

Natural preservation
The long-term survival of a sunken ship is entirely dependent on the nature of its watery environment – but it is difficult, nonetheless, to be definitive about the several factors which apparently influence the preservation of ancient wrecks. It was originally thought that deep water and/or a soft sediment were vital necessities in the preservation process, but well preserved remains of old ships have been discovered in shallow water sites, and others on apparently hostile sea beds, like the coral reef of the *Batavia* (see p.168). So the factors which affect ship preservation are far from straightforward.

However, many years of research and observation by maritime archaeologists in general have provided some clues as to what is required for an ancient hull and its cargo to survive the ravages of time. It seems that the rate of deterioration (or otherwise) of a sunken ship is initially dependent on the vessel's condition before being wrecked, the nature of the wrecking itself, and preliminary exposure to wind and water movements. Then, as the wreck ages, features of the burial environment increase in importance.

The two main threats then are physical movements of seawater, and attack by voracious marine wood-boring organisms such as the teredo worm. In order to survive, an ancient wreck must first be protected from physical destruction, either through being submerged in deep, still water, or protected by ocean sediment or some other marine layer such as algae. Burial in sediment or a secondary coating may go some way towards restricting the other major destructive process – the activity of marine organisms. This will also be reduced if the wreck is exposed to low temperatures, low salt levels and low oxygen circulation – unfavorable conditions for most of the wood-boring creatures and micro-organisms which cause so much destruction.

Survival of specific materials
A single shipwreck has several component parts, each of which will be subject to different rates of deterioration according to conditions on the seabed. Organic materials, including wood, and perhaps leather, skins and foodstuffs are all especially vulnerable to attack by marine organisms. However, if conditions are favorable, natural preservation of these substances can be truly remarkable. When the warship *Vasa* was raised in 1961, after having lain 120ft (36m) deep in cold, brackish water for 330 years, some of the archaeologists who investigated her claimed that they had eaten butter from her stores and tasted her beer.

Different metals have different survival rates, again depending on conditions. Shipwrecks can often be likened to giant galvanic batteries (in the words of one archaeologist) with the salt water acting as an electrolyte – hence deterioration of metals depends on what sort of electrolytic process (if any) the material has become involved in. Some interesting chemical reactions have been observed in ancient wrecks. At the Grand Congloué wreck, for example, the lead sheathing which had originally covered the ship beneath the waterline was almost completely transformed into sulfate of lead.

Usually though, only surface corrosion is suffered by metals like copper, bronze and brass – although, in the case of silver, even this kind of damage can be quite severe. Unalloyed gold, however, is always incorruptible.

One notable exception to this pattern is iron, which can be completely destroyed – iron from Roman times in the Mediterranean, for example, has almost always completely disappeared, leaving a negative cast under layers of concretion.

Pottery seems to last forever under the sea, vulnerable only to breakage by physical movement of sea water or ocean sediment – or perhaps the odd foraging octopus. Marble, on the other hand, is attacked by sea creatures – statues recovered from the wreck at Antikythera are perfect on the side protected by sediment, and pockmarked beyond recognition on any surfaces exposed to the sea.

The changes that glass undergoes after long-term immersion in water depends to a large extent on its particular chemical composition. Phoenician soft-glass beads from Cape Gelidonya seemed strong and well-preserved whilst still under water and just after they were raised, but exploded into particles of dust when they were left to dry out.

This last example illustrates the problem faced by conservators – the natural preservation of all these materials has occurred in an environment which is vastly different from the standard museum showcase or exhibition stand. Recovering the articles from a submerged site and re-exposing them to air can create vast difficulties. There are many sadly warped or corroding marine finds, either unconserved or improperly treated, tucked away from public view. They are testaments of the need for careful handling, treatment and storage of these delicate, irreplaceable artifacts. They are often the victims of ill-conceived excavations of sites which, left undisturbed, could have preserved the finds indefinitely.

From water to air
In most cases, that shipwrecks are able to be located is due to their "good state of preservation" in the seabed environment. What this actually means is that the newly excavated artifacts preserve their appearance, belying chemical or physical deterioration. If allowed to dry without treatment, waterlogged wood notoriously loses its form, if not its surface detail, through warping, shriveling, and cracking. This is because in the course of hundreds or thousands of years, water has shared with cellulose, and in some cases taken the place of cellulose in providing support for the wood's internal structure – if allowed to dry in an uncontrolled manner, that structure will collapse.

Corroded iron without proper cleaning, desalination and/or chemical stabilization can rapidly continue to corrode, upon drying, into a pile of rusted sweating fragments, or even explode, as in the case of the cast iron cannonballs raised from the *Mary Rose*.

Buried under the sea, the artifacts, after initially rapid reactions, become subject to very slow rates of reaction. Indeed the rate can be so slow that it is commonly but mistakenly described as a state "at equilibrium" with the seabed environment. This slow reaction state can be true for artifacts in sediments as well as those covered with chemical concretions. Upon excavation the artifact is introduced to a new environment: fresh or salt water, air, a clump of "original" sediment, some new storage elixir. Once again, the artifact can enter into rapid reactions, generally oxidative. The conservator, confronted with these rapidly changing artifacts, needs to know the different chemistry presented by each material that he handles. He is also obliged to apply as much wisdom and skill as possible to the task of interrupting the laws of thermodynamics.

Conservation and the customer

When the conservator examines and proposes treatment for a marine artifact, he or she has a watchful audience of clients. It is like being a gem cutter working on a big rough stone: you can either create the Hope Diamond or cover the table with a pile of worthless shards.

Naturally no one wants to see the artifact change for the worse. However, the definition of "worse" can become problematic. For instance, removal of obscuring or active corrosion layers from a metal artifact means different things to different people. The scholar looks for identifying details like inscriptions, which X-rays might not reveal. He or she will want the layer removed. A mineral scientist may argue against its removal since it contains potentially unique corrosion products, if only someone had the time to study them. The auction house wants some indication of sea burial retained to spark buyer interest. A collector agonizes over "patina," whether or not it should remain,

again prompted in part by market value.

So the conservator, in designing treatments, takes many interests into account. Then he consults his ethical training which has instructed him on the one hand to ensure that the artifact is physically and chemically stable against further deterioration. On the other hand, he is professionally sworn to preserve evidence of use/wear, of manufacture, of its history. If he employs a method to preserve the corrosion, will it resume corrosion at a later date? Can the preserving agents be reversed to allow future study or retreatment, if necessary? If he removes the corrosion, is he permanently altering the artifact and destroying potential information for future researchers? These are issues of real importance to everyone who has responsibility for artifacts, be they excavators, curators, or conservators.

What marine conservators can do: the state of the art

There has developed over the last 30 years

an international community of marine conservators who share information and brainstorm, visit and work in each others' labs, and console each other. Fortunately, there are several labs which have the benefit of scientific evaluations of treatments, and these ongoing results are always shared by means of conferences, publications, phone calls, and even beery confabs. The Japanese waterlogged wood conservator will be up to date on the Canadians' work and vice versa. If an excavator consults one conservator he gets the benefit of the others' experience. As well, if he alienates one conservator, he may rapidly find himself in awkward straits with the others.

Today the archaeological conservation community shares a series of common goals which can be enumerated in the following manner:

(1) To bring an artifact to the dry state with a minimum of physical distortion and chemical deterioration – probably

Triumphantly conserved within a specially constructed building in Stockholm, the *Vasa* (above) demonstrates the effectiveness of conservation techniques pioneered in Scandinavia. After three centuries on the seabed, the magnificent ship was raised to the surface in a purpose-built cage, and has become a national treasure. *Vasa*'s excellent condition is also due to the absence in Baltic waters of the wood-devouring shipworm, teredo.

the first practical goal both of the conservators and their clients. Following the minimum intervention ethic, a conservator will want to introduce the least amount of chemicals or consolidants and use techniques which require the least manipulation.

(2) Chemical cleaning and stripping of marine artifacts. This is a hotly debated activity. Cleaning is done most often to help confer chemical stability to an artifact. Secondarily, cleaning is done to reveal an artifact's form, appearance, and details. If cleaning or stripping is estimated to harm an artifact, other methods (e.g. technical photography) are recommended as the means of gaining information.

(3) All treatments should be able to be "reversed", that is it should be possible to undo them at a future date in case retreatment or scientific re-evaluation is required. Methods which involve irreversible processes are considered to be last-resort approaches.

In the achievement of these aims, there are not really any standardized techniques as such. One of the commonest procedures in the conservation of wood is the combined use of polyethylene glycol (PEG) and freeze-drying. After a lengthy period of soaking in PEG, the water within the cellular structure of the wood is gradually replaced by this waxy substance, which will eventually provide permanent support when the wood is subjected to the freeze-drying process.

Various treatments have been devised for the conservation of metals. Iron presents considerable difficulties when re-exposed to air, due to rapid chemical reactions which involve corrosive salts. Methods used to remove these salts include electrolytic reduction, chemical reduction, and even roasting in an atmosphere of pure hydrogen to a temperature of about 1,800°F (1,000°C).

It is obviously imperative that, whatever the substance to be treated, the conservation process should begin as soon as possible after the material is raised. Hence it must always be a pre-planned, carefully prepared part of any underwater archaeological project – and as such, it often seems to occupy a rather invidious role in that context. One marine archaeologist once described conservation as the "athlete's foot of archaeology".

Archaeology and conservation

Given that conserving the artifacts is a good thing, why does this apparent conflict between archaeology and conservation exist?

An obvious reason is that conservation is expensive and unpredictably so. Ironically, artifact conservation is no respecter of energy conservation. It is both laborintensive and one must supply energy to an unstable system (e.g. excavated artifacts) to prevent them from entropically

rejoining the universal pool of matter and energy. Electricity, chemicals, polymers, and leak-proof tanks, if ever they existed, cost money.

Another reason is that conservation poses a nightmare to planners. The durations of treatments are unpredictable but may often require a long period, as in the case of waterlogged wood.

Unfortunately, the quality of results is not always predictable or even attractive. Skilled marine conservators (rare commodities due to uneven employment opportunities), are not always easy to find or secure when one needs them. Generally, only government agencies can afford to keep a supply and then only when fulfilling a commitment to underwater archaeology. In some political seasons, expenditure even on underwater archaeology, let alone marine conservation, is viewed as political suicide.

Behind these issues lies the fact that marine conservation is downright difficult to perform technologically. While the methodology has been improving over these last 100 years, especially in the area of waterlogged organic materials, it still imposes limitations on what can be accomplished using proven methods. A dentist can perform an outrageously complex procedure in one hour because his treatment is standardized, and mouths appear to be reasonably predictable for dentists' purposes. The reason why there are few standardized procedures as yet in marine conservation is due to both the unpredictable variety of physical states that artifacts achieve in their various burials, and the lack of meaningful evaluations of treatments.

Another reason for conflict between archaeology and conservation involves power. In theory excavators can or should excavate only what can be preserved. If the conservator, for lack of funds or for lack of a proven treatment, says he cannot conserve the artifacts, the excavator can find his project limited or completely stalled by yet another constraint. If the excavator feels obliged to follow the conservator's advice, he may view the conservator himself as the stumbling block to his goal, which is the excavated, studied and displayed find; or he can take matters into his own hands.

Underlying all these reasons is a fundamental conflict between archaeology and conservation: archaeology alters the thing to be studied through excavating and dismantling, while conservation is dedicated to making or keeping things chemically and physically stable with a minimum of intervention. It is not hard to see why excavators and conservators may potentially be at loggerheads: the ultimate issue being not money, time, or aesthetics, but whether to excavate at all. Indeed, what intervention could be more minimal than no excavation?

Somehow, by mutual consent, conservators have accepted the responsibility

not only for providing care for the artifacts but for acting as the artifacts' advocate. We conservators remind people of the consequences of their actions, of their alternatives, we check up on how people handle artifacts, and it is small wonder that conservators have become notorious as the nagging consciences of the archaeological world.

If excavators have abdicated responsibility, it is the conservators' duty to return the responsibility for the finds' well-being to the excavators and lawmakers. For indeed, the ultimate responsibility for the survival of the artifacts resides with the people who disturb them as they lie in their burial environment.

So, given the fundamental instability of excavated marine finds, given their relative stability in the burial state, given the conservator's responsibility for preserving the finds, it should come as no surprise that most conservators are against excavation on principle. Paradoxically, while the practicing marine conservator enters into all the quandaries and pitfalls of treatment, at heart there is nothing he would like better than to put himself and his colleagues out of this particular line of work by declaring a permanent end to all excavation.

Additionally, marine conservation can

Two views of *Vasa's* upper deck (above). Although the ship's timbers were not affected by shipworm, the wood had undergone considerable chemical change in the course of its 300-year immersion. The conservators sought to protect the timbers against the attack of fungi, to reinforce the tissue of the wood, and to reduce damage likely to result from the process of drying. The final display of the ship in its own museum has proved that such a venture can be financially viable as well as providing an invaluable social and historical amenity.

even be threatening to life itself. There is a belief among chemists that choosing to follow this profession may cut off 10 years of life expectancy: by handling artifacts which may harbor unsuspected hazards, and by using solvents and chemicals which vary in toxicity, all marine conservators put themselves at risk and thereby endanger their health.

Why then are there practicing marine conservators? This is a thorny question. Nevertheless, an amateur would be able to ascribe any number of different motives to these conservators:

The altruism of curing sick things.
The omnipotence of magically accomplishing the impossible.
The fatalism of doing something now, no matter how ineffectual or wrong.

Finally, most conservators are genuinely curious, in the manner of humanists, about the history and reality of earlier men and how they did things. Here we see the conservator as latent archaeologist who shares in the thrill of the excavation and helps to piece the puzzle back together again. Perhaps evidence of an ancient repair will be discovered, or a formerly unsuspected approach to, say, foundry work, for example.

Scandinavian pioneering

Over the last 100 years, starting with Norway's Oseberg ship, and particularly over the last 35 years, with the massive *Vasa* (Swedish) and Roskilde (Danish) projects, versatile Scandinavian scientists and conservators have responded to the challenge of preserving wet archaeological finds with greater success than anyone had hitherto dared hope for. Now there are marine conservation labs throughout the world. We are still steering our labs by the great constellation of Nordic pioneers.

It might be instructive to inspect the Scandinavian approach to solving these problems. In nearly all cases projects were carried out through academically orientated institutions, usually government funded. Often, the academic approach coincides with the scientific approach, so necessary for archaeology and conservation, which asks the question, "What would happen if . . ."

Also, the state-supported institutions seemed to feel no conflict of interest in accepting aid from the private sector. A case in point was the Swedish chemical company, Mo and Domso, which published a glossy booklet on how their polyethylene glycol *Modopeg* was used by Bertil Centerwall in waterlogged wood

treatments. Centerwall worked from the University of Lund in Sweden. In North America, the situation is the opposite; government agencies and even many universities are positively squeamish about accepting support from corporations lest they even seem to indirectly endorse a product.

Further, I attribute the Scandinavians' great progress to the positive and very determined efforts of individuals and institutions in recognizing the cultural value of their finds (an easy matter in hindsight), and in making their projects work. If the United States has a less dazzling track record in underwater archaeology and conservation, I attribute this to a swaggering preoccupation with rugged individualism and a lack of commitment to cultural things. Even Canada, which is tiny in population but large in landmass and cultural heritage, has made great strides in these 30 years in marine archaeology and its conservation, due to a very strong cultural commitment.

There are exceptions to this generalization about the States, the Texas A&M Nautical Archaeology Program being the best example. But it is significant that Texas A&M is better known for its projects abroad than for those which it undertakes on American soil.

Before and after treatment on three 18th century French lead-glazed earthenware items. Recovered during the excavation of the French frigate *Le Machault* by Parks Canada under Walter Zacharchuk in the 1970s, the wares show the effects of 200 years of burial in a sulfide-rich estuarine environment (right). The lead-sulfur compounds were removed from the lead glazes by means of an elaborate chemical treatment. After chemical cleaning, the fragile glazed surfaces received a consolidating coat of reversible acrylic resin.

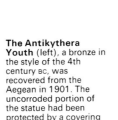

The Antikythera Youth (left), a bronze in the style of the 4th century BC, was recovered from the Aegean in 1901. The uncorroded portion of the statue had been protected by a covering of mud.

Dark Age seafarers/Introduction

In northwest Europe, ships played a key role in the vast population movements that characterized the so-called Dark Ages. From the Celtic tradition of skin-covered boats to the transoceanic maritime culture of the Vikings, waterborne activity was a central fact of life. Even before the collapse of the Roman empire in the west, seaborne raids and settlement by Germanic tribes had led to the construction of "Saxon Shore" forts along Britain's southeastern seaboard.

We know from isolated examples that different styles of boat-building were extant in northwest Europe from the mesolithic age, more than 6,000 years ago: at Starr Carr in Yorkshire and Mullerup in Denmark, hunter-fisher communities were building light-framed craft covered with birch bark, as well as using log boats. Excavation of the mesolithic settlement of Starr Carr has revealed evidence not only of fragile birch-bark boats, but also of leatherworking, suggesting the possibility that the two technologies may have been combined to produce a skin-covered boat. This is of course speculation, but in 1971 a skin boat, based generally on a group of Swedish Bronze Age rock carvings, was built for the BBC *Chronicle* television program, and sea trials demonstrated its ample capabilities in coastal waters.

From the early Bronze Age, distinctive pottery styles reflect the movement of small family groups across Europe and into Britain. Such groups would have made the difficult crossing of the Channel in small boats that must have been commissioned, bought or hired from local seagoing communities on the continental mainland, but nothing survives. Cross-channel contacts and trade must have continued and developed during the Bronze Age, but the only maritime evidence for this is a cargo of bronze tools and weapons of continental origin found on the seabed off Dover. Another possible Bronze Age wreck, at Salcombe Bay in Devon, again only survives in the form of a scatter of weapons.

In 1938, the discovery of a group of massive timbers belonging to a Bronze Age boat in the Humber estuary at Ferriby shows that sophisticated – if rather clumsy – boats were working in north Britain by the middle of the second millennium BC. Work over a 25-year period has recovered the remains of three boats, all built of massive oak planks fastened edge to edge with yew withies, and calked with moss.

Varieties of boat-building

At the same time that log-boats, extended boats and plank boats were developing (see p.123), light-framed skin boats must have evolved in northwest Europe as a practical response to available materials – boats that were able to make use of shallow waters and that were light and exceptionally easy to carry if need be.

By the late Iron Age immediately preceding the Roman invasion of Britain (AD43), coastal and riverine trade must have been relatively well organized, and luxury trade across the English Channel was flourishing. There is astonishingly little maritime evidence that reflects this particular aspect of life in pre-Roman Britain, but every archaeological find showing cultural links with the continental mainland is evidence in its own right of seaborne contact.

Throughout the Roman period, the logistics of maintaining long supply lines for the army in northern Europe implies substantial waterborne traffic, and it is clear that arterial rivers like the Rhine were alive with small boats, barges and lighters carrying a vast range of provisions and equipment. These cargoes would have been loaded onto larger merchant ships for the crossing to Britain. Such activity suggests a wide range of boats, built for specific tasks, which would have reflected local boat-building traditions.

Northern traditions

Precise evidence for local boat types in the Roman period is slender, but sufficient to show that sophisticated indigenous boat-building techniques were well established before the 3rd century AD. When Caesar fought the Veneti of northwest France in 56BC, in the first recorded sea battle in northern waters, he found to his cost that Mediterranean-style boats were totally unsuited to the rougher and less predictable tidal waters of Atlantic Europe. The Veneti's boats had oak hulls and leather sails, according to Caesar.

Recent work on a wreck that was found in the entrance to St Peter Port harbor, Guernsey, which burned to the waterline in the 3rd century AD after its cargo of pitch caught fire, shows it to be carvel-built of oak. This could be a later example of the kind of boats that the Veneti built – high-sided sailing ships also seen on some pre-Roman coins, such as the one dated to about AD20 and found at Canterbury in 1976.

Also from the Roman period are two 2nd century boats found in the Thames at Blackfriars and Guy's Hospital, and a 3rd century boat at Blackfriars. These provide further evidence of the existence of a north European boat-building tradition. Vegetius, a Roman author writing in the 4th century, refers to camouflaged boats, equipped with sails and rowed by 20 oarsmen, which the British called *pictae*,

perhaps after their northern homeland.

By the end of the 1st century AD, the Romans had established a British-based fleet, the *Classis Britannica*, which was to operate out of bases either side of the Channel, maintaining lines of communication and ferrying both troops and supplies to land-based legions.

Two centuries later, the population movements characteristic of the Migration Period appear to be already under way. In the 4th century, the "Saxon Shore" forts were set up by the Romans to keep out Germanic groups on the move from northwest Europe. In the post-Roman settlement of Britain, ships obviously played an essential part, and the Nydam boat (see p.113), represents the kind of vessel that may have been used to bring the settlers with their livestock and possessions to their new homes.

ATLANTIC OCEAN

A map of Northwest Europe towards the end of the 9th century shows how the massive population movements characteristic of the Age of Migrations were settling down into a period of consolidation. The map also includes wrecksites mentioned in the following pages, covering the period from the 5th century departure of the Romans to the 10th century emergence of more peaceful patterns of maritime activity. These finds, often of great magnificence, have not only enabled archaeologists to trace out the evolution of ship types; they also emphasize the power and wealth of the maritime world during a period which has yielded very few written records.

15°

NORWEGIAN SEA

Finns

Trondheim

Kvalsund

Norway

Halsnoy

Shetland

Vendel

Orkney

Valsgärde

Norway

Oseberg

Birka

Gokstad

Scotland

Skagerrak

Sweden

Strathclyde

Öland

NORTH SEA

Sweden

ish

Kattegat

BALTIC SEA

Dublin

Northumbria

Danes

York

Skudelev

Danes

Fyn

Zealand

Bornholm

Welsh

Gredstedbro

Danelaw

Hjortspring

Mercia

Nydam

Thames

Hedeby

Wessex

Caister-by-Norwich

Snape

Sutton Hoo

London

Hamburg

Blackfriars

Graveney

Elbe

Oder

Guernsey

Utrecht • Utrecht

Dorestad

Quentovic

Ghent

Rhine

Moravia

Bretons

Cologne

Seine

Paris

Germany

France

50°

Loire

0   300 Kilometers

0   200 Miles

KEY

• Wrecksites

Prevailing Winds

Strong Currents

Saints and skinboats

Boats made of skin have a very long ancestry in northern waters, going back perhaps to mesolithic times or even earlier. They are particularly associated with the Celtic West of the Dark Ages, where myth and history overlap. In the 6th century St Brendan the Navigator is said to have sailed an Irish curragh over the ocean to a land far to the west. In 1976 Tim Severin's *Brendan* showed that a medieval skinboat could indeed cross the Atlantic.

Literary sources suggest that by the late Iron Age (2nd century BC), long skin-covered boats were working around the coasts of Britain, and it is probable that round coracle forms had developed for river use.* Coracles similar to the ones described in these sources still survive on a few rivers in Wales, especially the Teifi, where they are principally used for fishing. At the beginning of the century they were common on other fishing rivers including the Dee, the Severn and the Wye.

The curragh
The curragh is a long banana-shaped sea-going skinboat, still used in parts of Ireland. The earliest description we have is that of Julius Caesar, writing of his Spanish campaign of 49BC.* To cross a river after the bridges had been destroyed, he instructed his soldiers to build boats "of the kind that his campaign in Britain (in 55 and 54BC) had taught him." When these light-framed skinboats were completed, they were carried on wagons to the river where they were used to transport Caesar's troops to the further bank.

The clear reference to information gathered during the British campaigns suggests that curragh-like craft, large enough to carry a number of men, were a familiar sight in southeast Britain (the area of Caesar's British campaigns), but not perhaps in Gaul or north Germania, the other coasts of Europe that Caesar knew.

The curragh was definitely regarded by classical writers as a seagoing boat. Pliny, writing in the first century AD, refers to a description from the historian Timaeus (d. 260BC), claiming that the British would sail for six days in light-framed, hide-covered boats, to an island called Mictis (perhaps Vectis, the Isle of Wight), from a part of Britain where tin was mined. This was presumably Cornwall, whose tin mines were famous even in the late Iron Age (see p.52). In his own times, Pliny writes, boats of wickerwork covered with hides were still being made around the British coasts.

There is ample evidence to indicate that curraghs were extensively used by the Celts of the southwest, as well as Ireland and perhaps Scotland, during the first centuries AD. It has been suggested that their gradual replacement by stronger clinker-built craft came about as the skills of wooden boatbuilding were acquired and the rapidly expanding ironworking industry enabled local smiths to make tools and iron fastenings. Curraghs finally survived only in Ireland, where they play an important part in mythology as well as in regular maritime traffic.

In pagan mythology, *Imramha*, the sea voyages of heroes such as Bran, Maelduin or Teigue, are among the oldest survivors of Irish storytelling, tales written down in the 8th century but originating in the pre-Christian era many generations before. In the *Voyage of Maelduin*, the hero sets out in a "three hide curragh" in pursuit of his enemies. Bran and his companions set sail in three curraghs each manned by a crew of nine. In contrast to these moderate-sized curraghs is the vessel of Teigue, who builds a massive curragh of "40 ox-hides of hard bark-soaked leather", fitted with 25 thwarts and capable of staying at sea

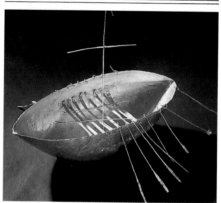

The Broighter boat, a tiny model (perhaps a votive offering) made of fine gold sheet (above), was found at Derry, Ireland, in a hoard of goldwork generally dated to the 1st century BC. Analysis shows that the tall mast and oars were made at the same time as the hull, which is rounded suggesting that the boat may be a representation of a coracle-type skinboat.

for a year. Even allowing for exaggeration, the details of the structure, particularly of the bark-tanned leather, are significant.

Saints and navigators
During the early Christian period, sagas of mythological heroes were augmented by tales of the extraordinary voyages of Irish monks. The most famous of these are the voyages of St Cormac and of St Brendan.

St Cormac, a follower of St Columba, is said to have set off in search of solitude on three voyages. After hoisting sail on his third voyage, he was carried north for 14 days and nights by a strong wind. During the voyage, his ordeals included "loathsome stinging creatures" (possibly Portuguese men-of-war) which slapped against the curragh with such force that the leather seemed in danger of failing. Fortunately for St Cormac, an about turn in the wind drove the curragh back home before disaster quite overtook it. St Cormac's voyages would have taken place in the last half of the 6th century, and were chronicled by Adamnan in the *Life of St Columba*, written nearly a century later.

A generation before Cormac, the most extraordinary *Imramha* of all had taken place. The voyage of St Brendan is of fascination to geographers, historians and boat archaeologists alike, for not only does it describe in some detail how a curragh of the early 6th century could have been built; it also suggests that St Brendan reached Iceland, perhaps even Newfoundland, the fabled land of plenty.

The *Navigatio Sancti Brendani Abbatis* describes St Brendan as the head of a community of 3,000 monks at Clonfert. He hears from a visiting monk, Barrind, of a voyage the latter made to the "promised land of the saints" in company with St Mernoc. The destination was reached by sailing westwards from Ireland until they entered a thick barrier of fog, beyond which lay a land rich in fruit and flowers. St Brendan decided to undertake a similar voyage, choosing 14 monks to accompany him and, of course, to work the boat.

Having obtained an essential blessing from St Ende, Brendan and his companions set up camp beside a narrow creek and began to build the curragh that was to carry them on their remarkable voyage. Using iron tools, the monks prepared a light frame of ribs with wicker infilling, which they covered with oak-bark-tanned cow hides. The seams between the skins, presumably sewn, were carefully tarred to make them waterproof.

Amidships they fitted a mast, equipping the boat with a sail and a steering oar. There is no mention of individual oars as part of the boat's gear, but these must have been included, since on several occasions during the voyage the monks had to row themselves out of difficulties.

Once completed, the curragh was stowed with provisions for 40 days, together with a supply of fat to replenish the dressing of the skins and to dress the spare hides carried in case repairs were needed. After loading the boat, St Brendan and his crew of monks set sail on the first leg of their seven-year voyage, which seems to have taken them at least as far as Iceland, via the Hebrides and Faeroes.

The descriptive details of the voyage have been an endless source of speculation. The description of the bombardment of the boat with hot rock may perhaps refer to Iceland, as we shall see, but how are we to interpret the details of the pillar in the sea, surrounded with a mesh having the appearance of marble? Even more important and fundamental to the core of St Brendan's voyage was the question of whether a skinboat could survive the hardship of such a voyage.

St Brendan's voyage recreated
The only way to prove or disprove the viability of any epic voyage, including one

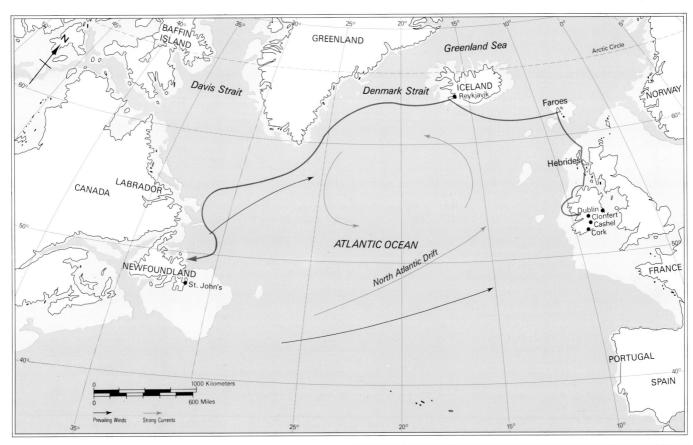

A transatlantic crossing by skinboat was made when Tim Severin's reconstructed *Brendan* reached Newfoundland in 1977 (map, top). Orkney, Shetland and the Faeroes make up a curving arc of islands from which Iceland can be reached with only a short open-sea crossing. Beyond lie Greenland, Newfoundland and the American eastern seaboard – all within the reach of a sea-going skinboat manned by a determined visionary crew.

Skinboats still being made in some parts of Wales and Ireland include coracles (above left), now used on Welsh rivers almost exclusively for trout and salmon fishing. In the past these also served as small ferries carrying people and goods from bank to bank at established river crossings. Curraghs (above right), with their long curved hulls, are essentially sea-going boats. Although they are now rare, some curraghs are still to be found in southwestern Ireland, where traditional boat-building techniques have survived in the face of modern competition.

like the *Navigatio*, is to recreate it. In the early 1970s, the germ of an idea was born that led to one of the most remarkable odysseys of the 20th century – the Brendan voyage shared by Tim Severin and his small but skilful crew.

A curious quality of the *Navigatio* is that, unlike other contemporary writings, it is not a vehicle for the description of miracles. Instead, it is a record of a series of remarkable voyages containing many passages of topographical detail and having the figure of St Brendan at its core. It was this difference, together with the wealth of practical detail, that caught Tim Severin's imagination. After a serious appraisal of the text of the *Navigatio*, and an equally serious investigation into the viability of the project, a skinboat to follow in St Brendan's wake began to be constructed in southwest Ireland, the modern home of the curragh.

The boat was built using traditional and still extant curragh-building techniques. First, double gunwales were made from seasoned oak, fastened with wooden pegs and shaped to the familiar curve of a Dingle curragh. The deep composite gunwale was then placed upside-down on the ground, and long single cross-frames of ash were fitted to it, delicately bent like giant hoops to make the characteristically U-shaped curragh hull. Next, lathes of ash were carefully tacked to the frames and then tightly lashed with alum-tanned thongs. In all, more than 1,600 ties were used, comprising nearly two miles (three kilometers) of leather thongs. Wool grease was splashed over the framework to protect and waterproof the ash, and to keep the thongs strong and flexible.

Now began the daunting task of covering the curragh. Modern research had shown that oakbark-tanned hides of the kind described in the *Navigatio*, treated with wool grease (almost pure lanolin), were highly resilient to the ravages of seawater. However, although the seams between the skins are described as being carefully smeared with fat, there is nothing in the *Navigatio* to suggest how St Brendan had joined together these hides to make a waterproof covering for the boat. After much experiment, Severin found that a waterproof join could be achieved by overlapping the trimmed hides by a "margin of one or two inches, and stitching a strong double line of flax thread along the joint."

The task facing him was immense, since 49 ox hides were needed to cover the ash framework, and each one had to be sewn meticulously to its neighbors to ensure the integrity of the hide covering, on which the lives of the crew would depend.

Finally the covering was complete, reinforced at bow and stern with a double layer of skin, and ready to be stretched over the ash frame and lashed with oxhide ropes to the gunwale. Then the curragh was turned the right way up, two ash masts were stepped in the hull, oars

(also of ash) were stowed aboard, and the *Brendan* was ready to put out to sea.

On January 24 1976, after the traditional blessing by the Bishop of Kerry and a naming ceremony in Irish whiskey, she was taken for trials on the River Shannon. Here Severin and his crew experimented with the oars and square sails, whilst growing to understand her behavior and her unorthodox response to wind and water. At last the *Brendan* was ready to go to sea. It had taken nearly three years of research and hard physical work to build this medieval skinboat, destined to sail into history.

The *Brendan* at sea
The first voyage began May 18 1976, visiting the Hebrides and Faeroes, and making landfall at Reykjavik, Iceland, on July 15. The curragh more than proved

The calm before the storm as *Brendan* leaves Iceland, drifting slowly westward before a gentle wind (above). After the first week, the weather began to deteriorate, bringing icy rain, fog, and huge swells with waves far higher than *Brendan*'s mainmast.

her staying power, skimming ahead of the wind across the surface of the water, and giving few problems apart from wear on chafing ropes and timbers.

The latter part of the journey threw new light on some of the *Navigatio*'s topographical descriptions. It has been suggested that the eruption of a sub-sea volcano may underlie the account of an "island of smiths" where St Brendan and his companions were bombarded by flaming rocks. In the text, this occurs near a description of a high coral-colored cliff, which could be interpreted as the soaring cliffs of the Reykanes peninsula, or of Dyrholaey, both of which lie on Iceland's south coast near the island's principal volcanoes – Hekla, Katla and Eyjafjallajoknl.

This may have been St Brendan's Icelandic landfall. The *Navigatio*'s account of an island "rough and rocky and full of slag, without trees and grasses" is typical of a newly born volcanic island, and the noise, boiling sea and foul smell suggest that the terrified monks may have witnessed the eruption of a volcano.

Whatever the truth hidden in the *Navigatio*, it is now clear that St Brendan could have reached Iceland in a skinboat with relatively little difficulty. But what of the "land full of promise", a fog-shrouded region with many fruit trees, that St Brendan finally reached? The *Navigatio*'s statement that the saint, after revictualling on the "island of sheep" (probably the Faeroes, whose name in Old Norse is the Sheep Islands), sailed *eastwards* for 40 days, is disconcerting. Could this be a transcription error, since the whole spirit of St Brendan's quest lay westwards?

The Atlantic crossing
When the *Brendan* set sail from Reykjavik on May 7 1977, heavily laden at the start of the second leg of her voyage, she ran into seas of such ferocity that the curragh almost foundered. Having survived this onslaught she ran into pack ice, and two floes converged on her, pinning her between them. Amazingly, the ash structure was not crushed, but a spur of ice tore through one of the skins, and the *Brendan* began to ship water fast. At length the leak was discovered on the waterline, and in sub-zero conditions a hide was trimmed to fit over the hole, and laboriously stitched onto the outside of the hull. The *Brendan* was watertight again. This ability to repair the vessel emphasized the practical ability of the curragh to survive in such adverse conditions.

Having passed through the pack ice, *Brendan* entered the Newfoundland fog bank. On June 26, the curragh dropped anchor at Peckford Island off the coast of Newfoundland some 50 days after leaving Reykjavik. Tim Severin and his crew had proved that an early medieval skinboat could have made the Atlantic crossing from Iceland to Newfoundland.

Moreover, the voyage raises further interpretations of passages from the *Navigatio*, suggesting that St Brendan's final voyage took him into Arctic waters far beyond Iceland.* Even the dismal fogs that surrounded the "promised land" of his quest can be interpreted as the notorious fog banks of Newfoundland. Of course, there is no direct archaeological evidence to support such a theory. The earliest Norse explorers of Greenland reported ruins of stone-built houses, stone tools and fragments of skin boats; but these cannot be interpreted as the remains of voyages from the Celtic West without supporting evidence of their material culture. Nonetheless, the fact that the *Brendan* proved able to survive the hazardous voyage to Newfoundland must open the doors of possibility even wider.

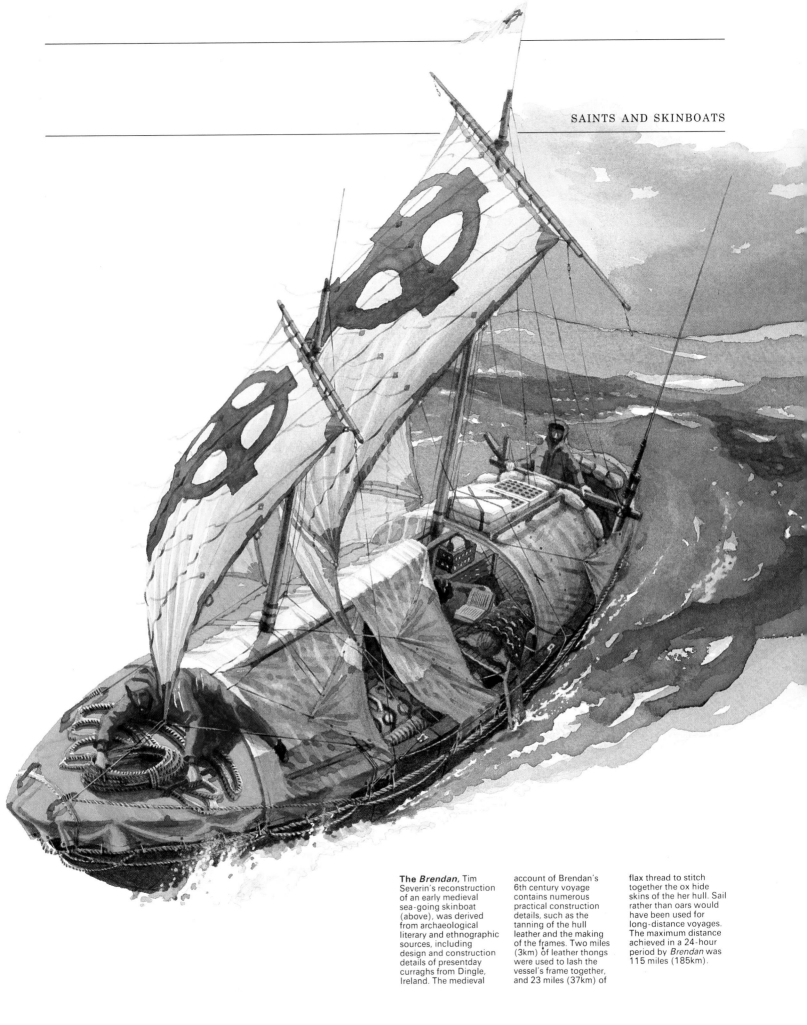

The Brendan, Tim Severin's reconstruction of an early medieval sea-going skinboat (above), was derived from archaeological literary and ethnographic sources, including design and construction details of presentday curraghs from Dingle, Ireland. The medieval account of Brendan's 6th century voyage contains numerous practical construction details, such as the tanning of the hull leather and the making of the frames. Two miles (3km) of leather thongs were used to lash the vessel's frame together, and 23 miles (37km) of flax thread to stitch together the ox hide skins of the her hull. Sail rather than oars would have been used for long-distance voyages. The maximum distance achieved in a 24-hour period by Brendan was 115 miles (185km).

The coming of the Anglo-Saxons

The "Englishing" of Britain began in the 5th century AD, when boatloads of Germanic peoples left the coastlands of western Europe to settle territories in southeast England, perhaps ceded to Anglo-Saxon mercenaries by British lords. Marine archaeology can tell us much about these early settlers, the ships in which they made the hazardous crossing, and their connections with their future enemies, the Vikings.

By the end of the Roman domination of northern Europe in the early 5th century, large groups of people were on the move throughout Europe, spreading south and west across the north European plain, and displacing local Germanic villagers. Many of these trekked towards the sea that separated Britain from Europe. Once at the coast, considerable numbers of Germanic families embarked from villages and trading entrepôts like Hedeby to a new land – an episode akin in many ways to the migration westward to America across the Atlantic during the 16th and 17th centuries.

Settlers and mercenaries
However, the process of Germanic penetration of Britain began before the 5th century. Towards the end of the Roman period, mercenary soldiers called *laeti* were brought over from the western coastlands of Europe to help defend the province against attackers from Ireland, Scotland and the continent. Several Roman military sites have yielded traces of their pottery, which reveals a connection with the pottery that has been found in their continental homelands.

The policy of employing mercenaries continued after AD409, the year which saw the official end of Roman rule in Britain. In 446, according to the *Anglo-Saxon Chronicle*, "The British sent men over the sea to Rome, and asked for help against the Picts, but they never had it, because they were on an expedition against King Attila the Hun. They sent then to the Angles, and the Anglian athelings [lords], with the same request."

In return for their services, the mercenaries were granted territory in the southeast of the former province. In 449 a large group of Angles, Saxons and Jutes arrived in Britain, apparently in response to a report that the Britons were poor fighters but had excellent land. These three Germanic peoples are mentioned by Bede, a very careful and exact historian probably relying on oral and legendary sources. He states that the Saxons came from North Germany and Holland, the Angles from the south of the Danish peninsula, and the Jutes from Jutland.

Thus the homeland of the Anglo-Saxons, who appear to have been culturally intermingled even before they arrived in England, was the coast of Europe between the mouth of the Rhine and central Jutland.

From the mid 5th century onward, the eastern part of Britain saw a continual and entirely successful process of settlement, suggesting the use of large numbers of boats to transport not only war bands but also entire families together with their possessions and beasts.

Most of the early landfalls would have been in Kent (the shortest Channel crossing), Sussex and East Anglia. Once ashore, many settlers tended to move along the rivers, which provided easiest access to inland territories, as suggested by archaeological finds and the distribution patterns of cemeteries.

Water, then, was used as one of the most convenient means of transport, and boats must have been an essential part of the campaign in the penetration and settlement of both southern and eastern

A superb brooch from Kingston Down, Kent (above), made of gold and decorated with a disciplined geometric pattern of cloisonné garnet and bright blue glass, shows the skill of the top Anglo-Saxon metalworkers in handling precious metals and stones.

England, as it would from now on be called. But what kind of boats were these?

Early Anglo-Saxon shipping
For the maritime archaeologist it is an exasperating fact that, while these incomers of Germanic stock have left behind a mass of information about their lifestyles in their remarkably fine metalwork and pottery, as well as in their burial sites and nucleated settlements, almost nothing survives of their water transport or their waterside structures. For example, archaeologists have yet to find London's Anglo-Saxon waterfront, and the large merchant ships they used for cross-channel trade have survived no better

than the mass of smaller boats and barges that must have been very commonly used both for fishing and for trade and transport along the coasts and rivers.

However, the very few boats that have survived enable us to reconstruct at least a framework of evidence, despite the lack of tangible material that would fill out our knowledge of maritime aspects of everyday life in Migration period Europe.

The Nydam boat, a heavy clinker-built oak vessel found in 1859 in a peat bog at Nydam, now modern Schleswig-Holstein, provides an early example of the Germanic or Anglo-Saxon sea-going ship. The technique of clinker-building, where one plank overlaps another, may have originated as a developed form of the log-boat – the simplest type of water transport in Europe for many centuries. By AD100 an extended log-boat – a dugout hull with an overlapping plank that increased the freeboard – was current in Scandinavia, as is shown by the Björke boat. Here, the single plank was held by iron rivets at each side of the hull in a sophisticated technique that itself suggests a considerable period of development, probably from hulls that were originally lashed together, as in the Iron Age Hjörtspring boat.*

These early boats were probably paddled, as there is no provision for oars, and they would have been used along rivers, in lakes, and in short coast-hugging voyages. But by about AD200 the small Halsnoy boat shows primitive "rowlocks", indicating that oars were by then in use.* Thus there seems to be a gradual technical progression in these hulls, though they are few and all from Scandinavia. However, different styles of construction and methods of propulsion could have been used at the same time, and it may be misleading to see these hulls in terms of chronological development. In mainland Europe, where different cultural elements were in close contact under the Roman empire, the patterns of development may well have been very different.

Nevertheless, by AD400 the Nydam boat, ancestor of the Viking hulls, shows that massive, sea-going, clinker-built hulls were being constructed by capable shipwrights in northwest Europe.

In fact, two boats were ritually deposited in the Nydam bog; one of oak and the other, destroyed during World War II, of pine. The oak boat, which is now on display at Schloss Gottorp, near Hedeby in Schleswig-Holstein, was almost 80ft (24m) long. She was rowed by 30 oarsmen and steered by a heavy after-paddle lashed to the hull. This hull was built with five massive strakes to either side of a broad keel-plank, and each strake was formed from a single slab of wood, fined down from an even thicker plank.* The oaks from which these long broad planks were hewn must have been immense. Even today, the boat maintains a feeling of dull strength that makes one marvel at the skill of the 4th century shipwrights in

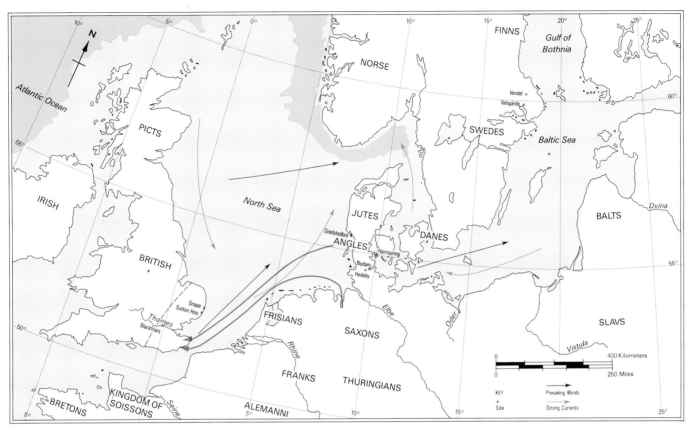

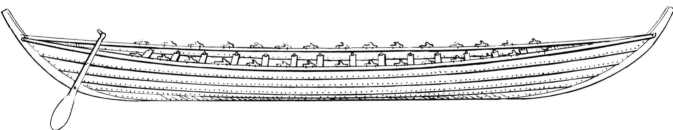

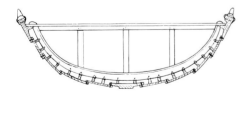

In the early 5th century, shortly after the collapse of the Roman empire in the west and the withdrawal of the Roman garrison from Britain, groups of Angles, Saxons, Jutes and Frisians from the north German plain and Jutland (modern Denmark) began a

wholesale settlement of the island (map, top). The Germanic tribes swarmed across the Channel, landing at first in Kent and then along the coast and rivers of East Anglia. Many displaced Britons themselves fled eastwards across the Channel into Brittany.

The Nydam oak ship (above), a heavy open rowing boat dating from AD350–400, is the kind of vessel that would have brought the Anglo-Saxons to Britain. Each side consists of five strakes cut from massive pieces of oak running the full length of the hull and held by iron rivets.

The presence of a large steering oar and 15 rowlocks on either side indicates a crew of at least 31 men. Such a boat would have been quite capable of crossing the Channel with family groups and their possessions and domestic animals. One of many boat types used along Germany's west coast during the late Roman period, it was found with another clinker-built vessel during drainage of the Nydam bog, Schleswig-Holstein, in the 1930s.

Livestock of all kinds from chickens to highly prized horses, would have accompanied Germanic family groups settling in Britain in the 5th century (above). There is little documentary evidence to show how this was done, but experiments with modern copies of

Viking ships show that ponies can very easily be persuaded on and off board in calm weather, and carrying livestock was perhaps more commonplace than we imagine.

cutting and handling such massive planks, and fastening them with iron rivets. Boat-building techniques of such an order argue many generations of evolution and technical experience.

The Nydam fir boat (which survives only in plans) contrasts with the heavy simplicity of the oak boat. The hull was built with narrow composite strakes for greater flexibility, the end posts were more curved and upright, and the keel-plank had a T-shaped cross-section that would cut more effectively through the water. This was the design that was to become the norm in the fully developed Viking ship (see p.131). Neither of the Nydam boats showed any provision for sail, although sailing ships were being used in northern waters by the 1st century AD.

It has been suggested that the Nydam fir boat may have been built in Scandinavia, belonging to the same tradition that ultimately produced the Oseberg and Gokstad ships (see p.122), whereas the oak boat belongs to a tradition which reflects the boat-building abilities of the North German tribes who went on later to build boats like the 7th century funeral ship found at Sutton Hoo and the 10th century Graveney boat.

What part did such ships play in the Anglo-Saxon migration? There is no evidence to indicate the kind of boats used to transport migrating Angles, Saxons, Jutes and Frisians to England in the 5th and 6th centuries. However, it is a reasonable assumption that boats similar to both the Nydam vessels were used, as well as smaller sailing boats like the depiction scratched in the fabric of a pot from Caistor-by-Yarmouth, East Anglia.

Ships and settlements

The Germanic incomers seem to have lost little time in making the new "English" territories their own, but very little survives of the boats they must have used. This absence applies equally to boats worked on a day-to-day basis for local traffic and also to those used for trading voyages to entrepôts on the continental homelands and Scandinavia, which archaeologists have shown were well established in the post-Roman period.

The presence of boats and their importance to the settlements may be apparent in the occasional finds, in East Anglia as in Denmark, of fragments of overlapping planks covering 7th and 8th century graves. These may be sections of boats, abandoned after serving a useful life along the coasts and rivers of the East Anglian kingdom, but their presence may reflect continental traditions seen more clearly in, for example, the complex of boat burials at Slusegård in Denmark, where, from the Iron Age, simple and extended log-boats were used as coffins or to cover burials.

The evidence shows that by the 7th century a boat-building industry was well established in East Anglia at least, although it now only survives in the form

of three "ghost ships" buried beneath large circular mounds in the cemeteries of Snape and Sutton Hoo on the Suffolk sandlings. The fabulous treasure of gold and garnet jewelry recovered in the excavation of the great Sutton Hoo ship burial (see p.116) has sometimes drawn attention away from the important fact that the ship itself belongs within the large family of clinker-built hulls current in the North Sea during the Migration period. Such ships are closely related to those found in the Swedish boat graves of Vendel and Valsgärde, and to the Kvalsund (Norway) boat and the fragmentary Gredstedbro (Denmark) boat.

Unfortunately, the Suffolk boats have survived only as shapes, shadows and lines of iron rivets – impressions in the sandy trenches dug to contain the hull up to the upper part of the prow and stern. Apart from this, only the remains of the untypically large royal ship in mound 1 at Sutton Hoo have been recorded in sufficient detail for an assessment of the

A 6th century brooch with scroll decoration (above). Metalwork and jewelry found both in England and in the North German homelands of the new settlers share identical characteristics, indicating continuity of culture.

original hull shape to be made. Excavations made during 1984 and 1985 from Sutton Hoo's mound 2 suggest that the boat shape may be the remains of the boat trench, the boat itself having been destroyed when the grave was ransacked centuries ago, However, the iron rivets that survive from the boat are identical to those found from the royal ship in mound 1 and to the few remaining fastenings from the Snape boat.

This, combined with the meticulously recorded ship remains found in mound 1, enables us to deduce a class of sea-going boat with clinker-built hull, low and raking stern and stem posts that thrust well clear of the planking (like the Nydam boat), and broad keel-planks projecting

chubbily into the water in a very narrow T-shape. Such boats probably had 8 or 9 composite strakes each side and were braced by heavy frames that fitted snugly into the hull and were fastened to the planking with wooden treenails (like the Gredstedbro boat), apart from an iron bolt holding the top of each frame to the uppermost strake.

We do not know whether the frames were single pieces of wood like those of the Nydam and Gredstedbro boats, or whether they were composite and made up of a floor timber scarfed into side frames, as in the 10th century Graveney boat* (see p.134).

Like the Nydam boat, the Suffolk boats were rowed, using tholes which, in the case of the royal ship, were nailed to an expanded upper strake with long iron spikes. The boats do not appear to have been worked with a sail, but since they were burial ships it is possible that any reusable and easily removed timber may have been cleared from the hulls before they were dragged to their burial grounds. The construction of a mid-ships burial chamber would almost certainly have required the removal of a heavy mast fish or mast to make room for it.

Steering-oars, probably similar to that of the Nydam boat, may also have been dismantled before the ships were dragged overland. The burial ship in Sutton Hoo mound 1 has a hull strengthened to take the thrust of the steering oar, and it is reasonable to assume that both the Snape boat and the Sutton Hoo mound 2 boat shared a similar steering system. However, it must be said that no other evidence of the steering arrangement has survived in any of the three boats.

The Sutton Hoo boats came from a royal cemetery, and the Snape boat held a burial of similarly high status, so these cannot be typical of ordinary craft used around the coasts of 6th and 7th century England. The latter were no doubt more akin to the smaller clinker-built boats of Scandinavia, as seen in the chieftains' graves from Vendel and Valsgärde; neat craft about 35ft (10m) long with four or five strakes each side and keels that were characteristically T-shaped.

It is not difficult to imagine the coastal waters of the time alive with such vessels. Rivers and lakes must also have had their water traffic, but for these there is only the evidence of the Utrecht boat (c.800), and depictions of similar hulled boats with a central mast which appear on early 9th century coins minted at Quentovic and Dorestadt. There were probably many local variations in structural detail, in the same way that variations existed between small regional boats 50 years ago, when such traffic was commonplace. This comparatively recent variety may give some idea of the flexibility and vigor of local boat-building traditions that must have been current during the pre-Viking era in northern Europe.

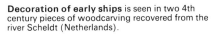

Decoration of early ships is seen in two 4th century pieces of woodcarving recovered from the river Scheldt (Netherlands).

An impression in the damp sand (above right) is all that survives of the Anglo-Saxon burial ship excavated in 1939 at Sutton Hoo, Suffolk. All the wood had rotted away, but the sweeping lines of the clinker-built hull are shown by the rows of iron rivets that originally fastened the planks together. The shape of the hull was remarkably undisturbed as the burial trench had been carefully dug to contain the entire ship apart from the ends of the stem and stern post. Small details survived as dark shadows made by the decaying wood which stained the yellow sand.

A pagan Saxon settlement of six farmsteads, perhaps comprising an extended family group of the Germanic settlers who established themselves in Britain, has been revealed by excavations at West Stow, Suffolk, and carefully recreated from the archaeological evidence (right).

A kingly burial

The extraordinary treasure discovered in the Sutton Hoo ship burial testifies to the wealth and power of the new English people, 200 years after the arrival of the first Anglo-Saxon immigrants. Buried beneath a large circular mound, the massive ship in which they placed the body of their king contained a wonderful collection of gold and garnet jewelry, silver plate, gold coins, magnificent weapons and a royal scepter.

The great clinker-built boat, buried in about AD625, was excavated in 1939 at Sutton Hoo, near Woodbridge in Suffolk. Although it survives only as a "ghost ship", a phantasmal set of impressions in the sand, this vessel is a magnificent example of Anglo-Saxon shipbuilding. It is believed to have been the grave of one of the rulers of East Anglia, perhaps Raedwald who died in AD625 or 626. At the time of his death Raedwald was one of the most powerful rulers in 7th century England, holding the position of high king

to whom other rulers of the English kingdoms owed allegiance.

First excavations

The story of the Sutton Hoo excavation is remarkable, both for its low-key beginning and for the gift of the ship's contents to the British people by Mrs Edith Pretty, who owned the estate containing the burial ground with its 16 barrows, and who sponsored two seasons of excavation in 1938 and 1939.

In 1938 Mrs Pretty employed a local freelance archaeological excavator, Basil Brown, to investigate the barrows, and in a short season he opened three of them with the assistance of two of Mrs Pretty's staff, Bert Fuller and Tom Sawyer, both laborers on the estate.

Unfortunately, all three mounds had been dug into in the past and only scraps and fragments of three high-status burials, each of a very different style, survived for Brown to record.

Nevertheless, he discovered that one of the mounds (number 2) contained a roughly boat-shaped pit and a small group of rusted iron rivets. He immediately assumed this to be a boat burial, identifying similarities with a boat grave excavated at Snape, a few miles away, in

1862–63. The robbers had left only a few grave goods, but these included decorated gilt-bronze devices from the front of a shield and one silver-gilt fitting from a drinking horn – evidence that the grave was of exceptionally high status. In this too it resembled the Snape ship burial, which had been robbed of almost everything except a few fragments of glass and a magnificent 6th century Anglo-Saxon gold filigree ring which contained an antique intaglio.

Although the Sutton Hoo barrows had clearly been systematically plundered, Mrs Pretty was sufficiently encouraged by the results of her first experience of archaeology to embark on another season of work. In the spring of 1939 she invited Brown to tackle the largest mound, which had a diameter of nearly 100ft (30m) and was just under 10ft (3m) high. In early May, he began exploring the barrow by opening a 7ft (2m) wide trench in its easterly edge and working west toward the center by removing all the soil that formed the barrow until he reached the buried Anglo-Saxon ground level.

On the third day of the dig one of his assistants, John Jacobs, who was one of Mrs Pretty's gardeners, dug up a corroded iron rivet. Almost immediately another five

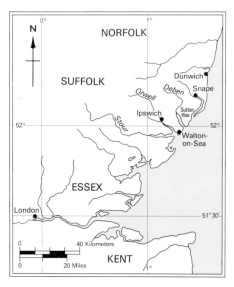

The Sutton Hoo gravefield lies at the edge of a plateau overlooking the river Deben, immediately opposite the modern county town of Woodbridge (map above). Within a few miles of the burial site on the Suffolk sandlings are many other Anglo-Saxon sites: Snape, the Anglo-Saxon mixed cemetery which also contained a princely burial, Rendlesham, the site of a 7th century royal "palace", and Ipswich, a thriving port.

The undisturbed ship-burial at Sutton Hoo presented the first excavators with a mass of archaeological material in a deposit of extraordinary complexity (right). Working under great pressure, they met the challenge of the collapsed burial chamber with a skill and delicacy that enabled them to recover even the most fragile, tiny and fragmentary finds.

were found lying in such a way as to suggest that they were in their original positions – Basil Brown had uncovered the extreme end of a buried boat.

The next few days were spent digging away the tons of soil that formed the mound and then roughing out the hull until the iron-stained sand surrounding each rivet told Brown that he was nearing the surface of the ship itself. This had survived only as a hardened but friable layer of sand, slightly discolored by the wood that had totally decayed. All that was left for Brown to excavate was a ship-shaped impression in the sand with lines of rivets showing where the overlap of each strake had originally been.

Brown was familiar with the publications about the two great Viking burial ships of Oseberg and Gokstad, which had been protected by the heavy blue clays of the Oslo fjord (p.122). He had also read the accounts of the Snape boat burial, but he had no real conception of the immense size of the boat he was uncovering until he had excavated almost 40ft (12m) before reaching the broadest part of the hull. Now he realized that his find was going to outstrip even the Oseberg ship itself in sheer size.

Still more astonishingly, in view of the three ransacked barrows excavated the previous year, this burial seemed to have escaped robbery. An attempt had been made to open it in the late 16th or early 17th century, when presumably the other large mounds in the gravefield had been robbed, for there was a filled-in shaft running from the top of the mound down as far as a point just above the level of the burial deposit.

At the bottom of the shaft, Brown found the remains of a fire and a couple of fragments from a Bellarmine jar. The robbers, misled by the depth of the shaft, may have thought that the grave was empty, or perhaps they did not dare risk extending the unsupported shaft any deeper into the unstable sand.

Gradually Brown began to suspect that, against all odds, the burial originally located in the center of the ship had survived intact. In this he was proved correct; reaching the central area of the ship, he uncovered a large iron ring and sheets of bronze that gave out a hollow sound when gently tapped. Brown realized that he had discovered the eastern end of the burial deposit.

The dig proceeds
However, sadly for him, he was not to excavate the burial. After the archaeologist Charles Phillips had visited the site, followed by a party from the Office of Works (now the Historic Monuments Commission), the British Museum and the Ipswich Museum, it was decided that the excavation should be put on a more professional footing.

Phillips was invited to take over and Brown was told to do no more work on the burial chamber but to concentrate on emptying the rest of the ship so as to establish its full length. In the meantime, Phillips gathered together a small but exceptionally able team of young archaeologists. Largely unfunded, but working on behalf of the Office of Works, they embarked on one of the most remarkable excavations that has ever been undertaken in English archaeology.

By the time Phillips arrived at Sutton Hoo to excavate the burial chamber, Brown had succeeded in the Herculean task of emptying the full length of the ship. He had revealed a huge open boat, surviving only as an impression in the very damp sand; the plank runs were shown by lines of iron rivets that had strengthened the boat. Amidships, a chamber had been built containing a burial of extraordinary complexity.

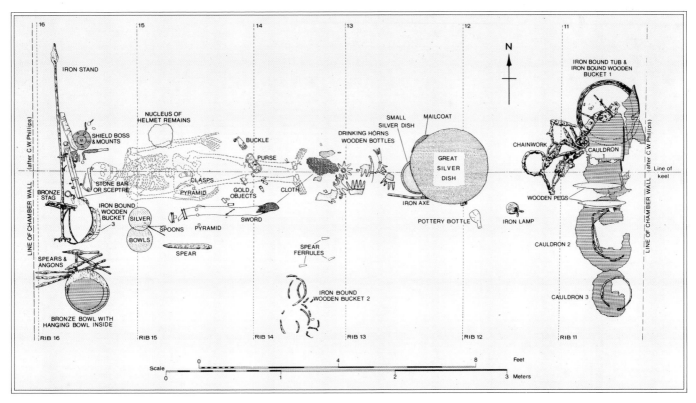

The Sutton Hoo burial chamber, built in the central area of the ship, was furnished with everything that the dead man would need in the afterlife (above): clothes, shoes, drinking horns, gaming pieces, a lyre for feasting and enjoyment, containers for food and drink, caldrons for cooking, weapons and armor to reflect his warrior status, Mediterranean silver to show his wealth, symbols of temporal authority in the scepter and stand, and symbols of royalty in the magnificent gold and garnet jewelry. The chamber was roofed with a double thickness of planks and probably contained a platform covered with textiles on which the body of the king was placed, accompanied by his most precious possessions. The body would have decayed rapidly in the acidic soil, to be finally destroyed when the burial chamber roof collapsed; no trace of it was found by the excavators. The burial, which emphasizes pagan Anglo-Saxon belief in the realities of the afterlife, would have been accompanied by elaborate ceremonies of the kind described in the contemporary epic poem Beowulf.

Equipment for the Afterlife

Very little is known of the beliefs and rituals that surrounded death and burial in the early Anglo-Saxon period, but the ship burial was one of the most complex burial practices. In the 6th and 7th centuries it seems to have been peculiar to the kingdom of East Anglia and the Uppland area of Sweden, where the high-status chieftains' graves of Vendel and Valsgärde contained very similar helmets, shields and decorative motifs. This suggests that the Wuffingas, who were the ruling caste of the East Anglian kingdom, may have had a Swedish ancestry.

At Sutton Hoo, the burial party furnished the dead king's tomb with a range of possessions that reflected every aspect of his life; gold jewelry to show his wealth and status, a scepter symbolizing his royal authority, weapons from his warrior past, a lyre and drinking vessels to express the delights of courtly life, and food containers to provide for his physical needs.

The strongly built chamber that filled the central area of the ship contained a vast range of possessions. But nothing survived of the chamber itself, apart from faint shadows in the sand made by the decaying remains of the end walls, and the crushed remains of the fallen cross-beams supporting the burial chamber roof. This was strongly made with two layers of planks, forming a low, almost coffin-like roof strong enough to withstand the immense weight of the mound heaped over the ship.

Sutton Hoo and Beowulf

There are descriptions in contemporary sources, especially the epic poem *Beowulf*, of the formal ritual and mourning that attended death in this period. At the beginning there is the account of the burial of the Danish king, Scyld, which tells how the body was laid out in the center of the ship by the mast, together with treasure from many lands as well as his weapons and armor. Then a gold pennant (signum) was hoisted at the mast head and the ship was pushed out to sea, consigning the king's body to the will of the wind and tide.

In contrast to this stark burial at sea, the poem closes with a description of the death of Beowulf, the hero, who eventually fell fighting the dragon guardian of a fabulous but cursed treasure. The poet describes how Beowulf's people built a funeral pyre on which they hung mail-coats, shields and helmets, as Beowulf himself had requested. They then placed Beowulf on the pyre and they set fire to it.

After the cremation, the pyre was surrounded by a stone wall, effectively creating a tomb. Here they placed the hoard of the dragon that had mortally wounded Beowulf, sealing the whole with a mound. Twelve high-born followers of the dead king then rode around the mound, declaring their grief and calling out Beowulf's many achievements.

Some of the descriptions of Anglo-Saxon burial rites in *Beowulf* can be applied to Sutton Hoo, which combines aspects of the burials both of Scyld and of Beowulf. For example, the dead king was placed in a ship which, although not pushed out to sea like Scyld's ship, was buried high on a headland beneath a mound in very much the same physical setting as Beowulf's mound. The high mounds of the Sutton Hoo gravefield must have been visible to any traveler on the River Deben in the 7th century.

The great ship seems to have been quite old, for it had been repaired several times. It may have been a royal barge – a massive broad-beamed ship, suitable perhaps for sailing in coastal and riverine waters, carrying the king on his regular progression through his kingdom, perhaps even voyaging south as far as the king-

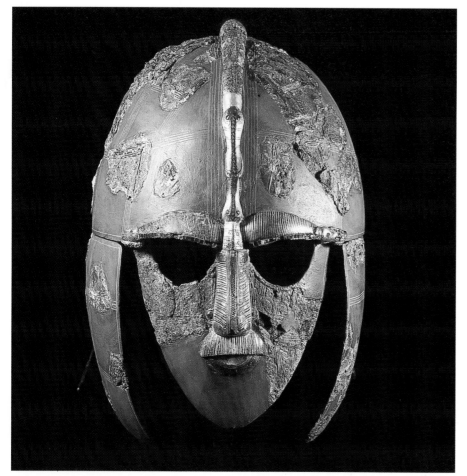

Anglo-Saxon helmets from Sutton Hoo (left) and Benty Grange (above) are both decorated with a boar motif, probably a protective emblem or device for the owners. The Sutton Hoo helmet has a small tusked boar's head, cast in bronze and heavily gilded, forming the terminal of each garnet and silver inlaid eyebrow. The Benty Grange helmet, in contrast, carries a small free-standing boar figure on its crest, a tradition known from the poem *Beowulf* and from Scandinavian helmet representations from Vendel and Valsgarde.

Magnificent gold and garnet jewelry from the Sutton Hoo burial demonstrates the astonishing ability of the jewelers and also the ingenuity of the master craftsmen in producing working pieces of such brilliance. The shoulder clasps (right), originally stitched to a leather cuirass, the great gold buckle (upper right) and the purse lid (below, far right) are essentially functional, besides being exceptional examples of the jeweler's art. A concealed hinge meshes together the two matching halves of the shoulder clasps; the great gold buckle is locked with an ingenious device of sliders; the purse lid originally closed a leather bag, using a golden tenon to engage in a gold locking piece attached to the bag.

dom of Kent, which Raedwald is known to have visited.

The ship must have been rowed as far as the water's edge and then laboriously dragged ashore. Its steering oar was probably dismantled for the journey to the gravefield, and its weight may have been reduced by the removal of some of its internal fittings – perhaps even a mast fish and mast. Ropes would then have been attached to the hull and the great ship would have been slowly hauled away from the water's edge, possibly over a corduroy of tree trunks, up to the gravefield that lay on the very edge of an escarpment overlooking the river.

The haul to the gravefield could have involved a journey of a little less than a mile if it had followed a gradual processional route. Alternatively, the mourners could have gone up one of the two narrow combes from the river to the plateau, a shorter haul but one so steep that there would have been considerable difficulty in handling the great ship.

Once on the plateau, the ship would have been dragged slowly towards the grave – a ship-shaped trench dug deeply into the bright yellow sand so that only the tip of the prow and stern were exposed above ground. Sand from the trench was piled carefully to each side to act as a marker for the barrow builders. The burial party may have lowered the ship into its closely fitting trench by slowly easing it out over rollers until the prow sank down into the eastern end.

The stern would then have been maneuvered into the trench. It seems that the ship may have slipped sideways while this difficult operation was under way, since she lies with a slight list to starboard, and the ends of the planks have sprung from the stern post – suggesting that the stern may have dropped heavily into the trench. Once in the trench, the ship would have had sand packed around it to support the hull while the burial was laid out amidships.

The chamber and its furnishings

The burial chamber containing the dead man's possessions occupied more than 16ft (5m) in the central part of the ship. A series of iron fittings suggests that a low bier filled the central area – a raised platform probably covered with heavy cloth, since some of the cleats have preserved a mineralized textile in the corrosion.

Once the formal surroundings for the burial had been prepared, the chamber would have been furnished with the possessions that the king needed for his unknown voyage to the afterlife. These were laid out at the foot of the walls forming the east and west ends of the chamber and along the central spine of the ship's broad keel-plank. In addition, a large bronze caldron with iron handles and a magnificent Celtic hanging-bowl were hung on the walls. The grave goods seem to have been positioned with great care and with a purpose or symbolism that is beyond recapture.

No trace of a body was found during the excavations because the damp conditions inside the chamber after it had been sealed would have led to the destruction of all organic remains. However, it seems that the dead man was laid out in the garb of a warrior, wearing a leather cuirass held at each shoulder by a magnificent gold clasp, decorated with garnets and millefiori glass.

At his waist the king wore a broad leather belt, which was fastened by a large and exquisitely made gold buckle decorated with a cunning design of interlacing animals. A leather bag or purse with a lid made of bone or ivory hung from the belt. The lid was bound with gold and set with gold plaques, also decorated with garnets and millefiori glass.

Two pairs of the plaques are representational, showing a bird of prey, and a man standing between two wolf-like beasts. These motifs, together with scenes on the helmet of dancing warriors and of a mounted man riding down his enemy, may have held a deep significance, but like so much Germanic and Scandinavian mythology the detail is lost.

The purse contained 37 tiny gold coins (tremisses) from Merovingian mints in Frankia, together with three unstruck blanks and two small billets of gold – payment perhaps for the 40 oarsmen and the steersmen who carried the dead king on his final voyage.

By the dead man's shoulder lay his spear and a magnificent sword with a pattern-welded blade and gold and garnet pommel fittings. The sword, buried in its wooden scabbard, hung from a belt fastened with a gold and garnet buckle and mounted with gold and garnet fittings. At the other shoulder lay a parade helmet made of iron, wtih deep ear flaps and neckguard and a realistic face-mask with eyebrows, nose and mustachioed mouth.

The surface of the helmet was covered with thin bronze plates, tinned to give them a silvery sheen. These were decorated with sinuous designs of interlacing animals (a favorite amongst the Germanic artists), two warriors performing a ritual dance, and a beautifully drawn scene of a mounted warrior hurling a spear while riding down a fallen enemy. Beyond the helmet lay the king's shield made out of leather-covered limewood, mounted with a heavy iron boss and decorated with several gilt-bronze devices, including a bird of prey as well as a multi-winged dragon.

The king's wealth and his far-flung contacts were represented not only by the gold and garnet jewelry and the gold Merovingian tremisses, but also by two groups of silver from the eastern Mediterranean. An inverted nest of ten shallow silver bowls and two spoons inscribed with the names *Paulos* and *Saulos* lay at his head. Beyond his feet was a massive silver platter, the Anastasius dish, covering a large silver bowl which was filled with numerous personal possessions. These included bone-handled knives, three combs, leather shoes and a set of walnut burr-wood cups with silver and silver-gold mounts. Beneath the silver lay a coat of mail made of iron links, fastened with tiny copper rivets, and a curious iron weapon, apparently an axe-hammer with a long iron shaft ending in a swivel that perhaps once contained a leather strap.

Elegant possessions

Between the two groups of silver objects lay a mass of folded textiles, including the remains of fine shirts and trousers, jerkins and cloaks, rugs and hangings. Amongst these were two magnificent drinking horns with bird-headed terminals, and at least five maplewood bottles, all decorated with gilded silver mounts.

There was also a set of drinking vessels that would have been used for banqueting in the king's hall, to the accompaniment of poetry and music played on a six-stringed musical instrument. This was made of maplewood and decorated with gilt-bronze and garnet-filled bird-headed escutcheons, and was found at the west end of the chamber inside a bronze bowl made in the Mediterranean. A large Celtic hanging-bowl, decorated with distinctive escutcheons filled with red enamel, contained a tinned-bronze fish marked with spots of red enamel and raised on an elegant pedestal, so that it was free to turn in the water that once filled the bowl.

Contrasting with these remarkable possessions, a range of domestic objects was laid out at the east end of the chamber. These included a large iron-bound wooden tub with silver escutcheons, within which were a wooden bucket and a wide caldron made from a single sheet of bronze strengthened with iron bands. Alongside lay an iron suspension chain, 15ft (4m) long and made of a series of

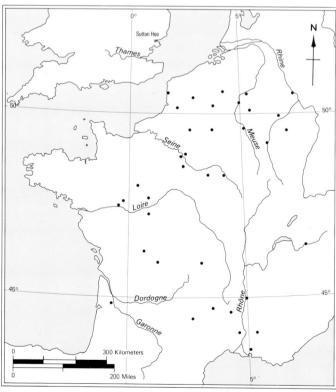

Contents of the purse included thirty-seven Merovingian gold coins called tremisses (above middle), three gold coin-sized blanks, and two small gold ingots.

Each of the tiny coins was minted at a different site (map, above left) and they appear to have been deliberately selected for the burial. They may simply be

tokens of the king's wealth, or they may have been payment for the ghostly crew of the dead king's ship.

Two silver spoons, found near the king's head, bear names inscribed in Greek: *Saulos* on one, *Paulos* on the other (above). This may be a direct

reference to the conversion of St Paul; alternatively, *Saulos* may be a mistake for *Paulos*.

highly complex decorative elements, which might have hung in the king's high-roofed hall. Two more bronze caldrons also lay at the foot of the east wall. A little way into the chamber, a narrow-necked pottery bottle had been placed alongside the mailcoat and axe-hammer, as well as a small tripod lamp made of iron whose bowl was filled with beeswax.

At the other end of the chamber, at the foot of the west wall, lay the large bronze "Coptic" bowl containing the lyre and hanging-bowl, and through one of its heavy drop handles were the long necks of three barbed throwing spears (angons). Alongside these lay five spears, all of different types.

A curious iron stand, about 5ft (1.5m) high was found a little further on, parallel to the wall and behind a second yew-wood bucket. This consists of a thin shaft with a voluted foot, at the top of which is a cage of twisted iron struts decorated with highly stylized animal heads. The stand may have been connected with the trappings of royalty, for it was found in the chamber in association with an object that has been interpreted as a scepter – a large carved whetstone, surmounted by a delicate bronze stag on a plaited iron ring. The scepter represents the dead man's temporal power, and the stand equally represents his authority in some shadowy way.

A powerful ruler

There seems little doubt that royalty is commemorated in the mound 1 ship burial at Sutton Hoo. The latest of the coins in the purse can be dated to AD625-630, and this makes possible an attempted identification of the dead man. The burial is essentially pagan and seems to celebrate the power and consolidation of the East Anglian kingdom, in that it reflects wealth, security and longevity. For these reasons, it seems likely that Raedwald, who ruled East Anglia from AD600 to 625-6 as a high king to whom all the others owed allegiance, was the ruler buried in such great splendor. But it is not possible to be absolutely certain of this.

The ship

A royal grave presupposes a royal ship, one perhaps not typical of Anglo-Saxon boat-building. But in fact the only abnormal feature of the ship is its great size.

Measuring nearly 100ft (30m) in the ground, it outstrips all but the Skuldelev warship (p.132), and is bigger than the Gokstad, Oseberg and Ladby ships. It is considerably bigger than the Nydam ship but, size apart, has no untypical construction details.* Her end posts were low raking, like those of the Nydam ship, with deep cutwaters that thrust forward beyond the planking, and she was steered by an oar which was slung to port high in the stern section of the boat.

Like the Nydam boat, she was rowed rather than paddled.* There is some debate about whether the positions originally existed amidships or whether there was a break in the rowing positions, perhaps, if the ship were the equivalent of a state barge, to provide comfortable space for her royal passengers.* If the rowing positions once occupied the full length of the ship, 40 oarsmen would have rowed her.

She would have been difficult perhaps to maneuver in narrow tidal river space, but she drew very little water, which would have reduced the risk of grounding. No evidence for the use of a sail survived, and although there is no reason why the Sutton Hoo ship should not have sailed, it is possible that she was used as a royal barge at the time of her burial.

Extraordinary though the Sutton Hoo ship is in size, scaled-down versions of similar construction and proportions were typical of Anglo-Saxon, Merovingian and Scandinavian vessels throughout the centuries following the collapse of the Roman empire, and hulls similar to Sutton Hoo were the direct antecedents of the magnificent Viking ships with their high rearing stern and stem posts, narrow flexible planks and deep keel.

A large carved whetstone or scepter (above left) was found in the burial chamber. It was topped with a beautifully modeled bronze stag standing on a ring of plaited iron wires and supported on a short bronze pedestal. A 5th or early 6th century classical fluted silver bowl with a *kymation* border design (above middle) was found together with many other items of silver.
Domestic equipment for the afterlife included a large yew-wood tub (above right) with ornate iron fittings, containing a bucket perhaps used for ladling out the tub's liquid contents. The exquisite gold and garnet sword pommel (below right) was mounted on the king's magnificent pattern-welded iron sword. The sword in its scabbard was placed alongside the dead man.

Swans of the Sea God

Ships lay at the root of Viking achievement. Indeed, Viking expansion was only possible because of the expertise in seafaring and shipbuilding for which the Vikings are famed. So important to these people were their ships that they even buried their dead in them, with exquisite works of art to accompany them on their final voyage.

In the spring of 1880 Norwegian archaeologists began digging into a low mound at the farm of Gokstad, on flat low-lying ground close to the southwestern entrance to Oslo fjord. Known in the district as the King's Mound, this was reputed to cover a royal burial: when locals attempted to break into it, the authorities launched a formal excavation.

On the second day of the excavation, an elaborately carved ship's prow emerged from beneath its protective covering of blue clay, and by the end of the summer an almost complete vessel, together with its contents, had been revealed. A burial it certainly was, and probably a royal one.

"Royal" burials
The individual concerned was a tall well-built man of about 50, who had been laid out in a bed within a wooden chamber built over the central part of the ship. His body had been decked out in fine apparel, and his weapons laid at his side. Other finds within the ship hint at the elaborate funeral ritual: dismantled wooden beds and three small boats; cooking utensils and tableware; gaming equipment; a sledge; ship's fittings and tools. Before the mound was closed a peacock had been sacrificed and placed within the hull, while at least 12 horses and dogs were killed and laid in the pit beside the ship.

A study of the finds suggested that the burial could be dated to around AD900, and that the ship itself had been built perhaps a century earlier. The presence of the peacock may indicate Viking trade with Arabs of the Middle East, who themselves traded with merchants from the Far East, thus enabling goods to travel all the way from India to northern Europe.

Twenty-four years later, in 1904, a similar burial was excavated at Oseberg, some 20 miles (30km) north of Gokstad. Again, blue clay, this time assisted by a layer of peat, had been used to seal and preserve a large wooden ship. This burial chamber contained the remains of two women – one in her late twenties, the other elderly and crippled with arthritis. The younger woman appears to have been of high rank, while her companion was probably a bondswoman or slave. The older woman may have been sacrificed to serve her mistress beyond the

grave. An Arab diplomat, Ibn Fadlan, witnessed such a sacrifice at a Viking funeral on the Volga in the early 10th century, when the deceased chieftain's slave woman was slain by his side, and buried with him in his ship. At Oseberg, the sacrifices certainly included animals, for the remains of 13 horses, three dogs and an ox were found associated with the ship; many of these sacrificed animals had been decapitated.

The ship itself probably dates from about AD800, although the burial appears to have taken place during the later part of the 9th century. Its contents were even more sumptuous than those from Gokstad; carved sledges, an exquisite four-wheeled cart, beds, a loom, tents, a chair, domestic utensils of all kinds, and a rich array of ship's fittings. Wild apples, wheat, cress and nuts were provided for the deceased's journey into the afterlife.

Both the Gokstad and the Oseberg mounds had been broken into in antiquity, long before these investigations, and the burial chambers had been disturbed in a search for the gold, silver and jewelry that they undoubtedly contained. But the most precious treasures – the ships themselves – remained marvelously complete, if somewhat crushed, beneath their hermetic shrouds of clay. Now painstakingly restored and rebuilt, both ships can be seen in Oslo's Viking Ship Museum. They are superb memorials to the great age of Scandinavian seafaring and also

to the technical accomplishments that made it possible.

Scandinavians and Vikings
Who were these people? The Gokstad and Oseberg ships, together with their contents, dramatically confirm what we know from contemporary accounts of Arab travelers, from Nordic sagas orally transmitted across the generations, and from other archaeological findings. All tell of social and economic structures that were deep-rooted and enduring.

The savage brutality of the Viking raids, beginning in the late 8th century, lives on in folk memory and language. But the Vikings also had strict laws which came into force as they began to settle in areas where once they had merely plundered. They were not only skilful boat-builders, sailors and traders, but also had long led a settled existence as farmers in their Scandinavian homeland.

Homestead settlements can be traced back as early as 4000BC, and by 1500BC Scandinavian peoples were trading with Britain and Ireland in flint and amber. The scattered groups of free peasant farmers lived under the control of local warlords or earls (*jarls*), whose dominating status is reflected in the elaborate burials they received. There was also an imported slave class, who provided the hard labor.

Intense loyalty to their families and social groups led to frequent warfare, but at the same time agriculture was practiced,

Tools and utensils (above) were among the many grave goods found in the Oseberg boat burial, from the ancient Viking kingdom of Yngling. The Vikings believed that the dead to whom such burials were dedicated had power over the living, and every care was taken to provide for their needs. Within the burial mound the dead person was surrounded with a host of grave goods, both simple and elaborate. The brass-handled yew-wood bucket in the center is of Irish origin. Its brass fittings depict a man seated cross-legged.

The Gokstad ship (above right) was found in a burial mound not far from Oseberg. The mound had stood undisturbed for generations, and when finally opened up in 1880 it was found to contain a huge oak ship, well preserved in the blue clay of the region and dating from c.850. The ship was reassembled, almost entirely using the original timbers. She was a sea-going vessel 79ft (24m) in length, with high sides and shuttered oar-holes. A replica made a highly successful voyage across the Atlantic from Norway in 1893.

yielding quantities of oats, barley and rye, cattle, pigs, sheep, goats and geese. These complemented the fish that formed an important part of their diet. They also bred reindeer and traded in furs, whale and seal products, locally produced soapstone, flint and amber, and the eiderdown which was "farmed" by providing nesting places for the birds.

Climatic change leading to warmer weather caused rapid population expansion in the 8th century. Early settlements, peacefully established, grew up on the Baltic coast, followed by many migrations to the west. The quest was for living space, not plunder, as the Shetlands, Orkneys and Hebrides, Iceland, Greenland, and even Newfoundland, were occupied by peasant Norse settlers who were prepared to work difficult soils in unkind climates.

This expansion was only possible because of the seafaring and shipbuilding skills for which the Vikings are so famed. Ships lay at the root of the Viking achievement, and they were accorded symbolic and imaginative names by Norse poets: *havsgudens svan* (swan of the sea god) or *havshasten* (sea horse) are typical.

The boat-building tradition
Early elements of the ships' long lineage are apparent in the Hjörtspring paddle-driven war canoe, deposited as a votive offering in the 3rd / 2nd century BC, together with a hoard of weaponry. This

The map (right) shows the Scandinavia of the Vikings. Although the idea of Scandinavia as a geographical entity goes back to the earliest times, the three countries have no obviously unifying geographical features. But their languages and cultures have always had more in common. The ruling families of the many different regions intermarried and interfeuded, and social organization was similar in all the Viking countries. Runic inscriptions indicate that these shared cultural and linguistic characteristics go back to at least the 3rd century.

vessel had overlapping sewn limewood planks and integral cleats to which the light internal frames were bent and lashed. Thwarts with supporting struts completed the structure and provided benches for the warrior crew, who manned what was evidently a light inshore raiding craft, probably used in local feuds.

The evolution of the Scandinavian vessel is seen in the late 4th century AD Nydam ship (another votive deposit), which is of true clinker build, its planks edge-joined with iron rivets clenched over square roves inside the hull. As with the Hjörtspring boat, framing is secured by means of cleats, although the frames now consist of shaped pieces of timber rather than bent branches. Rowlocks along the gunwale show that paddles have now been superseded by the more efficient oar, and a broad-bladed steering oar hung over the starboard side of the stern.

Three hundred years later, the Kvalsund ship displays a rudimentary keel, enabling the vessel to navigate open seas as well as inland waters. Once again we see the sharply rising stem and stern posts, turned back in the manner so characteristic of later Viking ships.

The Kvalsund ship shows another important development – a strong and efficient rudder mounting, with the tiller projecting crosswise into the ship. Cleats continue to be used for some of the frame/plank fastenings, but the keel itself is not attached to the frames, and the upper strakes are secured with wooden pegs. These features (elements of which may be seen in earlier boat finds) show a sophisticated understanding of the stresses involved, and of how strength could be obtained by combining lightness with flexibility.

There is no reason why a vessel of this type could not have been rigged for sailing, but the Kvalsund ship shows no sign of having carried a mast. Before the great Viking invasions of the 8th and 9th centuries AD, most of Scandinavia's maritime traffic was coastal, and it may be that the precise control and lack of dependence on wind provided by an oared ship was advantageous in an environment of narrow fjords and scattered islands. However, an early introduction of sail in this region can by no means be discounted. The earliest certain evidence of sails in Scandinavia comes from sculptured stones on the island of Gotland, dating from the 7th century AD. Thereafter their use spread rapidly, and by the late 8th century the ocean-sailing longboat had become a reality. The age of the Vikings had begun.

Viking vessels

The Oseberg and Gokstad ships have characteristics that we can identify as typically "Viking", but they are only two of the countless vessels of many kinds built in Scandinavia during their period. Many others of different sizes, functions

and designs must have been built, and it would be altogether misleading to see these fortuitous survivors as accurate reflections of all their vanished sisters. Indeed, the vast majority of Viking craft, like the three lesser boats associated with the Gokstad burial, will have been small in-shore vessels, and we may be sure that there were regional as well as functional variations in design.

An examination of the Gokstad and Oseberg ships shows many differences. Ornate, with richly carved stem and stern, the latter was essentially a pleasure craft designed for use in sheltered waters. Her mast was stepped on a short block spanning the two midships ribs, and further supported by a slender mast partner set across four cross-beams. This evidently proved an inadequate arrangement for sailing stresses, for at some stage in her career the mast partner had cracked, and had been repaired with two iron reinforcing straps. Since the ship is the earliest example yet discovered of a Scandinavian sailing vessel, this may possibly indicate that some of the complex problems of setting and working such a rig had not as yet been solved.

The Gokstad ship

They certainly had been solved by the time the Gokstad ship was built, around AD850. This vessel was slightly larger than the Oseberg ship, and more solid in a practical, workmanlike way. She had a

much higher freeboard, two runs of planking were set above the 16 oarports on each side, and each port was fitted with a hinged cover that could be sealed when the ship was under sail.

Built of oak throughout, the Gokstad ship was an ocean-sailing craft *par excellence*. A truly massive tree must have provided the T-shaped, single-piece keel, 60ft (17.6m) long. This was tapered towards the ends and arched slightly downwards so that the deepest draft was amidships. The effect was greatly to strengthen the ship longitudinally, increase her buoyancy, and make her easier to turn.

Stem and stern posts were scarfed, via transition pieces, into the keel, establishing her basic profile. Planks were then added from the keel upwards, the first (the garboard strake) being rebated and nailed into the T-section of the keel, with its ends fitted into the stem and stern. The succeeding strakes overlapped one another like slates on a roof, their edges joined with closely spaced rivets and roves, and sealed with a calking of animal hair and pitch. Each plank was split radially from its parent tree, a technique which, although wasteful of timber, produced pieces of great strength and reliability with tapered edges ideal for clinker joining.

Virtually all the work in making the boat was done with axe and auger. As the planks were assembled the hull took form,

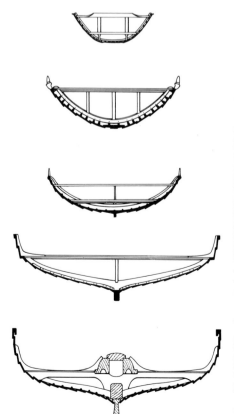

The development of the Viking ship is shown in this sequence of line drawings (left). From top to bottom: the **Hjörtspring** (c.300BC), the earliest Scandinavian ship yet found, is made of sewn limewood; the **Nydam** ship (AD350-400) is made of oak and its planks were fastened with iron nails; the **Kvalsund** vessel (c.AD700) had pine ribs and oak planks, a rudimentary keel and wide hull; the **Oseberg** ship (c.AD800), with its low freeboard, was probably a pleasure craft, the earliest Viking ship known to have had a mast; the ocean-going **Gokstad** ship (c.AD850) has a fully developed keel and strongly supported mast.
The 8thC rock carving (above) was found at Lärbro. Many of the carved and painted limestone blocks on Gotland depict single-sailed ships.

its shape entirely dictated by the way in which the boat-builder had fashioned his strakes. Each was made up of precisely calculated compound curves which, when joined to its lower neighbor, would bend and twist in one direction only – the direction that the builder judged to be right for the smooth and symmetrical hull he was creating.

The first nine strakes, carefully graded to a central thickness, formed the bottom shell of the hull. The tenth strake was almost twice as thick as these, and was known as the *meginhufr* or "strong plank". This reinforced the join between bottom and sides, gave longitudinal strength to the hull, and provided support for the cross-beams and standing knees which completed the structure. The 19-rib frames were lashed to cleats on the lower strakes with spruce roots, apart from the garboard. The keel too was left unattached. Now the cross-beams were fitted athwart the frames, tying the whole structure together and providing seatings for the standing knees. These supported the final six strakes on each side, which were pegged into place.

Directly over the midships part of the keel, and spanning the four central frames, was the *kerling* (old woman) – a massive block of oak into which the heel of the mast was set. Above this, supported by six cross beams, was the mast partner, an elegant and functional fish-shaped component designed to transmit to the hull

A sledge (above) was part of the Oseberg burial. Like three other sledges and a wagon from the same burial, it is beautifully made and as elaborately carved as the ship itself. The Viking sledge was used in winter for carrying goods and people. When the sledge was not needed, in summer, its box could be used as part of a wheeled cart. The grotesque finials kept evil spirits at bay.

This carved wooden animal head atop a post (below) was used for purposes unknown, but it may have been carried in processions. It has the same grotesque ferocity as the finial below. However, its strong form and the deep relief and serpentine elements of the decoration, hallmarks of Viking art in all its later manifestations, show a masterly hand at work. Its unknown maker is known to scholars as the Academician. The work is a striking foretaste of the stone-carving of later Viking masters.

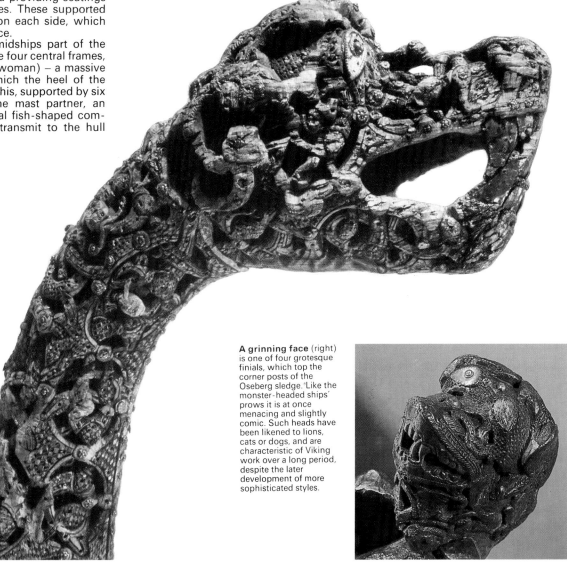

A grinning face (right) is one of four grotesque finials, which top the corner posts of the Oseberg sledge. 'Like the monster-headed ships' prows it is at once menacing and slightly comic. Such heads have been likened to lions, cats or dogs, and are characteristic of Viking work over a long period, despite the later development of more sophisticated styles.

the forward and side pressures delivered through the mast from the sail. An opening in the aft end of the partner allowed the mast to be lowered towards the stern so that, when necessary, the top hamper could be struck and the vessel's oak propulsion used to best effect.

A side rudder was fitted to the starboard quarter of the stern, pivoted on mounts secured to the specially strengthened aftermost rib and operated by a crosswise tiller. The ship's set of 32 oars, each pair of slightly different length to accommodate the gently rising sheer of the oarports fore and aft, were of pine. Loose pine decking covered the cross beams to provide both a platform for the oarsmen (who probably sat on their sea-chests to row) and a modicum of dry stowage in the hold.

Such a ship was useful for few purposes other than raiding – but for that purpose it was supremely well adapted. It could be beached or launched with ease, while its shallow draft (not much more than 3ft (1m) fully laden) allowed it to penetrate deep into estuaries and up rivers. Its composite construction of clinker planking, cleat lashing, and trenailing gave it a lightness and flexibility which made it a superb sea boat. It was primarily a sailing vessel, although the mast could quickly be struck to turn it into a rowing boat for inshore work, maneuvering independently of the wind, or sprinting to catch (or escape from) an enemy.

In 1893 a replica of the Gokstad ship – built, as closely as possible, in the manner of the original – was sailed from Bergen to New York. During the voyage the stresses of the North Atlantic demonstrated the genius behind the vessel's design and construction to the full. The replica's skipper, Captain Magnus Andersen, noted that when under sail (speeds of up to 11 knots were recorded) the keel and bottom planks rose and fell as much as 10in (20cm), while the gunwale strakes flexed up to 6in (15cm) although the hull remained safe and watertight. He praised the side rudder in particular, which he considered much superior to a stern rudder for a craft of this type. The Gokstad ship, he concluded, could scarcely have been improved upon, given the materials from which it was constructed and the purpose for which it was built.

Viking raids

In the closing years of the 8th century the Norsemen's purpose became horrifyingly evident to increasing numbers of people around the unprotected seaboards of northern Europe. The monks of a remote island monastery off the northeast coast of England were among the first to suffer, when, in AD793, their peaceful seclusion was shattered by the "ravages of heathen men" who "miserably destroyed God's church of Lindisfarne with plunder and slaughter". During the next few years other vulnerable religious communities, soft targets with the tempting combi-

nation of treasure and an unwillingness to fight back, were assaulted, notably Jarrow in Northumberland, once home of the Venerable Bede, and the holy island of Iona off western Scotland. By AD795 Norse raiders were striking the Irish coast in the vicinity of Dublin, and before the turn of the century the attacks had reached southwest France. In the early years of the 9th century the south Baltic coasts and the Frisian islands were being ravaged by the Danish king Godfred, and in AD834 the important Frisian trading town of Dorestadt was laid waste. About the same time the first of a series of attacks was launched against England.

Precisely what led to this wide-ranging outburst of violence is uncertain, although the causes were undoubtedly varied and complex. The seething heartlands of Eurasia often gave rise to widespread folk-movements, which usually had their strongest effect at the peripheries where displaced populations could move no further. Such population movements lay at the root of the collapse of the Roman empire in the west, and explain the Anglo-Saxon migrations which continued through the two centuries that followed. There is no firm evidence, however, of similar factors in the 9th and 10th

centuries. Perhaps pressures were more locally based; tensions caused by a vigorous and expanding population with restricted land resources, or by the defeat and dispossession of losers in the dynastic struggles which were carving out the great Scandinavian kingdoms. In Norway, the many local rulers finally submitted to one king in AD872; and in AD985 and AD993 single rulers were established in Denmark and Sweden respectively.

Such forces, together with the perennial human urge to obtain wealth, land, and fame (preferably all three), no doubt caused men to go *a-viking*. And, in war vessels like the Gokstad ship, they had an instrument uniquely suited to their purpose and vastly superior to that of any other race – an instrument which allowed two or three dozen determined and ruthless men to move swiftly through the seaways of western Europe, to strike without warning wherever they chose, and vanish just as quickly beyond the horizon. Churches, farmsteads, villages, and market towns – whether on the coast or further inland – had no defense against the fast-moving longships and their hard-hitting crews. "From the fury of the Northmen", prayed despairing churchmen in northern France, "God deliver us".

An illumination from an 11th century English religious history (left) shows heavily armed Norsemen, in their double-ended boats with carved prows, crossing the North Sea to England in AD866. They were led by Ivar, a Danish Viking chieftain, whose intention it was to conquer England. After three days at sea the Vikings landed in Kent, which they plundered, and then sailed on to the Northumbrian kingdom of York. In the illustration the two ships at the front have already reached land and Vikings can be seen walking across planks from their boats to the shore.

The hoard of Viking silver shown here (top) was found in a chest near the River Ribble, Cuerdale, Lancashire and dates from c.AD900. The Vikings loved gold, silver and beads and much fine work was done from early on in the Viking period. A complex of workshops at Helgö (near Stockholm) was producing objects on a large scale from AD400 onwards.

The head of a bishop's crozier (above), of Irish workmanship, was found at Helgö, near Birka in Sweden. The town of Birka was founded as a trade center c.AD800, with Irish from the west and Arabs from Spain and the east crowding at the port with their goods. The Vikings sold food and furs, plundered luxury goods, and bought silk and embroidery, glass, wine and horses" harnesses.

A silver cup (above), partly gilded and decorated with animal designs, comes from Laaland in Denmark. It is inlaid with niello, which is a compound of sulfur and silver, lead or copper. The cup dates from the 9th century and is in the southern English style. The south of England was frequently invaded by the Danish Norsemen from AD830 onwards. At first the Danes overwintered at home, but from AD850 they began to settle and farm in England.

127

The Viking world

The ferocity of Viking raiding, and the awful suddenness with which it could descend upon peaceful countryside, naturally evoked outraged complaint, on occasion spiced with colorful exaggeration, from contemporary chroniclers. But the individual pirate assaults which characterized the earlier phases of Norse expansion were relatively shortlived, and usually of little more than local consequence. As time passed the acquisition of short-term profit through plunder gave way to a larger scale and much more sustained effort to acquire and colonize territory and to initiate profitable trade.

Even before the close of the 8th century Norwegians were settling, apparently peaceably, in Orkney and Shetland. A saga finally committed to paper in the 13th century tells that these early settlements began during the struggles which led to Harald Fairhair's seizure of centralized power in Norway, in about AD872. One of the *jarls* had himself buried alive, rather than submit to Harald. Others set off in boats, with their families, slaves, goods and livestock, to make new livings for themselves. The saga tells that the Shetlands, Orkneys and Iceland all provided land for these settlers, and archaeological evidence confirms this.

Early settlements

A small settlement, no doubt typical of many, may be seen at Underhoull, at Unst in Shetland: here a family unit established a longhouse at what was evidently the center of a self-sufficient farming unit. At the edge of the bay below the house a *noost* was built for a 16ft (5m) boat, which was clearly a fishing boat – equipment for rendering down fish livers has been found on the site. Soon afterwards Norsemen were displacing those other great early North Atlantic seafarers, the Irish religious *peregrini,* from the Faeroe Islands, which the latter had reached a century or so before.

In England and Ireland the early invasions were soon followed by settlement, albeit less peacefully. In AD851 a Danish army wintered in England. By AD867 they had captured York, and during the century that followed they occupied or fought over much of the country. At much the same time a Viking kingdom established itself on the east coast of Ireland, with its main base and seaport at Dublin, on the River Liffey. From these incursions there emerged a unique realm surrounding the Irish Sea, extending through the Isle of Man and Galloway to the western coasts and islands of Scotland. Dublin and York were, in effect, the joint capitals of this kingdom, and modern excavations in the waterlogged strata below these two great cities have revealed the vibrant centers of their Viking predecessors, bustling with the activities of craft and commerce. Even to the settled Viking towndwellers, however, ships were ever close, as the much studied ship graffiti found in Dublin attest. It seems fitting that the favorite plaything of a Viking child should have been a toy boat.

Viking expansion

Seafaring, plunder, exploration, trade, settlement – these were all elements in the great age of Viking expansion. During the dynamic period between the late 8th and mid 11th centuries, Swedish adventurers penetrated by way of the Baltic and through the heart of Russia to the Volga and Constantinople, dragging their ships overland between the navigable waterways afforded by the great river systems. Other Scandinavian seafarers sailed down the Seine to occupy large parts of France and navigated the western seaboard of Europe to enter the Mediterranean.

To the North, settlement was particularly strong in the empty coastal areas of Iceland from about AD860–870, where the largely Norwegian population grew to 60,000 by the early part of the 11th century. Land was cleared and planted, sometimes with the help of Irish slave labor. Livestock was raised, and the plentiful local cod and salmon formed an essential part of the diet. Icelandic wood was mainly willow and birch, which soon became scarce, so that the settlers had to find other materials for their housebuilding. Turf was readily available, and was resourcefully used to make thick walls and roofs for long, low dwellings with sloping sides. These houses had a central hearth and a small opening at each end to let in light and air. The fire, burning dried sheep's droppings, was used for all the cooking, and partitions were arranged along the sides of the one room to provide sleeping accommodation.

From these uninviting homes the Nordic Icelanders began to add other industry to their farming activities and to produce goods for export. They spun their flock's fleece into wool from which they wove garments, they salted fish, hunted wildlife for fur and sealskin, and provided Europe with ivory from walrus tusks and with the down and feathers of the eider duck. The need to trade was perhaps reinforced by a dependence on the homeland, for the lack of building timber affected shipbuilding, which could only be done with timber from Scandinavia.

Many of the perilous voyages to Iceland were made not in the monster-prowed longships, but in the *knarr* This sturdy vessel was little more than half the length of the longship, but broad in the beam – about 15ft (4.5m) compared to the

The Viking expansion from about the 8th to the 11th centuries is shown on this map (above). The raiding expeditions on Irish monasteries from 793 were followed by many more raids, in England and France, in the early 800s. But settlement was beginning to take place in the islands off Scotland and by the late 9th century there was settlement by treaty in many parts of England; and a treaty granted Normandy to the Norsemen in 911. Trade routes extended around the Baltic and across Russia to the Black Sea. Iceland was colonized sporadically from c.870 into the 10th century. Settlement began in Greenland c. 985, and Vikings sailed to America c.986. The only settlement found there to date is at L'Anse aux Meadows in Newfoundland.

Objects from Coppergate (right), the main trading street of York in Viking times, have been found in large quantities. Already a major trading center, York fell to the Danes in 867. The town became the center of commerce for the large surrounding area which was settled and farmed profitably by the Vikings. The items include (left to right) Viking keys; arab coins, witnessing the extent of the Vikings' trading empire; leather boots and shoes, made by specialist tradesmen and sold in York's shopping center. The narrow plots of Viking traders are still occupied by shops today.

GREENLAND

Ivory
Furs
Hides
Falcons
Woollens

ttahlid

Fish
Fats
Woollens **ICELAND**

Arctic Circle

Faroes

Shetland

Orkney

NORTH SEA

SCOTLAND

Lindisfarne

Dublin   York

IRISH   Wool
        Fish

WELSH London

        Tin

NORMANDY Salt
BRITTANY Wine

Noirmoutier

FRANCE

Rhône

Venice

UMAYYAD
CALIPHATE

Mercury
Sugar

ZIRID EMIRATES

Sugar

Gold
Ivory
Slaves

Timber
Iron
Tallow
Furs   Birka

SWEDEN

*BALTIC
SEA*

Hedeby

Amber

Dorestad   *Elbe*
Copper
Lead
Silver
Beer   Gold

Wool
Wine
Corn

Rhine

GERMAN   Silver
EMPIRE

Slaves   HUNGARY
Timber

Danube

Constantinople

BYZANTINE
EMPIRE

Silk
Wine
Fruit
Spices

MEDITERRANEAN SEA

Jerusalem

FATIMID Cairo
        Corn   CALIPHATE

Nile

Ivory
Furs

Furs

Ladoga

Novgorod

RUSSIA

Bulgar

Dnepr

Tallow
Honey
Wax

Kiev

Slaves
Berezany

Don

KHAZARS

*BLACK
SEA*

Volga

*CASPIAN
SEA*

Chorezm

*ARAL
SEA*

Silver
Gold
Mercury
Iron
Copper
Slaves
Paper

Gurgan

Euphrates

Baghdad

Spices
Silk
Mercury
Iron
Silver

POLAND

DANISH EMPIRE

N

longship's 20ft (6.1m) – and with a deep keel. She had plenty of storage space in the hull, and was a sailing ship. Although she still had the high stern and prow of the longship, these were plainly, not ornately, finished, for it was thought that monster heads would frighten the spirits of the land. It is estimated that in such a vessel the crossing from the Norwegian coast would take five or six days in typical conditions, and so the Faeroes, about half way between Norway and Iceland, made a useful Viking base.

The stepping stones of Orkney, Shetland, the Faeroes and Iceland led the Norsemen to Greenland in AD982 and finally to North America (first sighted in about AD985), though the Vikings did not land there until some 15 years later. The sagas tell us that the Greenland settlement, which came to an abrupt end after nearly 500 years, was founded by the colorful Eirik the Red. Eirik, after feuding there, was banished from Iceland, and set sail with his followers to Greenland, which had been sighted before by Viking explorers. After crossing the cold, rough seas and navigating the icy coast, he finally found a grassy banked, habitable fjord on the western side of the southern tip of this huge island, and here he and his companions stopped and settled, calling the spot Eiriksfjord.

Eirik gave the name Greenland to the new territory, and after three years' banishment returned to Iceland to bring back more people to set up colonies along the west coast. These new Greenlanders built stone houses for themselves and lived on fish, mutton and beef, butter and cheese, as well as wild game. They produced the same commodities for trade as did the Icelanders, and braved the formidable high seas of the region to catch whales and pure white falcon, and to transport their goods back to the European market.

North America

It was Eirik's son Leif who first reached North America. Newfoundland, where he and his men eventually stopped for the winter, had a climate and growing conditions which seemed generously mild compared to Iceland and Greenland, with a less marked difference between summer and winter. In the spring Leif returned to Greenland and had to remain there on his father's death, though others settled in Newfoundland from Greenland, and later from Iceland. The hostile local tribespeople deterred them from establishing themselves as they had done en route, and therefore the Viking habitation of North America was sparse and shortlived; the lines of communication were too long, the number of colonists too small.

Only at L'Anse aux Meadows in northern Newfoundland has an authenticated Viking settlement been found. It consists of a group of three turf longhouses with outbuildings, set on a fertile terrace at the edge of a sheltered bay. Across a small

brook lay a blacksmith's shop and charcoal kiln. Two objects found during the excavation – a soapstone spindle whorl and a ring-headed bronze pin – are unquestionably of Norse origin, while radiocarbon tests point to a date in the 11th century. The site was probably inhabited for no more than 30 years; who its occupants were, and what became of them, is not known. What is certain is that they came by sea.

Boats found in Roskilde fjord

Until quite recently little was known of the type of ships the Vikings built during the later period, and almost nothing at all of the merchant vessels in which the great voyages of trade and exploration were carried out. That omission has in part been remedied by a remarkable discovery in Roskilde fjord, a long inlet on the north coast of the Danish island of Zeeland. Near the fishing village of Skuldelev the fjord narrows to about 3 miles (2km), and most of it is less than 3ft (1m) deep. Modern channels now accommodate large vessels, but in Viking times only one natural channel – the Peberrenden was navigable. At some time during the first half of the 11th century this channel was blocked by sinking five ships across it. In the first instance three vessels – two merchantmen and a longship – were filled with stones and placed across the 150ft (45m) wide channel; later a bigger longship and a small open boat were added to strengthen and consolidate the blockage. In this way the large and important town of Roskilde, 11 miles (17km) to the south at the head of the fjord, was protected from seaborne assault.

It is not known why the blockage was constructed, although it was doubtless related to the widespread warfare among the Scandinavian kingdoms which characterized the later Viking period.

In 1924 Skuldelev fishermen cut a passage through the Peberrenden, and brought up timbers which included a substantial keelson with an incorporated mast step. Then, in the mid 1950s, divers examined the site underwater. Some more timbers were brought up, and when these were studied in the National Museum at Copenhagen, along with the earlier finds, it became clear that the ships' remains belonged not to Queen Margrethe's time in the 14th century, as had been believed, but to the Viking period. Further investigation revealed that not one ship, but five, were involved. In the summer of 1962 a major archaeological excavation was set up under the direction of Drs. Olaf Olsen and Ole Crumlin-Pedersen.

Because the fjord was so shallow and its waters so muddy, it was decided to surround the blockage with a coffer dam and pump the water out to the level of the ships. Catwalks were then positioned over the remains so that teams of excavators could reach down to the wrecks and remove the mud, silt, and stones by hand.

The work was uncomfortable, grueling, and exceedingly dirty, but as it progressed the flattened-out and fragile remains of the ships emerged. As each piece was revealed, fine sprays of water had to be directed onto it to keep it from drying out – although the unusually cold and wet weather of the summer helped considerably. On the debit side, however, seas whipped up by storm conditions at times threatened to spill over the low sides of the coffer dam, and on one occasion the archaeologists had to down tools and frantically build up an emergency defense of sandbags to prevent the exposed and vulnerable remains from flooding.

Once the ships were exposed a meticulous record was made of their remains *in situ*. The site was surveyed photogrammetrically before the pieces were labeled, and then the painstaking work of disassembly and recovery began. Because of the wood's fragile state each piece had to be supported by an individually tailored masonite board before it was extracted and wrapped in heavy duty plastic sheet for transportation to the conservation

The longship (1) shown here (below) is one of five sailing ships found in the Roskilde fjord, near Skuldelev, Denmark, in 1959. It is low, long and narrow, with oarholes along the length of its gunwale, some of which had been blocked up ever since the ship was made. About 59ft (18m) in length, the boat could be beached and used for transporting and landing horses. Swift and easily maneuverable, vessels of this sort must have been used often in the Danish raids.

A *knarr* (2) or heavy cargo ship, (below) was also found at Skuldelev. It was capable of carrying much equipment, including livestock. These ships were used to transport Viking settlers across the Atlantic Ocean. This boat had no signs of scraping on her bottom, indicating that, unlike most Viking ships, she had never been dragged up a beach, being too large and heavy. She was probably an ocean-going vessel used in the North Sea and the Atlantic.

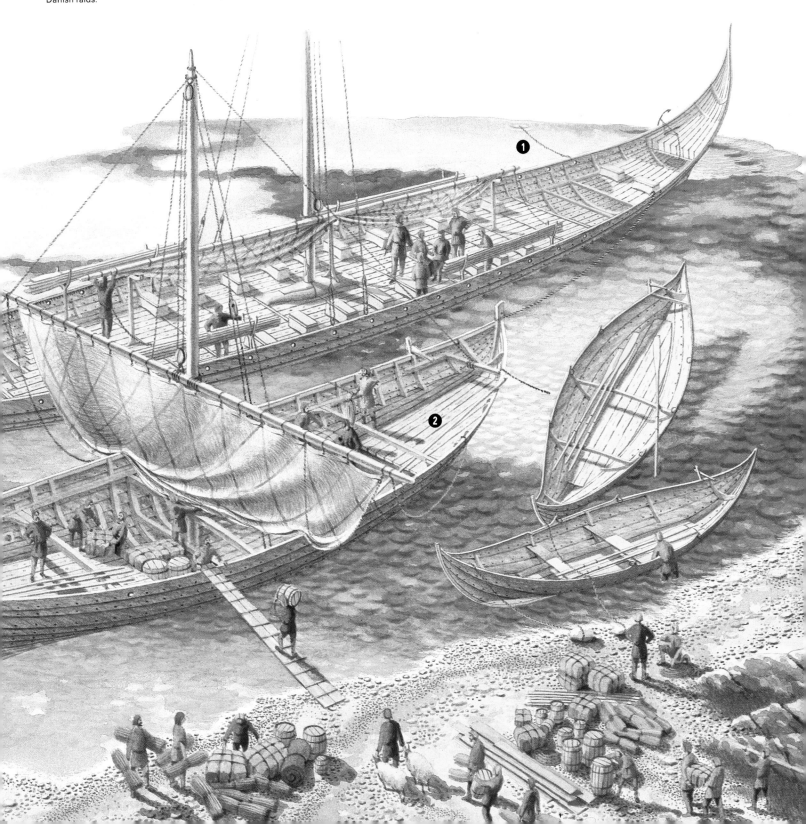

laboratory. Many of the 1,500 large components had been broken into fragments, and in all some 50,000 pieces of wood were recovered. Each had to be registered and identified so that in due course its exact location within the ship could be re-established.

Conservation work
In the laboratories of the National Museum at Brede, north of Copenhagen, the wrapped timbers were laid out and the long process of conservation began. Every piece was first washed and carefully measured, so that any subsequent distortion could be monitored – even slight variations from the original shapes of component timbers might radically alter the form of the reconstructed ships. The timbers were conserved in batches in a special tank which allowed them to be stacked in series while they went through a process of polyethelene glycol impregnation.

Meanwhile a special museum for the ships had been constructed at Roskilde, and in 1963 the conserved remains were moved there for their final reconstruction. With immense care the broken pieces were pegged together, and the shapes of the surviving components were used to determine the shapes of the vessels from which they came. Metal frameworks were then constructed to support the surviving structural elements, and on these the component parts were reassembled – a task of great complexity and precision in which the museum experts were assisted by professional boatbuilders. Now the five ships are displayed in a unique museum, overlooking the fjord in which they sailed almost a thousand years ago.

The builders of the blockade could scarcely have chosen five better ships as a sample of contemporary types. Two were warships. The smaller (Wreck 5) is a light, fast vessel of narrow beam, 52.5ft (17.4m) long and 8.3ft (2.6m) wide. It is made up of seven strakes on each side, the lower four of oak and the top three of ash. The method of construction is in some ways similar to that of the Gokstad ship – a clinker shell reinforced with inserted frames, deck beams, and standing knees. But there are significant differences. Unlike the V-hull of the Gokstad vessel, so well suited to the deepwater fjords of Norway, Skuldelev 5 has the flat bottom of a ship intended for beaching. The elastic but labor-intensive use of cleats and lashings to secure the frames has been replaced by pegging with treenails, and 12 narrow thwarts were provided above the deck beams for the vessel's 24 oarsmen. A mast step was set in the keelson.

This ship, like the others in the blockade, was old and much used, with her keel worn down by numerous beachings. Her three top strakes, moreover, had seen service in an earlier ship; the old oarports in the gunwale, which did not match the thwart spacings of the new vessel, had

been closed with patches, and appropriately positioned new ones cut. This ship was well designed for amphibious operations, easy to land on or launch from a beach. Very similar vessels are shown in the Bayeux Tapestry, landing William the Conqueror's army on English soil in 1066. This similarity is not surprising; William the Conqueror was a direct descendant of the Vikings who had invaded Burgundy from the Seine in AD885, and whose leader Rollo became Count of Rouen and ruler of Normandy in AD911.

Skuldelev 2, which lay in the shallowest part of the blockade, was the least well preserved of the five ships, although it was clear that she had been a ship of great length – perhaps as long as 100ft (30m). Such a vessel might have mounted 25 pairs of oars, and may well have been built as a royal warship.

Wreck 6 was an open boat built of pine, 37ft (11.6m) long and 7.6ft (2.4m) wide. Her cross-beams seem too low to have provided thwarts for rowers, and she may have been a ferry or a fishing boat.

The best preserved wreck, Skuldelev 3, was a small merchant vessel. She was 44ft (13.8m) long and 12ft (3.8m) wide, giving her much beamier proportions than the fighting longships. Her elegant and intricate stem post, cut to bring the lines of the strakes to a finely tapered upturned point, was carved from a single block of oak. The ship was light but strong, and in addition to the usual frames and cross-beams, further side support was given by fore-and-aft stringers, reinforcing the upper planks and gunwales. Stout triangular bulkheads strengthened the extremities, and a fixed mast was stepped into the keelson. Oar positions – seven in all – were provided fore and aft for maneuvering, but these appear to have been little used. With a central open hold capable of stowing up to 3.5 tons of cargo this vessel was clearly a small sailing trader, capable of plying the coastal routes of northern Europe or, with her shallow draft, of penetrating far into the river systems to further exploit trading opportunities.

Skuldelev 1 was a larger and much more substantially built merchant ship. Her massive pine planking could not easily have been obtained in Denmark during the Viking period, though it would have been readily available in southern Norway. She has been identified as a *knarr* – the kind of vessel in which the great Norse oceanic voyages of exploration and settlement to Iceland, Greenland and North America were made, built for strength rather than lightness. This particular ship is 63ft (16.5m) long and 10ft (3.2m) wide. Her keel and lower ribs are of oak, and her upper internal members of limewood. Capacious, high-sided, with fore- and after-decks and an open central hold, a ship of this kind could carry heavy cargoes, livestock, and emigrants far beyond the horizons of the North Atlantic.

Legacy of the Vikings
Many of the traditions of Viking ship-building survived and continued to spread long after the Viking era. The clinker boat-form permeated throughout northwest Europe, and survives to this day. The 12th century inhabitants of Perth, in Scotland, built and used boats indistinguishable from Viking types. A medieval boatbuilder on the island of Eigg placed two stepped stem or stern pieces of oak similar to those recovered from Skuldelev, in a peat bog, to season them. In the 1520s Alexander MacLeod was buried at Rodel in the Outer Hebrides beneath a representation of his war-galley which, apart from its stern-mounted rudder, might have sailed out of a Norwegian fjord six centuries earlier. Countless communities now living beside the sea in the Viking homelands, and in the lands where they raided, traded, or settled, still reflect in many aspects of their daily lives the influence of the vigorous seafarers who, a thousand years ago, passed their way.

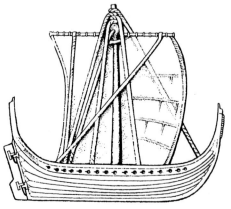

Sixareens (six-oared boats) were photographed at the settlement of Feideland, Shetland, in 1890. This timeless scene might have been echoed throughout the Norse world from AD800 until the recent past.

A detail from the Bayeux tapestry (above) depicts the Norman fleet which invaded England in 1066. King Harold and William the Conqueror were both descended from the Vikings. It is tempting to see William's invasion as being in the Viking tradition, especially as there was an invasion from Norway at the same time. Although the Normans had adopted the French language and culture, they had not forgotten how to build boats in the Viking manner.

A carving from Rodel, Scotland (left) on the 16th century tomb of Alexander MacLeod, shows a Highland galley and is typical of many tombstone carvings in the West of Scotland. These indicate that the Viking boatbuilding traditions persisted into the 16th century. This vessel is represented in closely observed detail, and has much in common with the Gokstad ship, except for its square sail and stern rudder. (The Gokstad ship had a side rudder and its sail was probably oblong.)

Present-day Swedish church boats (above) are part of a continuing folk tradition, despite many local variations. Their pointed prows date back to prehistory. Until recently, the boats were often built (during the slack agricultural seasons) from hollowed-out timbers, but now they are made of planks. The local parishioners, dressed in folk costume, launch the boats with great pride and sense of occasion, then the boats are used to convey the numerous members of the community in fleets to their parish church. More likely than not the tradition predates the adoption of Christianity in Scandinavia.

133

North Sea traders

We have seen how the Mediterranean provided a network of sea routes between the countries which surrounded it. Similarly, the North and Baltic Seas, where ships can move with relative ease around the coastal margins, joined together the nations of northern Europe. From the 10th century onwards, after the turmoil of the Age of Migrations, sturdy commercial vessels began to appear in northern waters. These ships were eventually to develop into the formidable warships and merchantmen of later centuries.

Trading contacts in the North Sea can be traced back into remote prehistory, developing during the Roman period both within and far beyond the imperial boundaries. In the unsettled period following the collapse of the Roman empire in the West, ships were used less for trade than they were for migration, raiding, or war.

A 10th century boat from Kent
During this time, however, new strong, seaworthy ship types emerged, and as more settled conditions began to prevail, new techniques were adapted to the construction of commercial vessels.

In 1970, the bones of one such vessel were discovered during drain-widening operations in the marshes of Graveney, Kent. Archaeologists, working against the clock while drainage operations were halted for 10 days, were able to record and recover the find.

The Graveney boat had been abandoned on a brushwood platform at the head of a silty creek some time around AD950. Enough ship's timbers survived to show that she had been clinker-built in the Scandinavian tradition, but in other respects she was quite different from contemporary vessels on the other side of the North Sea.* In particular, she was much more massively built, with heavy rectangular frames inserted into the shell-built hull. The frames were attached to the hull with a type of fastening quite unknown in Scandinavia, and some scholars have suggested links with earlier boat finds in Celtic Europe.*

A detailed program of recording, analysis and reconstruction has revealed a picture of the boat as she might have appeared in the 10th century. She was a substantial double-ended open vessel some 46ft (14m) long, with a beam of about 13ft (4m), capable of carrying at least seven tons of cargo. At some stage in her career she probably had a mast, which was later removed. Her strong hull, combined with fine lines and a capacious interior, suggests that she had been built as a seagoing trading craft.

Clues as to the nature of her cargoes included hop seeds, found trapped among her timbers, and fragments of millstones, from the middle Rhine area, lying in the bottom of her hull. There were also pieces of Kentish ragstone, some with traces of mortar still attached.

Scraps of Roman tiles may be no more

than the residue of ballast gravel from the Thames foreshore, but sherds of pottery from Belgium or northern France suggest wider trading contacts. Indeed, archaeological finds from contemporary Saxon centers like Thetford, Canterbury, or Hamwih (Southampton) confirm that eastern England had links with the Rhineland, Holland, and north Germany.

Is the Graveney boat's distinctive construction representative of a specifically English tradition of boatbuilding, or was she designed expressly for the transport of bulk cargoes? Was the ship local, or did she originate far from the Kentish creek in which she was eventually abandoned? All we know for sure is that she was a North Sea trader operating in the first half of the 10th century. Only further finds will broaden the picture.

Later medieval boats
By the later medieval period, the picture becomes broader and much clearer. At Kalmar, an important medieval harbor on the southeast coast of Sweden, excavations have revealed the remains of more than 20 ancient vessels. During the 16th century, the inner harbor basin silted up and was abandoned. Draining and clearing out the old harbor in the 1930s revealed 18 partially complete wrecks and fragments of six more.

The earliest wreck, which dates from the 13th century, was also the best preserved. It was a small coastal trader, a tubby clinker-built vessel 36ft (11m) long by 15ft (4.4m) wide, clearly of Viking ancestry but with several new features. These include a stern post, which is straight and raked slightly aft to accommodate a hanging rudder; a keelson,

A map of late 14th century northwest Europe, marking sites mentioned in the text. The Hanseatic League, a political-commercial association led by Lübeck, monopolized trade at this time, but gradually yielded to the Dutch over the next century. Most Hanseatic trade was carried in the belly of a humble but efficient bulk carrier – the cog. German merchants used these to supply west European urban centers with grain from Poland, timber from Russia and Poland, and herring from southern Sweden. Returning eastwards they carried Flemish cloth, French wine, and Breton sea salt – a preservative increasingly in demand as the herring fishery grew. The two trades complemented each other, and their need for cheap bulk carriage was a particular stimulus to the building and refinement of cogs.

An interpretation of the Graveney boat's stern section, shown in conjunction with its surviving part (in black). Ancient boat finds are usually fragmentary, but their remains can be used as a foundation for fuller reconstruction.

ATLANTIC OCEAN

SCOTLAND

Cornwall

Tin

15°   20°   25°   30°

NORWAY

SWEDEN

Gulf of Bothnia

REVEL (TALLINN)
Timber

60°

RIGA
Dvina

VISBY
Gotland

Fish

Timber
Tallow
Iron
Copper

Kalmar   Kalmar trader   BALTIC SEA

LITHUANIA

55°

Timber
Corn

Vigso remains   Kollerup grain cog

Kattegat

Amber

Fish

NORTH SEA

Vejby cog
DENMARK   Kyholm knarr-type
Samso

Kolding cog

Danzig ore hulk
Corn   DANZIG (GDANSK)

POLAND

Corn

Vistula

Coal

LÜBECK

Oder   Corn

HAMBURG   Elbe

Bremen cog
BREMEN

Corn

GERMAN EMPIRE

50°

ENGLAND
Thetford

Cloth

Salt   Flevoland mud barges   Lelystad beurtschip

London
Graveney boat
Thames   Canterbury
Wool
Southampton

BRUGES

Cloth
Wine

COLOGNE
Iron
Copper
Rhine   Lead

FRANCE

0   300 Kilometers
0   200 Miles

KEY   Prevailing Winds
• Wrecksites   Strong Currents

5°   10°   15°   20°

thickened amidships to provide a mast step; and a small bowsprit projecting forward. There were arrangements for raising and lowering the mast.* Decking was provided at bow and stern, and a windlass was situated aft to assist with the working of the mast and sail. Economy of operation is always an important consideration in the design of merchant ships, since large crews are expensive to maintain and occupy cargo space.

Some of these features relate the Kalmar boat to the cog family, an immensely important ship type whose origins may go back to the 10th century or even earlier. This distinctive type of vessel was the mainstay of Hanseatic merchants until it was superseded by the hulk around the beginning of the 15th century.

The Bremen cog
An almost complete example of a cog dating from about 1380 came to light in 1962, during dredging operations in Bremen harbor on the river Weser, West Germany. A rescue operation was set in train, and the vessel was successfully dismantled and recovered. In the process, an unexpected discovery was made: the ship was unfinished. No mast had ever been stepped, and the deck planking was yet to be laid. A stern platform was in place, complete with a vertically mounted windlass, but the staging at the bow – though evidently planned – had not been built.

Inside the ship, the excavators found shipwrights' tools, and a barrel of tar. They surmised that the almost complete vessel had been carried away from its builders' yard by a flood, to be engulfed by the river sandbanks downstream.

The loss sustained by an anonymous 14th century Bremen merchant has been posterity's gain; now reconstructed, the cog sits in a tank (with windows through which she can be observed) at the Deutsches Schiffahrtsmuseum, Bremerhaven, where she is undergoing a prolonged program of conservation.

Studies carried out during the reconstruction process have revealed much technical information about this type of vessel, for which the only previous source has been depictions on the seals of medieval Hanseatic towns. Now many puzzling features on the seals can be explained, from the evidence of this ship. The clench-nailed clinker sides, made up of short planks, explain the studded appearance with which the seals depict the angular hull, while the row of protruding cross-beam ends is often represented by appropriately placed blobs. In general, the seals proved to be accurate representations, subject only to the constraints of the circular format.

Some technical puzzles have been solved by wreck discoveries. Seals such as the mid 13th century Seal of Wismar, for example, show the forward and after ends of the keel tilted up. This has been explained as an artistic convention, but

exactly the same feature occurs in the Bremen cog, where the forward and after thirds of its flat plank-keel incline upwards so that only the central section lies horizontal. This feature would have countered any tendency of the keel to bow inwards, or "hog", thus immensely increasing the hull's overall strength. Thus the cog formed an efficient and seaworthy box structure, able to bear the stresses of the elements while afloat and the quite different strains of sitting, fully laden, on a beach to discharge cargo.

The cog was the mercantile workhorse of northern Europe, and since the Bremen discovery many more cog wrecks, or fragments of them, have come to light. The vessel discovered in Kolding fjord, Denmark, in 1943, and recorded in what was then unprecedented detail by Knud Hansen of the Copenhagen Maritime Museum, is now recognized as a cog. The Kolding ship is still safely buried in the fjord, ready to be reassessed in the light of the Bremen find.

The so-called Vejby cog was found in 1976, in less than 7ft (2m) of water off the North Sjaelland coast at Vejby, some 30 miles (50km) northwest of Copenhagen. Near the wooden remains of the wreck were a pewter plate and some gold coins, later identified as 14th century English gold nobles. The two teenagers who made the discovery most commendably kept quiet about their find, and hastened to report it to the authorities. Within 24 hours a team of archaeologists, disguised as a picnic party to divert attention from the find on a much frequented beach, were conducting a preliminary survey of the site and recovering more coins.

Wrecked around 1380, the Vejby cog had been quite a small ship – no more than 40ft (12m) along the keel – but she had evidently traveled widely. Two coins from the Danzig region had been placed in the mast step for luck by her builders, suggesting that she originated from this major Hanseatic port. The stone ballast

A small 13th century trader, abandoned in the mud of Kalmar harbor, was rediscovered when the dried-out basin was excavated in the 1930s. Such vessels were ideal for short-haul coastal work, being able to carry loads of several tons, yet needing a crew of only two or three, assisted by a stern-mounted windlass. Plentiful space amidships was combined with fine lines to ensure efficient sailing.

A cog under construction, based on the Bremen find. Several influences are apparent in this extremely successful design; the clinker sides (1) clearly derive from Norse tradition but the flat bottom, which gave the hull greater capacity and allowed it to sit upright when beached and dry, is flush-laid. Slight canting of the keel plank (3) fore and aft stressed the hull against any tendency to "hog", or bow upwards. Protruding cross-beams (2) lock the lower hull together, and allow the sides to be extended upwards to provide the vessel with greater depth. This combination of strength, capacity and ease of operation ensured the cog's success.

she carried on her final voyage, however, came from the Atlantic seaboard of Europe – perhaps Cornwall or Brittany. She was evidently homeward-bound in ballast after a successful trading venture to western Europe (represented by the gold coins) when she was driven onto a lee shore and smashed to pieces.

In 1974 at Vigsø, Denmark, two magnificent early 15th century bronze *aquamaniles* (ewers for hand-washing) were uncovered in a sand-dredging operation among dunes where the sea has receded since medieval times. A subsequent search located iron tools, locks, ship fastenings, and fragments of rudder-irons, but no part of the vessel itself had survived.

The remains of another vessel were uncovered four years later, at Kollerup, a short distance east of Vigsø, with scraps of pottery suggesting a 13th century date. Under the auspices of the local museum at Thisted, the water table was lowered and the remains extracted.

This time there was no cargo. The ship had beached high and dry, and she had evidently been stripped and partially salvaged immediately after the wreck took place: axe marks on the timbers show where local people cut away the upper parts of the hull.

However, enough survived of her lower structure to show that the ship was an interesting variant on the cog tradition. She had no keelson, but instead a massive transverse frame, set well forward, which incorporated the mast step. A groove was cut in the after edge of this frame to accommodate a removeable transverse bulkhead, and there was evidence of an internal lining of loose planking to keep the hold well clear of bilgewater. All this suggests grain as a likely cargo. She had been built with great precision, and was quite old when lost, for many cracks in the timbers had been carefully repaired.

Other medieval ship types
The cog was by no means the only commercial ship type in use. A wreck excavated in 1978 at Kyholm, Denmark, and dated to the 13th century, was not unlike the seagoing Skuldelev *knarr* of some two centuries earlier (see p.132) – for some classes of ship the older traditions still had a place.

But new types were emerging too. In 1969 Polish underwater archaeologists discovered, close to Danzig harbor, a wreck dated by c-14 analysis to the first half of the 15th century (though the objects she carried probably dated from about half a century later). Her clinker-built hull, with its rounded bilges, massive internal framing, and strakes curving sharply into the stern post, is quite unlike the cogs of a century earlier. Perhaps this is an example of the "mysterious hulk" – the ship-type which, according to documents, began to replace the cog as the main North Sea cargo carrier around 1400, and about

which we still know very little indeed.

The vessel had apparently been destroyed by fire, and melted pitch and wax from the cargo had percolated into its lower frames, preserving a wealth of evidence, including the remains of onions and garlic. The main cargo had been copper ingots, bundles of iron bars, and barrels filled with iron ore.

During the 15th century the three-masted rig began to appear, heralding the great warships and merchantmen which would dominate the oceans until the Age of Steam. But throughout this period large vessels were rare: most craft continued to be built along traditional lines, with modifications or adjustments as required. The great variety of ordinary workaday craft which developed is nowhere better seen than in 17th century Holland, where they have been depicted by many artists, especially Reinier Nooms.*

Recording techniques
During the past 45 years, the drained polders of the Zuider Zee have yielded some 350 wrecks dating from the last medieval period to the recent past. As each is discovered it is excavated and fully recorded. Only in exceptional circumstances can the wrecks be preserved, for the bulk of material is simply too great. The urgency and intensity of the rescue work has resulted in new and often ingenious excavation techniques being employed.

The results have been impressive. Of the 30 or so wrecks which date from the medieval period, nine show links with the cog traditions of northern Europe. Nine *waterschepen*, with their wet fishholds, have also been identified. Three, from the late medieval period, are remarkably similar to their 19th century descendants. Smaller fishing craft are well represented too. Most of the finds, however, are barges – the box-like bluff-bowed vessels so characteristic of the region from the Middle Ages to the present day*.

In 1980 the hull of a small coaster was discovered during the building of a canal in Lelystad. It had settled in the mud on its starboard side, which had been preserved, leaving an almost complete longitudinal section of the hull. The ship was 60ft (18m) long, with a beam of 17ft (5.5m), and had been equipped with lee boards to compensate for her shallow draft, though these had probably floated away when she was wrecked.

A small cooking hearth and several kitchen utensils indicated that the crew's living quarters were in the fore part of the ship. Coins found in this area suggest the ship sank around 1620. The vessel was probably a *beurtschip*, or Zuider Zee trader, built towards the end of the 16th century. Some of her cargo still lay in the hold: wrapped scythe blades, a box of eggs, brass cooking pots, pewter utensils, and leather bags.

For more than a thousand years, the

North Sea has throbbed with maritime commerce, and trade routes often transcended national boundaries. The small seaport on the east coast of Scotland where I live bears witness to this. A few years ago we conducted a small excavation in my back garden close to the waterfront, uncovering a rubbish deposit dated to about 1635. Here we found a great mass of broken pottery, containing sherds from almost every region in Europe: lusterware from Spain's Mediterranean coast; olive jars from Seville; tin-glazed wares from Portugal; exotic sherds from central and eastern France; functional stoneware from Normandy; cooking pots, clay pipes and delftwares from Holland; stonewares from the Rhineland; and domestic earthenwares from North Germany and Scandinavia. A seafarer from any of these regions would hardly have seemed a stranger on this bustling North Sea waterfront 350 years ago.

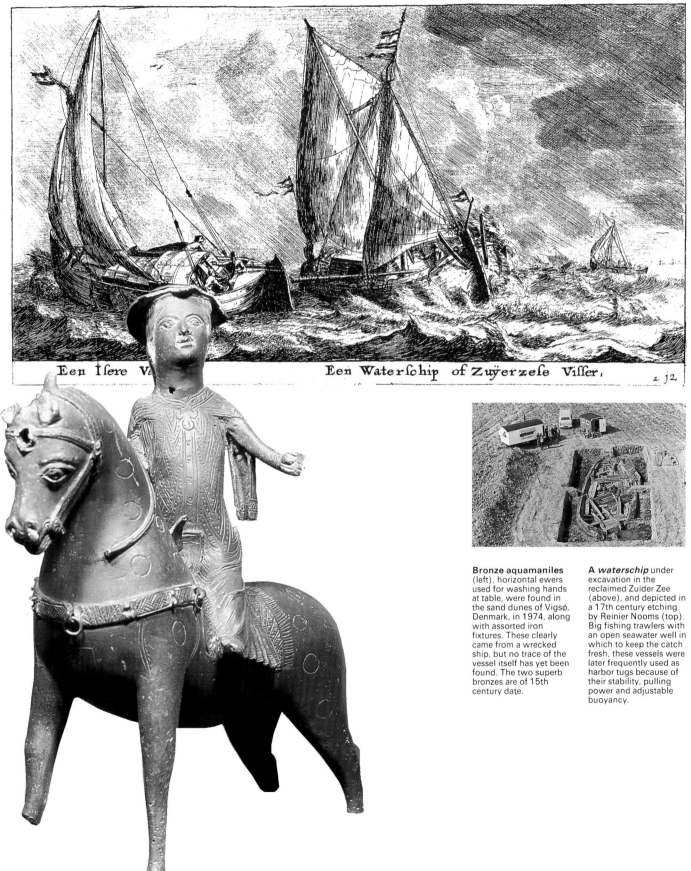

Een Ifere Ve··   Een Waterfchip of Zuÿerzefe Viffer.   a j2

Bronze aquamaniles (left), horizontal ewers used for washing hands at table, were found in the sand dunes of Vigsø, Denmark, in 1974, along with assorted iron fixtures. These clearly came from a wrecked ship, but no trace of the vessel itself has yet been found. The two superb bronzes are of 15th century date.

A *waterschip* under excavation in the reclaimed Zuider Zee (above), and depicted in a 17th century etching by Reinier Nooms (top). Big fishing trawlers with an open seawater well in which to keep the catch fresh, these vessels were later frequently used as harbor tugs because of their stability, pulling power and adjustable buoyancy.

Guns and sails

The use of firepower on ships was for long restricted to small pieces incapable of inflicting serious damage. But from these humble beginnings a close harmony was to develop between the sailing ship and the gun, enabling European nations to explore, conquer and exploit the rest of the world. Recent work in maritime archaeology shows how the technologies behind this power evolved, with particular reference to the *Mary Rose* and other ships of the 16th and 17th centuries.

Until the later Middle Ages northern ships were rarely used for fighting at sea. Even the Viking longships, though built for warlike purposes, were essentially a means of transport whereby soldiers could launch attacks on land-based objectives. Whether the operation was a free-booting raid by a single pirate ship on an unprotected monastery, or a huge military invasion such as that launched by William of Normandy against England in 1066, ships provided an attacking force with mobility and surprise, but decisive actions normally took place on land.

Of course there were exceptions. In AD885, according to the *Anglo-Saxon Chronicle*, a force of English ships encountered 16 Danish vessels off Harwich and enjoyed a short-lived victory. Ten years later the Anglo-Saxon king Alfred built a new fleet of 60-oared warships to counter Danish raids on his kingdom of Wessex. These specialized interceptors, with a high freeboard which gave them a telling advantage in ship-to-ship combat, were evidently effective. In one battle a Danish squadron was virtually annihilated, although at heavy cost.

Even when fighting did take place at sea, it was little more than an extension of land warfare. In 1340, at Sluys, Edward III ranged his fleet against the French in three lines in much the same way as he was to dispose his army at Crécy six years later. The front line was divided into units of three ships, with men-at-arms filling the middle vessel, and archers in the ships on each flank. Each unit thus constituted a self-contained assault group, supported on its flanks by concentrated arrow fire. The second line stood in close reserve to fill any gaps, while at the rear lay vessels for the knights' ladies and other non-combatants, together with a strong escort. The opposing French fleet was similarly arrayed, with its front-line ships chained together for mutual support. Once battle had been joined, little further maneuvering was possible, and the outcome depended on who won the ensuing hand-to-hand struggle. In this, Edward's skilful use of

heavily armed shock troops, supported on each side by archers, carried the day.

The 14th century warship

Edward's flagship at Sluys, the *Thomas*, is described as a cog. No remains of such warships have yet been discovered, but they probably had a basic hull construction indistinguishable from that of a merchant cog, with fighting platforms added fore and aft. The *Thomas* was probably not unlike the Bremen cog (see p.136), although she would have had more substantial fighting structures.

The 1325 Seal of Poole depicts a rather different type of warship, with characteristics suggesting a more direct link with Viking traditions. Her fighting structures comprise a level platform, protected by crenelated bulwarks, extending from the head of the stern-post to a point just aft of the mainmast. A smaller structure is located above the stem, while a fighting top is provided at the head of the mast. These arrangements gave troops the advantages of level space, height and protection during close combat. Such modifications could easily be made to existing merchant hulls, so that privately owned vessels could be requisitioned when necessary and almost instantly converted into warships.

The first quarter of the 14th century saw the introduction of guns in Europe. Edward III may have had some artillery aboard his ships at Sluys, but if so, the weapons were certainly small, few in number, and incapable of inflicting serious damage. Their early use involved no modification of tactics or ship design, and their effect was probably little more than psychological.

During the next four centuries, the sailing ship and the gun were destined to develop in close harmony, giving the European nations a unique and deadly combination, which would revolutionize naval warfare and open up the great continents beyond Europe for discovery, conquest and exploitation.

A landmark in this evolutionary process, which followed no single path or systematic development, occurred when Henry V of England ordered the construction of a huge new warship, the *Grace Dieu*. At her launch in 1418, this 1400-ton vessel was the largest ship ever built in England. But as far as is known, the *Grace Dieu* undertook only one short voyage.

Ordered to "set forth from the port of Southampton to the open sea" in 1420, her crew mutinied and forced her captain, the Earl of Devon, to put into St Helens on the Isle of Wight, only 20 miles from Southampton. There they remained, refusing all exhortations to sail. Thereafter the *Grace Dieu* was held in reserve on the River Hamble until 1433, when she was moved up-river to be retained in a fenced mud-berth above Bursledon. Six years later the ship was struck by lightning and burnt out.

The bottom of the *Grace Dieu's* hull has lain in the Hamble mud ever since. In 1874, in the mistaken belief that the remains were those of a Viking ship, an abortive and destructive attempt at excavation was carried out, of which no record was made. A few more timbers were removed in 1899. Then, in 1933, the site was examined by a group of pioneering nautical archaeologists, who surveyed, recorded, and convincingly identified the remains as those of the *Grace Dieu*.

She was truly enormous. The surviving portion of the hull measured 134ft by 38ft (41m by 11.5m), suggesting a keel length of some 127ft (39m) and a maximum beam of about 50ft (15m).*

These dimensions would readily accommodate the *Grace Dieu's* recorded 1400 tons, a figure which historians had regarded with some scepticism.

An Italian, Luca di Maso degli Albizzi, Captain of the Florentine Galleys, saw the ship in 1430 and estimated that the fore-stage towered 40ft (16m) above the waterline; he was told, moreover, that a further gallery would be added for sea service. He also noted that the mainmast was more than 7ft (2m) in diameter at the upper deck, and was about 200ft (60m) high so that, allowing for a taper of up to half this figure at top and bottom, the mast alone would have weighed about 90 tons. Luca di Maso thought the ship was the largest and most beautiful construction he had ever seen.

A warship depicted on the Seal of Poole, England, from a document dated 1325. The ship has a stern-hung rudder and integral castleworks, and the curved stem and stern posts suggest a vessel in the Scandinavian tradition. The depiction shows much technical detail, in spite of compression to fit the seal's circular design; short runs of clenched planking and triangular darts suggest through beams along the second wale.

The *Grace Dieu's* achievements did not match up to her appearance. But it would be altogether too rash to blame the ship's undistinguished career on her size, or on faults in her design and construction. The hostilities for which she was built were drawing to a close when she was commissioned: the need now was for small patrol vessels and not large warships. In a large-scale melee at sea the *Grace Dieu* might well have proved devastatingly effective, with her overhanging tiers of castleworks, particularly at the bow, providing secure and commanding positions for a strong contingent of archers. Her size, and her strongly built hull, would have rendered her virtually impregnable. But history never put her to the test.

New weapons, old tactics

Many influences are apparent in the concept and construction of the *Grace Dieu*. Her clinker build clearly shows her northern European origin, though in her size and shape she is probably more closely linked to the big merchant carracks of the Mediterranean. The towering forestage indicates that the type of warfare for which she was intended differed little from that of Sluys three-quarters of a century earlier. She was just bigger, with larger numbers of fightingmen placed at greater heights for close-range missile fire followed by boarding.

Guns were clearly still considered unimportant, for the *Grace Dieu* carried only three breech-loading pieces. A fully equipped archer or man-at-arms was probably still regarded as more effective than his equivalent weight in ordnance.

By the end of the century, a somewhat different view prevailed. In 1495 Henry VII's new ship *Sovereign* mounted no fewer than 110 serpentines and 41 stone-throwing guns, together with 200 bows. England's famous longbow had not yet been replaced by gunpowder weapons, but the two were increasingly seen as equal partners.*

Yet tactics had scarcely changed; the now numerous guns were very light, for they had to be mounted along the waist or in the relatively flimsy fighting castles. They would have had little effect on a ship's hull, and may be regarded as just another form of anti-personnel firepower. Ramming or hurling missiles from the fighting tops remained the sole means of effecting serious structural damage to the enemy's vessels.

By this time, however, the effectiveness of heavy artillery had long been known, especially for battering land fortifications, and it was obvious that it could have a similar effect at sea. But mounting heavy guns aboard ship would have presented problems of stability if they were placed in the lightly constructed upper works. To mount them low down in ، the hull, however, necessitated cutting ports in the sides of the ship, thus weakening her structurally, and risking a possibly disas-

trous influx of water should she heel unexpectedly.

The extensive rebuilding of the *Sovereign* in 1509, to accommodate heavy artillery, shows how these problems were being tackled. Her overlapping clinker planking – which could not easily accommodate gunports and their hinged lids – was removed and replaced with butt-jointed, flush carvel strakes. She now carried 16 bronze muzzle-loading guns in place of the earlier light iron pieces, and most of these must have been mounted below deck, with new gunports cut to accommodate them.

What are probably the remains of the *Sovereign* were discovered during the construction of Woolwich Power Station in 1912, at Roff's Wharf on the south bank of the Thames. Hereabouts, it is known, the old ship was laid up in 1521. The massive mainmast stump of the Woolwich ship certainly indicates a vessel of the *Sovereign's* size, and large-calibre stone shot shows that the ship was once heavily armed.

Most suggestive of all, the remains show that the vessel was originally of clinker build, and had subsequently been converted to carvel. Her notched clinker frames had been adzed almost smooth to accommodate flush planking, but traces of the original cuts – some filled with wedges – could still be seen. This process inevitably reduced the frames' thickness and weakened the structure, yet the

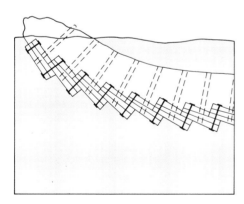

A section (above) through *Grace Dieu's* triple-skinned clinker planking, as recorded in 1933. The inner plank of each composite strake is left short to provide a recess for the strake below it. Tarred moss was used for calking.

War cogs in close action (above right), depicted in an early 14th century English manuscript. The height advantage provided by the forecastle is being used to good effect by the victorious cog on the left, which is also deploying effective missile fire from the stern. The archers' arrows are bundled in the same way as those discovered on the *Mary Rose*. The platform on the top of the mast, right, is for lookouts or for additional archers during combat.

The 1509 rebuild of *Sovereign* involved converting her clinker planking to carvel. A 1912 photograph (right) of the lower part of a frame on the so-called Woolwich ship, almost certainly Henry VII's *Sovereign* of 1488, shows how the notched frames have been trimmed almost flush, but the nicks of their inner corners are still visible.

whole point of the rebuild was to provide a strong hull which would be capable of bearing heavy artillery.*

The *Mary Rose*

The most important – and dramatic – evidence for this crucial stage in the development of the sailing warship is provided by the wreck of Henry VIII's prestigious battleship *Mary Rose*. The *Mary Rose's* keel was laid at Portsmouth in 1509, and in 1512 she was present off Brest when the 700-ton French warship *La Cordelière* and England's *Regent*, locked in close combat, were burnt to the waterline. In 1536 she was rebuilt to accommodate a new and even more formidable armament. This included 15 bronze pieces, ranging from 2-pounder falcons to full cannons – 50-pounders or more. She also carried 56 wrought-iron guns, 50 handguns, 20 anti-personnel hailshot pieces, and two guns designed to be used from the fighting tops. In addition she carried 250 longbows, 400 sheaves of arrows, and a miscellany of other weapons.*

Then, on July 19 1545, in Henry VIII's presence, she went down during an engagement with a French invasion force in the confined waters of the Solent. The circumstances of the disaster are unclear, although it would appear that she heeled over unexpectedly and sank quickly. Of the 700 or so men on board, fewer than 40 escaped.

An attempt by Venetian salvors to recover the ship failed (though they did bring up some of her guns), and the wreck gradually settled into the soft mud of the Solent. Since the ship lay heeled over to starboard at an angle of some 60 degrees, her bottom and most of that side became buried intact with many of the internal structures and contents remaining in place. Silt then piled up inside her, together with debris from the collapsed port side of the ship.

Thus the *Mary Rose's* remains became entombed within a series of deposits which held the key to understanding the sequence in which the ship had partially broken up and then stabilized. This, if systematically investigated and analyzed, would throw light on details of the construction and internal organization of the ship. Thus the *Mary Rose* could provide a window through which we might see at first hand one of Henry VIII's great battleships.

Between 1836 and 1840, the pioneer divers John and Charles Deane discovered the site of the wreck and tried to excavate it with the aid of explosives. Fortunately, their efforts met with limited success. A number of bronze and wrought-iron guns were raised, together with longbows, human remains, and various other finds, but the sheer bulk of the overlying silt deposits defeated them. Any damage they did proved later to have been largely superficial, and the *Mary Rose's* partly intact hull, with its precious contents, remained undisturbed, its exact location forgotten, for another 128 years.

In 1967 Alexander McKee, a diving historian who had launched a program to locate historic shipwrecks in the Solent, arranged with Professor Harold Edgerton to conduct a side-scan and sub-bottom sonar survey over the area suspected to contain the *Mary Rose*. A seabed anomaly, consisting of a mound and scour pit with a W-shaped feature beneath it, was observed; this was indeed the wreck, though physical evidence was not obtained until three years later. In 1971 the eroded tops of frame timbers were unexpectedly revealed by a slight shift of the surface sediments, just as they had been revealed to the Deanes more than a century earlier. The way was now clear for the largest underwater excavation yet to be mounted in Britain.

The enormous historic importance of the wreck was recognized from the outset. Under the direction of Dr Margaret Rule (a practicing archaeologist who learned to dive in order to conduct the project) the site was surveyed and tested. Assessment

A 1546 depiction of *Mary Rose* – posthumous, for she sank in 1545. Laid down in 1509 and extensively rebuilt in 1536, she is shown as a high-charged carrack bristling with ordnance. But a study of the ship's remains suggests she had a sleeker hull with lower castleworks.

was completed by 1978, when it was decided to excavate the ship and remove its contents: when that was done, the possibility of raising the entire surviving hull would be considered.

From 1979 until the end of the excavation, 24,640 individual dives were made by the archaeological team and their corps of volunteer helpers, amounting to a total of 9 man-years on the sea bed. Thousands of finds were recorded and conserved; loose timbers and internal structures were carefully surveyed, dismantled and stored for later reconstruction; and the complex stratigraphy of the wreck was revealed and interpreted by careful dissection. At last, on October 11 1982, the empty hull was successfully raised.

Guns at sea

The innovative nature of the *Mary Rose* and her armament stands out against the background of the development of guns during the previous two centuries. The very earliest firearms were probably vase-shaped pieces of cast bronze, but these were soon replaced by tubes of wrought iron. At first such guns were small, short, and usually clamped to a wooden stock. They were generally muzzle-loading weapons, and were carried and operated by a single gunner.

By the end of the 14th century, only the very largest pieces were muzzle-loaders – the great siege bombards which were now revolutionizing land warfare. But such guns were far too big and difficult to operate effectively afloat. Guns at sea were still few in number and universally small, but two distinct categories were beginning to dominate the maritime scene: one short and with a large bore compared to its length, the other long and of relatively small bore. The first was designed to throw stone shot, where the projectile was of low mass and could be of larger diameter than one made of denser material. It also required a smaller charge to propel it. Pieces designed to fire iron or lead, on the other hand, tended to have a much greater length in relation to their comparatively small bores.

Almost all these were breech-loaders with removable breechblocks, which held the powder charge. A wooden bung, or plug of wadding, kept the charge in place. The breechblock could be secured by bedding the gun in a solid block of wood, where the whole assembly formed a solid flatbed or sledge which would absorb much of the recoil.

Alternatively, an iron stirrup was constructed to provide a cradle for the breechblock, which was locked by a metal wedge. Guns of this type were usually mounted on a swiveling pintle set into the ship's side, which allowed them to be traversed or elevated with speed but limited their ability to absorb recoil – and therefore their size.

Hand-guns of various types were also used at sea, some of which could be hooked over a ship's rail (or the battlements of a castle) to check the recoil. Different types of ammunition were also used, including roundshot of various materials, scatter-shot made up of scrap metal, gravel, or sharp-fractured flint. Specialized projectiles such as darts, some of which were equipped with incendiary heads, were also known.

Many examples of such guns have survived, and more are now being recovered from wrecks, where the pieces are often found complete with their carriages or mountings, frequently preserving evidence of how they were worked and used.

A fine example comes from a wreck discovered during dredging operations in 1973 in the Cattewater, Plymouth's principal anchorage since at least the 13th century. Careful excavation over the next five years revealed the remains of a carvel-built ship estimated to have been of around 300 tons, and dating from the

Mary Rose at the moment of disaster, an imaginative reconstruction. The ship has passed through the critical point of no return, with water pouring in through her open lower gunports (2) to pull the hull even further over. A corresponding movement of loose deadweight across the steeply angled decks – including her guns and some 50 tons of doomed humanity – makes the outcome inevitable. The boarding nets (1) made escape impossible for the majority.

early 16th century. She was probably a merchantman rather than a warship, but among the finds were three guns of the bedded wrought-iron variety. The best-preserved of them, still loaded and ready for action, is of 5.5cm bore. Its bed of oak is carefully trenched to accommodate the ringed barrel, fixed to it with three iron straps, and the step at the rear of the tapered breechblock is reinforced with iron where recoil stresses were strongest.

A curved iron wedge-key locked the assembly firmly together. Such a piece could be made by a competent village blacksmith, with some help from a good carpenter, and would be cheap to produce; nevertheless it was a workmanlike and (by the standards of its day) useful weapon.

A breech-loading swivel gun recovered from the Spanish Armada wreck *La Trinidad Valencera*, although comparatively late in the history of its type, shows the distinctive characteristics of its kind and allows us to reconstruct in some detail the way in which it was operated. The gun itself, like the ship, is of Venetian origin. Apart from its barrel, which is of cast bronze, the piece is in all respects similar to swivel guns extending back some 200 years, a demonstration of the underlying success of the design. The gun was found loaded with a stone shot in the breech, and a twist of hemp jammed into the touch-hole to keep the priming dry.*

The full firing sequence can be deduced from information derived from this gun's remains, and from a study of wear marks on its various parts. Three men were probably involved. The gun captain stood at the rear, holding the aiming shaft or tiller at arm's length, and aiming along the barrel through a slot cut in the gun's flared wedge. No doubt the wedge helped to shield the gunner's eyes from the flying fragments which such guns tended to throw back on firing. The gunner must have had at least one assistant, probably standing to the right-hand side of the gun, to apply a burning linstock to the touch-hole at the word of command. If a third man was present to sponge out and reload the spare breechblock, the gun crew would have been able to maintain a fairly high rate of fire – two or perhaps even three shots a minute.

Such then were the guns that dominated the first two centuries of the use of cannon at sea, and which continued well into the next two. They are essentially anti-personnel pieces, and in this role evidently enjoyed considerable success, complementing and ultimately supplanting more conventional missile weapons such as the longbow. But they could not seriously damage ships.

For this, big muzzle-loaders were required. Large guns were coming into use by the last quarter of the 14th century, but these were of the cumbersome bombard type, massive tubes of wrought-iron (and later of cast bronze) which required bedding in special emplacements for bat-

tery work against fortifications. A gun of this type, cast in 1464 for Mahomet II, Sultan of Turkey, can be seen in the Tower of London; with an assembled weight of nearly 17 tons, it threw a projectile weighing almost 700 pounds.

Such guns could clearly not be used aboard ship, but the ability to produce big bronze castings, which became widespread after about 1450, led to the development of similarly effective heavy naval ordnance. By the end of the century, guns of the sort that would dominate sea warfare for the next 300 years were beginning to emerge.

The weapons of the *Mary Rose*

Ten such guns have been recovered from the *Mary Rose*; four by the Deane brothers a century and a half ago, and the remaining six during the recent excavations. They range from a 3-ton Cannon Royal capable of throwing an iron ball of some 65 pounds weight, to a 9-pounder "bastard" (i.e. non-standard piece).

Two were undated, and the remainder carried dates between 1535 and 1542;

The *Mary Rose*'s **watch bell**, cast in 1510, the year the ship was completed.

they had been cast by men like Francisco Arcanus, an Italian who had entered Henry VIII's service as a military engineer in 1522; Peter Baude, a Frenchman, who was casting guns at Houndsditch in 1529; and the English brothers John and Robert Owen. Henry had started his reign by purchasing foreign ordnance; then he brought the experts across to England; and finally he established a strong domestic industry. England, cut off from and threatened by the powerful Catholic states through Henry's break with Rome, could now defend herself with "cannon enough to conquer hell."

The *Mary Rose*'s bronze guns were mounted on compact four-wheeled truck carriages, each tailor-made for its particular piece and carefully adjusted to fit its ordained location within the ship. Such carriages, of which the *Mary Rose*

examples are the earliest known, are extremely efficient for use at sea: their design allows the gun muzzle to project well out of the port, while the rear part of the carriage scarcely extends beyond the breech. Sufficient room is therefore available, even within the cramped confines of a gundeck, to allow the gun to be worked and to be hauled inboard for reloading.

The *Mary Rose* also boasted a large complement of the more traditional wrought-iron, breech-loading guns, mounted on flatbed carriages, all of which were equipped with wheels. In addition, she also carried a number of hailshot pieces, three of which have been recovered. However, her main close-quarter weapon was still the traditional yew longbow: 138 of these were recovered from the wreck, together with more than 2,000 arrows.

One ammunition chest, found intact, contained no fewer than 52 bundles of arrows, each bundle containing 24 arrows. Also found were several round leather spacers, pierced to hold 24 arrows in a way that ensured that their feathered flights would not be damaged, and enabling the archers to achieve a rapid-fire rate of up to 12 shots per minute.

A broad outline of the ways in which the *Mary Rose* could fight is now becoming clear. Several stratagems might be employed, singly or in combination.

First, she could fight a stand-off action, bombarding her opponent with heavy broadside artillery. To this, if the range was sufficiently close, a blanket fire of arrows could be added, and at these closer ranges the smaller iron breech-loaders, with their relatively quick rate of fire, could be brought in to add to the confusion. Finally an enemy, softened up by the application of missile weapons, could be boarded and carried by storm. The ship's own defenses included removable wooden blinds, ranged along the waist deck, above which anti-boarder netting was stretched.

For all this weaponry, the fleet action with the French in which the *Mary Rose* foundered was inconclusive, as indeed were most major naval actions involving big sailing ships and heavy artillery until almost the end of the 16th century. Perhaps too little was understood of the complexities involved, for certainly the awesome potential of the new combination of guns and sails was barely touched at this stage.

The Spanish Armada

Twenty years before the 1588 Armada, a glimpse of the future came when an English merchant (the Spaniards would have called him a pirate) used artillery to blast his way clear of a much stronger Spanish fleet at the Mexican port of San Juan de Ulua. His escape was probably due to a combination of good seamanship, desperation and a strong element of luck, but the experience gained was not

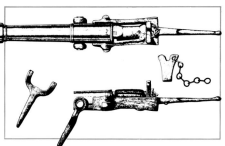

Breech-loading swivel gun (left), with bronze barrel and wrought-iron fittings, from the Armada wreck *La Trinidad Valencera*. Such close-quarter weapons were among the first seaborne firearms, surviving into the 18th century.

Personal possessions (below left) recovered from the *Mary Rose* include a pouch, a comb, a seal, a pocket sundial and a rosary.

A spoked wheel (above) from the mounting of a wrought-iron breechloading piece, being examined by an archaeologist from the Mary Rose Trust.

A bronze "bastard" (below) from the *Mary Rose*, inscribed as cast by the Owen brothers. The compact 4-wheeled truck carriage allowed most of the chase to protrude through the ship's side, providing

plenty of working space inboard. The Latin commemorates Henry VIII as King of England and France, Lord of Ireland, and supreme Head of the Church of England (drawing after Debby Fulford).

ROBERT·AND·IOHN·OWYN·BRETHERYN·BORNE
IN·THE·CYTE·OF·LONDON·THE·SONNES·OF·AN
INGLISH·MADE·THYS·BASTARD·ANNO·DNI·1537

HENRYCVS·OCTAV̅·DE I·
GRACIA·ANGLIE·ET·FRAN
CIE·REX·FIDE·DEFENSOR
·DNS·HIBERNIE·ET·IN·TER
RA·SVPREM̅·CAFVT·EC
CLESIE·ANGLICANE

forgotten. That merchant was John Hawkins, and when the Spanish Armada entered the English Channel, the lessons learned at San Juan proved to be England's salvation.

The two maritime powers which faced each other in 1588 viewed naval warfare in a very different light. Up until then, Spain had been the dominant nation at sea. Her traditions were rooted in the Mediterranean, where for more than 2,000 years the war galley had been a primary tool of naval strength.

Organized in fleets, and operating from secure bases, the Mediterranean galleys had become pawns on a great chessboard of balanced power. The bases rather than the fleets were the centers of that power, and major shifts occurred only on those rare occasions when bases changed hands. Serious warfare almost always revolved around attempted capture and defense of coastal installations.

The nature of the warfare was therefore essentially amphibious: galleys contested for localized maritime supremacy so that invasion armies could be landed and shore troops provided with close support. Like modern fighter aircraft, galleys were highly offensive weapons whose primary role was defense.

Galleys traditionally defeated their enemies by a combination of shock (by ramming) and assault (by physical boarding). The introduction of the gun around the end of the 14th century did not change the basic tactics. Forward-firing guns now provided an additional element of shock by discharging a single salvo just before the moment of contact.

The discovery of America shifted Spain's naval activity to the Atlantic. She adapted her concepts of sea warfare accordingly, but retained the same underlying philosophy: wars were won not at sea but by assaulting and capturing enemy bases. This view appeared triumphantly vindicated in 1583, when an amphibious task force landed at Terceira in the Azores, so completing Spain's annexation of Portugal.

What had been achieved at Terceira might therefore be attempted, on a much larger scale, against Spain's northern enemy England. In March 1586, detailed plans drawn up by the Marquis of Santa Cruz, commander of the successful Azores operation, were submitted to King Philip II for approval. An immense task force should sail direct from Lisbon to the Thames estuary, where it would secure a beach head at Margate and land an army strong enough to force its way through Kent and capture London. Ships would carry everything the army needed, from siege guns to spare shoes. Elements of the fleet would also provide the right flank of the army with close support as it moved up the Thames towards London.

Strict formation discipline, a mobile striking force, and the manpower of the invasion troops themselves would defend the Armada while it was at sea. Captains would be told that breaking station was a hanging offense, although a number of heavily armed fighting ships, dispersed among the fleet, would have authority to move at will against any threat without damaging the Armada's overall cohesion; and every ship, large and small, would carry a contingent of soldiers. Thus any attempt to board a Spanish ship would almost inevitably be repulsed, since the English ships had virtually no troops.

Santa Cruz calculated that 150 large ships and 400 support vessels would be needed to mount the operation, involving 95,000 men, of whom 55,000 would be front-line invasion troops. With six months' provisioning and an immense amount of equipment, he estimated the cost would be 4 million ducats.

This was too much for Philip's hard-pressed exchequer. He chose a cheaper alternative, whereby a much smaller Armada would sail from Lisbon, making its way up the Channel in the defensive formation already proposed. There it would rendezvous with a Spanish army already in the Netherlands under the Duke of Parma. The main invasion force would be provided by the latter, who would make the crossing in small craft escorted by the Armada. Once the beach head was secure, the fleet would off-load provisions, guns and men, and the operation would proceed as originally planned.

From the first, Spain's hardbitten naval and military commanders voiced their gravest doubts about this proposal. The plan was too complicated, too many things could go wrong, and the crucial rendezvous would be vulnerable to rebel Dutch attacks with their shallow-draft, heavily-armed flyboats. But the King's will prevailed, and a plan that might have succeeded was replaced by one bound almost inevitably to fail.

In the event, its failure was spectacular. Parma's force never set sail because the Armada, although it successfully penetrated the English Channel despite repeated English assaults upon it, was dispersed by fireships off Calais. This, coupled with an aggressive squadron of Dutch ships off Flanders, precluded all hopes of a rendezvous. After suffering a final trouncing from the English fleet's artillery off Gravelines the Armada, battered but still substantially intact (one captain was hanged to re-establish formation discipline), had no option but to return to Spain via the hazardous "north-about" route around the British Isles. Off the wild Atlantic coasts of Scotland and Ireland many of the returning ships, weakened by battle damage and manned by sick and starving crews, were lost in the unusually severe storms of that autumn.

The Armada wrecks
Several of the wrecks have now been found, and their excavation, coupled with a new examination of the voluminous documentary material which still survives in Spain, has allowed us to study the campaign afresh. Through the remains of the ships, their weaponry, and the equipment and possessions of the men aboard them, we can glimpse a style of naval warfare which, after the Armada, would vanish for ever. We can also see why, ultimately, it failed.

"The aim of our men," Philip II had instructed his fleet before it sailed, "must be to bring the enemy to close quarters and grapple with him."

To that end, the ships were provided with weapons for close-quarters fighting. In 1971 amateur divers from Northern Ireland discovered the wreck of one of the Armada's biggest fighting ships, La Trinidad Valencera, in Kinnagoe Bay, Donegal. Excavations have yielded a sample of weaponry which makes it clear how Philip intended his plans to operate.

The ship's guns were not designed to provide a continuous cannonade, trading shot for shot with an enemy in a drawn-out artillery duel; rather, they were expected only to provide a single close-range salvo just before clapping sides. Their carriages, unlike the compact truck mountings introduced into the English fleet more than a generation earlier, were cumbersome two-wheeled affairs with long trails extending inboard. Reloading was therefore difficult and extremely slow.

Spanish tactics did not foresee the need

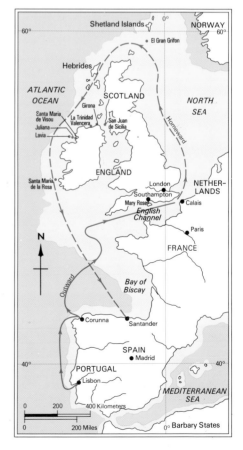

for rapid reloading of artillery during a general engagement. Loading of the large pieces, as opposed to the swivel gun previously referred to, was carried out unhurriedly before battle was joined by teams of soldiers, who then took up their boarding stations armed with musket, pike and sword. Each gun was left in charge of a single captain, whose sole task was to touch the priming with a lighted linstock on the word of command. There would be no need (thought the Spaniards) for a second discharge, for by then the enemy would be in their hands.

A variety of specialized weapons was provided for the boarding assault. The *Trinidad Valencera* has yielded a *bomba*, a ferocious incendiary device emitting fire and shrapnel, mounted on a long pole; and ceramic fire grenades containing a lethal mixture of gunpowder, spirits and resin – precursors of the modern napalm bomb. The bow had by now been wholly supplanted as a missile weapon by the musket and the lighter arquebus. Several hundred of these were sported by the larger ships, and were capable of producing sustained short-range fire.

But the tactic behind these weapons involved one fatal assumption – that the enemy could be forced, or induced, to come close. The English intended to do no such thing. During the course of the previous 30 years they had developed a new class of warship – the race-decked

galleon. Soldiers were dispensed with, and with them went the towering castle-works at bow and stern which caught the wind and made the ships slow and difficult to handle. Sail plans and under-water lines were refined to improve performance still further.

Unencumbered by the weight of soldiers, their equipment, and provisioning for long voyages, these ships would also carry an extremely heavy complement of guns. Mounted on their efficient truck carriages these guns could be reloaded as often as necessary during an action by their nimble and well-trained crews of seamen. The English ship was no longer a vehicle to bring soldiers to battle. It had become an integrated weapons system which could combine its superiority in mobility and firepower.

This revolutionary development was still in its infancy when the Armada came. On its own it might have failed to save England, had the Spanish plan – through Philip II's interference – not been so ill-conceived. But the new tactics, born of desperate expediency under the extreme threat of invasion, had come to stay. During the following two centuries they would develop to a level of sophistication unimagined by those who created them. The armed sailing ship had become a weapon of war in its own right, and this would give the northern European nations the key to their great global empires.

A ceramic firepot from *La Trinidad Valencera* indicates the close-quarter fighting methods favored by the Spaniards at the time of the Armada. Fitted with fuses and thrown by hand, such devices contained a mixture of gunpowder, spirits and resin which, on impact, would ignite, scatter and stick like napalm.

A 1586 drawing of an English galleon (below), emphasizes the ideal "cod's head, mackerel's tail" underwater design which, with reduced top-hamper, gave the English the maneuverable gun platforms needed for their new artillery tactics.

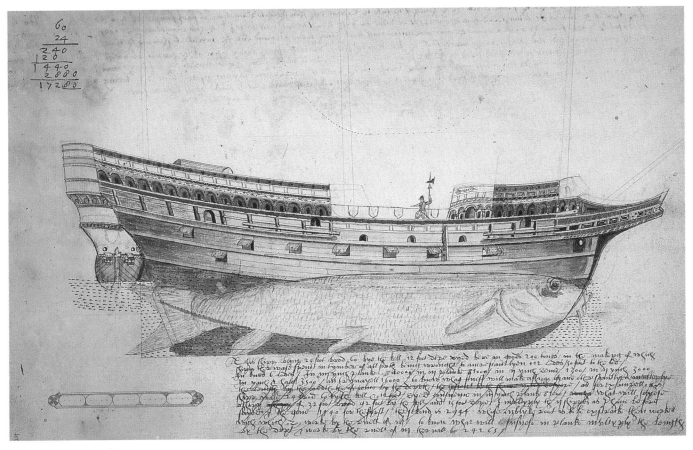

Ships of the line

The failure of the Spanish Armada demonstrated that merchant ships could no longer be successfully adapted as ships of war. They were too clumsy, and had not been designed for artillery warfare. Early in the 17th century, a new type of warship emerged in northern Europe, combining firepower, sailing performance and professional seamanship. Archaeology has done much to recreate these ships of the line and the lives of the men who served in them.

The requisitioned merchant ships which made up the bulk of the Armada were designed not for maneuverability and performance, but for the economic transport of heavy cargoes. When the function of ships had been to bring armies together for a seaborne melee, both sides coming to grips with each other hand to hand, such vessels had been ideal. The introduction of effective naval gunnery put an end to all that.

Armed merchantmen
Merchant ships could not be converted into effective gun platforms, even if troops were dispensed with. A wrecksite that we examined during the 1970s, in conjunction with members of the City of Derry Sub-Aqua Club, shows why this was so.

The wreck was that of the 1,100-ton Venetian greatship *La Trinidad Valencera*, the fifth largest and one of the most heavily armed ships of the Spanish Armada. She had been a grain transporter, whose normal run was the short haul between her home port and the grain-producing island of Sicily. Purpose-built for this highly specialized activity, the vessel's vast and capacious hull was designed to balance the conflicting pressures of water from without and the thrust of her cargo from within.

An archaeological analysis of her disjointed remains, coupled with historical research in the Venetian archives, has shown how this balance was achieved. These ships were mass-produced to standardized techniques; planks and frames were fastened together with rows of regularly placed iron bolts to give a tight, strong hull capable of standing up to heavy use. But the working life of such a vessel, though intense, was short; when the iron fastenings began to corrode, the hull would be a write-off. This was what the Venetians intended: cheap, low-maintenance ships which would give trouble-free service for a limited period – 10 years was the normal life expectancy.

The strength of these hulls was based on an elegant balance of forces: their shape enabled them to resist strong internal and external pressures but, lacking localized strength, they were prone to collapse if cracked. Their component parts were relatively slight, and the regular rows of fastenings set up serious lines of weakness along the grain of the planks.

La Trinidad Valencera's hull was at its strongest when it was filled with a cargo that exerted pressure equally in all directions. It was not well suited to the cargo of military stores, dismantled siege artillery and troops which the Spaniards had crammed into it. Still less was it designed to stand up to warfare involving the sustained use of heavy artillery.

Poorly adapted to take the punishment plentifully meted out by English gunfire, the method of construction also made her vulnerable to damage induced by her own artillery. With the guns lashed fast to the ship's side, the full stresses of recoil would have been transmitted into key structural components, particularly the knees which linked the frames to the deck beams. Such stresses could actually pull a ship apart.*

Not all the Spanish force's merchant ships would have been so vulnerable. The remains of the Guipuzcoan vice-flagship *Santa Maria de la Rosa* were discovered off southwest Ireland in 1968 by Sidney Wignall's expedition (on which incidentally I cut my own archaeological diving teeth). This was also a merchantman, but a much stronger ship than *La Trinidad Valencera*. She had been built at the north Spanish port of San Sebastian a year before the Armada sailed, and was pressed into service with the fleet the moment she was launched.

The *Santa Maria* was stoutly built for general cargo work in Atlantic waters, possibly even for the whaling run across to Newfoundland. Her structural remains certainly show close similarities with those of the better preserved wreck of the *San Juan*, the mid 16th century whaling mother-ship excavated at Red Bay, Labrador (see p. 173). Most of the *Santa Maria*'s lower forward hull survived intact beneath its mound of stone ballast, and the solidity of the construction is obvious.*

The mainmast had been ripped out during the wrecking process, breaking the ship in two. The shattered remains of the mast assembly have been closely examined, and show evidence of makeshift repair. This tallies with the fact, recorded by the Armada commander, that the *Santa Maria* had been damaged by storm during the voyage, and a new mainmast had been fitted at La Coruña.

Hardy – though evidently not invulnerable – as they were, these Basque-built Atlantic merchantmen were not ideal as fighting artillery platforms, for they were not designed for such a purpose. They were far too clumsy, and their capacity for mounting heavy guns – let alone their ability to use them – was restricted.

Vasa – a warship resurrected
Such ships were no match for the specialized sailing warships which were being built in northwest Europe during the late 16th century, notably by the English and the Dutch. So successful was the design of these ships that few were wrecked (unfortunately for maritime archaeologists!). However, early in the 17th century a catastrophe occurred that saved a single superb example almost intact.

On August 10 1628, the newly built 1,300-ton warship *Vasa*, pride of the Swedish King Gustav Adolphus's new navy, left the Royal Palace Arsenal in Stockholm harbor, where she had taken on ballast and armament for her maiden voyage. With all flags flying, gunports open, and the crew responding to cheers from the shore, the *Vasa* sailed majestically towards the sea. Suddenly she was caught in a squall, and began to heel over to port. An attempt was made to haul the portside ordnance to windward, but it was too late: the lower gunports tipped below water, and within minutes the ship had sunk. She had sailed less than half a mile.

In the ensuing enquiry, no one was blamed. After all, her builder had died shortly before, and the king himself had approved the ship's plans. Possibly the *Vasa* had been insufficiently ballasted or perhaps she was plain unlucky. Perfectly seaworthy ships could overset if caught by the wrong combination of forces.

Several unsuccessful attempts were made to raise the *Vasa* shortly after she sank, and in the 1660s most of her guns were recovered with the aid of a diving

A Mediterranean "greatship" of 1555 from a merchant's tomb in Padua, similar to the Armada's *La Trinidad Valencera* (see opposite). Mass-produced, mainly for the grain trade, such ships proved ill-suited to endure the recoil of heavy artillery.

An elaborate carving from the *Vasa* (above), one of many to have been recovered from the soft protective mud of Stockholm harbor, provides an impressive insight into 17th century ship embellishment. A view of the restored hull of the *Vasa* (right) emphasizes the flush top deck of a race-built galleon, its sheer rising steeply towards the stern. Two tiers of gunports can be seen, each with a hinged lid which, when opened, presents the face of a roaring lion.

Hull timbers (above) of the 1100-ton Venetian grain ship *La Trinidad Valencera,* pressed into service in the Armada and lost off the Irish coast. The hull has disintegrated completely, following the corrosion of the thousands of iron bolts that held it together.

A view of *Vasa*'s gundeck (right) looking aft. All the available space is utilized for the operation of truck-mounted guns; success in battle depended on the speed and skill with which they could be run out, fired and reloaded. The sailors lived, ate and slept beside their guns.

bell. There the matter rested till 1954, when the Swedish amateur historian and archaeologist Anders Franzen, who knew that the low salinity of the Baltic provided ideal conditions for ship preservation, began a systematic search for the *Vasa*.

Franzen proceeded to analyze contemporary accounts of the sinking, to look for seabed obstructions in the selected search area, and to test anomalies with an ingenious device he had developed.* In the summer of 1956, in the heart of Stockholm's dock area, he found a major obstruction that yielded samples of black oak wherever he dropped his device. An investigation was mounted by the navy, whose divers discovered the *Vasa*, upright and virtually intact in a bed of stiff clay, at a depth of 100ft (33m).

A huge recovery operation followed. Six tunnels were driven beneath the hull, through which steel wires were passed to form a lifting cradle. At the same time as this, many thousands of objects were recovered from inside and around the wreck, including the elaborate carvings that had decorated the ship, particularly at the stern. These had fallen into soft mud, to be preserved in pristine condition.

At length the ship was lifted from the seabed, though she was not yet ready to surface, and gently brought into shallower waters. There, divers worked for months to seal up the gunports, repair the damaged stern, and strengthen the weakened structure with steel bolts.

Finally, on April 24 1961, *Vasa* broke surface, and by May 4 was actually afloat. Her brief and long delayed voyage ended when she entered dry dock, less than half a mile from where she had been built 333 years earlier.

Ships of the line

Many years of work lay ahead. For the first five months, archaeologists worked through the mud-sodden shambles of the ship's interior, cleaning, recovering, recording and preserving all the evidence it contained. Divers continued to excavate the seabed where the wreck had lain, finding and recording further disjoined elements of the ship. By the early 1980s, the work of conservation and restoration was complete. *Vasa* now stands in her specially constructed hall, a supreme example of an early ship of the line.

For it was in line of battle that the *Vasa* was expected to fight. Everything about the ship was designed to a single end – the ability to bring maximum firepower to bear on the enemy.*

The twenty-four 24-pounders that made up the main battery on both decks had a length some 18 times the diameter of the bore. Experience had shown that this was best for use at sea. Attempts to use much longer pieces, which were thought (erroneously) to possess greater range and accuracy, had created much trouble in the 16th century.

The Armada battle had shown that shipboard guns were in any case only effective at very short ranges, and the best tactic was to come as close to the enemy as possible and pound him with broadsides. This doctrine was still valid until the end of the sailing warship era. In his instructions to the Fleet on the eve of Trafalgar, Nelson was to write: "No Captain can do very wrong, if he places his Ship alongside that of an Enemy."

Equally important to the number of guns was the speed at which they could be worked: a ship firing twice as quickly as its adversary would effectively possess double its firepower. And this too could be further enhanced if skilful maneuvering was used to allow each of the two broadsides to be presented in turn. It all hinged on weatherly ships, good seamanship, and efficient working of the guns.

In the 16th century there had been almost no standardization of types and bores. Loading techniques, too, were in their infancy. After firing, guns were either hauled back manually, or loaded by the terrifying expedient of clambering through the port to straddle the gun and charge it from this precarious position.

All this changed during the course of the 17th century, as standardized guns, highly trained crews, improved sailing performance and ship handling techniques were introduced. Most of these developments were already underway by 1625.

The new era also saw fundamental changes in the way warships were manned. Standing navies needed professional crews, and a fulltime career in the service of the state was now open to officers and seamen.* A warship's complement was determined by the number of men needed to work her guns and sails, which meant that except in time of battle she was grossly overmanned.

The *Dartmouth*

Through archaeology we can attain glimpses, frozen in time, of the closed wooden world in which such men lived. A good example is the wreck of the *Dartmouth*, a fifth-rate frigate built in 1655 and lost off Scotland in 1690. Following its discovery in 1973, an intensive excavation was mounted under my direction, yielding much information about the ship herself and the people on board.

Many details of the ship's construction did not tally with procedures laid down in contemporary manuals of shipwrightry. Such manuals were generally written by theorists, while shipwrights were above all else practical men. Not many of them could write, a fact that apparently did not limit their capacity to build large and complex warships. Ten generations of practicing shipwrights might lie behind the builders of such vessels, as attested by the contemporary diarist John Evelyn.* How they were built is therefore not to be found in books, but only through a study of their remains.

From artifacts distributed over the wrecksite, we deduced that the captain and his officers lived in the after part, where their higher social status was reflected in the quality of their domestic utensils and personal possessions: fine tableware, bottles of French wine, an elegant ivory snuff bottle.

In the forward area we found the ship's armory and the contents of the bosun's locker, including materials for emergency repair work. Here were no high quality plates, no bottles of wine: the crew ate from wooden platters with wooden spoons, washing down their rations with beer or cider (an empty earthenware jar from Devon hints at the latter).

The ship's galley, identified from a collapsed mass of bricks and tiles, was located in the upper part of the forecastle immediately below the belfry. The great bronze watch bell, which regulated the life of the ship, had fallen among the galley debris. The galley region also yielded a large collection of clay pipes, confirming that the Admiralty order restricting smoking to this area – where fire

precautions were strongest – was adhered to in practice. Pipes of a higher quality in the stern area show that this restriction did not apply to officers.

The *Dartmouth*'s history is known in detail, but some idea of where she had voyaged could have been deduced from the pottery she carried. Wares from Holland and England predominate, but there are also pieces from the Mediterranean, while sherds of Spanish olive jars no doubt relate to her spell of service in the Caribbean.

The first genuine written description of life on board a warship, as seen from the lower deck, does not occur until the early 19th century. However, life on the *Dartmouth* was probably similar in many respects. The description by William Robinson, an ordinary seaman who wrote under the splendid pseudonym of Jack Nastyface, makes fascinating reading.* The task of marine archaeologists is to attempt to produce an equally vivid human picture from the mute evidence of the shipwrecks they excavate.

A new *Vasa*? The warship *Kronan*, lost with 800 men in 1676 off the island of Öland, Sweden, remained undisturbed until Kalmar Museum's 1981 investigation. One of *Kronan*'s 126 bronze cannon, lying behind a skull (above) summarizes the power and tragedy of the find. Like other Baltic wrecks, the absence of marine worms has insured preservation of the woodwork, such as the grinning head (below), an external sculpture, and a cherub, seen in its original position (above right) and after conservation treatment (below right). Nearly 10,000 objects have been brought up from a depth of 85ft (26m), including cannon, clothing, gold coins, sculptures, bottles, plates and ceramics.

A wooden patch (above), inserted in *Dartmouth*'s hull to stop a crack from developing, provides an example of the way archaeology can show ships as they were, not as theorists thought they should be. Much of the technical detail was left to skilled but illiterate shipwrights, who applied ingenious and often unconventional solutions to problems of ship construction and repair that would otherwise not be known. A 1687 guinea and an onion-shaped wine bottle from the *Dartmouth* (opposite) show how shipwrecks can present a unique and varied cross-section of contemporary shipboard life, as well as providing a precise dating context.

In the Indian Ocean, the aqualung revolution came later and made less impact than in the Mediterranean or the Caribbean. It was not until the 1970s that important new maritime archaeological developments took place. Since then, detailed excavations have been carried out in Kenya, South Africa, Indonesia, China, Thailand and Australia, involving both local and European vessels.* This work has brought to light new and unforeseen patterns of ancient trade, and has revealed vital links in our knowledge of ship construction.

As we have seen, the exploration of the underwater world took on a new dimension with the development of modern aqualung equipment at the end of World War II. The aqualung enabled archaeologists to excavate wrecks scientifically, thus revealing facets of past lifestyles that had hitherto been entombed at the bottom of the sea.

At the same time, the invention of the aqualung also opened up possibilities for the sports diver, treasure hunter and salvage diver to explore and simply loot wrecksites. In the Mediterranean, the eastern seaboard of the North Atlantic and, especially, the Caribbean, many irreplaceable time capsules from the past have been – and continue to be – wantonly destroyed in excavations based purely on profit motives rather than archaeology.

Some legislation to protect the future of wrecksites has been initiated, but it is well known through existing archival evidence that the Indian Ocean conceals on its unexplored seabed large quantities of ancient and invaluable cargo. Such wealth constantly lures treasure hunters to move into the area.

Trade in the Indian Ocean

Traditionally the dhow, originating in Arabia and the regions adjacent to the Arabian Sea, is the vessel most widely identified with the Indian Ocean. Its presence there has been recorded since the 6th century AD. From the Tang dynasty (618–907), trading posts at Guangzhou (known to Europeans as Canton, to Arabs as Khanfu) bear witness to the extent of Persian and Arab trade. The Huaisheng Mosque in Guangzhou was built in AD672, according to legend, by an uncle of Mohammed.

Dhows brought across the Indian Ocean to East Africa a great variety of luxury items, including gold and silver jewelry, silk clothes, damasks, satin, copper objects, carpets, pearls, perfumes, glass beads, Chinese porcelain and glass vessels. These emanated from rich entrepôt towns in Southeast Asia, India and the Persian Gulf. Dhows also carried food and spices – wheat from Cambay (modern Khambhat in Gujarat, India) and cloves, nutmeg, mace and cinnamon from India and Malacca.

In 879, a massacre of foreign merchants in Guangzhou brought to a sudden end this flourishing sea trade with China. The Arabic merchantmen largely ceased to sail the China route, though some Arab vessels still continued to call at Khanfu for porcelain and silk, both of which were sought after throughout the Caliphate.

The maritime ventures of the Chinese

In the opposite direction, Tang dynasty annals of the period describe how Chinese vessels from Guangzhou were sailing to the Euphrates. It also appears that Chinese ships in equally early times voyaged as far as Aden. These voyages reached their zenith during the Ming period (1368–1644), in particular with the seven voyages of the Imperial Palace Eunuch of the Triple Jewel, Zheng He. These voyages, begun in 1405 and ended in 1433, may have been diplomatic in intention. They certainly were not exploratory, since the Chinese had already been frequenting these waters for hundreds of years.

The last voyage marked the ascendancy of the Confucian anti-maritime court faction, whose activities led, by the end of the 15th century, to the destruction of all records of these voyages. By 1500, it became a capital offence to build seagoing junks with more than two masts, and there was even a pronouncement made forbidding the Chinese to trade overseas. This policy has become known as the Ming Ban.

Europeans in the Indian Ocean

The change in Chinese policy, coupled with the entry of the European nations into the maritime theater at the beginning of the 16th century, created a fundamental shift in Asiatic trading patterns and shipbuilding techniques. The Portuguese and later the Netherlanders and the English rapidly filled the gap caused by the Ming Ban.

The first European voyage to the East was made by the Portuguese explorer, Vasco da Gama. He reached the port of Calicut (Kozhikode) on the west coast of India, via the Cape of Good Hope in 1498. The new maritime route meant that the Portuguese were able to control the East Indian spice trade, resulting in the decline of the camel caravans that had traditionally followed the great spice and silk over-

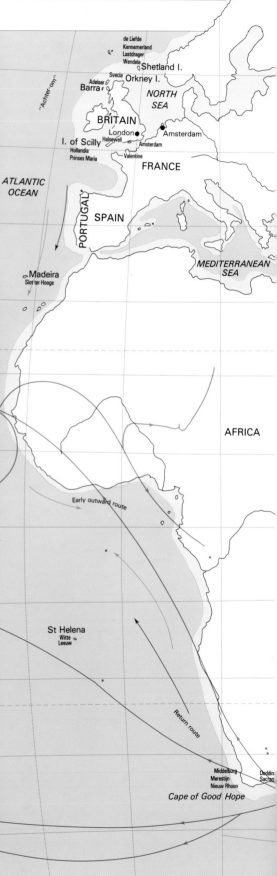

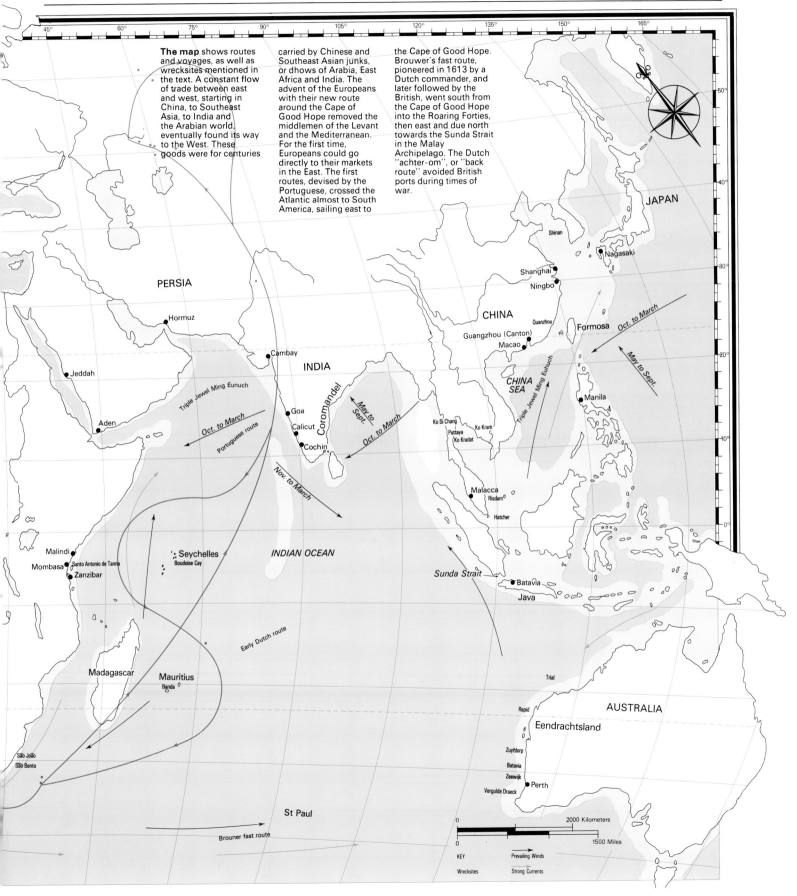

The map shows routes and voyages, as well as wrecksites mentioned in the text. A constant flow of trade between east and west, starting in China, to Southeast Asia, to India and the Arabian world, eventually found its way to the West. These goods were for centuries carried by Chinese and Southeast Asian junks, or dhows of Arabia, East Africa and India. The advent of the Europeans with their new route around the Cape of Good Hope removed the middlemen of the Levant and the Mediterranean. For the first time, Europeans could go directly to their markets in the East. The first routes, devised by the Portuguese, crossed the Atlantic almost to South America, sailing east to the Cape of Good Hope. Brouwer's fast route, pioneered in 1613 by a Dutch commander, and later followed by the British, went south from the Cape of Good Hope into the Roaring Forties, then east and due north towards the Sunda Strait in the Malay Archipelago. The Dutch "achter-om", or "back route" avoided British ports during times of war.

JAPAN

Shinan

Nagasaki

Shanghai

Ningbo

PERSIA

CHINA

Hormuz

Quanzhou

Formosa

Oct. to March

Guangzhou (Canton)

Macao

May to Sept.

Cambay

INDIA

Jeddah

Goa

CHINA SEA

Calicut

Coromandel

Cochin

May to Sept.

Manila

Aden

Triple Jewel Ming Eunuch

Oct. to March

Oct. to March

Triple Jewel Ming Eunuch

Portuguese route

Ko Si Chang

Ko Kram

Pattaya

Nov. to March

Ko Kradat

Malindi

INDIAN OCEAN

Seychelles

Mombasa

Santo Antonio de Tanna

Boudoise Cay

Malacca

Risdam

Zanzibar

Hatcher

Sunda Strait

Batavia

Java

Early Dutch route

Madagascar

Mauritius

Trial

Banda

AUSTRALIA

Rapid

Eendrachtsland

Zuytdorp

Batavia

São João

Zeewijk

São Bento

Vergulde Draeck

Perth

St Paul

Brouner fast route

0   2000 Kilometers

0   1500 Miles

KEY   Prevailing Winds

Wrecksites   Strong Currents

153

land route. Sailing ships proved faster, more reliable and cheaper, and enabled the end users to deal directly with the producers, and in so doing they cut out middle men.

This trade was reasonably stable for about 100 years, until 1581 when Spain annexed Portugal and soon embroiled her in Spain's wars with Protestant countries in Europe. This made it difficult for some European countries to obtain spices, and so at the beginning of the 17th century, the English and Dutch decided to start up trade independently with the East, forming the English East India Company (EEIC) and the Dutch East India Company (Veeringde Oost-Indische Company, VOC) respectively.

The Dutch rapidly became extremely powerful in the whole region and dominated the trade, the EEIC and other smaller European nations playing a minor role. Both the VOC and the EEIC were involved purely in trade and made no attempt to colonise or proselytize. The two companies eventually became bankrupt towards the end of the 18th century; they were taken over by their respective countries and incorporated into their colonial empires. The Portuguese and

Spanish, having lost their monopoly, were confined to minor local centers. Their approach was different in that they attempted to convert as well as trade, and in most cases this led to expulsion and persecution of their converts. They do still have one colony in the east – Macao – which is due to be handed back to China in 1991.

In the initial period of exploration, the English and Dutch trading ships came in a variety of types and sizes, selected for their availability rather than being purpose built. But by the early half of the 17th century, as the voyages became more routine, the Dutch East India Company standardized ships into various classes and sizes.

The trade was essentially three-fold in nature. The usual outward bound voyage would carry silver, lead and bulk goods that could be sold in the East, plus supplies for the company bases. The homeward bound trade comprised mainly spices and porcelain, and later other products such as tea and sugar. The third component was internal trade within the East Indies, with the European companies attempting to either remove or control the earlier existing trade patterns that they

had encountered on arrival in the area.

The incidence of wrecks
Maritime archaeological study of 16th century Portuguese shipwrecks in the Indian Ocean is limited to the *São Bento* and *São João*, found near Natal, and another unidentified site in the Seychelles, dated as being late 16th or early 17th century. The two sites are similar in their European ornament, but their cargo reflects the difference in destination. The Seychelles wreck was outward bound, carrying red Mediterranean coral and amber of European origin, while the *São Bento* and *São João* were homeward bound, their cargoes comprising Chinese porcelain. The Seychelles wrecksite yielded a small section of hull, which on closer examination was found to be calked in a most unusual method.*

In the 17th century, the number of sites increases, with a large number of Dutch East India Company ships being found, reflecting the amount of voyages being undertaken. Unfortunately, since many of these East Indiamen were regarded as treasure ships, excavation of these sites has more often than not been motivated by profit rather than archaeology.

Silver coins (left) were used by the Dutch to purchase trade commodities in the East Indies. Since the European nations had little of interest to the markets of the East, commodities like spices, porcelain and, later, tea, had to be bought with silver. Europe had a ready source of this metal, both within the continent and from the Spanish American mints. Chinese porcelain (above) from the VOC (Veeringde Oost-Indische Company) ship *Witte Leeuwe* (1613), is an early example of a new trade commodity brought from China for the European markets.

Arab dhows

Vessels of Arab derivation, known in the West as dhows, have been operating in the Indian Ocean from the time of Sindbad the Sailor. Some modernization has occurred in the last 40 years, but the dhow's cargoes and ports of call have remained remarkably constant. In 1980 the dhow's seaworthiness was demonstrated by Tim Severin in his skilful replication of a vessel from the time of Sindbad.

Even today, traditional and motorized dhows still navigate huge distances across the western Indian Ocean, to ports such as Zanzibar, Lamu, Aden, Muscat, Kuwait, Bandar Abbas, Karachi and Bombay. Their cargoes are as varied as ever they were. For example, from East Africa, Iranian vessels carry mangrove poles from the swamps of the Rufiji Delta of Tanzania to Kuwait, which is more than 3,500 miles (5,633km) away. Dhows from the Hadramat carry salt and dried fish to Mombasa, returning to their home ports laden with

ghee, lemon juice and various grains. From Kuwait, cars are transported across the Gulf to a number of Iranian ports, where fresh vegetables and fruit are picked up for the return trip.

Trade routes and dhows

Geography has favored the development of such Arab-borne maritime trade. Across the enclosed waters of the Red Sea and the Persian Gulf, the early Arabs could contact Egypt and Persia, two of the most ancient centers of wealth and civilization. Beyond Arabia to the southwest, it was easy to cross to East Africa and sail along the coast in search of tropical products. To the east, the coast of Persia led on to India, Indonesia and China. Most important of all, the Red Sea and the Persian Gulf were natural channels for through traffic between the Mediterranean basin and eastern Asia. Geographically, the Arabs were astride two of the world's great trade routes.

The advantages of this splendid geographical position could not be fully exploited until ships could be designed to sail close to the wind, using fore-and-aft rather than square rigging. They also needed to be constructed strongly enough

so as to endure the powerful blasts of the monsoon winds, which was extremely difficult to achieve in the absence of iron ore for nails or in the absence of suitable indigenous timber.

The earliest reference to these boats is found in Procopius's *Persian Wars,* written in the 6th century AD. According to this author, ships undertook direct ocean voyages to India from Arabia, using the southwest monsoon on the outward voyage from July to October and the northeast for the return trip from November to March. However, the 6th century *Periplus* points out that the southwest monsoon voyage (from June to October) is dangerous, as modern sailors of the Indian Ocean know well, for the wind is generally boisterous and the sea rough. Arab vessels today, and almost certainly in medieval times, tend to set sail from Arabia in winter, and after going along in the lee of the Hadramat coast, to fall away before the northeast monsoon, from a point sufficiently north and east. Modern dhows bound for East Africa from Arabia run south with this northeast wind, and leave for home just ahead of the southeast monsoon.

During the 9th and 10th centuries, the

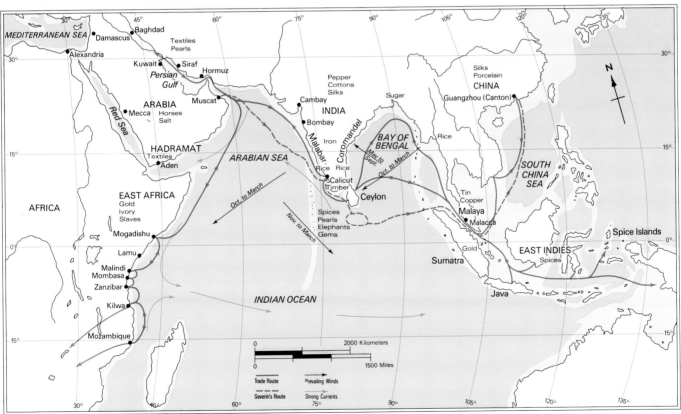

The monsoons, seasonal patterns of winds in the Indian Ocean, were exploited by Arab seafarers for centuries before the arrival of the Europeans. Thus, dhows sailed down the East African coast on the NE monsoon in December and January, and returned with the SW monsoon in April and May. In their medieval heyday, they criss-crossed the Indian Ocean, carrying spices, sugar, rice, aromatic woods, timber for ships, gems, gold, ivory, copper, tin, porcelain, silk, horses and even elephants.

Persian port of Siraf, now known as Tahira, was recognized as the center for fitting out trading vessels bound for India, China and East Africa. Many popular tales and scientific descriptions stemmed from this seafaring capital.

It is thought that the design of the dhow was modified soon after the first Europeans arrived in the Arabian Sea in 1498. The European claim that the influence of western shipwrights led to the use of nails in the construction of previously sewn dhows has been disputed. Written Portuguese descriptions, which date back to 1509, mention the use of nails only 11 years after the arrival of the Portuguese. This technique could have come from the Chinese junks which had been in contact with the Arab world for hundreds of years.

However, it is possible that the Europeans did influence the overall design of dhows, and a square-sterned shape gradually replaced the traditional sharp, two-ended model that had previously been characteristic of shipping in the Persian Gulf and the Indian subcontinent. The new shape gradually became popular for humble dinghies, as well as for the great cargo ships.

In more recent historical times, the principal ocean-going kinds of dhow have been the *baghla* and the *boom*. The *baghla*, with its transom stern, is now extinct, but it is thought to have reflected the influence of 18th century European merchantmen in its design and decoration. The double-ended design of the *boom* seems to be the most successful and is the only ocean-going traditional Arabian vessel still widely used for trade today. The homeland of the *boom* is Kuwait, in the Persian Gulf, but the same kind of vessel is known to have sailed extensively, over long distances to the south, along both the Indian and African shores. There were many examples of dhows in Africa, the most interesting being the *mtepe*. This breed survived until the 1930s and continued to use sewn plank construction such as traditional dhows are always identified with. There are a number of other small boats still in existence that use the sewn construction method, but it is a tradition that only just survives today.

The *Sohar* – a replica of a dhow
To substantiate our knowledge of dhow design and capability, during 1980–81 Timothy Severin triumphantly sailed from Oman to China in a reconstructed sewn boom, the *Sohar*. He chose this route because he believed it to be relevant to the origin of some of the famous stories based on *Sindbad the Sailor*, which date back to the 9th century. *Sohar* was based on details culled from early Arabian texts and pictures and from illustrations on the first Portuguese maps that were made of the Indian Ocean.

Besides successfully retracing early Arabian navigational routes, Severin also experimented with the techniques by which early Arabian seafarers determined their position at sea. *Sohar's* crew used the stars to calculate latitude and a *kamal* – the Arabian equivalent of a sextant – to measure the angle of the North Star, Polaris, above the horizon. Using such unsophisticated early techniques, they were able to ascertain their whereabouts remarkably accurately – to within 30 miles (48km) of their true position, according to modern sextant observations.

The heyday of the dhow
There were many main dhow-linked maritime centers between the mid 14th century and 1500, spanning both sides of the Indian Ocean, the Red Sea area, Ceylon, the Coromandel coast, lower Burma, Malacca and nearby ports in

An ocean-going dhow of the *boom* type was faithfully reconstructed by Tim Severin, who sailed her from Oman to China in 1980–81. The final stage in her building, shown here, was to swab vegetable oil onto the coconut stitching as a preservative.

Malaya, Sumatra, Java and the Spice Islands. The principal ports (see map) and regions were linked by large ships, carrying cargoes of merchandise and these ports were host to large groups of merchants, mariners, shipwrights and artisans.

Abundant staple products formed the backbone of this mature intercontinental trading economy. Not only were compact commodities of high value such as aromatic spices, opium, pearls, fine textiles, ivory and porcelain widely exchanged, but dhow-borne trade in bulk commodities, including rice, sugar, copper, tin, iron and salt, was equally buoyant. Horses, for example, were exported in large numbers from Somalia, Arabia and Persian Gulf ports to Indian shores, where they were needed for the cavalry of various rulers, while Ceylon and Burma sent elephants overseas to both the east and west coasts

of India. Timber, needed especially for shipbuilding, was a continually important export from the west coast of India to Arab shores.

Although the overall pattern of commerce remained unchanged over several centuries, the second great wave of Islamic expansion, from the 13th century on, saw the Red Sea area becoming the main western terminus of Indian Ocean trade, with a corresponding decline in the role played by the Persian Gulf ports. The continuing process of Islamization along the East African coast, through the efforts of the Arab and Somali traders, had created many new converts of the merchant class, who felt it necessary to make at least one pilgrimage to Mecca and Medina during their lifetime. This increased the importance of the Red Sea route, for merchandise and pilgrimage went hand-in-hand. Together with the Islamic penetration of India and the Islamization of the Hindu town cultures of Malaya, Java and Sumatra, the greater part of the Indian Ocean trading system gradually passed into the hands of Moslem Arabs.

The cultural decline
After the arrival of the Europeans, dhows in the Indian Ocean were required to carry Portuguese permits, and traded goods were taxed. Most of the towns on the East African seaboard were supposed to pay tribute to Portugal but, due to the interference in their economies and domestic policies, most retrogressed during the 16th and 17th centuries. Some cities, once great, such as Kilwa sank into near oblivion. A few towns, including Pata and especially Mombasa, fought hard for their independence, although for the most part unsuccessfully because the Portuguese were such resourceful and aggressive colonists.

In spite of this, by 1600, the northeast and northwest corners of the Indian Ocean were slipping from the Portuguese grasp, and in 1622 they were finally ejected from the Persian Gulf. By the mid 16th century, Arab seafarers from the maritime state of Oman were regularly raiding Portuguese outposts even as far south as Zanzibar itself.

And so, by the 18th century, the East African coast, north of Cape Delgrado, had generally resumed the late medieval pattern of its external relationships. There was a re-emergence of Swahili city states, mostly under Arab dynasties owing a nominal allegiance to the rulers of Oman. But, the wider commercial connections with India and Indonesia, which had given a special lustre to the late medieval culture of the coast, had been thinned and diminished. The Portuguese had upset the trade relationships of the Indian Ocean, with the result that the towns in the hub of the trade routes had lost many of their customers. The dhow trade suffered accordingly.

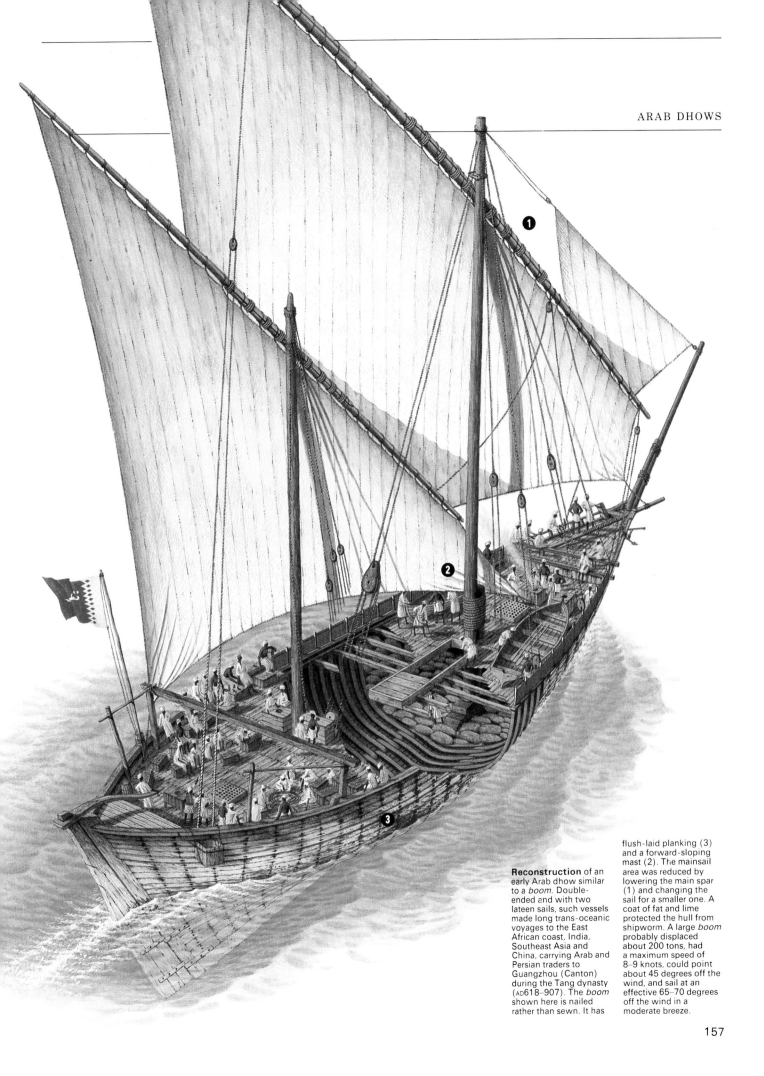

Reconstruction of an
early Arab dhow similar
to a *boom*. Double-
ended and with two
lateen sails, such vessels
made long trans-oceanic
voyages to the East
African coast, India,
Southeast Asia and
China, carrying Arab and
Persian traders to
Guangzhou (Canton)
during the Tang dynasty
(AD618–907). The *boom*
shown here is nailed
rather than sewn. It has
flush-laid planking (3)
and a forward-sloping
mast (2). The mainsail
area was reduced by
lowering the main spar
(1) and changing the
sail for a smaller one. A
coat of fat and lime
protected the hull from
shipworm. A large *boom*
probably displaced
about 200 tons, had
a maximum speed of
8–9 knots, could point
about 45 degrees off the
wind, and sail at an
effective 65–70 degrees
off the wind in a
moderate breeze.

Chinese ocean-going ships

Between the 8th and the 15th centuries, an unknown number of Chinese sailors and merchants visited Arabia and the east coast of Africa. Contemporary travelers' accounts suggest that ships, cargoes and crews deployed in this transoceanic trade were far larger than anything known in the West. Two recent finds of ocean-going ships have enabled archaeologists to confirm and fill out this little-known chapter of history.

The Chinese records of trade routes and shipping are notably sparse, and the archives that do exist are difficult for Westerners to decipher. However, it seems that, before the 8th century, the Chinese did not possess ocean-going ships. Vessels operating in transasiatic trade and visiting China were not local but mainly from Southeast Asia and the Indian Ocean. It seems probable that the southern Chinese evolved an ocean-going vessel that incorporated elements derived from Chinese coastal vessels and these visiting ships. This shipbuilding tradition reached its zenith in the Sung and Yüan dynasties (960–1279 and 1279–1368).

Chinese texts as early as AD860 described the south coast of the Gulf of Aden and the Somali coast. Malindi (Mo Lin) was known about 1060 and the Zanzibar coast (Tsheng-Pa) and Madagascar (Khun Lun Tsheng-Chhi) about 1178. Coins dating from the 7th century onwards (the majority from the Sung dynasty of 960–1279) have been found in such numbers along the East African coast that they must have been used for payment of goods. However, they may have been old coins. Many coins have been found in 14th century wrecksites in Thailand. There is also an immense quantity of ceramics, dating from the 10th century onwards, to provide further physical evidence that the Chinese had ancient trade relations with East Africa.

Medieval ocean traders

One of the first western accounts of Chinese ships comes from the Venetian traveler Marco Polo, writing at the end of the 13th century. He provides a full description of the ocean-sailing traders that went from China to India.

. . . They are built of the wood called spruce and of fir. They have one deck, and above this deck, in most ships, are at least 60 cabins, each one of which can comfortably accommodate one merchant. They have a steering-oar and four masts. Often they add another two masts, which are hoisted and lowered at pleasure.

The entire hull is of double thickness, one plank being fastened on top of another, and this double planking extends all the way round. It is calked outside and in, and the fastening is done with iron nails.

Some of the ships, that is the bigger ones, have also 13 bulkheads or partitions made of stout planks dovetailed into one another. This is useful in case the ship's hull should chance to be damaged . . . In that event, the water coming through the breach will run into the bilge, which is never permanently occupied. The sailors promptly find out where the breach is. Cargo is shifted from the damaged compartment into the neighboring ones; for the bulkheads are so stoutly built that the compartments are watertight. The damage is then repaired and the cargo shifted back . . .

The crew needed to man a ship ranges from 150 to 300 according to her size. They carry much bigger cargo than ours. One ship will take as much as 5,000 or 6,000 baskets of pepper. At one time their ships were even larger than those now in use.

When a ship is in need of refitment . . . they nail on another layer of planks all round, over the top of the original two, so that there are now three layers. They then calk her afresh. This process is repeated yearly till there are as many as six layers, after which the vessel is rejected as no longer seaworthy.''

Very close to the time that Marco Polo's *Travels* were written, a ship was wrecked near the port that he called Zaiton, known today as Quanzhou. Discovered in 1973, the ship was found while dredging a canal at Houzhou, about 6 miles (10km) from the port. The excavation was completed in August 1973 and the ship was then dismantled and transported to Quanzhou, where it was rebuilt under a temporarily constructed shelter.

Between 1977 and 1979 a building was constructed which included the ship, a display area, and administrative quarters. The hull structure was completely rebuilt, cradled by six massive iron supports. The remains, measuring 80ft by 30ft, consist of the keel, part of the transom, 12 bulkheads, and the sides of the ship up to and slightly beyond the turn of the bilge.

It is thought that the Quanzhou ship was originally 112ft (34m) long, 36ft (11m) wide, and had a displacement of around 380 tons. She can be dated to c.1277, and has a design radically different from the types of ships recorded by Europeans in the 19th and early 20th centuries. Before the Quanzhou find, it was thought that the Chinese had always built flat-bottomed ships without any form of keel. However, this vessel has a distinct V-shaped hull cross-section and a pronounced keel, enabling her to make long journeys through heavy seas.

Polo in the 13th century, made frequent voyages across the Indian Ocean before the 15th century Ming Ban drastically curtailed Chinese transoceanic maritime activity. According to Marco Polo, the vessels had 13 compartments (3), each of which was allocated to a merchant. The crew ranged in number from 150 to 300 men. The ships had a transom stern with axial rudder (1) that could be raised or lowered with a windlass (2). The masts were angled so as to give better sailing characteristics. Marco Polo reports of the Chinese that "at one time their ships were even larger than those now in use."

Reconstruction of an early Chinese ocean-going ship similar to the Quanzhou find. These huge vessels, which excited the admiration of the European traveler Marco

159

The archaeologists ascertained that the keel was made of pine and constructed in three parts. They then discovered that the vertical faces of the joints holding together the keel hid a deliberately arranged set of seven bronze coins and a bronze mirror. The coins were placed in such a way as to represent the constellation of Ursa Major; the mirror is thought to represent the moon.

These symbols have a Taoist significance, either bringing good luck and fair winds, or representing the so-called Seven Star Ocean where there are many dangerous rocks; the mirror is there to reflect light and ensure a safe journey. Apparently, this tradition continues today in modern shipbuilding, with the stars represented by nails and the moon by a silver coin.

The vessel has 12 bulkheads, creating 13 compartments (just as Marco Polo described) roughly equal in size. A series of edge-joined cedar planks form these bulkheads, and each one is penetrated at its lowest point by a waterway – a small hole enabling the water to flow to the lowest part of the ship, where it can be pumped out. This again is quite contrary to what was previously thought.

The bulkheads were calked, but obviously the presence of waterways indicates that water was meant to pass freely between compartments. The planking of the bulkheads was also dovetailed exactly as Marco Polo described.

Heavy wooden frames were set on one side of the bulkheads, and these had a waterway cut into them to match the waterways of the bulkheads. A series of thick camphorwood blocks, forming the outer layer of the transom, contain a round vertical groove which took the (missing) axial rudder. This method of mounting enabled the rudder to be raised or lowered without affecting its operation, and is a common Chinese tradition.

Again in accordance with Marco Polo's description, the hull is double-planked up to the beginning of the turn of the bilge, where it becomes triple-planked. The planking is made of cedar, and is constructed in an exceedingly complex manner. In a sense, the outer planking becomes the inner planking, and the whole structure is arranged according to a type of mixed clinker-carvel construction (see diagram opposite).

The foremast and main mast steps were set on the keel. A square section was cut out of the upper remaining plank of the bulkhead forward of the main mast step, perhaps to allow the mast to be lowered. This would be lowered forwards, because the height of the mast from the step to the deck is over twice the width between the bulkheads.

Iron appears to have been the main fastening material. The edge joints of the rabbeted inner planking were nailed diagonally from the outside through the joint. The strakes were nailed to the edges of the bulkheads, which were also attached to the hull by an arrangement of iron fastenings bent at right angles in order to form an L-shape.*

The cargo
The main cargo consisted of 2 tons of fragrant woods (*lac* sandalwood and *aloes* eaglewood) thought to come from Indonesia or Southeast Asia, together with pepper, betel nut, cowries, tortoise-shell, cinnabar and ambergris (identified as coming from Somalia). There were also ceramics of Chinese origin.

Provisions included coconut, olives, peaches, plums and lychees. Animal bones were found, indicating the presence of cows, pigs, goats, fish, dogs, birds and rats. Items that may have been ship's supplies included a wooden ruler, an axe, a lock, a bronze ladle, celadon bowls and plates, a narrow stoneware wine jar, Chinese chessmen, a rattan hat, bamboo matting, linen, and glass beads.

A total of 540 brass cash coins were found on the site. These provide the main dating evidence, the last coin dating from the reign of Duzong (1265–74). All the evidence indicates a date of about 1277, almost at the end of the Sung Dynasty.

The Quanzhou ship appears to be a departure from the normally accepted Chinese form of shipbuilding, but this is probably because almost all the available literature is based on accounts of Europeans visiting China after the so-called "Ming ban". Such accounts are likely to reflect the post-ban bias toward craft designed for inland waterways, river and coastal trading.

The Shinan ship
In 1976 a shipwreck was discovered near Shinan in southwest Korea which could be dated to 1352, making it virtually a contemporary of the Quanzhou ship. The site attracted much attention because of the large and varied ceramic cargo that was found. This included one of the largest collections of Chinese ceramics ever excavated outside China, celadon and porcelain wares, lacquered wares, silver and iron ingots, and bronze cooking utensils. But the murky waters that kept the ship and her cargo safe for 600 years now make excavation conditions extremely difficult.

It is interesting that, like the Quanzhou ship, the Shinan ship's design is radically different from those of Chinese vessels recorded by Europeans in the 19th and 20th centuries. In fact, the two ships share many common features: bulkheads, iron fastenings, waterways, etc. Moreover, both have a V-shaped hull and a similar type of construction.

The Chinese ocean shipbuilding tradition reached its zenith in the Sung and Yüan dynasties, and the Quanzhou ship is particularly representative of this period with its bulkheads and multi-layered planking, iron fastened with complex rabbeted clinker and carvel. The Shinan ship is similar in age and design

The Shinan wreck yielded celadons or greenware covered jars, decorated with incised lotus and arabesque designs (front) and ribbed design (rear). This immense Chinese ceramic cargo was destined for the markets of Japan and the Philippines.

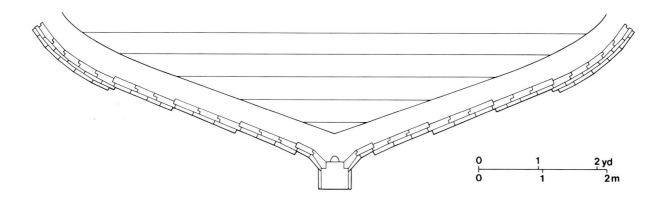

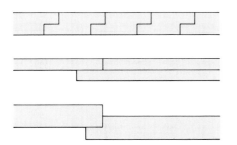

Complex construction of the Quanzhou ship's hull profile (above), combining clinker and carvel work. The latter lays the planks edge to edge with a rebate or groove, but with a resultant smooth surface (left, above). In the former, planks are joined by placing one plank on top of another (left, center). A small rebate resulting in a discontinuous surface joins the planking together (left, below).

Artifacts (below) from the Shinan site, one of the richest ever recorded, include a bronze incense burner in the shape of a lion (top, left), a bronze plate with a design showing a hare milling under a cinnamon tree (bottom, left), a white glazed vase with flower and arabesque design in underglaze black; and a celadon vase with a design of diamond-shaped flowers and two rings (handles).

but shows a simpler rabbeted clinker.

Vessels following another tradition in Chinese shipbuilding have a square-shaped, flat-bottomed hull without a keel. The other major tradition appears to be Southeast Asian in origin and has a structure that is edge-joined with dowels – the South China Sea tradition. The lack of examples of true ocean-going ships of the Quanzhou type might have been the result of the rise of power of the anti-maritime party, in the reign of Hangxi until 1425 and Xuande, from 1426 to 1435, which culminated in the so-called Ming Ban. The reasons for the Ming Ban are politically complex but the effects were catastrophic in terms of maritime development. The Chinese navy was abandoned and by 1474 only 140 warships out of a total of 400 were left.

Finds from the Gulf of Thailand

In 1976 looters discovered a 16th century shipwreck sited off Pattaya. Over the years this site was systematically looted of its ceramic cargo.*

In 1980 I visited the site, which was then selected for formal excavation. This began in 1982 as part of a three-year programme to investigate wrecksites in the Pattaya area. The excavation was undertaken by a joint Thai-Australian team of maritime archaeologists.

We found that the Pattaya ship had a number of features in common with the Quanzhou ship. A comparison of these inherent similarities is remarkably revealing and helps in interpreting the Pattaya hull structure. The Quanzhou ship even helped us to establish which end of the Pattaya wrecksite was the bow and which was the stern. Other similarities between the two ships include the waterway through the bulkhead as well as the large mast sockets.*

The Pattaya wreck lies in the Gulf of Thailand, approximately midway between Ko Lan and Laem Pattaya, near a group of rocks called Hin Ko Lan. It is on the direct tourist boat route to the coral areas west of Ko Lan and as such, makes an ideal spot for tourist diving. This explains, to some extent, the deteriorated state of the wrecksite.

Excavation began at the southern end of the wrecksite and systematically proceeded northwards, uncovering timbers using an airlift. The positions of artifacts found during the excavation were recorded, in relation to the initial base line. However, not surprisingly, due to years of looting, very few artifacts were left to be found. The few remaining relics that were recovered included ceramic sherds of earthenware, coarse stoneware, one porcelain fragment and a number of lead ingots that were conical in shape.

By contrast, the hull structure was exceedingly interesting, with a large amount of complex structure. Thus the emphasis on excavation was to uncover the hull so that it could be fully recorded.

This was achieved using the usual measuring techniques for the recording of profiles as well as by producing a photo-mosaic.

In all, a 29ft (9m) length of hull was uncovered with a maximum width of 15ft (4.5m). The hull profile had a marked V-shape next to the keel, which flattened out, finishing in an upward curve at the turn of the bilge. A sample of wood from the bulkhead was brought back to the Western Australian Maritime Museum for identification. It was found to be beech (*Fagus*), probably Japanese beech (*F. oblique*), which is a widely distributed tree in Southern China, Japan, Thailand and Korea.

The Pattaya Pottery wrecksite represents an example of an Oriental ocean-going ship. As with the earlier Quanzhou and Shinan ships, the V-shaped keel again challenges the widely held view, based on 19th and 20th century European descriptions, that most Chinese vessels were flat-bottomed.

The bulkheads and dowel edge-joined planking of the Pattaya site are a complete departure from any Chinese and European tradition of boat-building of the equivalent era. The major difference is that the Europeans relied on regular frames to provide some or all of the lateral strength of the ship. These frames were clamped to the keel with a keelson and in some cases, additionally strengthened with a layer of internal planking, known as the ceiling – a so-called "skeleton-first" technique of boat-building. The Chinese use of edge-joining with nails, and the Southeast Asian joining with dowels is slightly akin to mortise and tenon edge joining, typical of Greco-Roman boat-building. The fundamental and unique difference, however, is that Oriental ships obtained most of their strength from a series of regular bulkheads which divided the ship into compartments.

The Ko Si Chang site

During the 1982 Pattaya expedition, we were informed of a wrecksite to the north of Pattaya. Towards the end of the two-year excavation, we decided to briefly investigate the site, making a day-trip visit in a small motorized flush-decked boat that took us offshore, where the depth of water was about 114ft (35m). Here amidst the sea, looking back upon a featureless island, the local fisherman indicated the location of the site.

With considerable scepticism, the first diver rolled off the edge of the boat and sank into the sea, to try to locate the site. All our doubts were completely confounded. The diver surfaced with a set of blue and white porcelain plates and dishes. There was indeed a wrecksite down below.

Unfortunately, the diving time for such a preliminary excursion was limited to only 20 minutes. To our astonishment, more artifacts were raised in that short

time than during the whole of the excavation of the Pattaya site.

It was interesting that each of the five divers who inspected the site came to the surface with different selections of material. Three bowls were found as part of a series, stacked together and lying on their sides. Some kendis were found in one group and the blue and white porcelain in another. Another extraordinary find, especially in such a short space of time, were the large structural timbers, photographed on the seabed.

Their presence was remarkable because one would expect that timbers in such warm water would be completely eaten away by teredo worms and other marine organisms. Even from such a brief examination of dimensions and their general configuration, there is no doubt the timbers represented some form of integral hull structure. But, from such a superficial survey, it was not possible to draw any conclusions as to what part of the ship they represented.

Speculations on the origin of the ship were made by examining the ceramic material. The porcelain plates were most revealing in terms of the age of the vessel. According to their general style and shape they are known as Swatow ware. Decorations in their center – a gourd and a fan – are Taoist emblems of the Eight Immortals. The other porcelains are not Swatow ware, the most significant being

The Ko Kradat site
before excavation shows the ballast mound with coral growing among the ceramic sherds. This 16th century shipwreck was one of several sites found in the area (see map opposite).

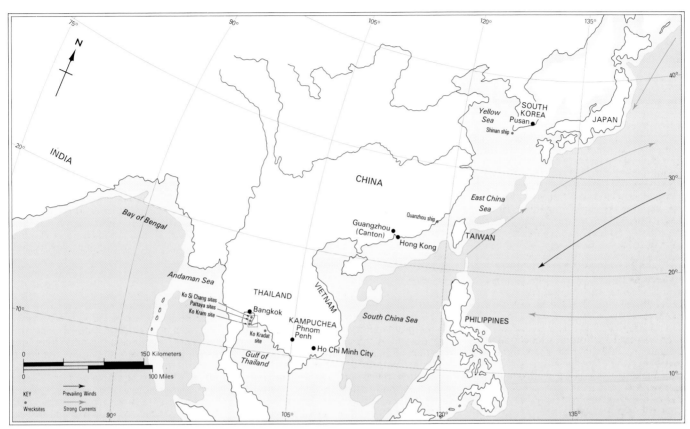

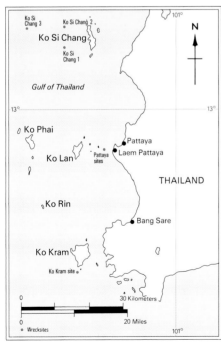

The map (top) of Asia shows the main underwater sites that have been excavated in recent times. A detail of the Gulf of Thailand (above) shows where the Fine Arts Department of Thailand and a Thai-Australian underwater archaeological project have investigated a number of important sites. This project has been supported by the Australian Research Grants Scheme.

The Pattaya site (above) showing the mast step of the wrecked vessel. This was one of the first sites investigated which contained extensive hull structure. Thus, although looted for its ceramic cargo, this site provided valuable evidence on the construction of Southeast Asian vessels.

a bowl of the Wanli reign. This clearly dates the site to a period around 1573–1620. The other artifacts recovered include fragments of eggshell porcelain with decorations that are both interesting and curious.

The paired Taoist plates indicated that the ship was carrying trade porcelains – the plates being part of the cargo. This and the lacquer ware point to a Chinese origin for the ship. However, the lids are certainly Thai in origin and have also been found on a wide variety of sites, including Ko Kradat and the Pattaya site.

Also among the finds were large storage jars, some containing large quantities of fish vertebrae. Possibly the jars contained food or provisions for the voyage. The jars are thought to be Sawankhalok ware and have also been found on a number of wrecksites, including the *Batavia* site. They are also familiar in Indonesian collections from Sarawak, and even as far away as Fort Jesus in Kenya and on the Portuguese ship *São Bento*, which was wrecked in 1554 on the Pondoland coast of South Africa.

Following its initial discovery, a formal expedition to the Ko Si Chang site was made in 1983. The wrecksite was rediscovered on the first day of diving, but a number of problems were encountered during the course of the work. An unseasonal monsoon caused very rough seas and heavy rain, and as a result diving was so difficult that it sometimes had to be abandoned. Also, the rough seas increased sediment levels in the water and so lowered visibility.

This was heightened by the heavy rain causing an increase of muddy water flowing into the area from the Chao Phraya River, some miles to the north of Ko Si Chang. We also experienced problems in mooring the boat, due to the conflicting direction of the tidal stream and the prevailing wind. This meant that there was considerable uncertainty in the location of the position of the boat relative to the wrecksite, and consequently great care had to be exercised during dives and in the amount of time the divers spent underwater.

Crow cups

A large group of bowl fragments were found on the site. They are known in the Netherlands as *Kraaikoppen* or crow cups, because of the resemblance of the bird depicted in their center to a crow. Remarkably, we found that two particular fragments, one from the 1982 and the other from the 1983 expedition, actually fitted together. There were variations of the bird imagery, some with the bird perched on rocks, with the moon above. Other decorative themes included bamboo, furniture and scenery. A fruit that occurs on some of the ceramics is possibly a pomegranate.

The Ko Si Chang wrecksite shows a completely different style of construction

to that of the Pattaya ship, with a waterway hollowed out in the top of the keel. The hull was multi-layered with compartmentalized bulkheads, and a large number of compartments.

The cargo was also unusual. In addition to the Chinese porcelain and lacquer wares, and Thai lids with lotus bud handles, there was much material of uncertain origin. The kendis for example are thought to be Chinese, but there are no exact parallels. Clearly, the ship had been trading with China. But the interesting question remains: Why was there so much non-Chinese material on board?

One site leads to another

During the joint Thai-Australian excavation of the Ko Si Chang site, two other wrecksites were discovered in the vicinity. One of the sites, Ko Si Chang 3, was first found in 1985 in clear water, on a sandy sea bed at a depth of 80ft (24m). In January 1986 an international team of underwater archaeologists began a formal excavation of the site.

The artifacts found from this site included some earthenware jars and a small selection of porcelain, mainly originating from Vietnam, but some also came from China and Thailand. Other items included metal ingots, elephant tusks and duck eggs, some of which were still intact. A total of more than 1,600 individual items were recorded.

Conclusion

From the variation in data derived from the excavation of wrecksites, it is clear that there is a great deal of variety in Asiatic shipbuilding technology but a number of definite kinds of construction. In its most evolved form, Chinese ocean-sailing activity culminated in the 15th century with the seven mighty expeditions that took place between the years of 1405 and 1433.

Thereafter, the inward-looking, anti-maritime Confucian faction was in the ascendant, with its Ming Ban policy. It regarded as superfluous the importation of such commodities as elephant tusks, rhinoceros horns, pearls, aromatics and spices. By that time, some Chinese captains may have doubled the Cape of Good Hope and sighted the West African shore – at a time when even the most informed European traveler had only the vaguest notion of the true shape of the vast continent of Africa.

This xenophobic mentality resulted in a fundamental change in oceanic trade patterns. It disrupted, temporarily, the Chinese export of ceramics, and it brought about the disappearance of the traditional ocean-going vessel of South China. However, Southeast Asia took over much of this trade, and the arrival of the Europeans on the Asiatic maritime scene at this time had considerable impact on the situation.

Stoneware jars from the Ko Si Chang 3 site. These jars were carrying a variety of food products and domestic supplies, including incense and duck eggs. The ship has been dated to the early 15th century, and was probably a small coastal trader.

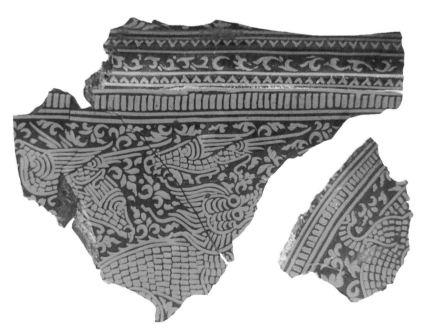

Chinese trade goods from the Ko Si Chang I site, including red lacquer ware (center). Porcelain was a major trade export from China, and a consignment of fine bowls recovered from the site includes some bearing the frequently seen motif of a bird on a rock with the moon above (top). Various styles from the same wreck can be seen (top right), but the plate (center right) is particularly useful to archaeologists for it helps to date the ship: the reign mark refers to the "Great Ming Wan Li Year", and we know that Wan Li reigned 1573–1620. From the Ko Si Chang 3 site (above) came duck eggs, dated over 100 years earlier. Comparison of ceramic styles from these sites have enabled archaeologists to build up important chronologies.

Kublai Khan's invasion of Japan

For many years, fishermen trawling in the Bay of Imari, off the island of Kyushu in the western part of Japan, have been discovering relics from the fleets of Kublai Khan, that came in the 13th century to invade Japan.

The Kamikaze and the invasion of Japan

There are detailed legendary accounts of the two Mongol attempts to invade Japan. Both were launched by Kublai Khan, whose grandfather, Genghis Khan, founded the Mongol Empire. In 1268, having conquered northern China and Korea, Kublai Khan demanded submission from Japan. The Japanese ignored the command and the Khan prepared to invade their island stronghold. Finally in 1274, a fleet of 900 ships and more than 40,000 Mongol, Chinese and Korean troops arrived at Kyushu's Hakata Bay.

After a day's successful fighting, the invaders retired for the night. That evening a storm threatened the fleet at anchor, forcing the ship captains to flee out to sea. The storm eventually overtook the fleet, sinking 200 ships and bringing the total cost in lives to 13,500.

Despite this staggering death toll, Kublai Khan prepared another attack – a vast armada of 4,400 ships and 142,000 troops – which was assembled by 1281. As they prepared to invade mainland Kyushu, the Mongols found themselves in the path of another typhoon. Their fleet was again devastated and the Mongols have never seriously threatened Japan since then.

The Japanese considered that the typhoons that overwhelmed the Mongol fleets were due to divine intervention, in response to their prayers and elaborate Shinto ceremonies. On account of this the winds that saved the defending Japanese have since been known as "kamikaze", meaning divine wind.

The Takashima project

For seven centuries the remains of the Mongol fleet lay largely undisturbed, on the seafloor, off Takashima. However, in 1980 Tarao Mozai, a Professor of Engineering with an active interest in marine archaeology, set out to locate formally the remains of the Mongol fleet.

Funded by the Japanese Ministry of Education, he had the idea of using a sonoprobe – a device familiar to geologists, that uses sound waves to map formations of rock beneath the ocean floor – to locate buried artifacts. Using this instrument mounted on a boat, Mozai and his team surveyed an area of ocean where Chinese and Mongol artifacts had traditionally been found by local fishermen. The sonoprobe was able to locate small features such as scattered debris or shells up to a depth of 90ft (30m) beneath the seafloor. But results were not substantial enough, being merely recorded on black-and-white recording paper, inadequate for the purpose of identifying artifacts. Clearly, the instrument needed to be modified for use in underwater archaeology.

The color probe

In response, Mozai had the ingenious idea of combining the sonoprobe with a color sonar device that had originally been designed to locate shoals of fish. This combination had never been attempted before and was a revolutionary approach to the problem of locating shipwrecks below the seabed. The color screen enables the resolution of very fine sound differences which can detect objects buried up to 33ft (10m) below the sand and silt of the seafloor.

The sonar system consists of an acoustic mirror which is floated in the water on the side of the survey boat and any buried objects show up clearly on a video screen. Objects made of the hardest materials, such as stone, metal or porcelain, register on the color probe's screen as bright red. Softer materials such as wood, appear orange and even softer materials such as sand and silt, register yellow or light green. At the end of the scale in terms of softness, water appears on the probe's screen in its natural color.

Using this instrument for the first time, divers began recovering sunken artifacts almost immediately. The positions of sonar targets were recorded on a positional map so that they could be relocated. A diving team made a systematic search of the area around Kozaki, thought to be one of the most likely places to find traces of the lost fleet.

All finds were carefully recorded and they included ceramic sherds, porcelain and earthenware pots and vases, stone anchor stocks, iron ingots and round stone balls. A cavalry sword was found that had landed in the upright position, with its point and part of its blade embedded in the sand. The buried section was in remarkably good condition, whereas the exposed handle of the sword was so heavily encrusted that it was almost unrecognizable.

It so happened that the search coincided with the 700th anniversary of the invasion of 1281, an event that is celebrated every 50 years with a festival. The local islanders of Takashima became so fascinated with the recovery work and its importance that a number of fishermen came forward with finds they had made. These finds included ceramics from the Yüan period, resembling those from the Shinan wrecksite that date back to 1352 (see pp. 160–162).

A number of round stone ballistae balls that were recovered present an interesting archaeological and historical problem. They date back to around the time when the Mongols first began to use cannons. It is known that the Mongols used stone shot in a type of gun known as a mangonel. There are several anonymous references and paintings depicting Japanese being slain by iron firearms in the first Kublai Khan invasion.

One of the donations was an almost unbelievable treasure. It was a bronze object trawled up by a fisherman some years earlier, which he had kept in his tool box. On examination, it was found to be an inscribed Mongol seal revealing that the bearer was a leader of a group of 100 to 1,000 horsemen. The seal is of great historical importance and was donated to the island of Takashima by the finder. It has been declared as one of Japan's national treasures. The inscription on the seal was in a written form of Mongolian language, commissioned by Kublai Khan himself. The dynasty had had no official written language until the year 1271, when the Khan ordered a Tibetan monk to create one.

Although there have been numerous discoveries of relics from the Mongol fleet, as yet the actual wrecksite has not been located. Fishermen report that in some areas of deep water they trawl up complete pots. The trawlers operate to collect sea cucumber which are only found on deepwater seabeds. It is in these deep waters that important discoveries regarding the lost fleets are likely to be made in the future.

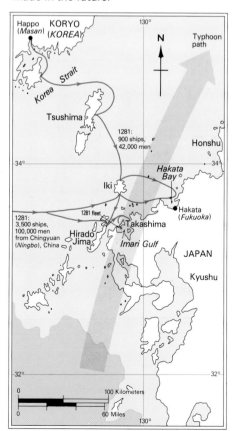

An exploding shell (left) bursts over a Japanese Samurai warrior in one of the earliest depictions of the use of gunpowder. The warrior is Suenaga, who commissioned this scroll.

A bronze statue of the Buddha (below), now in a small shrine on the island of Takashima. It was dredged from the sea at a site near where the Mongol fleet was destroyed by the "Divine Wind" typhoon in 1281. Deepwater finds by local fishermen suggest that important discoveries still remain to be made in the area.

The two invasions by Kublai Khan (opposite), in 1274 and 1281, centered on Hakata on both occasions, and included Chinese from South China and Korea. Vastly outnumbered, only the exceptional bravery of the Japanese warriors and, more importantly, the advent of a typhoon wind, called the Kamikaze or Divine Wind, saved Japan from occupation and incorporation into Kublai Khan's Mongol empire.

A bronze seal (above), belonging to a Mongolian officer in charge of cavalry, was found by fishermen and relates to Kublai Khan's ill-fated "Kamikaze" invasion of Japan, 1281.

167

East Indiamen

The late 17th century marked the heyday of trade for the Dutch East India Company (VOC) and English East India Company (EEIC). Both companies had fleets that ranged from Aden and Persia, eastward to Korea and Japan. Inevitably, the sea journey was dangerous, and many ships were lost. The Western Australian Maritime Museum has studied a number of East Indiamen wrecks, notably the *Batavia* with its extraordinary cargo, which sank in June 1629.

Each year fleets shipped out goods such as butter, bricks, tablecloths and tack to supply the company's needs in the Indies. Silver and other items were used in exchange for all kinds of Asian goods. On reaching Java, Dutch ships would unload at Batavia (modern-day Jakarta), which was the headquarter port of the Dutch East India Company.

The journey at sea was a dangerous one and many ships sank or ran aground. So far, divers have found 24 East Indiamen wrecks, but according to detailed records, this number only represents a tiny fraction of the losses. Many East Indiamen ships have now been studied and their details are outlined in the East Indiamen wreck chart (p.170).

The preponderance of Dutch wrecks reflects the vigor with which the Dutch tried to dominate trade to the east. One of the most interesting of these wrecks to be excavated is the Dutch East India Company ship, *Batavia*.

The *Batavia*

On 4th June 1629, two hours before sunrise, the VOC ship *Batavia* was wrecked on the Houtman Abrolhos, 40 miles (75km) off the Western Australian coast. The shipwreck and mutiny that followed became famous in history. The journal of *Batavia*'s commander Francisco Pelsaert describes how the ship broke up, what happened to the survivors and how much of the ship was salvaged. Leaving 268 passengers and crew safely ashore on nearby islands, Pelsaert and the senior officers sailed off in a ship's boat, seeking water and help. They returned about 100 days later, to find that the undermerchant and a gang of followers had mutinied and senselessly massacred 125 men, women and children. Although none of the passengers or crew died of hunger or thirst, due to the massacre and the executions that resulted from it, only 68 of the original 316 people aboard the ship survived.

In 1963, divers found the *Batavia* wreck in a shallow dip in the coral of Morning Reef in the Wallabi Group, one of several groups which make up the Houtman Abrolhos. A short excavation followed and in 1972, the Western Australian Museum launched a four year excavation programme that managed to investigate most of the wreck.

A formidable Indian Ocean swell tends to break dramatically on reaching the shallower Western Australian waters and so pounds any wrecks in the area into scattered fragments. It was fortunate that the *Batavia* was found in a depression in the reef and was protectively covered by coral. Museum archaeologists managed to salvage one-third of the port side of the ship and part of the transom, which had survived buried under many tons of dead coral. Constructional evidence from these remains indicates that the vessel used heavy framing at the stern end and a double layer of planking throughout the ship.

During the excavation, sandstone blocks from part of a building were recovered. After conservation the excavation team attempted to reconstruct the blocks. It was found that they comprised a prefabricated portico. Subsequent studies of historical documents revealed that the portico was destined for the gateway to the waterport of the castle at Batavia.* One of the most conclusive pieces of evidence supporting this is an etching of Batavia that shows the castle with the unfinished water port, awaiting the arrival of the ship.

Early attempts to reconstruct the façade were unsuccessful, but after conservation treatment, special details, such as the original mason's marks (B1 to B7, which corresponded to seven layers in the columns), enabled workers to deduce how the columns of stone were supposed to fit together. Another major problem in the reconstruction was how to hold the façade together because most of the blocks were so badly eroded that it was impossible for it to stand freely. Eventually, however, a steel framework was engineered to support each layer of blocks. The steel support system is even designed to withstand local earthquake tremors and enables any one block to be extracted without having to dismantle the whole of the portico.

In December 1979, the last block was put in place and the façade was completed – three and a half centuries late. It forms the entrance to the Western Australian Maritime Museum, which also houses the recovered remains of *Batavia* and her cargo. The vast collection of recovered artifacts includes a selection of silverware, destined for the Mughal Emperor Jehangir. Among the navigational instruments found at the *Batavia* wrecksite were four astrolabes and a meridian ring for a globe.

Divers raised bronze and iron cannons, including two examples with a composite construction of copper sheeting, wrought-iron band and staves, and a type of lead solder. References to such cannons appear in lists of Netherlands patents for the 1630s, but the *Batavia* discoveries gave modern scholars their first chance to assess these weapons directly and at first hand.

Scholars have also learned a good deal from the navigational instruments found on many of the East Indiamen wrecks. The *Kennemerland* carried a relatively crude form of backstaff in 1664, by which time this kind of design was supposed to have been obsolete. But, the octant found on the *Hollandia* which was wrecked in 1742, provides us with another picture in terms of development because this kind of device had only been invented a few years prior to that date. The VOC's supposed resistance to innovation at that time makes this find especially interesting in a historical context.

Written records of cargo material are more complete than wreck material, but wrecks preserve miscellaneous items, such as personal possessions, that would be omitted from official lists. Aboard the *Batavia* were ornately engraved ornaments, featuring Oriental scenes, which are known to have been made for the Mughal Emperor Jehangir. Equally fascinating are the pocket sundials found aboard the *Lastdrager*, all designed to operate in European latitudes. They would have been useless and were obviously intended as prestigious gifts for people in the East.

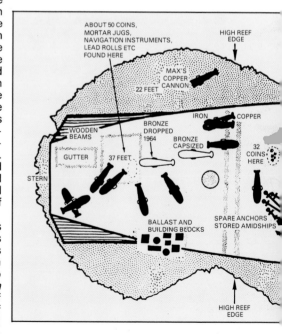

The wrecksite of the *Batavia*, lost in 1629 off the Houtman Abrolhos Islands, 80 miles west of the Australian coast. Archaeologists have been able to reconstruct the break-up of the ship through the disposition of bronze, iron and composite guns, the anchors and the cargo. They can also show where the items were stowed on the ship.

Killed by mutineers on the *Batavia*, the grave of a Dutchman (left) provides a grim reminder of the dangers that could emerge in long ocean voyages. During the 200 years of the Dutch East India company's operation, about 1,770 individual ships sailed to the East Indies, making a total of nearly 4,800 voyages to the Indies and about 3,400 voyages home. Of these voyages, a total of 250 ended in disaster. An archaeologist (below) holds two stoneware jugs from the *Batavia* site. The ship also carried a portico facade (bottom, left), now re-erected at the Western Australian Maritime Museum, destined for the gateway to the company's castle at their headquarters in Batavia, Indonesia.

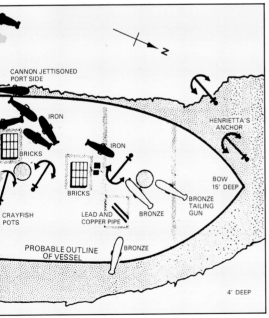

Items from East Indiamen. Part of a pocket sundial (above, right) from the *Lastdrager*, lost 1653, must have been intended as a novelty present in the Indies: designed to tell the time in Europe, it was useless in the Indies because of the different latitude. Ornate smoking pipes (right) from the *Vergulde Draeck*, lost 1656, are from N. Thailand and suggest a long-established tradition of smoking.

EAST INDIAMEN WRECK CHART

Name	Origin	Lost	Found	Location	Direction
São João	Portuguese	1552	1980	Natal, S.A.	Homeward
São Bento	Portuguese	1554	1968	Pondoland, S.A.	Homeward

One of the few early 16th century sites to have been excavated and studied. Finds include bronze breech loaders and rather primitive muzzle loaders.

Seychelles wreck	Portuguese	16thC	1976	Boudoise Cay, Seychelles	Outward

Finds include a range of armament, some with marks of founders working in 1515 and 1550, copper and lead ingots, German and Thai pottery, brass bowls and copper containers, an elegant green glass cup, red coral and amber beads. Coral was often used as a trading commodity carried by Portugal to the Orient, and amber was traded on the East African coast.

Santiago	Portuguese	1585	1977	Bassa, Da, India	Outward
Witte Leeuw	Dutch	1613	1976	St Helena	In battle

Sunk in an engagement with two Portuguese ships off St Helena in the South Atlantic. During the battle the *Witte Leeuw* exploded. After investigations in the archives and an extensive search, the site was discovered in deep water. Finds include vast quantities of Chinese porcelain, Rhenish and Indonesian stoneware, spices, personal possessions and natural history collections. The wide range of objects found on board this earliest known Dutch East India Company wreck indicates how the young trading company was still experimenting with many different kinds of cargo.

Banda	Dutch	1615	?	Mauritius	Homeward
Trial	British	1622	1970	Western Australia	Outward

The earliest known wreck of any British East Indiaman, and the oldest known site in Australian waters.

Campen	Dutch	1627	1979	Isle of Wight	Homeward
Sacramento	Portuguese	1647	1977	Port Elizabeth, S.A.	Homeward

Sunk while sailing home from Goa. Finds include 26 bronze cannon, Ming china, peppercorns, turmeric and gunpowder.

Lastdrager	Dutch	1653	1971	Shetland	Outward

Went down while rounding northern Scotland on the *achter-om* ("round the back") route. Finds from the wreck included taps, spoons, puddles of mercury, navigational instruments, stoneware flagons, clay pipes and coins, mainly Dutch and Spanish.

Vergulde Draeck	Dutch	1656	1963	Western Australia	Outward

Struck a reef off Western Australia while on her second voyage to the Indies. A group of survivors reached Batavia in a small boat. Extensive finds from the cargo included lead, ivory, bricks, amber and coral beads, and 10,000 coins.

Kennemerland	Dutch	1664	1971	Out Skerries, Shetland	Outward

Foundered when only six days out from Holland, traveling by the *achter-om* route around the north of the British Isles. Following contemporary salvage by locals, a court awarded the main treasure chests to King Charles II. The court evidence, together with a lively local tradition, led a team of student divers to the wrecksite. Iron bars, spare anchors, building bricks and lead ingots (one of the largest surviving collections of 17th century lead) were found at the wreck's point of impact. Farther north lay smaller personal items and personal baggage, including a graduated wooden rule, part of an early Dutch backstaff.

Prinses Maria	Dutch	1686	?	Isles of Scilly	Outward

One of the largest East Indiamen, she ran aground and was pillaged by local Scillonians, with King James II apparently sharing in the plunder. Archaeologists have discovered large amounts of mercury, some contained in stoneware flagons.

S Antonio de Tanna	Portuguese	1697	1960s	Mombasa, Kenya	In battle

A 42-gun frigate assigned to the rescue of Portuguese besieged by Omani Arabs in Fort Jesus. Having relieved the fort, she ran into trouble and sank while at anchor. A large part of the ship's structure has been excavated. Finds include some ceramics, a huge concentration of cannon balls and other small items. The lack of material suggests extensive contemporary salvage.

'tHuis te Kraijenstein	Dutch	1698	?	Capetown, S.A.	Outward
Meresteyn	Dutch	1702	1971	Cape Town, S.A.	Outward

Divers have combed the site and auctioned the finds, but there seems to have been no systematic excavation of the wreck or proper report of the work. Items sold at auction included part of a swivel gun, a musket, a sword, dividers, taps and spoons.

De Liefde	Dutch	1711	1964	Out Skerries, Shetland	Outward

Lost with only one survivor, the ship's location passed into folklore. Lerwick museum contains some material and information about this wreck, little of which survives. However, thousands of silver coins have been found on the site.

Zuytdorp	Dutch	1713	1920s	Western Australia	Outward

One of the world's most difficult sites, the wreck lies below high cliffs battered by waves, backed by uninhabited bush. Tackling this wreck in the few calm days available each year has involved building a road, an airstrip and a wire flightway from the clifftop down to the divers' base. Archaeologists found the site carpeted with silver coins, minted in 1711. Nearly 8,000 coins were recovered in one three-hour dive alone.

Slot ter Hooge	Dutch	1724	?	Madeira Is	Outward

Archives and a copy of engravings from an old silver tankard helped in the discovery of the wreck. Finds included a unique collection of silver bars, as well as coins, tobacco boxes, pipes, candlesticks, spoons, forks, bricks, taps and stoneware.

Akerendam	Dutch	1725	?	Rondoe, Norway	Outward
Risdam	Dutch	1727	1984	Mersing, Malaysia	Internal

An extremely well-preserved example of an 18th century Dutch East Indiaman, this is the only known example of a hull of a *fluit* (see p.136). Finds include Thai storage jars, tin and lead ingots, Dutch bricks and elephant tusks.

Zeewijk	Dutch	1727	?	Western Australia	Outward

In addition to the wrecksite, a study has been made of the camp at Gun Island established by the survivors, but 19th century guano diggings have removed most traces of the camps. Cannons and anchors lay on the outside of the reef where the ship originally struck, while a second group of articles was found in the shallows inside the reef, including Chinese porcelain, German and Southeast Asian stoneware, and several iron cannons.

Adelaar	Dutch	1728	1972	Barra, Hebrides	Outward

Discoveries include lead ingots, iron cannons, and a small bronze swivel gun, as well as pipes, domestic utensils and tools. However, the general lack of material reflects the probability of salvage work soon after the wrecking.

Wendela	Danish	1737	1972	Fetlar, Shetland	Outward

Lost five years after the founding of the Danish East India Company while on route for the East with a general cargo. A large number of coins was recovered, many from a variety of European states, reflecting the weakness of Danish currency at the time.

Svecia	Swedish	1740	1975	N. Ronaldsway, Orkney	Homeward

Lost a few days before she was due to arrive home at Göteborg. The cargo included large quantities of dyewood.

Hollandia	Dutch	1743	1971	Isles of Scilly	Outward

Lost with no survivors and no clue as to her precise position, the wreck was located near Gunner Rock after extensive searching with a magnetometer. One of the few sites in European waters to have escaped the early salvagers. A survey revealed a cluster of three anchors, several bronze and iron cannons, some small bronze swivel guns and quantities of military equipment. There were also fragments of Chinese porcelain, small pewter objects and many coins.

Reijgersdaal	Dutch	1747	1979	Capetown, S.A.	Outward
Amsterdam	Dutch	1749	1969	Hastings, U.K.	Outward

Lost in the English Channel while on route for Batavia. Most of the passengers and much of the cargo were saved. The ship sank deeply into sand before much salvage was possible. She was found intact by men working at low water on a nearby sewer.

Geldermalsen	Dutch	1752	1985	Indonesia	Internal
Doddington	British	1755	?	Port Elizabeth, S.A.	Outward

Foundered at Bird Island, off Port Elizabeth, while carrying treasure and cannons for the British army in India. Twenty-three survivors lived on the island for seven months, eventually sailing to Mozambique in a small boat that they had built. Finds include coins (*reals*), brass penknives, mirrors, navigational instruments, and four brass guns.

Nieuw Rhoon	Dutch	1776	1970	Capetown, S.A.	Homeward

Finds include a large variety of roundshot and clay pipes, a pottery jar, and Kwangtung Chinese porcelain bowls.

Valentine	British	1779			

Sank while returning on her fourth trip from the east. Finds include cannons, lead ingots, dyewood, Chinese porcelain and a large number of worked and unworked agates.

Middelburg	Dutch	1781	1970s	Saldanha Bay, S.A.	Homeward

Set alight by the ship's commander when a British navy squadron trapped a Dutch fleet in Saldanha Bay, she exploded and sank.

Halsewell	British	1786	?	Seacombe, Dorset, U.K.	Outward

Sank in a southwesterly gale soon after starting the voyage. The area makes systematic recovery very difficult.

Captain Cook in the Pacific

The qualities which are so outstanding in James Cook are perhaps a reflection of the industrial age which was emerging in the 18th century. Farmer's son, naval captain and Royal Society gold medalist, Cook was the greatest explorer-seaman the world has ever known.

In 1755 Cook, aged 27 and largely self-educated, had thrown up command of a Whitby collier to volunteer for the Navy. Within a month he was promoted to master's mate, and a year later passed his examination for master. For the rest of his life he was to be a navigator.

In an era when new philosophical ideas were shaking the foundations of society, and new technology was changing its structure, James Cook found himself in the mathematical intricacies of celestial navigation and astronomy. He was a brilliant marine surveyor who loved the craft of mapmaking, a pragmatic perfectionist who pushed the technology of his day to its very limits.

Exploring the Pacific

Since 1520, when Magellan had sailed into the Pacific after going through the straits that bear his name, dozens of bold navigators had challenged the Pacific from the east, only to meet destruction at the southern end of South America or starvation in the vast reaches of that ocean. From the west, the road into the Pacific had been explored by the Dutch, among others, especially the great navigator Tasman, who had reached Tasmania and New Zealand in the 1640s. But the Dutch East India Company had decided against further exploration, staying with the well-known Indian Ocean passage to the Spice Islands.

In 1768 rumors of a great continent to the south, the so-called Terra Australis Incognita, had recently re-emerged when a British ship had visited Tahiti, and reported the loom of a great continent to the south. The French were not far behind (Bougainville visited Tahiti shortly afterwards), and their English rivals had no desire to see them claim this southern continent and thus acquire a new colonial empire in the far Pacific. It was decided to send an expedition to follow up on the reported discovery of a new continent as soon as possible.

Warships, designed essentially for inshore operation within reach of dockyards, had fared badly in the Pacific. Their commanders tended not to be professional explorers, chartmakers or sophisticated navigators, and their crews had taken terrific losses from scurvy.

The Admiralty's solution was to find a cheap, expendable but suitable ship; to outfit her for exploration, with particular attention to the problem of scurvy; to put her under the command of a professional explorer and mapmaker; and to send her out as an official scientific expedition with the cooperation of the Royal Society.

For a ship, what else but a Whitby collier, one of the little barques famous for their seaworthiness? For a commander, who else but the renowned navigator and mapmaker, Warrant Officer James Cook, a Whitby collier man? So Cook was appointed commander of the *Endeavour*, and instructed to carry members of the Royal Society to Tahiti in order to observe the transit of Venus across the Sun. He was also told to locate Terra Australis on the same voyage.

On this voyage Cook established that there was no southern continent. He also circumnavigated and charted New Zealand, sighted the southeast coast of Australia, and successfully navigated the hazardous Great Barrier Reef. During the three-year expedition not one of his crew died of scurvy.

James Cook was not at ease with "philosophers", as scientists were then sometimes called. Yet he was as good a scientist as any of them. Besides being the finest navigator and surveyor of his age, he was perhaps the first anthropologist of the Pacific, a nutritionist who tested and proved the remedies for scurvy that have saved countless lives. His magnificent charts were made with primitive navigation equipment; on his first voyage even Harrison's chronometer was not available to him. In an age before the term "scientific method" had been coined, Cook used what was to hand in order to do good science.

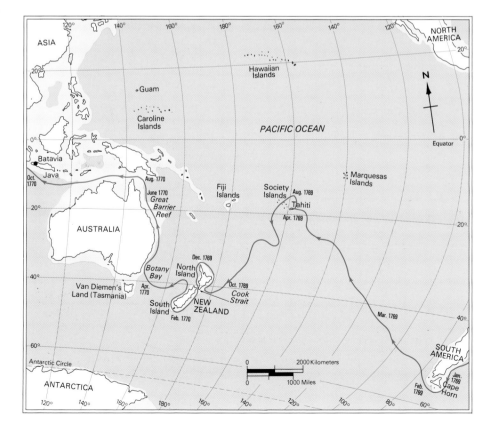

A portrait of Captain James Cook (above), "painted at the Cape of Good Hope" by G. Webber, shows the great navigator suffering from the strain after several years of seaborne exploration. Cook's first voyage (left) 1768–71, brought greater fame to his passengers, such as the gentleman-scientist Joseph Banks, than it did to Cook himself.

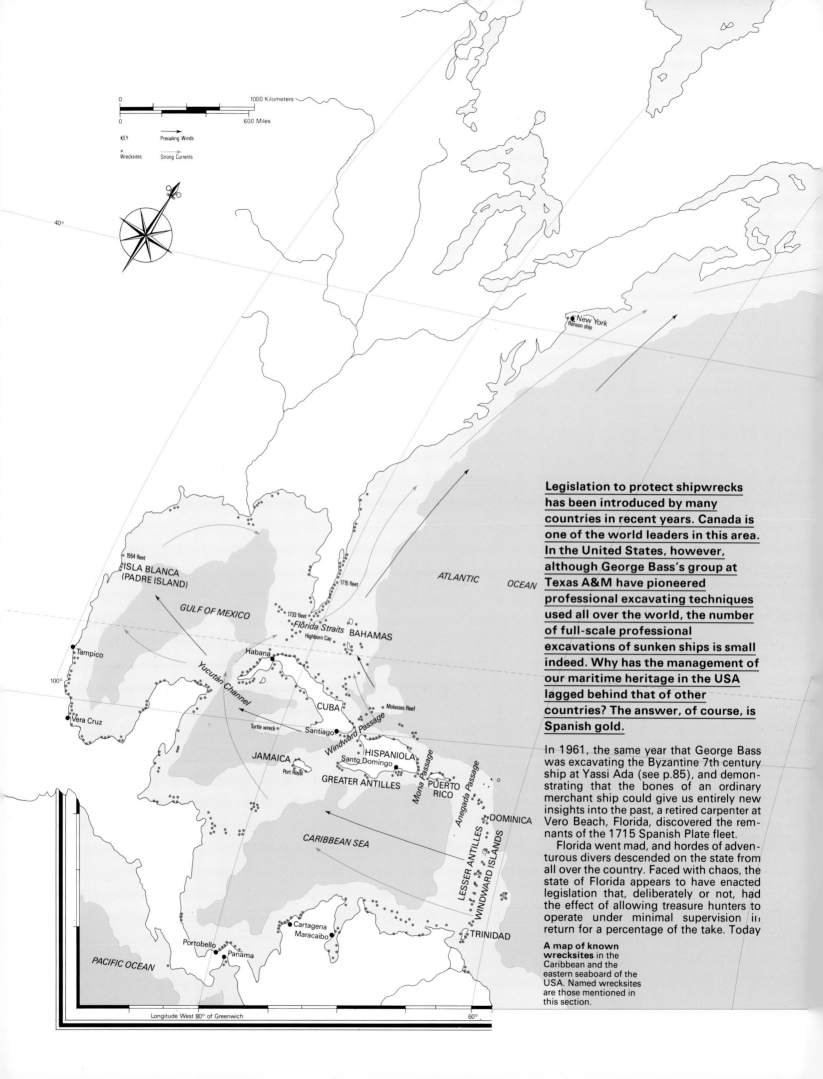

KEY

→ Prevailing Winds

• Wrecksites ⇉ Strong Currents

40°

New York
Ronson ship

ATLANTIC OCEAN

1554 fleet
ISLA BLANCA
(PADRE ISLAND)

1715 fleet

GULF OF MEXICO

1733 fleet

Florida Straits BAHAMAS

Highborn Cay

Habana

Tampico

100°

Yucután Channel

CUBA

Molasses Reef

Vera Cruz

Turtle wreck Santiago

Windward Passage

HISPANIOLA

JAMAICA

Santo Domingo

Port Royal

GREATER ANTILLES PUERTO RICO

Mona Passage

Anegada Passage

DOMINICA

CARIBBEAN SEA

LESSER ANTILLES

WINDWARD ISLANDS

Cartagena

Maracaibo

TRINIDAD

Portobello

Panama

PACIFIC OCEAN

Longitude West 80° of Greenwich

60°

**Legislation to protect shipwrecks
has been introduced by many
countries in recent years. Canada is
one of the world leaders in this area.
In the United States, however,
although George Bass's group at
Texas A&M have pioneered
professional excavating techniques
used all over the world, the number
of full-scale professional
excavations of sunken ships is small
indeed. Why has the management of
our maritime heritage in the USA
lagged behind that of other
countries? The answer, of course, is
Spanish gold.**

In 1961, the same year that George Bass
was excavating the Byzantine 7th century
ship at Yassi Ada (see p.85), and demonstrating that the bones of an ordinary
merchant ship could give us entirely new
insights into the past, a retired carpenter at
Vero Beach, Florida, discovered the remnants of the 1715 Spanish Plate fleet.

Florida went mad, and hordes of adventurous divers descended on the state from
all over the country. Faced with chaos, the
state of Florida appears to have enacted
legislation that, deliberately or not, had
the effect of allowing treasure hunters to
operate under minimal supervision in
return for a percentage of the take. Today

**A map of known
wrecksites** in the
Caribbean and the
eastern seaboard of the
USA. Named wrecksites
are those mentioned in
this section.

The Age of Discovery/Introduction

Red Bay, Labrador. Canada's achievements in maritime archaeology include the excavation of a ship in the Great Lakes (the Mallorytown wreck) by Walter Zacharchuk, and that of the frigate *Machault* in the St Lawrence estuary by Zacharchuk and Robert Grenier of Parks Canada in the mid 1960s. After a season at Kyrenia with Michael Katzev (see p.55), work continued on the *Machault*. Then Grenier did a brilliant excavation of the *San Juan*, a 16th century Basque whaling ship at Red Bay, Labrador, in collaboration with James Tuck, who excavated the land part of the whaling station.

The Parks Canada conservation lab at Ottawa leads the world in innovative conservation of underwater material. Unlike her big neighbor to the south, the Canadian government gives considerable financial support to archaeology.

Map labels: Moore Point, Penney Island, THE HARBOUR, RED BAY, San Juan, Lighthouse, Saddle Island, Saddle Island Rocks, Twin Island Rocks, Twin Island

the state museum in Tallahassee is brimful of Spanish gold and silver, and store-rooms are packed with tons of smashed pottery and rusting iron. A few shriveled chunks of wood remind the visitor, faintly, that all these goodies came from ships.

Of course, there is big money in the treasure business, although it does not always come the way of the investors. The ones who have profited most from the great treasure craze have been the lawyers: in the last 25 years more money has been spent on lawsuits over treasure in Florida than has been spent on maritime archaeology worldwide.

American treasure hunters are blasting holes in the sand all over the Caribbean. The device which does the work is a giant pipe elbow, rigged so that it can deflect the propwash downward. A really big one can be 6ft (1.8m) in diameter, and in a few minutes will dig a hole in soft sand or mud 10ft (3m) deep and 30ft (9m) around. The standard platform for such a rig is a surplus oilfield supply vessel. It is hard to estimate how many such vessels are operating in the Caribbean at present, because the treasure salvors' world is a secretive one. A good estimate might be somewhere in the region of 25.

Caribbean activity

Newly independent Caribbean island governments, beset as they are with the typical post-colonial problems of poverty and disorganization, generally have little time for or interest in maritime archaeology. Thus they are vulnerable to the blandishments of treasure hunters. A chance for millions in return for a permit may seem a good investment to governments beleaguered with chronic balance of payments problems.

At the time of writing, a British group with a successful track record for salvaging modern vessels has raised $4,000,000 on Wall Street for work in the Turks and Caicos, and is operating there with the permission of the government. An American group is operating in the Bahamas, also with full permission from its government, and a treasure hunting concession for part of the Dominican Republic has been obtained by another US group.

Elsewhere in the Dominican Republic, however, the story is rather different. In 1985, an American company by the name of North Caribbean Research obtained a concession for shipwreck exploration from the Dominican government. The area consisted of 100 miles (160km) of coastline west of the Haitian border, and the aim of the group was to promote research in coordination with commercial development, including not only archaeology but also marine biology and mariculture.

In 1986, working as a consultant in collaboration with local fishermen, I was involved in the location of 18 shipwrecks in the area between Monte Christi and Manzanillo. These ranged from an early 17th century Dutch cargo vessel to a 19th century American sailing ship. Two mid 18th century French wrecks have been identified, both carrying cargoes of high quality faience pottery, possibly from Nantes. A museum of underwater archaeology, financed by NCR and Manzanillo city, was opened in January 1987.

Maritime archaeology in the USA

In the United States itself, treasure hunters and their lawyers have established a powerful lobby claiming that their activities are just good old American enterprise. The archaeologists, meanwhile, are attempting to get a law passed that will take shipwrecks buried in the seabed out of the jurisdiction of the federal admiralty courts and give jurisdiction to the states.

Nevertheless, apart from the general confusion caused by treasure fever, maritime archaeology is doing well in the United States. Most states are being responsible about protecting their shipwreck heritage. Dozens of bright young archaeologists from Texas A&M are getting their PhDs elsewhere and taking their places in the archaeological hierarchy. At East Carolina University, another MA program in nautical archaeology has been started by the brilliant young archaeologist Gordon Watts. One of its projects is to identify and evaluate all the ships sunk during the American Civil War (786 so far), so that the most important ones can be protected.

It seems, then, that the orgy of destruction which began on Vero Beach in 1961 has reached its crescendo, and the United States will soon join the majority of civilized countries in definitively protecting its maritime heritage.

Trade and piracy in the West Indies

New World riches came to Spain along a tenuous maritime lifeline, as witnessed by recently excavated wrecks replete with weaponry, valuables and personal possessions. But the Caribbean was not allowed to remain a Spanish lake for long. Other European nations challenged their monopoly, and privateers, smugglers and pirates flourished. The drowned city of Port Royal, destroyed in 1692, is proving a "pirates' Pompeii" for marine archaeologists.

Within a decade of the discovery of America by Christopher Columbus, Spanish mariners had charted most of the Caribbean's major islands, noting that winds and currents moved in a prevailing direction from east to west. They found that the Caribbean Basin is in fact a large enclosed sea, similar to the Mediterranean, and one that cannot easily be exited from the same entrances under sail.

Entering through the Windward or Leeward Islands, early navigators found that their ships could not efficiently retrace the same routes to regain the Atlantic by beating upwind. Instead, they discovered that three main avenues between the Great Antilles – the Anegada,

Mona and Windward passages – permitted ships to leave the basin through the Old Bahama Channel, which would take them northward into the Atlantic to catch the trade winds back to Europe.

In the process of exploration and discovery, Spaniards also found that the Caribbean Sea, unlike the Mediterranean, contained vast banks of shoal waters lined with hazardous coral reefs, which were more difficult to chart than cloud-covered islands, and which also threatened to wreck any unsuspecting vessel venturing in the vicinity, especially at night or in stormy weather. One unfortunate ship that did sink on just such a reef-lined bank is now named the Molasses Reef wreck and has recently been excavated. This and the Highborn Cay wreck together represent a major archaeological breakthrough in our knowledge of how early 16th century vessels were built, and give us new insight into the kind of ship that was first employed by Europeans to explore the New World.

The Molasses Reef wreck
In the 16th century, a small Spanish ship was sailing northwest through the deep waters of the Old Bahama Channel, when she struck the reef-strewn edge of the Caicos Bank, north of Hispaniola. This vessel now represents one of the earliest shipwrecks yet found in the New World.

Isolated from any land, the site eventually became known as the

Molasses Reef, an area that even today remains poorly charted. Spilling ballast stones, torn lead sheathing and bent iron fasteners as she ground over coral spurs, the unlucky vessel finally came to rest in a small sandy canyon on the reef's outer edge, in 20ft (6m) of water. As the ship keeled over on the seabed, her artillery and ammunition tumbled from the deck to the sand below.

Centuries passed before the site was discovered in the 1970s by wreck hunters, who recognized the antiquity of the early wrought-iron ordnance, and took several pieces as souvenirs. Treasure hunters claiming to have found the site of Columbus's *Pinta* (and thereby hoping to raise funds to work the site) arrived at the reef in 1980. Their unsuccessful attempts to mount an expedition prompted the Government of the Turks and Caicos Islands to invite the Institute of Nautical Archaeology (INA) at Texas A&M University to give the wrecksite the scientific attention it deserved.

After a brief survey, systematic excavation of the Molasses Reef wreck began in 1982, under the direction of Donald M. Keith. The site consisted of a mound of ballast stones 39ft (12m) in length and 10ft (3m) in breadth, upon which were situated an anchor, and two large wrought-iron cannons, or *bombardetas*. A scatter of 15 smaller wrought-iron swivel guns, or *versas* were spread over the seafloor, alongside the ballast pile.

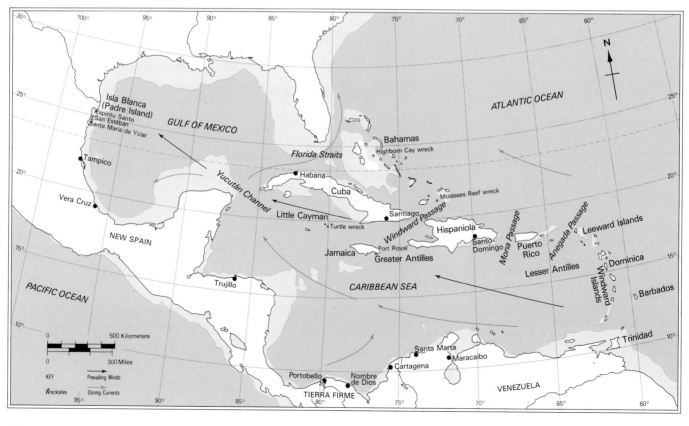

Lead and iron shot, as well as powder chambers for each kind of ordnance, were distributed throughout the site.

Typical of artillery commonly carried on European vessels during the first half of the 16th century, the *bombardetas* had represented the main battery of the ship's weapons system, while the smaller *versas* served as anti-personnel ordnance, mounted on swivel yokes along the vessel's railings. Each type of artillery was designed to be loaded from the breech with interchangeable chambers that allowed rapid and repetitive firing. Unlike later artillery cast in a mold, each had been laboriously forged by hand, long iron staves being welded together to form the barrel, which was reinforced by a series of sleeves and rings.

Ammunition for the guns consisted of cast and wrought-iron solid shot, solid lead shot, and lead wrapped around an iron cube, which formed a hard core. The two-part shot molds that were discovered on the wrecksite indicate that the ship's crew had been capable of casting ammunition at sea. In addition, fragmentary examples of shoulder arms were found, including two octagonal-barreled *haquebuts* (an early form of matchlock musket), and two crossbows. These portable weapons, along with edged weapons, would have accompanied the mariners during any reconnaissance they carried out on shore.

The site began to reveal other secrets as excavation progressed. Fragmentary sherds of utilitarian ceramic vessels were carefully collected from the ballast pile and surrounding nooks and crannies in the seabed. Rather than being cargo, they represented storage containers for the ship's provisions – basins for washing, pots for waste, and common tablewares that served the men on board. Despite the wreck's exposed situation in the shallow forereef zone, fragile portions of tiny glass medicinal vials turned up. They may have belonged to a pharmaceutical chest carried on board to relieve common ailments at sea.

Concurrent archival research in Spain is being undertaken to determine whether the identity of the ship can be ascertained through records of early voyages to the New World. Comparative analysis of the wreck's ordnance, ceramic and glassware with known examples from Europe and other early Spanish terrestrial sites in the Americas dates the Molasses Reef Wreck to the first half of the 16th century, and tentatively, to the first quarter.

The Highborn Cay wreck

Occasional losses of ships, such as that wrecked on the Molasses Reef, did not impede the Spanish mariners' increasing knowledge of the islands and shoals north of the Greater Antilles, as they sought Indian slaves from the Bahamian archipelago to replace the dwindling numbers of aboriginal laborers on Hispaniola. But other dangers awaited early European navigators among the myriad islands and reefs: tidal currents racing through narrow channels, and squalls and storms moving unimpeded over the low-lying land forms. Even with the modern navigational aids of today, sailing at night or in bad weather among the Bahama banks is considered tricky. Thus it comes as no surprise that other wrecks have been salvaged from this hazardous stretch of sea, adding vital information to our knowledge of the Age of Discovery.

In 1965, three skindivers discovered a small ballast mound with several pieces of encrusted artillery and an anchor, sited in the lee of a tiny island called Highborn Cay, on the edge of the Great Bahama Bank. The shipwreck's wrought-iron ordnance, the lead ammunition and simple hardware, all suggested that the vessel dated from the 16th century.

The discoverers obtained a salvage license from the government of the Bahamas and sought assistance from Mendel Peterson, formerly of the Smithsonian Institution. Beginning in 1966, all the visible iron materials were raised from the site, and portions of each end of the ballast pile were excavated, revealing remnants of the ship's wooden hull beneath the stones. Recovered artifacts were taken to the United States, a brief report was written, and the site was forgotten until researchers at the Institute of Nautical Archaeology (INA) began work

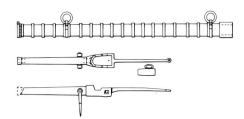

The Caribbean is a hazardous sea and difficult to chart (map far left). Many of the Spaniards who first explored the area came to grief on its coral reefs. The homeward-bound Spanish ships, carrying treasure from the New World, would follow prevailing winds and currents from Vera Cruz to Havana, sailing along the western shores of the Gulf of Mexico as far as the 28th parallel. They then sailed due east until the coast of Florida was sighted, and Cuba could be approached from the north. The 1554 fleet was taking this route.

Wrought-iron swivel guns, or *versas*, like the one above, were found at the Molasses Reef wrecksite. Similar weapons, used as anti-personnel ordnance, were found at Highborn Cay and at the 1554 fleet wrecksite.

Air-filled lifting bags help members of the Institute of Nautical Archaeology team to raise an early 16th century wrought-iron cannon from the seabed (right). It was part of the weapons system carried aboard the small Spanish vessel that was wrecked on the edge of the Caicos Bank – the Molasses Reef wreck.

on the Molasses Reef wrecksite in 1982.

Hoping to learn more about the High-born Cay wrecksite and to contrast its artifacts with apparently similar objects simultaneously being uncovered at Molasses Reef, the INA research team contacted several members of the original salvage team for comparative data. They found that ordnance from the vessel, such as *bombardetas* and swivel guns, was very similar to that found on the Molasses Reef wreck. Unique among the weapons was a wrought-iron barbed harpoon with a shaft 5ft (2m) long. The few personal effects recovered from the Highborn Cay vessel were also similar to those found at Molasses Reef.

In both sites, the similar distribution pattern of the large wrought-iron anchor and the *bombardetas* suggested that small seagoing vessels of this period tended to carry their heavier ordnance and anchors below deck to lower their center of gravity while underway.*

The Highborn Cay wrecksite was similar to that of Molasses Reef, and most of the ballast had been left undisturbed, so we decided to reinvestigate it in order to see if we could find out more about 16th century hulls. In 1983, with permission from the government of the Bahamas, the site was relocated, and exposed fragments of ship's timbers were found to be protruding from beneath the ballast stones. Returning to the wreck in 1986, we discovered that the hull of the ship had been well preserved over the centuries, despite the shallow, warm Caribbean waters and heavy tidal current moving across the site.

Our brief examination of the remains provided us with precisely the kind of crucial structural details that were missing from the Molasses Reef wreck. Both vessels offer a vivid picture of the kind of ships that were used to cross the Atlantic in the 16th century.

The tragedy of the 1554 Fleet

The discovery of another exit from the Caribbean Sea, the Yucatan Channel, occurred with the circumnavigation of Cuba in 1509. The channel led into the Gulf of Mexico, opening another area for Spanish maritime exploration. As Spanish soldiers marched inland toward Aztec riches, Spanish navigators coasted the perimeter of the Gulf, noting unusual landmarks and charting river deltas, anchorages and roadsteads. However, although American treasures began to find their way back to Spain, the new shipping route still held many unforeseen dangers, especially the devastating tropical hurricanes.

In the spring of 1554, four small Spanish merchant vessels, *Santa Maria de Yciar, San Esteban, Espiritu Santo* and *San Andres*, were sailing from Mexico to Spain, via Havana, with cargoes of silver, gold, sugar, silk, wool, cochineal and cow hides, as well as official documents and private letters. There were 400 people on board, including elderly conquistadors, wealthy merchants and settlers, and Spanish citizens returning home, however, only a quarter of them were to see their homeland again.

Following the normal route from Vera Cruz to Havana, the four vessels were caught after only 20 days at sea in one of those vicious storms that typically haunt the Gulf of Mexico during April. Blown off course by raging winds and seas, the ships were forced due west toward the desolate shores of southern Texas and Isla Blanca, now known as Padre Island.

Despite the mariners' desperate efforts to avoid grounding by casting anchors overboard as they approached the beach, three of the ships were dashed to pieces on the sands and only the disabled *San Andres* managed to reach Havana.

The shipwrecked survivors may well have thought themselves less fortunate than their drowned companions as their ordeal continued. Harassed by bands of hostile Indians, burned by the sun and weakened by exhaustion, the castaways set out southwards, along a shoreline of wind-swept sand dunes and little fresh water, to the Spanish missionary outpost of Tampico. Few reached civilization to tell of their terrible experiences.

The loss of the three ships was a major blow to the Spanish economy, since their cargoes contained precious metals urgently needed by the Crown to settle

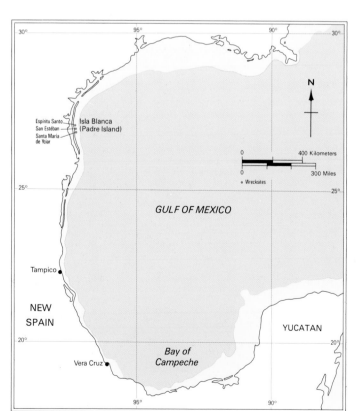

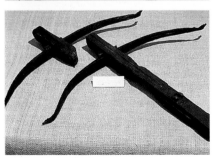

The wrecksites of the 1554 fleet are shown (map far left). A fierce storm in the Gulf of Mexico blew the ships off course towards the shores of southern Texas. Three of them were wrecked at Padre Island and the unfortunate castaways began a tortuous march south to the Spanish missionary outpost at Tampico.

Precious metals, including silver discs, gold ingots and silver coinage (left), were found at the 1554 fleet wrecksite. The coins, minted in Mexico City, were in denominations of one, two, three and four *reales*. Wooden military crossbows recovered from the 1554 fleet wrecksite were remarkably well preserved, and even the main stock of one survived (below left).

A small pneumatic chisel is used by a conservator at the Texas Archaeological Research Laboratory (right) to clean an artillery piece, a wrought-iron cannon or *bombardeta*, also found at the 1554 fleet wrecksite.

debts with other nations. A salvage fleet of six vessels was soon despatched, reaching the wrecksites in July 1555. Divers worked on the vessels in shallow water until September, when all remaining cargo that could be located had been recovered from the vicinity.

For almost 400 years the wrecks lay hidden beneath the sands of Padre Island, the only clues to their existence being occasional coins washed up on the beach. Then, in the late 1940s, the United States Army Corps Engineers came across the wreckage of a ship as they were dredging a cut through Padre Island. The wrecksite was largely destroyed as ship's timbers, chains and anchors became caught in the dredge; but the silver coins and other artifacts from the spoil suggested that the ship had been Spanish.

However, her identification remained unclear until, in 1964, similar coins discovered along a section of Padre Island prompted a treasure hunting company, Platoro Inc., to search for their source offshore. Dates and denominations on the coins led to archival documents connected with the loss of the three merchant ships in 1554. Platoro located one of the wrecks and began to recover more coins as well as bullion, artillery, navigational instruments and numerous other artifacts, before being halted by a court order. Little or no effort had been made to record or map the site, and the recovery of artifacts concentrated on valuable objects, which

were subsequently taken to the Platoro company base at Indiana.

The removal of the artifacts from Texas caused a public outcry, leading to the establishment of the Texas Antiquities Committee whose aim was to protect cultural resources. The salvaged materials were returned to Texas where they were safely conserved in 1971.

During the following six years, the Antiquities Committee conducted conclusive archival research and archaeological investigations on the 1554 fleet. Translation of hundreds of documents helped to piece together the story of the tragedy, and tentatively to identify the shipwreck destroyed by dredging as the *Santa Maria de Yciar*, and that salvaged by Platoro as *Espiritu Santo*. Extensive magnetometric measurements of the shallow, turbid waters off Padre Island revealed scattered and buried wreckage of a third ship, presumed to be the *San Esteban*.

Under the direction of archaeologists Carl Clausen and J. Barto Arnold, a large assemblage of 16th century weapons, instruments, goods, ship's hardware and cargo were carefully plotted, excavated and conserved for public display. This combined inventory of restored artifacts from the wrecksites, and the massive archival documentation, made possible the most comprehensive study yet to be published of colonial Spanish shipwrecks.

The artifacts were x-rayed to determine their nature and then carefully extracted

from the conglomerate in which they were encrusted, after centuries on the seabed. As work progressed, under the supervision of conservator D.L. Hamilton, remarkable details of weapons systems, cargoes and personal possessions carried aboard 16th century Spanish merchant ships, gradually came to light.

The 1554 wreck had several features in common with the ships at Molasses Reef and Highborn Cay. Hand-forged wrought iron *bombardetas* formed the bulk of the vessel's defensive artillery and lighter swiveled *versas* had been mounted as rapid firing anti-personnel weapons. In some cases, iron and bronze breech chambers were found to have been plugged with wooden stoppers to protect their powder charges from moisture at sea. Also preserved were military crossbows (including one with a unique "goat's foot" cocking mechanism), as well as fragments of a sword, a knife and chain mail, all embedded in concretions that had to be carefully cleaned.

The fleet had been carrying an official cargo of precious metals – including silver coinage from Mexico city, crude silver disks and marked gold ingots. Among the personal possessions of the passengers were pewter plates, porringers, ceramics, German stoneware, a small silver thimble, brass buckles, a small gold crucifix and a tiny wooden cross trimmed with gold.

Interesting objects of aboriginal nature were also recovered, such as obsidian

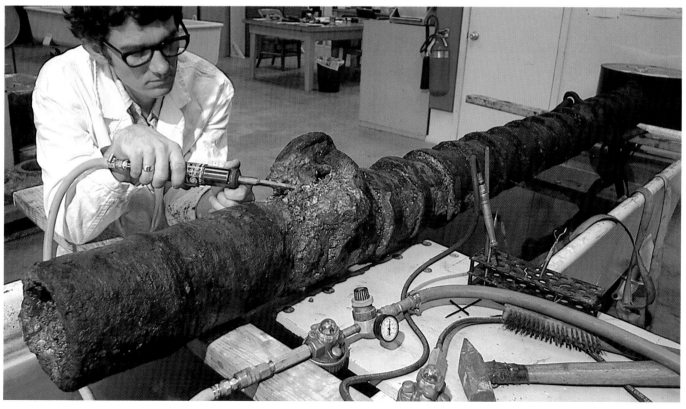

blades, an iron pyrite bead and a polished pyrite mirror. These probably represent native souvenirs being taken home by an ethnographic-minded collector. Mariner's equipment included three brass astrolabes (ancestors of modern sextants), brass navigational dividers, and numerous tools such as hammers, pincers and a pick adze – all indispensable for repairs at sea.

Scientific treatment of the 1554 vessels by the Texas Antiquities Committee represented a major advance in New World shipwreck archaeology. Patient and systematic laboratory procedures, combined with careful recording and painstaking archival research allowed jumbled pieces of the historical puzzle to be reassembled. Even the smallest components of the wreckage, such as the remains of 16 stowaway cockroaches with egg cases which represented both Old and New World species, did not go overlooked. An impressive museum display presently resides in Corpus Christi, Texas, displaying the earliest remains of Spanish maritime endeavors yet to be found in the United States.

Information on the constructional nature of the ships was derived from a portion of the *San Esteban*'s keel assemblage. After cleaning and conservation, fragments of the vessel revealed clues as to its dimensions and method of construction. Even minute details came to light, such as how the calking of the hull planks had been accomplished with a mixture of oakum and animal hair, held in place by a resin-soaked fabric covered by thin strips of lead to prevent teredo worm infestation of the hull.

European rivals in the Caribbean

Spain's newly found wealth soon brought jealous European rivals in the wake of her growing maritime convoy system. Early in the 16th century, French corsairs began to congregate in the Mona Passage, between Puerto Rico and Hispaniola, ready to pounce on Spanish ships beating their way into the Atlantic.

Soon England's merchants began to seek a share in the market created by Spain's American colonists. Slave-trading expeditions under Sir John Hawkins in the 1560s ended in a disastrous battle with the Spaniards along the Mexican coast, so that for the next three decades English ships came to the Caribbean as raiders rather than traders. Foremost among the privateers was Sir Francis Drake (of Armada fame), who organized annual raids against the Spanish colonies, ultimately sacking Santa Domingo and Cartegena, as well as disrupting trade in both the Caribbean and the Pacific.

Intrusion into the West Indies by smugglers, pirates and privateers indicated to Spain that her monopoly in the region would soon be openly challenged, as the establishment of new foreign settlements grew. By the early 17th century, England, France and the Netherlands had gained footholds along the South American coast and, later, settlements in the Lesser Antilles.

In 1655, an official English expedition succeeded in taking Jamaica, at that time an underpopulated and poorly defended Spanish colony. Mariners soon began to congregate at Port Royal, a strategic spit of land situated at the entrance to Kingston Harbor. Some ventured to the neighboring Cayman Islands, where they learned from French mariners how to collect sea turtles – a vital food source in pre-refrigeration days since they could be kept alive for weeks aboard a ship or in salt water pens. Other newcomers turned to buccaneering, and the money and merchandise taken from passing Spanish ships began to pour into Port Royal.

Elsewhere, a growing network of French and English adventurers, disaffected planters, and runaway sailors had begun to gather on the tiny island of Tortuga, a few miles off the coast of Hispaniola, where there was a promise of fresh water and victuals, and a place to hide and to refit their vessels. These *flibustiers* or buccaneers, loosely-knit bands of desperadoes, traded cow hide, meat and plunder from passing Spanish ships in return for liquor, guns and cloth from Dutch and English vessels calling at the outlaw post.*

Tortuga quickly became notorious, and the pirates' headquarters began to be

Captain Kidd, the 17th century British privateer who became a legendary pirate, sailed the renowned *Adventure* (above). Kidd was originally a legitimate privateer, commissioned to attack French traders and Red Sea pirates. His ship, launched in 1695 at the Thames River shipyard, Deptford, England, was designed for speed, firepower and maneuverability and so was equally well suited to piracy. By 1697, Kidd had still not taken a prize ship and so resorted to piracy. He reached Anguilla, in the West Indies, in 1699, after scuttling *Adventure*, by then unseaworthy, only to learn that he had been denounced as a pirate. *Adventure* was a hybrid vessel, combining a modern hull and sail rig with oar power. Under full sail, with 3,200 yards (2,900m) of canvas, she could make 14 knots. Without wind, but with two or three pirates straining at each of her 46 oars, she could still move at three knots. Apart from the captain's cabin (1) and a nearby cubby for the first mate (2), the interior of *Adventure* was spartan to the extreme. There were no crew quarters as such and at night the 150 or so crew were crammed into the 124ft (38m)-long hull and slept wherever they could. The shot locker, with its six tons of shot for the 12-pounder cannon, and the huge water casks (3), each weighing a ton, were located amidships to help ballast the ship.

179

constantly attacked by Spanish ships, forcing the buccaneers to look for a new base of operations. They soon found an ideal retreat at Port Royal.

Raids by English privateers against Mexico, Central America and Cuba from this new stronghold persuaded Spain to mount a reprisal against the English in Jamaica, a virtual declaration of war.

The Turtle Wreck

The Spanish authorities issued a privateering commission to the Portuguese-born corsair, Manuel Rivero Pardal, who arrived at the Cayman Islands with five ships, flying false English colors, and opened fire on a guard ship *Hopewell*, stationed at Little Cayman. The Spanish took the ship and captured the crew. Three months later, they attacked the Cayman Islands again, raiding and burning houses and taking prisoners.

In 1979 the Institute of Nautical Archaeology found, at South Hole Sound, Little Cayman, wreckage thought to be associated with Rivero's attack.

Outlines of ship's timbers and ballast stones were visible along the edge of a low mound of turtle grass, which extended into a large depression in the sandy floor of the lagoon. As the digging began, evidence of fire damage to the upper surfaces of buried planking and

frames was immediately apparent. Also, turtle bones, some charred around the edges, began to emerge from the sand.*

Fortunately, the sediment overburden was minimal and a compacted grass root structure had provided a protective mantle, preserving the buried remnants of the wrecked vessel. We even found an intact segment of hemp line and a worm-eaten pulley sheave – part of the ship's rigging and tackle.*

Careful recording at Turtle wreck enabled us to deduce that the wreck represented the remains of a small sailing ship, solidly framed and fastened with iron and measuring some 60ft (18m). The discovery of a cannon carriage wheel indicated that the vessel was armed, like most of the ships that ventured into remote waters during colonial times. However, the rest of the vessel's armaments and her anchors were not found, and it seems possible that the cannons and anchors were salvaged shortly after sinking or in subsequent years.

The evidence suggests that the crew were seamen engaged in turtling on the island. Limited provisions were stored aboard the ship in wooden barrels and earthenware jars. The crew members smoked tobacco in clay pipes; ate fish, dried fruit and turtle; and carried a cargo of live turtles, kept on their backs and

lashed together by their flippers. Had the live turtles not been bound by their flippers, they would have escaped when the vessel sank. Our analysis of the clay pipes and ceramic fragments suggested that the ship was destroyed in the mid 17th century, apparently by fire.

A systematic magnetometric search of the vicinity led to further test excavations, recovering a spent lead musket ball, flattened by impact, some "slow match", and a 17th century musket barrel found with a Spanish jar. This suggested that the Turtle Wreck represented a fire following the arrival of Rivero's punitive fleet in 1670.

Rivero's activities led to renewed conflict with the Spaniards, bringing about the destruction of the city of Panama by the celebrated privateer Henry Morgan. Rivero himself was shot later, apparently by one of Morgan's henchmen, and his frigate *San Pedro y La Fama* was taken to Port Royal. Documents found on the ship, including personal letters and reprisal commissions, were sent to England as proof of Spain's organized intentions, and can still be seen in the archives.

The demise of the corsair Rivero marked the end of a unique chapter of West Indian rivalry in which Tortuga buccaneers, Port Royal privateers, and Cayman Island turtlers played a central role in the power struggle.

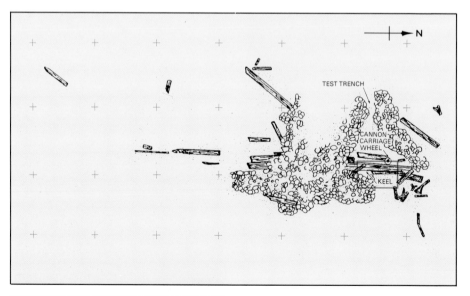

The abundance of turtle bones and shells (above) found at the Turtle wrecksite gave support to historic accounts of local turtling operations and helped to identify the vessel as one lost during the first

recorded battle in Cayman history in 1670. The cargo of live turtles had their flippers tied together, otherwise they might have been able to escape when the vessel sank.

The wheel of a cannon carriage, uncovered amid other hull remains of the Turtle wreck, is measured *in situ* (left). This discovery indicates that the vessel was carrying at least one piece of heavy ordnance to protect her crew and cargo.

A plan of the Turtle wrecksite (above) shows the surviving timbers in relation to the remains of the ballast, giving an insight into the character of the vessel. Her narrow beam and shallow draft had let her enter the Sound with ease. The red square indicates the diver's location.

The sunken city of Port Royal

Ratified in 1670, the Treaty of Madrid proclaimed peace between England and Spain, and the two rival colonists revoked all reprisal commissions and licenses to take prize ships. Moreover, Spain at last legally recognized England's possession of Jamaica, the Cayman Islands and other satellites. Yet, piracy continued, centered at Port Royal, until Henry Morgan himself, knighted by Charles II, returned to the region as Lieutenant-Governor of Jamaica, and proceeded vigorously to suppress his former pirate colleagues.

Jamaica's importance in Atlantic trade continued to grow, and Port Royal became one of the most cosmopolitan cities in the West Indies. Commerce in sugar, slaves and raw materials made her the "hub of the Caribbean", a wealthy maritime center. Yet her reputation as one of the most wicked cities in the New World lingered on, as former pirates rubbed shoulders with countless sailors, merchants and craftsmen, along water-front wharves and in taverns, brothels and accounting houses. At the height of its prosperity, Port Royal had an estimated population of 6,500 people and as many as 2,000 buildings, concentrated in 51 acres at the tip of a sandy peninsula projecting from the island. Many of the buildings were brick-built, and some were several stories tall, crowded together on narrow streets which lay between the sea and the harbor.

That period of prosperity came to an abrupt end at 11.40am on June 7 1692. At that instant a severe earthquake shook Port Royal, causing almost two-thirds of the city to slide into the ocean. Shock waves radiated throughout the island, and the compacted sand foundations of the city rapidly turned into a jelly-like fluid of sediments that could no longer support the weight of manmade structures. It is estimated that 2,000 people were killed instantly by the earthquake and the subsequent tidal wave that came ashore from the harbor. An additional 3,000 people died of injuries and disease in the days following the initial disaster.

Then, while survivors combed through the devastated townsite, salvage seekers worked in the drowned harbor, beginning a tradition of underwater recovery that was to continue for years afterwards.

Today, that tradition is beginning to come full circle with the recognition that the sunken city of Port Royal is perhaps the most important 17th century English archaeological site in the world. The cataclysm that sent Jamaica's pirate port into underwater oblivion perfectly preserved its 17th century character. In terms of archaeology, her underwater remains can be compared to Pompeii and Herculaneum – prosperous cities which were suddenly buried by volcanic ash, to become time capsules entombed from the day of their disappearance and waiting to be unearthed.

After the initial looting phase had ceased, the drowned city was virtually forgotten until 1859, when a Royal Navy helmet diver identified the remains of Fort James, marking the northwestern edge of the original city. This was not followed up for another 100 years, when, in 1959, underwater explorer Edwin Link employed United States Navy divers to bring up artifacts from the fort and the nearby King's Warehouse. However, it was not until 1966 that a serious excavation of the sunken city began, under the auspices of the government of Jamaica.

The site was faced with imminent dredging for a modern deepwater port, but after two years of intensive work by the American diver Robert Marx, thousands of 17th century artifacts were recovered from the southwestern portion of the site, where the fish and meat markets had originally been located. A trove of English pewter, glass and ceramic wares emerged from under Port Royal's fallen walls and buried foundations.* Catalogued by Marx, the vast collection formed the basis for the first museum of

A treasure trove of 17th century English pewter utensils (above), paralleling those unearthed by archaeologists from land sites of an equivalent age, was recovered from the southwest portion of the sunken city of Port Royal in the 1960s.

An eye-witness account, and a moralistic one at that, of the earthquake that befell Port Royal (right) was published a century later in The London Times. In the illustration buildings are shown toppling to the ground and being swallowed up, and boats being wrecked against the coastline. A circle of people can be seen on their knees, praying. The account contains horrifying details of what became of certain individuals: the author sees the earthquake as a terrible warning from God that Man should mend his ways.

historical archaeology in the Caribbean. Later, a portion of St Paul's Church, destroyed in the earthquake, was unearthed by Philip Mayes, an English archaeologist who installed a pump system to lower the water level of the sandy spit sufficiently for a dig on land.

Archaeology and the records
In 1981, the Institute of Nautical Archaeology was invited to continue excavations on the sunken city. Port Royal's Old Naval Hospital, constructed in 1817 to combat yellow fever and other maladies, became the project's headquarters, museum and laboratory. A field school for students of underwater archaeology was established under the direction of Dr D.L. Hamilton.

The field school offers students from many different universities a unique opportunity to learn the techniques and procedures of underwater archaeology. Excavation teams are responsible for unearthing and recording finds, and these are sorted and catalogued after each dive. The Old Naval Hospital complex contains conservation and photographic libraries, and staff members coordinate cleaning, stabilizing and eventual display of the recovered artifacts. Location and excavation of the entire sunken townsite will require decades of dedicated work, but

the establishment of the field school represents a precedent of cooperative international research which will hopefully continue elsewhere, not only in the Caribbean but on a global level.

At the outset of the Port Royal project, Hamilton was concerned to carry out controlled archaeological excavations on the sunken city, and to match submerged features of Port Royal with 17th century real estate records. His group found that they could easily identify the remains of the drowned city, lying in shallow clear water beneath a layer of post-earthquake deposits, which included a lens of dead coral marking the destruction caused by one or more early 18th century hurricanes. Below the coral, the foundations of old Port Royal were revealed like pieces of an architectural puzzle.

As work continued, careful dredging gradually unearthed a large multi-room structure. The foundations and brick floors suggested that the building had originally contained three rooms, with three more added later. Fallen walls and architectural debris covered the building's floors, indicating the existence of an upper story, while wooden door jambs were still in place in the doorways between the walls of the rooms.

Within the building, the team discovered pewter utensils, glass and ceramic tablewares, butchered animal bones, turtle shells, hand tools, pipe stems and a complete wicker basket, preserved within the earthquake layer. One room yielded a Bellarmine jug, two wooden kegs, a gun, lead shot and, within a walled enclosure, over 60 liquor bottles, many still corked and containing liquid.

Comparing the dig's location with 17th century maps of Port Royal, Hamilton concluded that the building had been situated in a central business district adjacent to the harbor. The architecture and artifacts suggest that this was a typical English terraced or row house that had been expanded to meet the economic opportunities of a booming colonial outpost, in response to the varied services that its location demanded. In this one building, it appears that shops and living quarters alternated with taverns and storerooms. Confined geographically to a natural sandspit, buildings and their occupants had been crammed together in a geologically unstable but economically lucrative situation.*

Excavation of the entire sunken townsite will require decades of work, but the establishment of the field school represents a precedent of cooperative international research which hopefully will continue elsewhere, not only in the Caribbean, but on a global level.

A pewter tankard, candlestick and wine bottle illustrate the variety of 17th century household objects that fell into the sea during the 1692 earthquake.

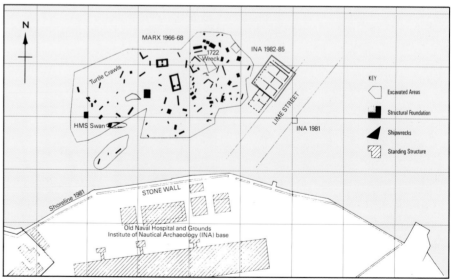

A plan of Port Royal (above) shows the portions of the sunken townsite that have been excavated. The red square designates the site of the excavation of the doorjamb.

Divers excavate a doorjamb (left) from one of the sunken Port Royal buildings. The jamb was so well preserved, retaining sharp corners and smooth edges, that the divers were able to ascertain from the absence of wear normally caused by foot traffic over a long period, that the building was probably not very old when it slid into the sea.

Spanish treasure fleets

The quest for precious metals, which Europe had run dangerously short of by the end of the 15th century, was the principal driving force behind Spain's ventures in the New World. The annexations of Mexico and Peru brought discovery and control of substantial gold and silver reserves, especially the fabulous silver mines of Potosi, south of Lake Titicaca. Between 1503 and 1660, some 35 million lb (16 million kg) of silver arrived at Seville – enough to triple the existing silver resources of Europe.

Within a few decades of the conquest, Spain had constructed an extensive bureaucratic regime for her American possessions. The Spanish Crown organized the American trade into a monopoly controlled from Seville, the *Casa de la Contratación*, which prescribed every detail of ships, armament, cargo and crew. The most highly prized of the imports from America, which included dyestuffs, pearls and sugar, were of course gold and silver. The standard vessel used for this trade combined the bulkiness of a carrack, the lines of a galley, and the sails and rigging of a caravel. Called a *galeon* when it carried a large number of cannons, and a *nao* when employed as a merchant ship, its average size lay between 300 and 600 tons, with some ships ranging up to 1,200 tons or more. Galleons were built with two or three decks, and large castles fore and aft. They carried either three or four masts, and were able to make about three or four knots on the transatlantic run if they were not overloaded.

The *flota* system
From an early stage, the majority of these ships were organized into *flotas*, convoys of merchant ships and armed escorts. A guard was essential to protect the increasing quantities of bullion being shipped back from the Indies. Also, the registration of cargoes was more easily managed with a regular convoy system starting out from Seville and Cadiz, and making for one of the three chosen ports of the New World, namely Vera Cruz, Cartagena and Nombre de Dios.

The convoy system was very expensive, but in terms of security it fully proved its worth. Despite folklore to the contrary, surprisingly few treasure galleons fell into enemy hands. However, a good number were wrecked on the numerous reefs, shoals and coasts that flanked the great routes from the Caribbean Basin to the Gulf of Mexico. The official treasure fleets were always heavily laden, often excessively so, and consequently were badly prepared to face a region notorious for violent changes of the weather, and particularly for hurricanes.

The convoys were probably most vulnerable at the beginning of their voyages when, having assembled at Havana, they sailed up the relatively narrow Florida Straits, taking advantage of the three-knot, northward-flowing Florida current, and on past the Bahamas before striking out across the Atlantic.

By 1600, decades of warfare had drained Spain's resources. Large quantities of American silver had reached Spain in a century when shortage of liquid capital was one of the severest obstacles to economic growth, but too little of this had been invested in productive enterprises at home. Much of it went on conspicuous consumption; and an increasingly large proportion fell into foreign hands, and left the country without conferring any benefits on Spain's economy.

As the 17th century continued, the whole elaborate economic network of the Spanish Atlantic began to unravel, and Castile's chances of using New World wealth as a cushion against further

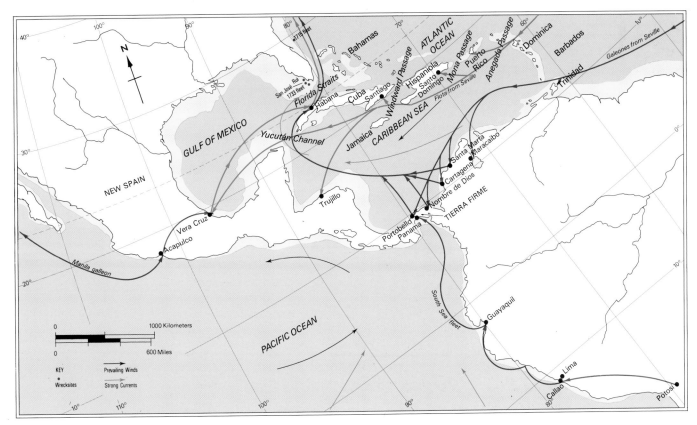

Spain's trade with the Indies waś at its height between 1550 and 1650. Each year Spanish ships were organized into a New Spain *flota* and a Tierra Firme *galeones* convoy. They carried Castilian textiles and Andalucían wine, oil and corn to colonists in the New World, returning after the winter with gold, silver (mainly from Potosí) and pearls, dyestuffs, and sugar. Chinese porcelain was shipped via Manila.

economic hardship were correspondingly lessened. There was a decline in New World silver as the first mines to be exploited became worked out. Depopulation caused a shortage of crews and ships for transatlantic voyages. Spanish vessels became the target for attacks by buccaneers and hostile powers.

By 1650 the New Spain *flota* and the galleons sailed only once every four or five years. In 1661 Spain had become so weak that she used a Dutch squadron to protect the returning treasure fleet. During the War of the Spanish Succession (1700–13) there were only five fleet sailings to the New World. Spain was unable to provide her fleets with sufficient defense, and this task was performed by her ally, France. Between 1715 and 1736 small fleets sailed to Mexico once every two or three years, but in this same 21-year period only five small armadas sailed to what are now Colombia and Panama. In 1740 the Spanish stopped sending out armadas, and thereafter large solitary galleons sailed directly out and back to Peru. As for the Mexican *flotas*, only six sailed to Vera Cruz between 1754 and 1778. In that same year the Spanish Crown declared the *flota* system to be extinct, although single Spanish ships, or *sueltos*, continued to sail the trade routes of the Indies.

Treasure wrecks

The wrecks of those vessels that came to grief are prime sources for gaining insight into the detailed workings of Hispano-American trade. They can reveal what was actually carried to Europe, and the quantities and qualities of the goods involved, thus supplementing the evidence of the mountains of dusty documents surviving from the bureaucracy of the *Casa de la Contratación* at Seville.

Unfortunately, the legendary wealth of the treasure fleets has led to the plundering of many of these sites by treasure hunters motivated solely by profit. The practice of dynamiting wrecks has resulted in an irretrievable loss of information, often quite pointless since a study of the abundant archives would soon have revealed whether or not bullion formed part of the cargo.

Two major fleets lost during the 18th century reflect the considerable value of Spain's receipts, even at a time when Spain was losing control of and profit from her American possessions.

The earlier catastrophe occurred in 1715, when the cargoes were especially valuable because of the resumption of convoys after the end of the War of the Spanish Succession. The 12-ship convoy that left Havana on July 24 1715 was made up of five ships of the New Spain

flota, six ships of the Tierra Firme (Panama) *galeones*, and a French vessel. Six days out, the convoy was making its way up the Straits of Florida when a hurricane wrecked all but the French ship on the Florida coast. More than 1,000 people were drowned, and many of the 1,500 who reached the shore died from thirst, hunger and exposure. Since 1961, various salvors have recovered many thousands of gold and silver coins, gold ingots, jewelry and other valuables from the wrecksite.

The loss of the 1733 fleet, consisting of 17 or 22 ships (records vary), was an even greater blow. On July 14, two days out of Havana, all but one of the ships were dashed to pieces against the reefs and shores of the central Florida keys. A contemporary chart led to the identification of one vessel from the fleet, the *San José*, off Plantation Key.

Excavation revealed how the *San José* was wrecked. After striking an offshore reef, she was carried intact towards the shore by huge seas, losing her rudder and five cannons on the way. She then sank on a sandy bottom in 35ft (11m) of water. Much of the lower hull is well preserved. Artifacts recovered from the wreck include silver coins and rosaries, gold rings and jewelry, a large collection of silver and pewter tableware, and Chinese porcelain shipped via Manila.

A Spanish-American royal, or 8-escudo gold coin (below), recovered from the 1733 treasure fleet wrecked on the Florida Keys. Gold coins were made with milled edges to discourage the practice of shaving metal from coinage. The loss of the 1733 fleet – at least 17 ships went down – was a heavy blow to the finances of an already debt-ridden Spain. The gold necklace pendant (right), set with eight amethysts and depicting the Virgin Mary, is one of many items of personal jewelry recovered from Spanish fleet wrecksites in Florida waters.

The ship beneath Manhattan

In 1981 property developer Howard Ronson acquired a piece of land in New York City on which to build a 30-story office block; he also unknowingly acquired, beneath the fabric of the city, a unique archaeological find – remains of a sailing ship that sheds interesting light on transatlantic maritime activities more than 200 years ago.

In the early 18th century, New York was a small English colonial trading port with only a sparsely populated hinterland to produce surplus goods and buy imports. But its flour and wood products were in demand overseas, especially in England and the British West Indies. New York also had a good harbor, which was centrally located in the 13 colonies, and was therefore used by the British as an important military terminal.

Exports included beaver pelts, whale oil, and some tobacco to England and flour, bread, peas, pork, and horses to the West Indies. Imports included manufactured goods from England and rum, molasses, and sugar from the West Indies. Some trade was also conducted with the Iberian Peninsula and its islands for salt and wine as permitted by the British trade laws. By 1720 New York's hinterlands had established themselves enough to produce significant amounts of export goods. The port expanded accordingly, as did its need for larger, more economical ships. Colonial New York port records show that prior to 1720, few ships entering the port were registered as weighing more than 100 tons. But in the next few years the larger ships became increasingly more common.

New York's port expands

The New York port facilities needed to grow with the increase in commerce. In Manhattan, large ships could only meet shore at a stone dock, which was too small to service all the ships. Many of the vessels were still serviced by lighters, small flat-bottomed boats which ran into the numerous slips to meet horsedrawn wagons. In order to service ships efficiently, the colonists needed to expand their harbor facilities. By filling the intertidal and shallow subtidal areas of the shoreline to the street level they could load and unload trading vessels directly from wagons, instead of using lighters. This provided quicker and cheaper lading of the vessels and also provided land for new storage buildings to allow merchants and shippers to hold large quantities of import and export cargoes.

Extending the shoreline was an organized affair. The city government issued a deed to a water lot, usually to the person whose land came to the present shoreline. The agreement generally included the

stipulation that the lot be filled within a specified number of years and that a municipal street be included along the newly created shore line or quay. The lots were then cribbed with an interlocking structure of logs and filled with stone, soil, and refuse from the land, and excess ballast from visiting ships. Old ships were often incorporated into the lot as a substitute for cribbing.

During the 19th and early 20th centuries, merchant stores, warehouses, and apartments occupied the newly created land along the East River. This was a bustling area of import merchant trade. As the 20th century progressed, lower Manhattan grew vertically. Skyscraper office buildings began to surround a block between Fletcher and John Streets and the 19th century buildings on the block were leveled to form an asphalt-paved parking lot. In 1981 developer Howard

A large breast hook, a timber which held the two sides of the bow together, is lifted out of the bow (above). Most of the pieces of the bow, including this half-ton timber, could only be removed with the use of nylon crane straps or a wooden tray lifted by a mechanical digger.

Ronson applied to the city to construct a 30-story office building which would cover the whole block, now called 175 Water Street. He was required by the New York Landmarks Commission to conduct a preconstruction archaeological investigation of the site.

Discovery of the ship

Ronson contracted with Soil Systems, Inc. to conduct the investigation which would include the careful excavation of approximately 15 percent of the block. In the rest of the site they would dig "deep test" holes, 6 × 10 × 12ft (2 × 3 × 4m) deep, and check the stratigraphy to compare it to the stratigraphy in the area which was carefully excavated. In the last deep test to be made, in the eastern part of the block, the eastern wall of the hole fell away to reveal the outside of the hull of a wooden ship.

Shortly after discovering the ship, Soil Systems called me and asked me if I would look at it. In the bucket of a mechanical digger, I was lowered into a 4 × 10 × 12ft (1 × 3 × 4m) deep test hole. I could see the outside of the hull of a vessel, including exposed sheathing planks, used to protect the ship from shipworms. An examination of the ship's framing and planking indicated we were looking at the outside midship section of an 18th century merchantman.

Excited by the integrity of the exposed hull and the degree of preservation, Soil Systems agreed that we should excavate a 10 × 10ft (3 × 3m) test pit within the hull. But all archaeologists were to be out of the site by February 1, when the bulldozers were contracted to move in. We wanted to discover the size of the vessel, the amount of preserved inboard structure, and the type of fill inside the hull. Sheli O. Smith, my wife and fellow nautical archaeologist, left our home in Maine to join me and Soil Systems archaeologists Bert Herbert and George Myers.

During the second day of excavating the test pit we uncovered the lower deck of the ship, 10ft (3m) below the present street level. Eventually the pit revealed a gunport on the western side, a large cargo hatch on the east side with a monkey pole ladder protruding from it, and a companionway (personnel hatch) that had been planked more than 200 years earlier. By measuring from the monkey post, assumed to be in the center of the ship, to the outside of the hull we calculated that the ship had a beam of 25ft (8m) and a length of 72 to 125ft (24 to 41m). We estimated that she was extant from well above the waterline to probably the keel, but her orientation indicated that she lay on an approximate north-south axis with her eastern side (starboard) and most of her southern end (stern) under Front Street. We realized that this was the first major discovery of a colonial merchant ship which had a chance to be thoroughly studied. But there was only a week remaining to us before the archaeological deadline.

We decided to ask for more time, presented a proposal to the Ronson people and the New York Landmarks commission, and were granted the time and budget necessary to excavate and record that part of the ship not directly under Front Street and its sidewalk.

The excavation

Knowing that any delays would cost the developer thousands of dollars a day, we conceived a plan which would be both thorough and quick. We split the crew into four units: an excavation team of 35 people; a wood recording team of four who measured, sketched, and photographed each piece as it was removed from the site; a hull recording team of four; and a support staff of three. The plan also called for an extra month to work

(February), a six-day working week, two mechanical diggers, five pumps to keep the water level down, and much other essential equipment.

The operators of the mechanical diggers immediately began to clear away six to eight feet of asphalt, concrete, and rubble that lay over the ship. On February 1 the crew assembled to begin hand-excavation. During the gruelling New York winter the team braved freezing temperatures, mudslides, cave-ins, and picket lines to complete their work on time. By February 28 most of the ship was excavated and Mayor Koch led the way as 12,000 people viewed the site from a special balcony erected by the Fuller Construction Company.

The future of the ship's remains was still a problem. It could not stay *in situ* because the office building was to be supported by more than 300 steel piles. We had carefully recorded the dimensions and shapes of every timber so that the ship could be recreated on paper and studied later. But future research innovations and the public would be deprived of an important piece of American history if it were destroyed, or removed and left to disintegrate (which would happen in a few months if left untreated). We could remove the hull, but conservation of that much wood would cost an estimated three million dollars. Building a controlled-environment museum to house it in lower Manhattan and supporting continued maintenance would cost many times more.

Saving the bow

After long consultations among the various parties and with outside consultants from all over the United States and Canada, it was agreed that the bow was such an important treasure it had to be saved. The rest of the ship, after careful study, was to be let go. Developer Howard Ronson stepped forward and offered to underwrite the removal and conservation of this unique relic.

When the crew had finished studying the ship, a team took the bow and beak apart piece-by-piece in a 24-hour marathon to meet our deadline of March 4. We transported the carefully wrapped timbers to a conservation laboratory in Groton, Massachusetts. There the timbers were immersed in tanks of water to begin a long conservation process, planned to allow the timbers to survive eventual drying and, ultimately, exhibition.

Once the timbers were safely in the laboratory we had time to consider the ship we had excavated. She was 82ft (26m) long on the lower deck (approximately 100ft (33m) overall), had a beam of 26ft (8m) and would have been registered in America at between 150 and 210 tons. She was larger than the average colonial merchantman, yet not as large as the great East India ships. Three southern latitude species of ship worm were found

in her outer wood sheathing, indicating that she had sailed at least once to southern waters.

The bow of the ship was so full as to be almost square and had a massive, fully intact beak protruding 10ft (3m) in front. The foremast, now gone, was stepped far forward. Three posts (bitts) remained standing directly behind the foremast and a wonderfully intact, all-wood capstan lay unstepped on the lower deck forward of the mast. Just aft of the bow area a section of the upper deck also remained, collapsed onto the lower deck. The cargo hold was extensive – 7½ft (2.2m) high and at least 50ft (16m) long with no indication of any cargo-separating bulkheads, except in the bow.

We could see from the vessel's position in the land fill that she had been carefully stripped of her hardware and ballast, and brought into shore at high tide. There, workers spiked her to a set of pilings parallel to the shore. Then crews of other ships unloaded their excess ballast into her to fill the hold. Layers of beach stones, coral sand, volcanic black sand, and English flint composed most of the fill in the vessel's hull.

A ballast pump was still in place and internal lower deck scuppers, which directed rain and splash water from the lower deck to the bilge pumps, were positioned just below three gunports along the port side. The gun ports indicated that the ship had been armed with six 6-pounder cannons on the lower deck, and probably more smaller guns above. Armament was necessary in the 18th century to repel pirates and privateers in many waters. Tongue-and-groove panelling lined the cabin area in the stern, pierced in one spot by a lead pistol ball still in position. Beneath a shelf in the cabin area we found an 18th century rum bottle intact, but empty.

In June 1982 we gathered an interdisciplinary team of specialists from around the United States to help extract information from this important find. Archaeologists, conservators, an historian, a wood specialist, and a ship reconstructor began studying, treating, researching, and testing the ship. By autumn 1982 the bow timbers were cleaned, recorded, and ready for chemical conservation treatments.

Conservation process

The wood was placed in a bath of weak acid to remove iron salts without destroying its cellular structure. The wood then went into a solution of water and polyethylene glycol (PEG), a synthetic microcrystaline wax, where it spent two years soaking. The bow timbers arrived at The Mariners' Museum in April 1985 to begin a long, controlled drying process before being reconstructed in a major exhibit. As the timbers slowly dry, the museum staff coats them with more PEG every two weeks to ensure their stability. To date, the PEG solution has penetrated approxi-

mately one inch into the wood, the optimum distance for the wood's condition. When the timbers are eventually dried, the PEG will remain in the wood cells, giving them strength so that they will retain their shape.

Meanwhile further research of the ship continues. Analysis of the ship timbers is difficult because the wood cells have been subjected to more than 200 years of abuse. We now know that the hull timbers were mostly oak, probably much of it southern live oak, and that many other species of wood were also used, including southern yellow pine. Although the wood specialists cannot be certain of some of the key species because of the wood's condition, it appears that the only place all of the species were easily available in the early 18th century was the Chesapeake.

Historically, we know of no shipping of large amounts of southern hardwoods or yellow pine either to Europe or for long distances in America. We do know that English tobacco companies sent English shipwrights to the Chesapeake to build tobacco ships in the late 17th and early 18th centuries.

Sheli Smith records the hull of the Ronson ship (above). Details taken of the hull shape, fastening positions and timber provided much information about shipbuilding and trade in the early 18th century. It was decided that to remove the hull and conserve it would be too expensive so after careful recording it was let go, along with the rest of the ship's remains, except the bow.

A transatlantic tobacco ship

The Ronson ship fits easily into this story. She was larger than most ships of her day, yet the normal size for a transatlantic tobacco ship. Moreover, the builder's attention to detail, something we noted during the excavation, was typical of English, rather than colonial shipwrights. As she was probably made of a variety of woods natural only to the Chesapeake region, our hypothesis is that the ship was built as a tobacco ship in the Chesapeake, probably Virginia, for an English or Scottish tobacco company.

How did she find her way to a land fill operation in New York? Most ships spent much of their active life shuttling between two ports, carrying cargo of a specific nature. But economies change and ship owners had to remain flexible. For example, the merchants of Glasgow were slowly gaining control of the American tobacco trade during this period. If the ship was owned by London merchants who were losing some of their tobacco trade, she may have been sent to New York to participate in the growing flour trade. There, she may have been

condemned as unfit for a return voyage. As an American built merchant ship, her owners could recoup her cost in two voyages and only expect the ship to last eight to fifteen years in the Atlantic trade before becoming structurally too weak. Remains of two resheathings of the ship's hull indicate that the Ronson ship was used at sea for a period of approximately nine to twelve years.

In New York the ship may have floated at her mooring, or have been run ashore, until used by the colonists to bulk some fill where they were extending the port facilities. In 1737 the lot owners on the East River waterfront between Fletcher and John Streets received water lot deeds to the shallow water area in front of their properties. As with other standard water lot deeds, they were required to fill the lots within a specified time. From contemporary maps of Manhattan one can see that the area was filled between 1745 and 1755. Evidently they coordinated their efforts to crib six of the lots at the deep end with an old merchant ship by stripping it of its hardware and ballast, floating it in at high tide, spiking it to some piles,

and filling it with excess ballast from other ships and soil and refuse from the city. New Yorkers appear to have used her as a wharf for a while, placing the small capstan in her bow and using the vessel's mizzen (rear) mast as a cargo boom. Eventually the shore line was extended outwards another block and the ship was covered with eight feet of rubble and asphalt until found again in 1982.

To test this hypothesis we have studied the New York and much of the Chesapeake port records in an attempt to identify the ship, but we have only narrowed the search down to eight possibilities. We may never know exactly which ship this is. Background research in America and Britain has bolstered the tobacco ship hypothesis but no hard proof exists. In fact, further research may lead to an entirely different explanation of the ship's history.

During the next few years we will continue the archaeological analysis and historical research so as to interpret the site for the public and professionals through The Mariners' Museum's planned programs.

The site of the Ronson ship excavation, looking northeast, is shown in this photograph (above, far right). The East River and the Brooklyn Bridge can be seen in the background.

A merchantman rides at anchor in this 1712 engraving of New York harbor (above). Note the three gunports in the ship's side. The Ronson ship would have looked something like this in her day.

As a bow timber is slung out of the hull for preservation, archaeologists dismantle the beak and frames (right). The ship is facing the camera with its beak protruding center, front.

A detail of the beakhead structure is shown in this scale drawing (far right). The colored area shows the part of the beak in the photograph (right). The damage caused by shipworm is also indicated.

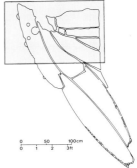

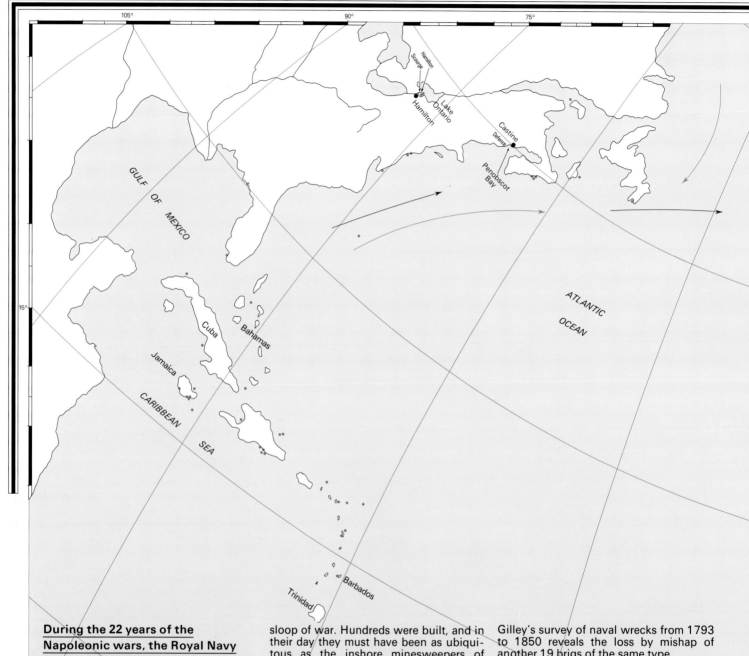

During the 22 years of the Napoleonic wars, the Royal Navy lost far more ships by mishap than by enemy action. A survey of Royal Navy shipwrecks between 1793 and 1850 lists more than 370 naval ships destroyed through accident rather than war. The bones of the ships commemorate Nelson's navy, while the wreck of the *Colossus*, with its wonderful trove of classical antiquities, recalls a chapter from the life of the hero himself.

A common type of warship in the Royal Navy of Nelson's time was the 18-gun sloop of war. Hundreds were built, and in their day they must have been as ubiquitous as the inshore minesweepers of World War II. I was able to study the remains of two of these ships, both of which were lost in the Mediterranean.

Ships of the Columbine class followed a 1797 design by Sir William Rule. They were rigged as brigs, and measured 100ft (30m) long on the deck. Copper sheathed, they were usually built of oak with copper fastenings, and carried a complement of 121 men and 18 guns.

A merchantman of that size in the early 1800s seldom had a crew of more than 25 men. We might expect a naval ship to be better maintained and have stronger gear than the average merchantman; yet of 70 Columbine-class brigs built between 1803 and 1809, 19 were lost by mishap.

Gilley's survey of naval wrecks from 1793 to 1850 reveals the loss by mishap of another 19 brigs of the same type.

HMS *Columbine* and HMS *Nautilus*
In 1963 I was in the little harbor of Porto Longo in the southwestern Greek Peloponnesus, looking for the wreck of HMS *Columbine*, the name-ship of the large class of 18-gun brigs already described. The ship had sunk there on January 25 1824, and I hoped to salvage some copper and bronze for chemical experiments, and to learn something about deterioration processes in a wooden ship.

We had copies of her builder's specifications, the captain's court martial, and her log on the day she sank, so we were optimistic about finding the site. HMS *Columbine*'s mission to Porto Longo was

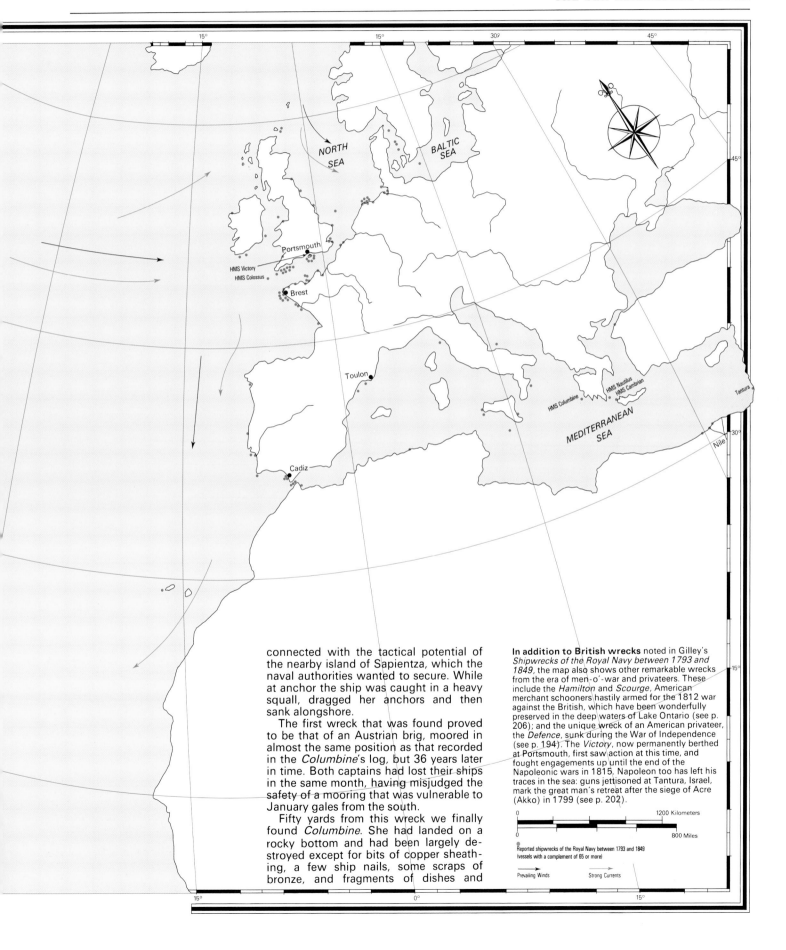

connected with the tactical potential of the nearby island of Sapientza, which the naval authorities wanted to secure. While at anchor the ship was caught in a heavy squall, dragged her anchors and then sank alongshore.

The first wreck that was found proved to be that of an Austrian brig, moored in almost the same position as that recorded in the *Columbine*'s log, but 36 years later in time. Both captains had lost their ships in the same month, having misjudged the safety of a mooring that was vulnerable to January gales from the south.

Fifty yards from this wreck we finally found *Columbine*. She had landed on a rocky bottom and had been largely destroyed except for bits of copper sheathing, a few ship nails, some scraps of bronze, and fragments of dishes and

In addition to British wrecks noted in Gilley's *Shipwrecks of the Royal Navy between 1793 and 1849*, the map also shows other remarkable wrecks from the era of men-o'-war and privateers. These include the *Hamilton* and *Scourge*, American merchant schooners hastily armed for the 1812 war against the British, which have been wonderfully preserved in the deep waters of Lake Ontario (see p. 206); and the unique wreck of an American privateer, the *Defence*, sunk during the War of Independence (see p. 194). The *Victory*, now permanently berthed at Portsmouth, first saw action at this time, and fought engagements up until the end of the Napoleonic wars in 1815. Napoleon too has left his traces in the sea: guns jettisoned at Tantura, Israel, mark the great man's retreat after the siege of Acre (Akko) in 1799 (see p. 202).

0   1200 Kilometers

0   800 Miles

Reported shipwrecks of the Royal Navy between 1793 and 1849 (vessels with a complement of 65 or more)

Prevailing Winds   Strong Currents

wood fixtures from the captain's cabin.

Columbine was not the only British sloop to lie on the Mediterranean seabed. The story of HMS *Nautilus*, lost in 1807 while carrying dispatches to the Cadiz fleet from Rear Admiral Louis's Dardanelles squadron, was well known. The survivors had suffered dreadful privations after she ran onto an uncharted rock between the islands of Pori and Antikythera. The subsequent court martial revealed that the dead captain of the ship, Edward Palmer, had been entirely responsible for the disaster.

Nautilus reef, named after the lost sloop, has no anchorage. When a calm spell allowed us to moor there, we explored it. From accounts of the wreck, I judged that the remains must be inside the eastern point of the bare islet called Nautilus Rock. After a brief search in the clear water, I saw, peering down to the ledge 20ft (6m) below, a heap of iron ballast bars, scattered over the bottom, and then a cannon. We had found what was left of HMS *Nautilus*.

It seems likely that the wreck was picked over by sponge divers soon after the ship sank, for we located only seven cannon out of the total armament of 18. However, I found the bronze cheekpiece of a block and two bronze pins, one of them satisfyingly stamped with the Royal Navy's broad arrow.

On our very last dive I spotted some-thing gleaming white, wedged under a stone. It was a silver spoon concreted to a lump of iron. After cleaning, it was possible to distinguish Captain Palmer's crest, a greyhound *sejant* (seated). Hallmarks showed that the spoon had been made in 1805.

HMS *Cambrian*

In classical times and right through to the 19th century, pirates had traditionally thrived in the dangerous area between Cape Malea and Crete, the gateway to the Aegean. From the 17th century onwards, the straits were infested with mustachioed Maniots from the mainland, fierce men in small fast rowing boats which they concealed, when they took to the hills, by filling them with stones and sinking them in shallow bays. When cornered, the Maniots fought like wolves. It took the Royal Navy to stop the Maniot pirates, but not before the loss of HMS *Cambrian*, a 48-gun frigate, off Grabusa, Crete.

The ship had formed part of Sir Edward Codrington's squadron at the battle of Navarino in the previous year, when combined Russian, French and British fleets had destroyed the Turkish fleet and decided the Greek War of Independence. At the time of the sinking, in February 1828, she had been bombarding some Greek pirate schooners in Grabusa bay at the north end of Crete when she had missed stays, hit the rocks, and sunk.

The wrecksite yielded a scatter of bronze and copper equipment, evidence of the sophisticated finish of a ship of this type in 1828. Coins found on the site apparently date to later than the wreck, suggesting that the ship had been salvaged before the excavation – hence the absence of cannon.

When she went down, *Cambrian* had on board a case of watercolor paintings made by Lusieri for Lord Elgin, the notorious acquirer of the Elgin Marbles. They showed various classical monuments of Athens, many of which were destroyed soon after the watercolors were made. The paintings have of course not survived, but collections of antiquities, assembled by these early antiquarians, may yet be recovered from the sea. Seventeen cases of treasures acquired by Lord Elgin were salvaged from the wreck of the *Mentor* by naked sponge divers soon after she went down in 1802. In recent years, the spectacular recovery of Sir William Hamilton's collection on board the *Colossus* has added another chapter to the archaeological story.

The hero and the connoisseur

Sir William Hamilton (1730-1803), the long-serving British envoy at the court of Naples, is traditionally remembered as the elderly husband of Nelson's celebrated mistress, Lady Emma Hamilton. However, his real claim to fame is as a connoisseur,

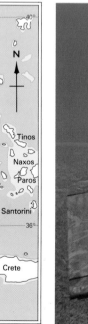

Recovered from the Columbine, an elegantly made door is brought to the surface by a diver (left). Most of the artifacts from the sloop of war, lost 1824, had disappeared after the ship had landed on a rocky bottom, but pieces of wood, including the door and a wooden pulley block, had been preserved in some mud.

A silver spoon (below) belonging to the commander of the *Nautilus*, Captain Palmer, was found concreted to a lump of iron. The crest of a greyhound *sejant* (seated), stamped on the spoon, revealed that it had belonged to the unfortunate Palmer, who was lost with his ship in 1807.

The gateway of the Aegean (above), the area between Cape Malea and Crete, was a region of dangerous reefs, treacherous squalls and marauding pirates. Hundreds of vessels have been lost here, including several Royal Navy ships: *Columbine* was sunk by a heavy squall, *Nautilus* hit an uncharted rock, and *Cambrian* missed stays while in action against local pirates.

scholar and amateur archaeologist, whose collection of antique "vases" (ceramics) had a great influence on contemporary art and design, and in particular on the work of Josiah Wedgwood.

Hamilton's appointment at Naples in 1764 coincided with the excavation, or plundering, of Pompeii. Here he showed himself far ahead of his time in his concern for careful excavation and recording of objects before their removal. His First Collection of antiquities was acquired by the Trustees of the British Museum in 1772 for £8,400. He then began his Second Collection, an even finer assemblage of more than 1,000 vases, which he judged to be "far more beautiful and complete than the series already in London."

In the summer of 1798 Horatio Nelson, the wounded hero of the recent victory over Napoleon at Aboukir Bay (the Battle of the Nile), came to Naples with his battered fleet. Despite this famous victory, Napoleon was making gains in north Italy, and Hamilton sought Nelson's permission to send the cream of this Second Collection aboard a homeward-bound ship.

Nelson arranged for the collection to be shipped on board the 74-gun armed storeship HMS *Colossus*, which was about to set sail for England. Securing his permission would not have been hard. The value of the collection was one factor; another was Nelson's friendship with Sir

William and his beautiful second wife.

The shipping of this consignment delayed the departure of *Colossus*, and the vessel did not set sail until November. As a warship in Nelson's fleet, *Colossus* had seen much service and was no longer sound in timber and cordage. On December 10 1798, she ran into a fierce storm off the Scilly Isles, foundered on a spit of submerged rock, and sank. Only one life was lost, but the priceless cargo of ancient Greek "vases" went to the bottom of the sea.

The remainder of Hamilton's collection was saved, and elegant illustrations of selected specimens, drawn in 1787 by Wilhelm Tischbein, have helped to identify some lost pieces. But what exactly went down with the *Colossus* when she sank that December day was a mystery and remained so for nearly two centuries.

Discovery of the *Colossus*

In the late summer of 1974, Roland Morris and a team of professional divers located traces of an 18th century wreck at a depth of about 30ft (9m) off Samson in the Scilly Isles. The site was immediately secured under the Protection of Wrecks Act, and in 1975 the team was granted a licence to survey and, at a later stage, to excavate the wreck. From the very beginning they were confident that this was the wreck of the *Colossus*.

This was confirmed in 1975, when Dr

Ann Birchall and Brian Cook of the Department of Greek and Roman Antiquities at the British Museum positively identified some of the decorated pottery sherds that had been found. Later that year, Dr Birchall was appointed archaeological director of the excavation. So began one of the largest jigsaw puzzles of all time.

In 1976 work started on a total of 32,000 pottery fragments recovered from the site, all carefully marked, labeled and sorted. Fragments were grouped into different categories consisting of the section of vase from which they came, the stylistic shape of the vase, and also its place of origin.

The Tischbein drawings proved invaluable, but omitted certain important features such as the shapes of the vases from which the drawings had been made. However, more than 100 distinct groups of fragments were assembled, with each group representing the nucleus of an individual vase.

Of these, 23 had figured scenes that matched the Tischbein drawings, and 80 made up parts of previously unknown vases. Featuring numerous aspects of Greek life and mythology, and painted on a variety of vessels, cups and jugs, this magnificent collection, now in the British Museum, is one of the finest and most unusual troves that has ever been wrested from the seabed.

Nelson as hero (left), celebrating with his men after the Battle of the Nile, August 1798, when the British captured 11 out of 13 French warships in Aboukir Bay. A contemporary print by Thomas Rowlandson shows the affection as well as the admiration that Nelson inspired.

"**The return of Hephaestus** (the smith god) to Olympus" features in Tischbein's 1795 drawing of one of Hamilton's finest Greek vases (above left), lost with the *Colossus*. The 440BC krater (above) was reconstructed after comparison with the drawing.

Nelson's flagship

Launched in 1765, HMS *Victory* saw action for the first time in 1778, against the French, who had just entered the American War of Independence on the side of the colonists. In 1782 she took part in the relief of Gibraltar and the Battle of Cape Spartel. In 1793 Britain joined the First Coalition against Napoleonic France, and *Victory* fought engagements in the Mediterranean under Lord Hood. In 1795 she engaged in the indecisive action off Cape Hyères, and in 1797 served as Admiral Jervis's flagship at the British victory of Cape St Vincent. From 1798 to 1800 *Victory* was stationed at Portsmouth as a hospital ship. Recommissioned in April 1803 after a refit, by July she was serving as Lord Nelson's Mediterranean flagship. For the next 18 months she took part in the blockade of Toulon and the

pursuit of Villeneuve's Franco-Spanish fleet to the West Indies. The fleets finally clashed off Cape Trafalgar on October 21 1805. The Franco-Spanish force of 33 ships turned back towards Cadiz in an irregular line five miles long. Nelson, in two divisions, each in single column, on a course at right angles to his adversary's, drove directly into the center of the long enemy line, cutting it in two – a great tactical innovation. In a five-hour battle, 18 French or Spanish ships were taken; the remainder fled, only 11 reaching Cadiz. No English ship was captured. Nelson was killed as the *Victory* closed in furious combat with the French *Redoubtable*. At Trafalgar Napoleon lost his colonies, any chance of invading England, and all hope of getting control of the important sea-route to India.

HMS *Victory*, which had led Nelson's

column into battle, was so severely damaged that she had to be towed into Gibraltar for temporary repairs. Once back in England she underwent an extensive refit, and was recommissioned in 1808. For the next five years she was employed, largely as the flagship of Admiral Saumarez, in journeying to and from the Baltic, though in January 1809 she helped to bring home Sir John Moore's expeditionary army from La Coruña in Spain. In 1812 *Victory* returned to Portsmouth for another refit, but the end of the Napoleonic Wars in 1815, and the advent of steam propulsion, finally concluded her long fighting career, and she remained in reserve until 1824, when she became the flagship of the Portsmouth naval command. Until 1922 HMS *Victory* was berthed in Portsmouth Harbour. By this time her timbers were in poor shape, but

in that year she was removed to a graving dock. An appeal launched by the Society for Nautical Research led to her restoration, by 1928, to the appearance she bore at Trafalgar.

HMS *Victory* in her prime was a self-sufficient but uncomfortable world – damp, insanitary and overcrowded, reeking of tar, bilgewater, sodden timber, old salt meat, rum, gunpowder and about 850 closely packed human bodies, with no provision whatever, except in the officers' well-furnished cabins, for any physical comfort: this ship was built to fight. Many of the sailors were very young men: the average age of the crew of the *Victory* was 22. Most lived on the dank, dark and noisy lower gun-deck. When the gun-ports were opened for battle or practice, light and air were admitted; otherwise only a dim light filtered down through gratings.

Victory's 104 guns were mounted on the quarter-deck (twelve 12-pounders), the forecastle (two 12-pounders and two 68-pounder carronades or "smashers"), the upper gun-deck (thirty 12-pounders), the middle gun-deck (twenty-eight 24-pounders) and the lower gun-deck (thirty 32-pounders), where most of the crew lived, manning the capstan, pumps and galley. The senior ratings and junior officers lived on the orlop deck, which was used in action for the treatment of the wounded. The surgeon's cabin(6) was close to the mess(5): the mess table was used for amputations during action. Nelson occupied a day-cabin(8), dining-cabin and sleeping-cabin, and Captain Hardy had his own quarters(1). The ship's officers lived in the wardroom(7). Before the ship went into action, hammocks and mess-tables were stowed, the gunports opened, powder brought up from the magazines(4) (lit by separate light rooms), and shot from the lockers(3). The ship was controlled by steering wheels(2) linked to the tiller, and made way using sails rigged to the mizzenmast, mainmast and foremast. The pikes surrounding the foot of each mast were used for boarding or repelling boarders.

Privateers, not pirates

During the American War of Independence, the business of privateering boomed. America was clearly unable to meet the threat of British sea power, due to the inadequacy of the fledgling United States Navy, despite the efforts of individuals like John Paul Jones. So the authorities resorted to privateering to augment their battle fleets. One such ship, recently excavated, was the *Defence.*

Privateering was especially encouraged by the government at the peak of the war effort when the Continental Congress authorized the States of America to issue letters of marque* and reprisal. Merchant ship owners from as far afield as Massachusetts and the Carolinas were quick to respond. According to archival records, as many as 1,600 privateers were enrolled, ranging in size from whaleboats and sloops to large three-masted ships, with the majority consisting of schooners and brigs or brigantines.

Being a legalized profession, privateering could be profitable for the shipowner, captain and crew. Each capture was judged in a "prize court", which tended to rule in favor of the captor, giving a percentage of the captured cargo to the owners, officers and crew of the privateer. Privateers generally operated alone and most often preyed upon merchant vessels that were slower and undergunned. In the case of a confrontation between a privateering and a naval vessel, the outcome would most likely be to the misfortune of the privateer, mainly because the crew tended to be untrained and undisciplined for battle conditions.

The birth of *Defence*
In Massachusetts alone, some 600 letters of marque were issued and among the recipients were two merchants, John Cabot and Israel Thorndike of Beverly, a small town north of Boston. They launched a vessel designed and built for the sole intention of preying upon enemy shipping. Her maiden voyage was to have been to the Gulf of St Lawrence.

The Cabot-Thorndike vessel was a fairly typical brigantine of 170 tons, carrying 16 six-pounder carriage guns on her deck. She was launched in 1779 and christened *Defence*. Unfortunately, her maiden voyage as a privateer was not as intended. The brigantine sailed no further than the upper reaches of Penobscot Bay, on the coast of Maine, only 200 nautical miles from her home port. There, in an inlet, now known as Stockton Harbor, just west of the mouth of the Penobscot River, she sank on August 14 1779, in just 24ft (7m) of water. Over the years her hull became deeply embedded in silt and mud, and she

remained forgotten until 1972, when the wreck was discovered.

The Penobscot expedition
The demise of *Defence* in Stockton Harbor had not been a solitary incident, but part of a major naval disaster. Four years into the American Revolution, a fleet of 44 American ships, comprising naval vessels, privateers, troop transports and supply ships, embarked from Massachusetts, up the coast toward Penobscot Bay. *Defence* was one of the privateers enlisted to augment the naval vessels.

This armada, the largest military and naval expedition ever assembled by the Americans during the War of Independence, was heading toward a small British garrison at Castine, which they planned to attack. The British had established themselves here, on the eastern approaches to the mouth of the Penobscot River, to fortify and protect the small harbor which they planned to use as a base against privateering activities in the Gulf of Maine. They also wanted to ensure access to the interior, via the Penobscot River, where precious and sought-after mast pines grew in abundance.

Due to inadequate leadership, poor planning and dwindling morale among the troops, this American effort to dislodge the British garrison at Castine resulted in an abysmal failure. The arrival of a relief squadron of five Royal Navy vessels put the American fleet to flight.

Initially, this was an orderly retreat up the river, but it was soon transformed into a rout. By the evening of August 13 1779, all the American fleet had been scuttled except for two vessels, and these had been captured. Ships were either driven ashore and set ablaze or were abandoned at sea, left adrift as burning hulks, the relics of a self-imposed holocaust.

One particular American vessel, *Defence*, apparently sought to escape and, running west along the coast, slipped into an inlet – Stockton Harbor. However, this attempt came to nothing as she had been sighted and followed by a British warship, HMS *Camilla*. The warship anchored near the mouth of the harbor and sent a smaller boat to investigate. During the boat's approach towards the trapped American brig, there was an explosion aboard *Defence* and she sank. Apparently her skipper, John Edmonds, had scuttled the vessel to avoid the inevitable capture by a British man-of-war ship. So the one survivor of the river expedition had been forced to scuttle with the rest.

Defence is discovered
The story of the discovery of *Defence* is unusual in that the wreck was not found by wreck or treasure hunters, but by a group of students. It was 1972 and they were participating in a summer engineering course based at Castine and hosted by the Maine Maritime Academy. One of their projects was to build a simple sonar

device, and while they were testing their unsophisticated equipment, they noted an interesting anomaly.

Divers investigated the source and found a square brick structure that barely protruded above the silt. It was the top of a galley cookstove that enclosed a large built-in copper caldron. Forward of the stove was the eroded stump of a mast.

The Maine State Museum, in Augusta, granted a permit to carry out further reconnaissance work on the site, to ascertain the age of the wreck. During this phase more diagnostic material was recovered, including two cannons (one of which bore the casting mark of a Massachusetts foundry), ceramic material, 18th century bottles and parts of wooden mess kits – some bearing carved initials. The artifacts, coupled with historical research, indicated the wreck was the Beverly-built privateer, *Defence*. A rough plan of the site revealed that the ship's hull remains were completely buried and that few structural elements protruded above the silt – only the mast stumps and an occasional frame along the periphery of the embedded hull. All the recovered artifacts connected with the site were to be conserved and eventually displayed by the Maine State Museum.

Great advances in the field of conserving waterlogged wood and other material of an organic nature had recently been made during the restoration of the Viking

The stump of *Defence*'s foremast was discernible in our first exploratory dive, during which visibility was 6ft – the clearest conditions throughout the entire excavation. Remarkably, the original mortise and tenon joint that had held the sailing ship's mast in place, attaching it to the keel, was still intact, even after 200 years under the water.

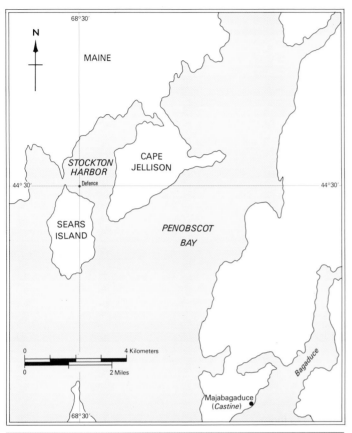

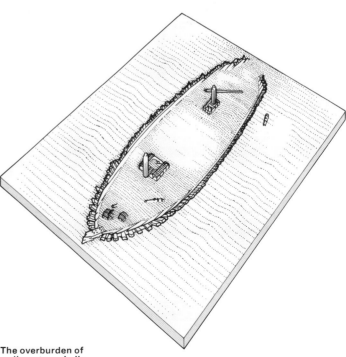

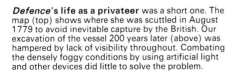
***Defence*'s life as a privateer** was a short one. The map (top) shows where she was scuttled in August 1779 to avoid inevitable capture by the British. Our excavation of the vessel 200 years later (above) was hampered by lack of visibility throughout. Combating the densely foggy conditions by using artificial light and other devices did little to solve the problem.

The overburden of sedimentary shells was vacuumed up to the surface and emptied into a constantly monitored floating sieve box (top). This proved ideal for exposing the hull structure (above) and the end frames marking the periphery of the embedded wreck. The dominant features are the cookstove in the bow area, the mast stump and the extent of explosion-caused damage in the stern.

ships at Roskilde (see p.130) and the recovery of the Swedish warship *Vasa* (see p.148). The conservator at the Maine State Museum, Stephen Brooke, made a study of these techniques, with a view to applying them to the *Defence* site.

Logistical arrangements were as vital as the conservation effort, and the Institute of Nautical Archaeology (INA) formally assumed responsibility for conducting and coordinating the excavation. George Bass, one of the founders of the INA, suggested I should direct the project and use it as field school experience for students of nautical archaeology, the first of its kind in the United States. I was happy to accept the challenge. As a final part of this task force, the Maine Maritime Academy was to provide expedition vessels, and large work floats to be anchored over the site with space for temporary wet storage holding tanks for the retrieved artifacts.

The first glimpse
I soon realized that my previous and initial experience in underwater archaeology at Yassi Ada (see pp.86–87), where visibility was perfect at great depths and the wreck was only covered by a relatively shallow deposition of sediment, was not comparable to the poor visibility and deeply embedded remains encountered at the *Defence* site. During our first dive at the site, in February 1975, visibility was only five or six feet, but it was enough to see the stump of the foremast and the upper part of the cookstove located immediately aft of the foremast.

Also discernible and jutting a few inches above the seabed were some eroded ends of frame timbers. Even more impressive were well-preserved planks that formed the interior of the hull. The cold winter conditions ensured this preliminary dive was short. Nevertheless, it was particularly exhilarating because it gave us confirmation that the remains of *Defence* did have enormous archaeological potential.

The site would be a perfect testing ground for the innovative archaeological methods that had been so successful in the warm waters of the Mediterranean. We were about to apply this kind of approach for the first time to the systematic excavation of a wreck in the United States.

By recording the artifacts found within the hull area, we hoped to gain a clearer understanding of the various facets of life and work at sea during the era of the American Revolution. We also hoped to unravel and record details of ship construction techniques typical of the period, which had been lost through time and change.

Finally, we considered the feasibility of raising, preserving and exhibiting the hull of *Defence* as had been done with *Vasa* and more recently with *Mary Rose* (see p.142). However, it soon became apparent that this would be enormously costly –

due to the engineering involved in lifting and transporting the hull and the need to build a specially designed conservation laboratory. Moreover, as a national symbol the *Defence* lacked the status of *Vasa* or *Mary Rose*. So we decided to preserve the ship through thorough and meticulous documentation, culminating in a set of naval architectural plans, from which a model of the hull could be built and its features analyzed.

The dig begins
During the first of six field seasons, we acquainted ourselves with the site characteristics and ascertained the volume and variety of artifactual material that would eventually be encountered during more intensive future excavation work. The most difficult aspect was the lack of visibility, a problem that became even more acute when seafloor sediments were disturbed during our efforts to probe the interior of the hull. Even in prime conditions visibility was only 6ft, while disturbance of the sediment, causing the unreflective black mud to explode into clouds, created a virtually total black-out.

Initially, we attempted to overcome the problem of poor visibility by constructing various ingenious devices, including a "clear water box" to enhance photographic documentation, an "underwater current producer" to carry suspended silt away from the work area and a "visual acuity tent." But not one of these contraptions was effective. We simply had to resign ourselves to dealing with the situation by using conventional excavation tools and basic mapping procedures to create an accurate plan of the hull. However, the nearly constant gloom that overhung the site meant that mapping operations could not be achieved through photo mosaics; sadly, it was never possible to view the hull structure of *Defence* in its entirety.

Our most effective excavation tool was an airlift made from 20ft sections of 4in diameter PVC pipe which emptied into a constantly monitored floating sieve box. In the event of an excavator inadvertently intruding into a sensitive area, pouring artifacts into the sieve and possibly disturbing the conditions, a signal to shut down the compressor could be given. The pause in suction would alert the excavators that something had occurred and they were to surface for instructions.

During the first field season, airlift excavation was limited to digging test trenches, exposing the extent of the upper limits of the hull structure and the ends of the frames that marked the periphery of the embedded wreck. Test trenches were completed in the bow, at the mainmast, outside of the hull and at the stern, from which we recovered samples of diagnostic material. These gave us a clearer idea of the amount of organic material such as wood, leather, and animal remains that would all require time-consuming

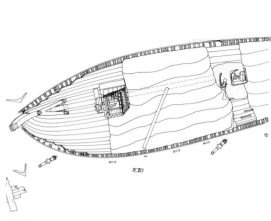

A site-plan of the *Defence* (above) shows lines similar to the so-called Virginia-built privateer of the later Revolutionary period, seen in this reconstruction. She was a two-masted brigantine of 170 burden tons, with wide decks, a row of 6-pounder carriage guns running along each side and square lofty sails towering above. Although she had heavy interior sheathing, made of 10 × 2in planks, her build was generally light-boned. The kind of innovative features seen in the *Defence* made important contributions to the design of sailing ships and the search for speed under sail.

treatments to preserve properly. During subsequent field seasons, airlifts were used to clear the entire hull of overburden.

Ceramic, glass and iron remains need totally different kinds of treatment and stabilization procedures, and the material recovered from the test areas was vital in gauging the extent and the kind of conservation work that would be required as the excavation progressed.

The excavation
A special conservation laboratory was set up, based on the information provided by the preliminary site reconnaissance, and was used in conjunction with the excavation work to enhance the archaeological value of the project. Equally important, in view of future work, was the completion of a map of the site. This was done by labeling each frame end as soon as it was exposed and then using triangulation to plot its location – the standard plan-making method used by archaeologists working on land.

The main problem we encountered was eliminating spurious measurements due to the tapes becoming snagged or being misled in the murky underwater conditions. In spite of the number of "retake" measurements, a plan of the wreck gradually began to take shape. The site plan was steadily modified and enhanced as more structural details came to light, giving us the opportunity to appreciate the full extent of the site.

More than 40 percent of the 72ft-long hull was structurally intact and in its original "as-built" condition. Further investigations ascertained that the jumble of timbers in the stern had been caused by the explosion that sent *Defence* to the seafloor. The distribution of the artifacts in the hull was recorded graphically and the resultant depositional pattern provided us with clues to the events in the hull of *Defence* after she sank. The bow section of the vessel was treated in the same way – being cleared and measured so that we could preserve the wreck through documentation and scaled drawings.

Eventually, the tedious removal of the accumulated sediments revealed the artifacts in the hull area. Interesting finds included several pulley blocks, a brass pot lid, grapeshot, and a lead apron used to cover the touch hole of a cannon. In addition, the excavators recovered more personal artifacts that were not connected with the ship's rigging or ordnance, such as portions of shoe, pewter spoons, small tubs that were later identified as the crew's mess kits, pieces of furniture and a unique bone whistle. These types of find were vital in providing a clearer understanding of life and work at sea during the colonial-revolutionary era.

A time capsule
The artifacts and structural information recovered from *Defence* have a special archaeological significance: no other 18th

century American vessels that have been excavated reveal comparative data. The *Machault*, for example, was excavated in Canada between 1969 and 1972, but the data derived from this site represents a ship of a different nature – a French armed merchantship, typical of the 1760s.

The *Philadelphia*, an 18th century ship recovered in 1935 (the hull and associated artifacts are on display at the National Museum in Washington DC), is also not comparable to the *Defence*. The *Philadelphia*'s hull is of a type known as a gundalow, a flat-bottomed single-masted vessel of the 18th century and later, common in New England rivers, lakes and estuaries. It was basically an undecked craft, propelled by oars or sail and carrying three cannon, not a seagoing vessel like *Defence*. In terms of structural characteristics, nothing comparable to the inherent features of *Defence* exists in any vessels yet excavated in the United States.

A tribute to ship design
Our excavation of the hull of the ship verified some earlier suspicions about the nature of the construction of *Defence*. We thought that the privateer might have been speedily and economically built to meet her wartime demands, and several intrinsic features of the vessel confirmed this theory. We found evidence of time-saving constructional methods such as a partially adzed oak crotch that formed the breast hook, bark remaining on many of the frames, as well as a startling lack of iron nails. These are normally used to fasten ceiling strakes, and their limited number may indicate wartime shortage.

Near the mainmast, the bilge, pumpwell and shot locker areas appeared to have been almost "thrown together", using mismeasured pine boards that were even

placed slightly askew of the center line of the vessel. Other evidence suggested possible short cuts taken by her builder, such as the method employed in setting up the frames. But these can only be confirmed by comparative structural data derived from other ships of a similar age.

Such potential evidence may come to light from the excavation of the well-preserved hulls of *Hamilton* and *Scourge* that have lain undisturbed in Lake Ontario since 1813, at a depth of 240ft (see p.206). Up to now, these vessels have only been examined photographically, but when raised and excavated in a safer environment, both vessels will yield all kinds of important comparative data.

Structural curiosities noted during the excavation of the Massachusetts-built privateer indicate that the lightly-built vessel was unlike naval vessels typical of the era. Interestingly, a more traditional, heavier vessel may well have withstood the damage caused by the internal explosion, allowing the ship to burn down to the water line, prior to sinking – depleting her potential from an archaeological viewpoint, especially in terms of hull contents.

Final analysis of the remains strongly suggests that *Defence* represented a breed of vessel unique to New England waters in the 18th century. The hull lines indicate a sharply-built vessel designed for speed, similar to vessels built in the Chesapeake area of the colonies and refined after the Revolution. These vessels, referred to in naval architectural parlance as "Virginia-built", were the forerunners of the famed Baltimore clipper brigs and schooners of the early 19th century. By the 1850s, these vessels had developed into the clipper ship – America's most important contribution to the search for speed under sail.

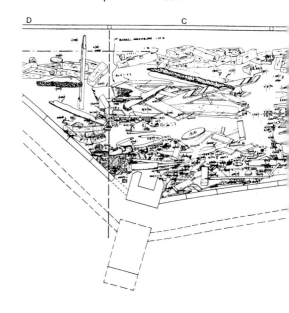

Life at sea

Sailors have always lived a life apart. After the discovery of the New World, mariners were separated from their land-based mother cultures for long periods at a time. This, and the closed community formed aboard a ship, necessitated the modification of certain contemporary cultural norms.

By the 18th century, landsmen had modified or discarded many medieval customs and traditions, which sailors, for reasons of efficiency, still followed. Thus there emerged a distinctive subculture.

Before the advent of mass communication, sailors were often the transporters of cultural ideas, carrying the customs of their homeland around the world and bringing back curios and stories of exotic cultures to their families and friends. Ships, cargoes and the crew's clothing and belongings were floating material expressions of their mother culture, as well as their own distinctive subculture.

Unfortunately, much information about life at sea during the colonial period and earlier has been lost or stylized beyond recognition. However, some 18th and early 19th century journals and diaries have survived. John Nicols, Nathanial Fanning, Richard Dana and Herman Melville all recorded what they saw, but even these perceptive observers quite often neglected the more mundane details of life, or made reference to them in such a casual manner that the modern reader misses the significance. Factual documents such as muster lists and port records throw light on some of the problems, but even the two sources of information combined are not fully comprehensive.

So historians and archaeologists have turned to a third source of information: the intact shipwreck. Shipwrecks often yield remnants pertaining to every aspect of contemporary shipboard life. When used in conjunction with historical records and journals, these remnants provide an authoritative source which can clarify or add missing information concerning this important segment of society.

The *Defence* shipwreck

The 170-ton brigantine *Defence*, scuttled by her crew in 1779 during the Penobscot expedition of the American Revolutionary War, is an excellent example of an intact shipwreck. The thick mud into which the wreck settled helped preserve almost 50 percent of the hull. Within the vessel, archaeologists recovered more than 5,000 well-preserved artifacts representing a wide range of shipboard activities and materials. Bay sediments quickly sealed off the ship from harmful oxygen with the result that fragile potato peelings, leather goods, delicate glass bottles and ceramics survived their 200-year submersion. Unfortunately, many artifacts made of iron could not withstand the corrosive properties of salt water.

Most of the tools, however, had wooden handles which did survive. The durability of other wooden items depended on what sort of wood they were made from and the length of time they had remained exposed to oxygen underwater.

Before thorough analysis could begin, archaeologists sought to identify all the artifacts. In most instances this process was relatively easy. However, a few groups of artifacts remained unidentified for years. At least one group has never been identified. In the case of 20 small, initialed wooden tags, identification finally came from the journal of a prisoner of war aboard the British prison ship *Jersey*, moored in New York harbor. The prisoner, one Captain Durig, described the messing procedure in which each mess captain whittled a distinctive wooden tag which he then secured by twine to the mess allotment of meat. The meat was then lowered into the ship's large caldron. Later, at mess, the tag and the meat were hauled out and dumped into a serving tub, called a mess kit or messkid, with appropriate portions of peas and potatoes.

With the identity of the tags secured, other journals by Melville, Dana and Nicols were reviewed. All three journalists mentioned the tags, but only in passing, and so their significance was missed by our researcher on first perusal. Once identities were assigned, all the artifacts and their categories, ranging from personal belongings and tools through provisioning and food preparation to ordnance, were examined with regard to their manufacture, the general context in which they were used, and the way in which they reflected the physiological as well as the psychological traits of the crew.

Layout of the ship

The general distribution of artifacts aided archaeologists in determining the layout aboard the 85–90ft (26–27m) long *Defence*. Dividing bulkheads had deteriorated long ago. Only the ways in which the artifacts had been distributed hinted as to the ship's original layout. Information about the exact locations of bulkheads was further enhanced by patterns of artifacts blown out of the stern by the force of the scuttling blast. Thin-walled aquamarine case bottles tumbled out of

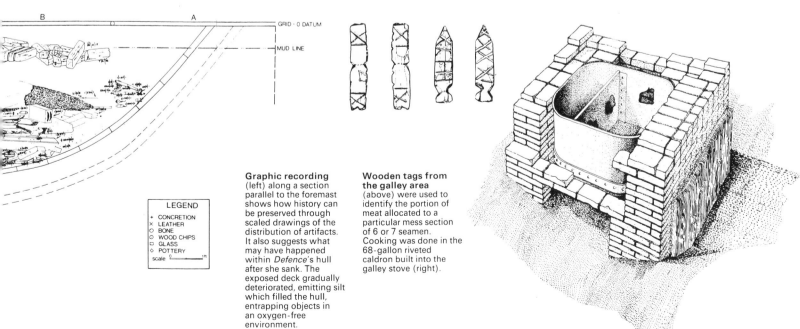

LEGEND
+ CONCRETION
× LEATHER
○ BONE
○ WOOD CHIPS
□ GLASS
◇ POTTERY
scale 0 _____ 1m

Graphic recording (left) along a section parallel to the foremast shows how history can be preserved through scaled drawings of the distribution of artifacts. It also suggests what may have happened within *Defence*'s hull after she sank. The exposed deck gradually deteriorated, emitting silt which filled the hull, entrapping objects in an oxygen-free environment.

Wooden tags from the galley area (above) were used to identify the portion of meat allocated to a particular mess section of 6 or 7 seamen. Cooking was done in the 68-gallon riveted caldron built into the galley stove (right).

GRID - 0 DATUM

MUD LINE

the stern and flew across the open amidship area before smashing on the bulkhead which partitioned off the galley.

Originally, Captain John Edmonds and his officers, Nathanial Swasey and John Boardman, berthed in the stern alongside the "spirit room" and over the magazine. A massive brick cookstove with a large copper caldron dominated the first 25ft (7.6m) of the hull.

Alongside food preparation utensils and casks of provisions were tools and personal effects. Several seamen, most likely the cook and at least one or two other craftsmen, often referred to as the "idlers", probably bunked in the bow. The bulkhead aft of the cookstove provided these men with a modicum of privacy. The remaining 95 sailors slung their hammocks in the 20ft by 20ft (6m by 6m) open midship area along with most of the provisions stored in wooden casks.

Although the four-hour watch system ensured that not all the sailors were off duty at any one time, at least half the crew would have been off duty during each watch. The cramped quarters, smells and sounds that must have assailed the *Defence* are a far cry from modern concepts of personal space and privacy.

Colonial manufacturing

Information on contemporary manufacturing techniques and styles garnered from the precisely dated shipwreck is an invaluable tool of comparison for both terrestrial and nautical archaeologist alike. Large collections of casks, ceramics and bottles found aboard the *Defence* provide an additional insight into the colonial economy and its trade connections. For example, the aquamarine case bottles, found predominantly in the American colonies, are thought to be French in origin. The subtle differences among the bottles in terms of size, shoulder shape and neck form suggest that even within the small group that was found aboard the *Defence*, two different craftsmen or glass houses were represented.

In contrast, the majority of ceramics appear to be domestic products. The consistency in form, body and glaze of the redwares suggests they were made at a local potting house near Beverly, Massachusetts, owned by the Bayley family.

The *Defence* collection also provides information on contemporary fashions: the shoes and spoons display discreet style changes over a 40-year period. This information is particularly significant as the *Defence* was on her maiden voyage. Unlike land sites, which often represent many years of occupation, the *Defence* was only at sea for a month before she sank; yet the artifacts found aboard cover a 40-year period. Determining the lifespan of particular fashion styles is therefore very useful in this context.

Archaeologists recovered a large number of artifacts related to eating and food preparation in the galley area and throughout the amidships. Among these were 19 pewter spoons found mainly in context with other personal belongings.

Stylistically, the spoons represent only three styles: Hanoverian (Rat-tail), Trifid and Neoclassical. The Trifid and Rat-tail spoons represent styles from the first three quarters of the 18th century and were already old-fashioned when the vessel sank; the Neoclassical style, on the other hand, had only recently become popular.

Each of the spoons found was engraved with a distinct set of initials. Two spoons had clipped handles allowing them to fit neatly into someone's pocket. Although the lack of stylistic variety may partially explain why the initials were necessary, the practice of owning a private set of utensils was already outmoded on dry land. Furthermore, the absence of forks suggests a more medieval manner of eating, in which the spoon was used as the primary utensil.

The most likely reason for making individuals responsible for their own utensils was so as to render the feeding process more efficient. This theory is borne out by the engraved spoons found on the Dutch East Indiaman *Amsterdam*, driven ashore at Hastings in 1748. In this case, spoons were found that belonged to both the crew and the passengers.

The majority of spoons also show signs of wear on the side of the bowl. Side wear reflects how the sailors used their spoons, for the bowls of 18th century spoons are too large to fit easily into the mouth sideways. The wear pattern suggests the spoon was held stable or tipped while the owner sucked food from it.

Communal eating

Additional information about attempts by the crew to assert their individuality, and also information about their habits, can be obtained from five intact oak mess kits and a single pewter plate. (Mess kits were the single serving containers for the five men who shared a mess.) All but one mess kit were located in the galley area and all were identical. The pewter plate would appear to have been blown forward from the stern quarter by the scuttling blast.

Multiple sets of initials were engraved on the base of the mess kits. One mess kit owner, a certain I. L., conveniently (for us) carved the date 1779 next to his initials. In contrast, the pewter plate had no markings besides those made from cutting up portions on the plate. The groups of initials found on the mess kits probably represent the men who made up the different messes and possibly the gun crews. It would take only 20 mess kits to feed a crew of 100 men.

The mess kits were probably returned to the galley for storage after each meal, judging from where they were found aboard the wrecked ship. While the size of the mess kit suggests how large the allotted portions were, the bucket-like shape, in conjunction with the food remains and the large caldron found in the cookstove, show us the type of food served. Boiled stews of peas, potatoes and large cuts of meat were convenient for feeding many mouths at one time. Communal eating also reduced the number of serving containers as well as the number of individual cuts of meats required.

The presence of the pewter plate, however, suggests that some of the people aboard the *Defence* were not obliged to eat communally or partake of the medieval-type stew fare. In spite of the restrictions imposed on the rest of the crew, it would seem that the right to retain his individual place setting was an officer's perquisite.

Buttons and buckles

In contrast to the food-related objects, items of clothing found aboard the ship reveal that the sailors were generally in step with contemporary colonial fashions. Although most of their garments have not survived, the more durable objects such as buttons, buckles and shoes exhibit styles and subtle wear marks that say much about the physical characteristics of the *Defence*'s crew.

The ratio of home made to commercially manufactured buttons suggests that most of the seamen, or their landbased families, made their own. Even some of the plain cast pewter buttons could have been made at home. However, the presence of the more ornate buttons among the regular sailors' belongings shows that they had access to more finely crafted items – and could afford them.

Apart from the buttons which fastened the sailors' clothing, there are only a few buckles to shed any additional light on the type of trousers worn by some of the

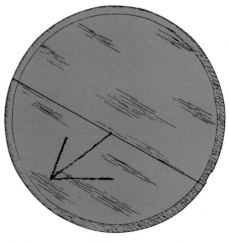

The base of a mess kit, a small stave-built container used to distribute allotted portions of food to a mess section.

sailors. Among the eight buckles recovered were two small copper buckles, one with gold leaf, that most likely adorned some sailor's knee breeches.

Knee-length breeches fastened with buckles were very fashionable on land in the 1770s. However, most sketches of sailors from the period show calf-length, wide-legged trousers. The presence of the two small buckles among the common sailors' belongings suggests that some sailors wore breeches or had an extra set of "Sunday best" clothes. On the other hand, the breeches may have belonged to landsmen lured into a privateer cruise by the promise of prize money. After all, the navy required that at least one third of any privateer's crew be landsmen, so as to leave some trained sailors for naval duty.

The remaining buckles once fastened shoes. Although only six shoe buckles survived, at least 19 fairly complete shoes were found. All except one were buckle-style shoes and all except the one example appear to have been made in the American colonies.

Shoe styles and sizes

Shoes, like the buttons and buckles, represent individual tastes among the sailors. Twelve latchet styles (with leather straps/thongs) were discovered, as well as four vamp styles (a style covering the upper part of the front of the foot). The combinations of various buckle, latchet and vamp styles probably made different pairs of shoes distinctive. However, the abundance of shoes left aboard the scuttled vessel raises questions about the sailors' attitude to the wearing of shoes and the number of pairs of shoes owned by each sailor. Wearing shoes aloft could be dangerous and many shoes have their counters broken down so that they could be slipped off and on with ease. The habit

of not wearing shoes aboard ship may account for the many shoes left behind when the sailors hastily abandoned ship.

The shoes also provided information about the physiology of the sailors. Ranging in size from a modern size 3 to $8\frac{1}{2}$, the shoes seem quite small by today's standards. Furthermore, the average C width of the shoes is wider than the average modern shoe. Thus the shoe collection suggests that the *Defence* crew were shorter and had wider feet than their modern male counterparts.

In addition to reflecting different styles and sizes, the shoes also suggest two methods of manufacture and tanning processes. Shoe stores did not exist in the colonies in 1779. Most shoes were made to order, although some shoes were made on speculation. The latter required that the design account only for size. In fact, most people wore "straights", which were originally constructed for either foot. However, at least three of the shoes in the *Defence* collection were constructed with a specific foot in mind. These were referred to as "crooks" and represent a more expensive type of shoe.

All of the "crooks" and some of the "straights" are made of good quality leather, smooth side out. In fact, one of these shoes bears a tanner's stamp, with the words *bourg cuir*. The French stamp most likely denotes a leather tanned outside the city of Paris and thus not in keeping with guild standards.

From a modern vantage point, the stamp of inferiority on one of the better quality shoes is ironic. Many of the shoes are made from a thin, flimsy leather and the use of cheap leather does not appear to go hand in hand with a plain design. For example, one thin leather shoe sports a striped woven ribbon carefully sewn around the tongue. The reason for the use

of poorly tanned leather is unclear since the better quality leather appears in styles and shoes throughout the wreck. The answers may lie in the infancy of the colonial tanning industry and the availability of products during the Revolutionary War.

The *Defence* collection serves a dual purpose. Firstly, the variety of artifacts found helps to date accurately and, in the case of the mess tags, to expand the archaeological record. Secondly, the results of the *Defence* collection study together with the documentary data and journal descriptions, should remove forever any vague 20th century notions of clouds of billowing sail and pristine wooden hulls. In their place, the image of 100 men crammed into a small space and living a spartan existence will emerge. The layout of the *Defence* shows that privacy was non-existent. Add to the claustrophobic spatial arrangements the constant creaking noises of a wooden ship, the smell of damp wool, rotting food, and 100 unwashed men, and the image is not very romantic. Rather the archaeological data reveal a particularly earthy lifestyle.

Although sailors shared many of the same fashion tastes as their contemporaries on land, they had to be continually aware of the dimensions of space and time in order to survive. They achieved this through various means, notably the four-hour watch system, the open berthing area and the medieval messing practices, all of which contributed to the efficient manning of a sailing ship.

Yet the various styles of artifacts found and the initials engraved on some of the objects indicate a desire for identity and ownership. In this way, the crew of the *Defence* adapted objects and customs from their mother culture to suit the unusual needs of life at sea.

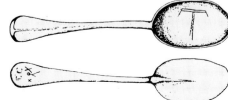

Life on shipboard (above), as portrayed by a contemporary British observer, Thomas Rowlandson. Women were allowed on board while ships were in port. A pewter spoon from *Defence* (left) with the maker's mark EC and possibly the initial of the owner. Note the wear-induced indentation.

Napoleon's guns

Remains of land battles are not normally found underwater. The discovery of 18th century military hardware beneath the waves of the Mediterranean along the coast of Israel was first considered to be part of a shipwrecked cargo. Further study of the site, however, introduced us to a fascinating footnote in Napoleonic history.

Spurred by a growing interest in diving, underwater archaeology has become an established field of research in Israel. The Department of Antiquities set up its sea base at the Tantura lagoon near Kibbutz Nahsholim, in a disused old glass-bottle factory built by Baron Edmond de Rothschild in 1893.

In the beginning, we dived frequently in the Tantura lagoon and in the large bay to the south of the nearby ancient maritime city of Dor. We were practicing basic work techniques by carrying out an underwater survey of this area.

In the course of these dives, we were surprised to find items of military hardware scattered on the seabed – similar finds had already been brought to the surface during a survey by the Israel Undersea Exploration Society in 1961–1964.*

At that time a number of heavily concreted muskets, two swivel guns, a mortar, and mortar balls had been found. This was assumed to have been part of a ship's cargo which had sunk nearby, but no remains of the ship itself were found. During our dives, we removed four flintlock muskets, several lead musket balls, and an iron cannon ball for purposes of identification. We also began researching the history of Tel Dor-Tantura in an attempt to find a historical event which would perhaps explain the preponderance of weaponry on the seabed.

Among the sources studied were various old maps. Of particular interest to us was one prepared by Napoleon Bonaparte's cartographer, Jacotin, during the Egyptian campaign. The map shows the Carmel Coast, and along with other details, indicates the route of the French army's retreat from Akko. A crossed saber and musket indicate Bonaparte's camp on the evening of May 21 1799, not far from where we were finding military hardware in the sea. Excitedly, we began delving into the happenings at Tantura on that date; finally, we were able to reconstruct the events of that fateful day.

Napoleon at Tantura

As darkness fell on the eve of May 20 1799, a disillusioned Napoleon Bonaparte raised his unsuccessful siege of Akko. Stealthily evacuating its positions around the walled city, the battered French army struck out south along the coast in a forced march. Many of the soldiers were incapacitated from wounds received during the fierce fighting or by having fallen victim to the plague which ravaged the French camp. At midnight the army arrived at Haifa. In a letter to his mother a French officer described the march:

> . . . We hoped that we should no longer have before our eyes the hideous sight of dead and dying men . . . when, as we entered Haifa in the dark of the night, we saw about a hundred sick and wounded who had been left in the middle of a large square. The poor, desperate people filled the air with their screams and their curses . . . some were tearing off bandages and rolling in the dust. This spectacle petrified the army. We stopped for a moment, and men were designated in each company to carry these men in their arms to Tantura.

The march south took place under horrifying circumstances. The historian of this campaign, Louis Antoine Fauvelet de Bourrienne, wrote:

> . . . I saw with my own eyes officers who had limbs amputated being thrown out of their litters . . . I have seen amputated men, wounded men, plague stricken men, or people merely suspected of having the plague, being abandoned in the fields. Our march was lit up by torches with which we set fire to the towns, the villages, the hamlets, and the rich harvests that covered the land. The entire countryside was on fire . . . We were surrounded by nothing but dying men, looters and arsonists. The dying, by the roadside, were saying in a barely audible voice, "I am only wounded, I haven't got the plague", and in order to convince those who were marching by they opened their wounds or inflicted fresh ones on themselves. Nobody believed them. People said, "He's a dead man," and passed by . . . To our right was the sea; to our left and behind us, the desert we were creating; ahead of us, the sufferings and privations that awaited us.

Early on the morning of May 21, the van of Napoleon's army straggled into the small harbor town of Tantura. Bonaparte had earlier sent specific orders to the officer in charge of his fleet, Admiral Perrée, to meet the troops at Tantura with ships in order to evacuate the army and its equipment to the rear bases at Jaffa and Damiette in Egypt. But instead of ships, the exhausted army found an additional 700 to 800 wounded and sick soldiers lying on the beach at Tantura.

Bonaparte soon realized that in order to

A view of Akko (Acre) from the sea during the siege (above) shows how it would have appeared to Sir Sidney Smith's fleet. Napoleon thought at first that the city would not be difficult to capture. However, the tactics of Sir Sidney Smith, and the resistance offered by the handful of intrepid Turks who had remained in the city during the siege, caused Napoleon to realize that the capture of Akko would cost the French troops dear. The siege was abandoned.

A view of Tantura lagoon as it is today (above right) shows part of the ancient harbor of Dor. During Napoleon's Egyptian campaign Tantura was used as a staging post for the French army's unsuccessful siege of Akko. It was at Tantura on May 21 1799 that Napoleon's retreating troops were obliged to rid themselves of their weapons so that they could continue to march on foot. To ensure that the weaponry would not fall into enemy hands, cannons were thrown into the sea and guns buried hurriedly in the sand.

extricate the army and to bring it safely to Jaffa, he had to find a way to make it more mobile. Sufficient water and food were lacking for an extended march, and many of the soldiers were disabled. Accordingly, he ordered all the beasts of burden to be allocated for carrying the sick and wounded, marching himself on foot to set a personal example.

However, using the animals for transporting the wounded meant that the army's weaponry had to be abandoned. Throughout the night of May 21 and the morning of May 22, Bonaparte's men toiled to dispose of the weaponry to prevent it from falling into enemy hands.

Cannon carriages together with the caissons of gunpowder were burnt on the beach. One caisson exploded, badly burning several of the soldiers who were standing nearby. Some twenty cannon were jettisoned into the sea. The remaining two (of a total of five) "24s" (24-pounders) – the largest of the siege cannon – were hastily buried on the beach. In the words of de Bourrienne:

> The remains of our heavy artillery were left in the moving sands of Tentoura . . . The soldiers seemed to forget their own sufferings at the loss of these bronze guns which had enabled them so often to triumph, and which had made Europe tremble.

A flintlock musket, one of four concreted to the seabed in the Tantura lagoon, is examined and recorded by a diver (above) before being brought to the surface. The muskets were subsequently identified as French service muskets of the 1777 type.

Jacotin's contemporary map of the Carmel coast (right) shows the route followed by the French army retreating from Akko – the words *"Route suivie par l'Armée d'Orient à son retour d'Acre"* are just legible. The march south was a terrible ordeal by all accounts, with many sick and wounded soldiers.

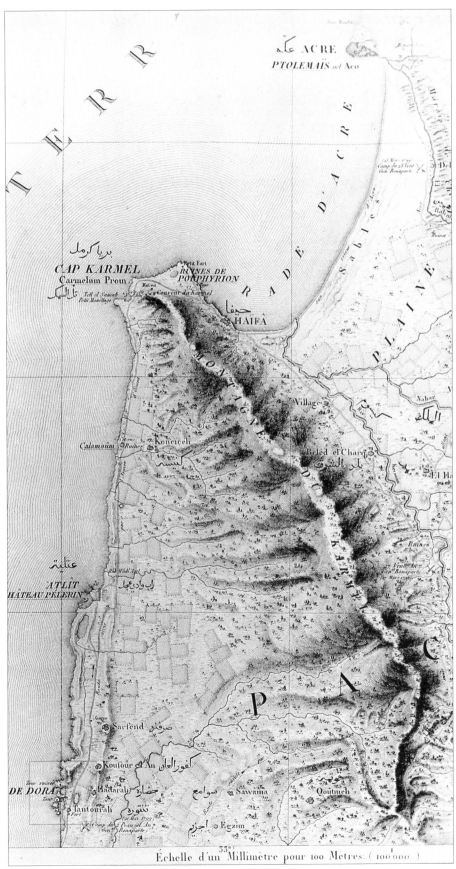

Grenadier's saber

At 10am on May 22 1799, Bonaparte left Tantura with his army on the way to Jaffa, Sinai, and to his final defeat in Egypt. Of particular interest to us were the two "24s" which had been cached on the beach. Since they had such high sentimental and military value, we reasoned that the French might have recorded the burial site of the guns with the intention of retrieving them one day. A simple metal detector found only rusted sewage pipes, iron nails, aluminum foil yogurt tops, and other assorted debris.

Colonel Willing, of the Hôtel des Invalides, identified the four flintlocks as French service muskets of the 1777 type. This same model, with several modifications, continued in use until 1840. The concreted remains of a saber scabbard proved to be of a type used by French infantry grenadiers from 1789 to 1800. Unfortunately, no known map remained of the burial spot of the "24s". If one did indeed exist, it must have been lost, along with other records, during the French army's evacuation from Egypt.

Our search for the cannon jettisoned into the sea bore fruit in March of 1981. A 5ft (1.6m) long bronze cannon was found lying upside down with its markings buried. With the enthusiastic assistance of members of Kibbutz Nahsholim and the University of Haifa's Sea Workshop, the cannon was raised from the sea.

Turkish guns

At last we had found one of Bonaparte's cannon; or so we thought. Our jubilant mood rapidly dissipated; for, as the cannon's markings were cleaned, the crescent and star symbol on the barrel showed it to be Turkish. The cannon also had a Turkish sultan's monogram, or *tugra,* near the priming hole. Reviewing once again the available eye-witness reports, we found that we had overlooked a basic fact: some of the pieces jettisoned into the sea at Tantura were Turkish cannon which had been captured at Jaffa and brought before Akko prior to being "deep-sixed" at Tantura. Thus wrote Louis-Alexander Berthier:

> . . . it (the French army) arrived at Tentoura, the port where the objects to be forwarded to Damiette and to Jaffa had been evacuated along with forty Turkish campaign pieces, captured at Jaffa, some of which had been brought before Acre.
>
> There were not enough horses to draw this quantity of Turkish artillery. Bonaparte decided that all the means of transport would be preferably employed for evacuating the sick and the wounded. Consequently he kept only two howitzers and a few small Turkish pieces, and he had twenty-two thrown into the sea; the caissons and the carriages were burnt at the port of Tentoura.

Lieutenant-General (Ret.) Bahaddin Alpkan of the Turkish Prime Minister's Office, informed us that a cannon with similar markings in the Turkish Military Museum dates to the reign of Sultan Selim III (1789–1807). Independently, the *tugra* on the Tantura cannon was tentatively identified by Myrian Rosen-Ayalon and Amnon Cohen as that of Selim III or one of his immediate predecessors, Mustapha III (1757–1774). There can be little doubt, therefore, that our cannon found its way into the sea at Tantura through the hands of Bonaparte's soldiers on May 21 or May 22 1799.

Since there has been little research on the subject of Turkish artillery, the Tantura cannon is interesting in itself. Frank Howard, an authority on early European artillery, has noted that the cannon's dimensions are very similar to an English ship's 4-pounder cannon. The bore is slightly smaller and, consequently, the shot would be somewhat lighter than four pounds. This may be due to differences between Turkish and English measures.

Although the cannon dates from the late 18th century, its appearance is somewhat old-fashioned by contemporary European standards. Loop handles, also known as dolphins, had disappeared from English and French cannon by the mid 18th century. The position of the trunnions, on which the cannon swiveled, low on the barrel, is another archaic feature reminiscent of English practice in the 17th century, rather than a century later.

Placing the trunnions low on the cannon caused an undesirable downward stress on the carriage when the gun was fired. Because of this, trunnions were later placed one-third of the gun's diameter up from the underside . . . "hung by the third", as the saying went. The gun's old-fashioned appearance is not surprising, for Turkish arms lagged behind Western European ones in the 18th century.

The cannon was probably a field piece rather than a ship's gun originally. It was common practice then to mount naval guns on land carriages and contrariwise. However, the Turks were not particularly active at sea in the Eastern Mediterranean during this period.

Spanish mortar

The story does not end with the Turkish gun. In January 1983, we recovered a second artillery piece at Tantura. This time it was a Spanish bronze mortar, bearing five separate inscriptions. The most interesting of these states that mortar "No. 3162" was made in "SEVILLA" on December 12 1793 – only five years before Bonaparte disposed of it in the sea.

One of the trunnions bears the inscription "COBRE DE LIMA" – that is, the piece is made of copper from Lima, Peru. The other trunnion bears a number "Pº. 725". According to Colonel Willing, this number refers to the weight of the mortar in pounds; the mortar weighs 333.7kg.

On the forward part of the barrel is a pennant with part of an inscription which has, for the most part, been erased by time. All that remains is "——IV". This apparently refers to Carlos IV, the king of Spain at that time. Another inscription is

The concretion and cast (left) of the lower part of a French infantry grenadier's saber scabbard, found on the seabed, was identified as a type in use from 1789–1800. The cannon (above), found lying with its markings buried, was at first thought to be French. It was in fact Turkish.

located near the priming hole. It contains an "R" and a "Q", inscribed one within the other, and capped by a crown. This has also been identified by Lieutenant-Colonel Neuville of the Hôtel des Invalides as the monogram of King Carlos IV of Spain (1788–1808).

The historical significance of an artillery piece made in Spain during the latter part of 1793 cannot be ignored. Louis XVI was decapitated in that same year, which led to war between Spain and France. It was apparently during this war that the mortar was cast. We hoped that some information on the mortar might still exist in the Musée de l'Armée since it bears a serial number, but no record of it remains.

How did a Spanish mortar fall into the hands of Napoleon's army? Colonel Willing suggests that it may have been captured by the Armée Française des Pyrénées Orientales, which fought under General Sherer in the region of Bilbao and Vitoria in Spain in 1794. The mortar has been defined by Willing as a "six-inch", a type generally fired at an angle of 45 degrees with a load of 1lb 14oz (850g) of gunpowder. Its standard ammunition was a hollow iron ball that weighed 1lb 15oz (880g), and which was packed with 1lb 7oz (675g) of gunpowder. Its maximum range was 1.5 miles (2.3km).

Bonaparte's visit to Tantura is admittedly little more than a historical footnote. However, the story behind the elegant weapons recalls the horrors of this long-forgotten war and bears witness to the ruthless dynamism of a man who was to shape the annals of modern Europe.

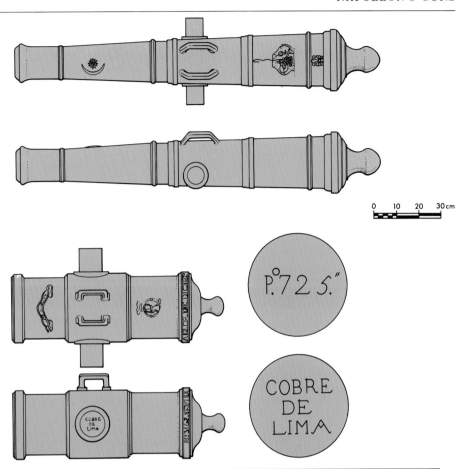

Nº 3162. SEVILLA. 12. DE. DE. DICIEMBRE. 1793.

The Turkish cannon and a Spanish mortar (above), also raised from the lagoon, are now on display at the Center for Nautical and Regional Archaeology, Kibbutz Nahsholim. The cannon was captured from the Turks at Jaffa; the mortar may have been seized in northern Spain in 1794.

Line drawings of the Turkish cannon (top) show the star and crescent and the *tugra*, or sultan's name; drawings of the mortar (above left) show the pennant and the royal monogram of Carlos IV, king of Spain when the cannon was cast. The pennant in detail (above) shows only the roman numeral "IV", the rest of the inscription having worn away. "COBRE DE LIMA" and "Po.725" on the mortar's trunnions indicate that the copper used in casting the weapon was from Peru and that the cannon weighed 725 Spanish pounds.

Naval wrecks from the Great Lakes

The Anglo-American War of 1812 grew out of the life-and-death struggle in Europe between Britain and Napoleon's France, and involved a number of naval actions on the Great Lakes, notably the battle of Lake Erie. However, the two wrecks discussed here were sunk by a storm, not by enemy action. *Hamilton* and *Scourge* were patrolling Lake Ontario when they went down in 1813, to be discovered in 1971 by an officially commissioned Canadian research project. The ships are in an extraordinarily good state of preservation, due largely to the depth of the lake, and plans are being made for their recovery.

In the early morning hours of Sunday August 8, 1813, *Hamilton* and her fellow schooner *Scourge*, were hove to with 11 other ships of Commodore Isaac Chauncey's American squadron 6 miles (9.6km) off present-day Port Dalhousie on Lake Ontario.

They were awaiting first light to renew action against the British-Canadian squadron of six ships commanded by Commodore Sir James Lucas Yeo, RN. Around 2am, a sudden squall swept up the lake, and caught both schooners beam on, capsizing them and sending them to the bottom, 50 fathoms (300ft) below, along with 53 hands. There were 19 survivors, which made this the largest single loss of life on the Great Lakes during the War of 1812.

Discovery of the ships
A search for the schooners, initiated in 1971, resulted in their discovery two years later and the find was confirmed in 1975. A brief exploration of *Hamilton* using a remotely piloted vehicle and sonar recording instruments established that the vessels were intact, upright and in a remarkable state of preservation.

Factors responsible for their preservation are fresh water, the constant near-freezing temperature, and the nearly utter darkness in which they lie. In addition, the vessels lie approximately 260ft (80m) deep, beyond the reach of hobby or semi-professional divers. They are protected by stringent provincial legislation pertaining to archaeological sites, and a radar surveillance system has been installed to keep watch over them.

Cousteau and his team investigated *Hamilton* in 1980. In the same year, title to the schooners was transferred from the United States Navy to the City of Hamilton, Ontario, and the Royal Ontario Museum through the United States Con-gress. Enabling legislation was passed by the Provincial legislature.

Wide range of artifacts
In 1982, a *Hamilton-Scourge* Foundation/National Geographic Society survey of both vessels was conducted. Only then was it discovered what a full range of artifacts the schooners contain: guns stand upon the decks, ladles just to one side as if laid down yesterday; cutlasses are crossed above *Scourge*'s guns; shot lies in the shot-racks; pikes are scattered upon the decks; boarding axes stand in their racks; a platter lies next to *Hamilton*'s rudder.

Computer-indexing of visual materials, using seven variables, was completed in June 1986 and led to a re-drafting of the preliminary plans made at the time of the National Geographic Society/*Hamilton-Scourge* Society survey.

Search of local records
At the same time, because original plans for the schooners (if indeed they do exist) would be of great use to archaeological investigators, first priority was given to historical studies essential to interpretation. A data-base analysis of Upper Canada Customs records for the Lake Ontario ports between the years 1801–1812 was made. These records and the business records of the firm which operated the American portage around Niagara Falls after 1808 were combined to form an on-going main-frame index, "Lake Traffic", through which the whereabouts of all the lake's schooners in the years 1801–1812 can be traced using a wide variety of sources.

This search of local history records yielded findings such as the accounts for the construction of one vessel and what appear to be complete shipping records for the other. A search of naval records turned up material related to maintenance and supplies. Gradually, project researchers have developed a detailed knowledge of the schooners from historical records.

Alias *Diana*
Hamilton is the former merchant schooner *Diana*, constructed at Oswego, New York, in 1809 by the shipwright Henry Eagle for the merchants Matthew McNair and P.D. Hugunin. Eagle, who came from the Baltic port of Memel, had worked for the great shipwright Henry Eckford in New York. After the War of 1812, he became a very prosperous Oswego merchant/shipowner. By an insurance agreement, the Porter-Barton firm (which operated the American portage around Niagara Falls during this pre-canal period) entered into part-ownership of the vessel.

The *Diana*'s regular run was from Oswego, New York, to Lewiston, at the base of the American portage, and return; her cargo was salt from Salina (near today's Syracuse), destined for the burgeoning new farms of Ohio, Western Pennsylvania, and Michigan. She also carried luxury goods from the great wharves of New York, forwarded up the Hudson-Mohawk waterway, and passengers. There were three categories of the latter: settlers, investors and tourists. The tourist trade at Niagara Falls was brisk even at this early date – one Lake Ontario schooner took $5,000 for passenger trade alone in the 1810 season.

In October/November *Diana* was purchased by the United States Navy, and converted into a warship by the addition of ten 18-pounder carronades. Later, two guns were removed, and replaced by a 12-pounder long-gun which was mounted amidships. She participated in the American attack on Kingston in November 1812, the capture of York in April 1813, and of Fort George the following month. On August 8, 1813, she capsized and was lost.

Alias *Lord Nelson*
Scourge is the merchant schooner *Lord Nelson*, constructed at Niagara, Upper Canada, in 1810–1811 by the shipwright Asa Stannard for the merchant brothers, James and William Crooks. Stannard, a native of Connecticut, was brought from Hudson, New York, by Augustus Porter, to construct two schooners for the Porter-Barton firm. Subsequently he went across the river to build for James Crooks. Accounts for the construction of *Lord Nelson* indicate that her cabin was nicely finished, and it is likely that she had passenger accommodation typical of the lake's schooners, and which contemporaries considered comfortable.

Perfectly preserved in a freshwater, near-freezing environment, an 18-pounder carronade peers through the side of the converted merchant schooner *Hamilton*, 300ft below.

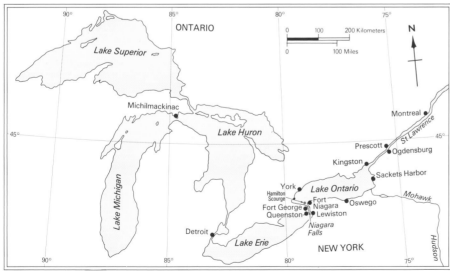

The figurehead (top) of *Hamilton*, originally the merchant schooner *Diana*, shows the right side of the goddess in an Empire dress. On her left side she wears only a quiver and strap (as seen on p.224). Together with *Scourge*, another merchant schooner pressed into naval service and sunk at the same time, the almost intact vessel represents a unique archaeological treasure.

A drawing of *Hamilton* complete with ship's boat, can be accurately made from the wonderfully preserved remains on the lake bed. Areas featured in the photographs are marked on the drawing.

The map (above) shows how the Great Lakes were part of a riverine system, with Lake Ontario as one section of a route from the Atlantic to Quebec, to Montreal, across the lake, over two great Niagara portages, across Lake Erie, and thence deep into the continent and linking up with the Mississippi river. The Mohawk-Hudson waterway joined the Great Lakes to the wharves of New York City; from Genesee (now Rochester, New York), an inland waterway led to Philadelphia, then the greatest of all American cities. Furs, flour, whiskey, salt pork and staves passed down the St Lawrence; tea, coffee, wine, iron, glass, china, textiles, chocolate and salt, the essential preservative, came up the Mohawk-Hudson waterway. Control of Lake Ontario, and thus the waterways, was seen as the key to success in

Lord Nelson's regular run was from Niagara to the new forwarding port of Prescott opposite Ogdensburg on the St Lawrence, and back to Niagara, although she may also have put in to Forty-Mile Creek (now Grimsby, Ontario), where William Crooks owned a flour mill. Although there is no record, she is almost certain to have carried to Prescott flour, potash, pearl ash, staves and skins. Bills of lading indicate that for the return trip she loaded merchandise forwarded from Montreal: china, bar iron, tools, glass, and a variety of personal effects – including a bride's trousseau which was captured with the ship on June 6 1812.

The capture of the vessel, on suspicion of smuggling, resulted in a lawsuit which preoccupied the Crooks family until it was finally settled (in an international treaty court) and payment made to family members in 1930. It also resulted in *Lord Nelson*'s libeling and subsequent purchase in October 1812 by the United States Navy. After this, bulwarks were raised in her, and she was armed. She participated in the American capture of York in April 1813, and that of Fort George in May. By July 1813 she was armed with ten 4- and 6-pounder long-guns.

A member of her crew, Ned Myers, was an old shipmate of James Fenimore Cooper, and in the 1840s he related his life's story to Cooper, including an account of the schooner's last ten months and her capsizing (see *Ned Myers; or A Life Before the Mast*, first published in 1843). Myers describes how he and a few other men escaped from the sinking ship: "The lake had swallowed up the rest . . . and the *Scourge*, as had been often predicted, had literally become a coffin to a large portion of her people."

Structure of the schooners
In terms of design and construction, *Hamilton* is the larger schooner with a length on deck of approximately 73ft (22m); *Scourge* is approximately 16ft (4.6m) shorter. Both schooners were once said to be approximately 20ft (6m) wide amidships, but it is now estimated that *Scourge* is about 2ft (0.6m) narrower than *Hamilton*. Naval records dated July 1813, list *Hamilton*'s tonnage as 76; *Scourge* was estimated at 45 tons; James Crooks estimated her at 50 tons.

Scourge's lines are old-fashioned – similar to those of the well-known *Sultana*, while *Hamilton* is transitional in design – sharper (although not as sharp as the government ships *Tecumseth* and *Newash*, constructed above the Falls only a few years later, and for which we have no plans). Her masts are raked back, although not to extreme angles.

The lake's schooners were typically shallow-draft, to enable them to ease over sandbars at the mouths of the lake's harbors, and these two vessels are no exception; the draft is as yet unknown since the bottoms of both schooners lie on the lake's floor. Perhaps because of the necessity for a shallow draft, and the need to provide comfortable accommodation for passengers, both schooners have raised quarterdecks, although the vessels were constructed after these had gone out of fashion in east coast schooners.

Behind *Hamilton* lies her ship's boat, fallen from her davits; this could be sailed or rowed. (*Scourge*'s boat was used to rescue sailors at the time of the capsizing.)

Figureheads
Both schooners have fine figureheads: *Hamilton*'s is a bust of the goddess Diana, who is naked on her left side, save for a quiver of arrows slung over her shoulder; on her right side, she wears an Empire dress, fashionable at the time, with a low-cut neckline, puff-sleeves, and a high belt. *Scourge*'s figurehead is the full-length striding figure of a merchant of the period, wearing Hessian boots, and a sailorly queue. Accounts indicate that the latter carving was imported from New York.

Importance of the project
The schooners are archaeological treasures of international importance, as the vessels, together with their artifacts, provide a blueprint for naval practices of the period. They are also connected with the early days of western exploration and the development of two great nations. The *Hamilton-Scourge* Project is, along with *Vasa* and *Mary Rose*, among the four or five most important underwater archaeology projects in the world. Like the other two, it excites enormous popular interest.

At present, plans and safeguards of excellence are as follows: a Steering Committee (set up in 1986) oversees the work of a Technical Study Team (set up in 1987), whose mandate it is to produce a feasibility study, including archaeological analysis and conservation and engineering recommendations, with financial guidelines. On the Steering Committee sit representatives of the Federal Government (Parks Canada); the Provincial Government (Ontario Heritage Foundation and the Ministry of Citizenship and Culture); and the City of Hamilton. The Technical Study Team is comprised of working specialists, supported by a larger group of aides and advisors.

A small staff is employed by the City of Hamilton; a Special Committee to administer the *Hamilton-Scourge* Project sets policy for the City's input; this committee reports to City Council. The *Hamilton-Scourge* Foundation is an allied but independent fund-raising board and the *Hamilton-Scourge* Society is a volunteer group open to membership; by its constitution the latter supports the Foundation. Attached to the *Hamilton-Scourge* Project are six advisory task forces; Project Planning; Archaeology; Conservation; Museum Planning; Engineering; and Historical Research.

The conclusions of the Technical Study Team, to be received and reviewed in two years' time by the Steering Committee, cannot be anticipated. It is expected, however, that archaeological study will continue by means of remotely operated vehicles and an electronic grid; that divers will be used in the final stages of archaeological exploration; artifacts will be raised to test conservation methods; wood-conservation methods will include the use of varying molecular weights of PEG (polyethylene glycol); if the decision is made to raise the vessels, slings will be used, and the ships put into a water-filled floating dry-dock which will provide tank transportation to land; the vessels will be transferred to tanks constructed per aquaria and/or swimming pools where conservation can commence.

A lake-side museum
It is expected that the schooners will eventually be exhibited dry. Holography and photography will be used to examine them further and the artifacts will be displayed during the conservation process. A lake-side site has been set aside in Hamilton for a *Hamilton-Scourge* museum, which is expected to become an international tourist attraction and a showpiece of Canadian museum technology.

Detailed plans as outlined above are essential to the success of an endeavor such as the *Hamilton-Scourge* Project. But the continued progress of the project depends on the meticulous seeing through of tested plans, together with the use of up-to-date equipment by experienced professionals. It also depends on the coordination of skills and gifts, on expert management, and a sound financial basis, and on the carrying out of archaeological investigations, conservation, and, if possible, recovery.

The *Scourge* was originally the *Lord Nelson*: the figurehead (opposite, top) depicts the famous admiral with both arms, although he had lost his right arm in 1797. A Canadian schooner operating from Prescott on the St Lawrence, she was captured on suspicion of smuggling and prized by the Americans on June 5, 1812, two weeks before hostilities were

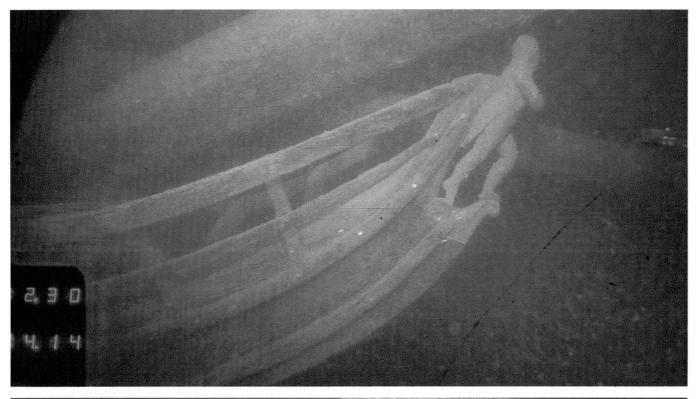

declared. At the time of her capture she was carrying an assorted cargo, including the bridal trousseau of a Mrs. McCormick of Queenston, Upper Canada. After capture she was immediately armed, renamed, and served against the British. The perfectly preserved bilge pump (above) has a cutlass stuck beside it. On the side of the wooden pump is its outlet for bilge water. Directly in front of the pump is *Scourge*'s mainmast. Cleats for halyards are attached to the mast.

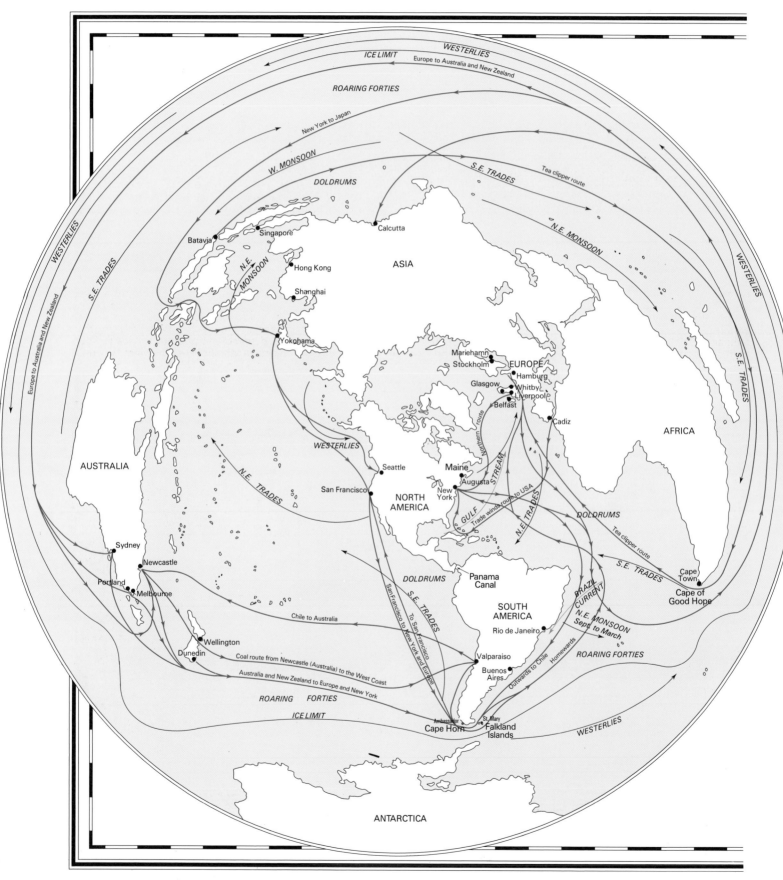

It is a comparatively recent idea that ships are artifacts with a value of their own, and that the craftsmanship which went into their creation deserves careful study. Yet this is now one of the foundation stones of modern maritime archaeology. Increasingly, maritime museums are beginning to retrieve and reassemble entire vessels, keeping them in good condition as "live" ships. The world's greatest resource of 19th century ships' bones is to be found around the Falkland Islands.

Saving ships

Ever since maritime museums began to save ships, there have been different schools of thought as to how to go about it. In the 1930s, when scholars of naval architecture were beginning to record the remnants of the 19th century maritime tradition, some believed that the best that could be done was to make careful drawings and perhaps a model. Others, like Carl Cutler of Mystic Seaport Museum,

believed that ships should be saved and kept in operating condition.

In Scandinavia, it was thought that ships should be preserved as artifacts in themselves. The discovery and excavation of the magnificent Viking ships at Gokstad (1880) and Oseberg (1904) led to their elegant restoration in the 1930s. These were exhibited under cover in the Oslo Seafaring Museum. Since then, a number of superbly reconstituted vessels have been rescued and displayed as artifacts, notably the 17th century Swedish warship *Vasa*.

Gradually, museum curators began to realize that the most effective way of preserving the memory of ships too large to be kept under cover, and financially impossible to maintain as part of an open-air museum, was to recover parts of them before they were scrapped or discarded. Thus Mystic Seaport Museum salvaged the beautiful joinery work from the captain's quarters of the Maine-built square-rigger *Benjamin Packard*.

The real father of the movement to exhibit parts of ships under cover was Gerhard Albe of the Stockholm Maritime Museum, who in the 1930s created exhibits incorporating the real thing among the ship models. It was Albe's work that inspired Karl Kortum to create

similar exhibits using actual ship parts at San Francisco.

The ghosts of Cape Horn

Three hundred miles east of Cape Horn lie the Falkland Islands, where sailing ships damaged off the stormy headland could lick their wounds. The English had taken possession of the islands in the 1830s, when trade with the west coast of South America was increasing, and more and more ships were trying to make the rounding, not always successfully.

In 1849 an estimated 777 vessels took part in the Gold Rush to California, and at least half of this flotilla tried to make it round the Horn. There were many cripples, and the superb Falklands harbor of Port Stanley at last had an industry. The repair of ships at the harbor boomed during the Gold Rush, and continued, sometimes fitfully, for 60 years afterwards.

Some of these vessels were so badly damaged that, although they had reached the Falklands, they were not worth repair or further investment on the part of their owners or insurers. The craft were then condemned and put into service as jetty-heads or storehouses. The most famous of these hulks was Brunel's wonderful iron ship the *Great Britain*, which served as a floating storehouse from 1886 until 1933.

Global trade routes of the 19th century (left) owed much to seamen's knowledge of world wind systems, collected over the centuries since the first oceanic voyages of discovery. Trade winds were used to travel north or south, and for westing across the North Atlantic, Indian and Pacific oceans. Passages to India and the Far East required knowledge of the monsoons, and Australian voyages an understanding of the prevailing westerlies south of the Cape of Good Hope and Cape Horn. Clipper ships made for the Roaring Forties in search of speed.

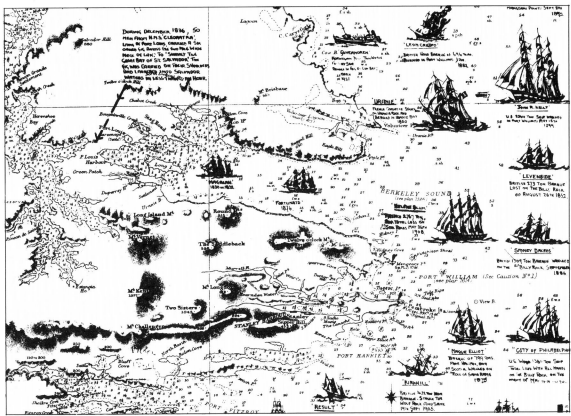

A map of Falkland Island wrecksites and remains by Falklander John Smith, shows the scale of Cape Horn danger for sailing ships.

Of these, some were lost completely, while others, though not sunk, were too damaged to be worth keeping in maritime service.

Karl Kortum of the San Francisco Maritime Museum was largely instrumental in rescuing this ship, but a huge range of other vessels left at Port Stanley and the Falkland Islands have been mapped by a Falklands resident, John Smith.

The rescue of the *St Mary*

In 1976 I returned from the Falkland Islands to Maine. I had just completed surveys on the remains of what I believed to be three of the most important American maritime artifacts left in the world: the *Snow Squall*, a clipper ship abandoned in 1864; the *Charles Cooper*, a Western Ocean Packet ship sold at Port Stanley in 1867; and one of the last full-rigged wooden ships to be built in the United States, the *St Mary*, which was wrecked in 1890 on her maiden voyage from New York to San Francisco.

In the course of a slide show that I gave then, I remarked that the remains of a ship such as the *St Mary*, professionally reconstituted, could be ideal raw material for a museum exhibit: they were unique; they were simple to salvage if the logistical problems could be solved; and there would be no conservation problem.

By a happy coincidence, the assistant curator of the Maine State Museum, Ron Kley, was present at my talk. The museum, which concentrates on Maine life in the 19th century, is one of the best of its kind in the United States, and is visited by some 120,000 people every year. Much of this success is due to the work of the curator Paul Rivard, a Maine native with great experience in managing museums.

In the 19th century, ships were a major end product of Maine's forests, and Kley and Rivard both felt that a ship exhibit was essential. They had recently been debating the problem, and had been considering a mock-up of a vessel. But this would be prohibitively expensive, and would lack the impact of the real thing.

A location 40ft (12m) long and 16ft (4.5m) high was available in the museum, enough space to take in a part of the surviving side of the *St Mary*, 140ft (42m) long, as it lay on the beach in the Falklands. Thus began the project to ship a part of this historic vessel back to the USA.

In 1978, with the aid of an enthusiastic volunteer crew and some donated equipment, we removed the required pieces from the shingle beach where they rested. An amazing collection of organizations, including the Royal Navy, the Royal Engineers, the Maine Maritime Academy and a corps of the US Army Engineers helped us to bring the future exhibit to its new home at Augusta, Maine.

It was a moving moment in 1981 when the exhibit was formally opened by Ada Minott Haggett, granddaughter of the famous Maine ship-builder who had built the *St Mary*, Charles Minott.

The end of an era

By 1900 the technical ingenuity of Western man had turned to powered vessels. Sailing ships were old hat. Yet the last sailing ships built were among the most perfect and marvelous of man's creations. The quality of their construction would be amazing to a modern shipyard. Great sailing ships of the last period of development were so good that they outlived their designers, their crews, and the trades they were built for. The last trading square-rigger, the four-mast bark *Omega*, was lost at sea by fire in 1958. She had been built in Scotland as the *Drumcliffe*, more than 60 years before.

Like all merchant ships, these last sailing ships were the products of commercial need. By the 1880s and 1890s the best cargoes had been taken by steamships, which could run to an exact schedule. The wonderful "down easters", big square-rigged American bulk carriers, could not compete with steel ships. However skilfully constructed, wooden ships leaked, cargoes got damaged, and insurance rates went up.

By the end of the century, British shipowners estimated that steamships could earn three times as much per pound sterling of capital investment. They were selling their sailing ships as fast as possible, mostly to Scandinavia, or to small British one-ship companies usually run by ex-skippers and their relatives.

The Germans, however, thought that sailing ships could be made to pay, especially in the nitrate trade to South America, and were increasing their sailing ship tonnage. The famous Laetz line, which specialized in the nitrate trade, had 16 sailing vessels totaling 10,995 tons in 1885. By 1910 Laetz still owned 16 sailing ships, but they were four times as large, with a combined tonnage of 39,485.

These "Flying P" clippers (they all had names starting with P) were the product of continual development in design, and showed what could be done when real thought was put into the modernization of sailing ships.

The giant *Preussen*, built for Laetz by Tecklenborg at Geestemunde in 1902, was especially designed for the Cape Horn nitrate trade. Capable of carrying more than 8,000 tons of cargo, she was a full-rigged ship (with square sails on every mast); her five masts were 9ft (2.7m) in circumference at the base, and rose to a height of more than 213ft (62m) from the keel. It took 1,260 wooden and steel blocks to control her 43 sails, which presented a combined area to the wind of nearly 60,000 sq ft (5,574 sq m). In the right conditions she could sail 17 knots, as fast as a clipper ship.

For all her efficiency in the Roaring Forties, *Preussen* was, like any other sailing ship, at a disadvantage in the confined waters of the English Channel. On her last voyage she set sail from Hamburg in October 1910 with a cargo of coal, cement and bulk furnace coke, bound for the west coast of South America. Off

The *Snow Squall*, built in Maine 1851 and abandoned at Port Stanley 1864, is the only genuine American clipper to have survived (above). She is now the focus of an ambitious marine archaeological program under Dr E.F. Yalouris. The photograph shows the retrieval of the forward section, which was shipped back to Maine in 1987.

The *St Mary*, photographed in 1890 (above) at South St, New York, before her fateful maiden voyage around Cape Horn to San Francisco (which she never reached). One of the last full-rigged wooden ships to be constructed in the United States, she was built in Maine by the famous shipbuilder Charles Minott.

Abandoned in Port Stanley, many superb vessels were kept as storehouses and have now become subjects of interest to marine archaeologists. The contemporary photograph (above) shows, from left to right, the composite clipper *Vicar of Bray*, the *Margaret*, the *William Shand*, and the only surviving American clipper *Snow Squall*.

The bones of the *St Mary* (above), as she was before excavation and reconstruction in 1978. In that year, the surviving starboard side of the vessel (above left) was brought back to her place of origin by Peter Throckmorton with the assistance of numerous individuals and organizations, to become an exhibit at Maine State Museum.

The British barque *Lady Elizabeth* (right), built in 1879, struck a rock off Port Stanley in 1913 and is now being surveyed by the *Snow Squall* archaeologists under Dr E.F. Yalouris.

Hastings, late at night, she had the misfortune of colliding with a largish steamer, went ashore near Dover and became a total loss.

Steam ships often failed to realize how fast the big sailers could travel, and this led to the loss of other Flying P liners. On March 12, 1912, just a few miles from the site of *Preussen's* accident, the *Pisagua* collided with the P&O liner *Oceania*, and had to be sold for scrap. Ten months later, the *Pangani* collided with the French steamer *Phryne*, sinking instantly and taking 30 of the 34-man crew to the bottom with her. In all three cases, the steamer was legally at fault. However the real fault lay in the circumstances. Something as unhandy as a big sailing ship should not have been operating in the busiest waterway in the world.

In the early years of the century, only the Germans took up new ideas and applied them to their sailing ships. For example, a system of power winches, operating from the center of the deck so that men did not have to work at the edge of the deck, where they risked being swept overboard, was partially realized on magnificent Cape Horn sailers like *Pamir*, *Passat* and the magnificent *Moshulu*, which has survived as a floating restaurant in Philadelphia.

Last of the big sailers

In 1905, anyone predicting that sailing ships were doomed would have been laughed at. On a typical day of that year, *Lloyd's List* noted the movements of 3,600 large sailing ships. Square-rigged ships, and the way of life that went with them, were part and parcel of the world's seascapes. An ocean without sailing ships would have been as difficult to imagine as one without seagulls.

Yet the writing was already on the wall. The surviving British sailers were disappearing fast and not being replaced. All the square-riggers were being forced into the bulk cargo trade around Cape Horn. Many of the 10,000 British seamen who died at sea between 1900 and 1910 were lost in that dreadful stretch of ocean.

In his expedition of 1908, Sir Ernest Shackleton arrived in a bay on the southern side of South Georgia when his ship was crushed in the Antarctic ice. He found a bay full of sailing ship debris, the only witness to dozens of vessels missing with all hands. There were teak handrails with turks' heads still on them, hatch boards, teak skylight benches, lifeboat oars, rudders and smashed planking, as well as remains from ships of earlier times. That year, a dozen sailers had gone missing off the Horn, and the master of one survivor, the Italian *Cognati*, reported seeing much wreckage near the place where he had collided with an iceberg.

In 1906 it had been proposed that a fleet of tugs be stationed in the Straits of Magellan to tow ships through. Nothing came of it: parsimonious and set in their ways, sailing ship owners calculated that men and time were cheap. The cost of feeding a square-rig crew and paying them for a month or two was probably less than a fast tow through the Straits. As we have seen, only the Germans were receptive to new ideas.

Captain Alan Villiers, square-rig shipmaster and talented journalist, was one of the few educated men to take the opportunity still on offer in the 1930s to learn at first hand the great and wonderful art of big sailing ships, and to write about it from the standpoint of the professional seaman as well as of the historian. He wrote the following:

The opportunity to continue to the final victory of the great wind ship over wind and sea was not so much lost as no longer noticed . . . The traditions of designing them and sailing them were broken and flung aside. Man discovered how to ride winds of his own making in the sky; he became power mad at sea and in the air.

Yet the great patterns of the world's trade winds produce more natural energy than all the world's power plants combined. The westerly winds of the southern ocean continue to blow right around the world. It may well be that, in a world running out of fuel and clean air, industrial man will some day wake up and harness that enormous resource.

A typical Cape Horn casualty, the big sailer *Wavertree* limps into port after a terrible battering, strikingly recorded in two contemporary photographs (left and above). Thousands of lives were lost in the stretch of ocean around the Horn, but owners were reluctant to improve conditions for their crews. A scheme to tow vessels through the Straits of Magellan, mooted in 1906, came to nothing – presumably because seamen's lives were considered cheaper than the outlay required.

The clipper ship

The clippers of the mid 19th century were the most beautiful ships ever built. They represent the high point of the search for perfection in the nautical cultures of both England and America. Delicate and expensive, they could bankrupt their most talented builders, such men as Donald McKay and Hercules Linton, designer and builder of *Cutty Sark*. But this did not prevent men building them.

The eminent American nautical historian Howard Chapelle defines a clipper ship as a "large, very fast sailing ship . . . built without much regard to cargo capacity and operating costs."

There were several kinds of clipper ship, each representing shipbuilders' and owners' responses to economic challenge. Before the Californian Gold Rush, the American and British merchant marine consisted mostly of small wooden ships, which were adequate for the Atlantic or West Indies trades and an occasional Cape Horn passage. Following the California Gold Rush of 1849 there was a terrific boom in the round-the-Horn sailing ship trade. This gave great designers like William Webb and Donald McKay scope for creating ships like the

Challenge and *Flying Cloud*. These ships made money for their owners on speed: fast passages paid off in higher freights, which compensated for the extra expense of running what was in today's terms a monster racing yacht.

Birth of the clipper

In the 20 years preceding 1850, large numbers of both British and American ships were smuggling opium from India to various places on the China coast. This trade, horrible in its final implications, represented smuggling on the grandest scale. Like the slave traffic 50 years before, or today's heroin trade, it was deplored by many but proved nearly impossible to control because the profits were so vast. The circumstances of the trade created, in the 1830s, a demand for faster, more weatherly sailing vessels, built to carry freights at very high prices. In sailing ships, just as in architecture, form must follow function!

In the 1830s, an Aberdeen shipwright and designer, William Hall, had proposed that ships should have hollow rather than round bows, and should be longer, narrower and shallower. The *Scottish Maid*, a fast schooner embodying Hall's revolutionary ideas, was launched in 1839. She was a great success, and soon other yards in Aberdeen were building fast, small vessels incorporating the so-called "Aberdeen bow". There was an immediate demand for these in the opium trade.

However, by that time the trade was in its last decade, and until the opening of the Suez Canal, in 1869, tea was to be the principal clipper trade from China. The first tea clipper to be ordered by the famous firm of Jardine Mathiesson (the *Stornaway* built by Hall's) was commissioned in 1849 – the same year that gold was discovered in California.

The first American clipper with a hollow bow was the 750-ton *Rainbow*, designed by J.W. Griffiths of New York. As with the *Scottish Maid*, controversy surrounded her building, but in 1846 her second China voyage settled the matter; she went to Canton and back in a mere six and a half months.

Rainbow foundered off Cape Horn with all hands in 1848, on the passage from New York to Valparaiso, but her early success had convinced her owners of the value of the new clipper type. A second clipper, ordered a year after the launching of *Rainbow*, was the famous *Sea Witch*, built specially for one of the up and coming young skippers of the time – Captain Robert Waterman.

The California Gold Rush of 1849 caused gold freights to San Francisco to rise to $60 per ton. The Donald McKay clipper *Stag Hound* paid for herself on her first voyage and made a net profit of $80,000 for her owners. By the mid winter of 1850 the shipping boom extended from Nova Scotia to Maryland. Anything that could float was engaged at a premium.

San Francisco harbor, photographed in 1853 (left), resembles a waterborne ghost town of clippers abandoned in favor of the gold fields. The Gold Rush of 1849 enormously expanded the West Coast economy and brought clippers in their hundreds. These rounded Cape Horn from New York and New England, laden with merchandise that earned their owners stupendous profits. Seamen infected with gold fever were known to jump ship even before anchoring.

The Gold Rush was on. Ten thousand shipwrights were at work in New York alone. Thirteen clipper ships were launched in 1850 and 1851.

These clippers were run, as we have said, like racing yachts. Speed out and back was worth big money in the tea trade, and even more in the California trade. In order to perform to capacity, clipper ships had to be driven, just as a racing skipper drives his yacht, continually tuning it up. The racing skipper can never relax, never cease squeezing his ship. In variable weather, a big racing yacht might hand and reset different sets of sails every half hour for days.

A big 50ft modern racing ketch or yawl sails with three watches of four men each, who have to handle a total of about 1,500 to 2,000 sq ft of sail area at a time, divided up in a maximum of five sails set at any one time.*

A clipper ship had a crew of up to 50 men, who might have to handle nearly 13,000 *yards* of canvas in over 70 sails, of which 60 required work aloft every time they were hauled in or reefed. These sails were controlled by over 300 major, and an equal number of minor, ropes of various kinds. It would take a computer to figure out how many possible permutations existed for handling these sails.

The skipper of such a ship was like a jockey riding an immensely complicated race horse, and he had to remain on deck almost all the time. Clipper ship captains made terrific money, but they earned every penny of it. A sailor's instinct is always to shorten sail or slow down before the ship is damaged. Carrying sail to the limit of a ship was a responsibility that only the skipper could accept.

Some skippers cracked under the strain. The famous captain of the *Sea Witch*, Bob Waterman, turned into a maniac on *Challenge*'s maiden voyage around Cape Horn to San Francisco in 1851, beating his men with a heavy mallet for minor or non-existent offenses. Eight men died before they reached San Francisco, where Waterman was tried for murder but acquitted (after apparently managing to bribe the jury).*

The Cape Horn passage put a cruel strain not only on the men but also on the wooden vessels in which they sailed, and shipwrights like Webb and McKay wracked their brains for solutions to the problem of how to build a long narrow wooden vessel that would keep its shape.

McKay from the beginning never built a failure. His masterpieces sailed faster than any wind-driven ocean-going ships had ever sailed before. *Flying Cloud* was the most famous of these clippers. Only one vessel, namely the *Andrew Jackson*, ever exceeded *Flying Cloud*'s double record of 89 days to San Francisco.

However, by 1853 the California boom was over. *Flying Cloud*'s owners were glad to get $10 per ton in 1854. Then, in the fall of 1854, the Panama railroad was opened, and a fleet of steamers running from Panama to San Francisco put an end to the Cape Horn yachts.

Clippers in competition

British tonnage laws, formulated in 1773 and still in force until 1854, taxed ships by length and breadth but not depth, thus encouraging slow ships. Vessels of clipper dimensions, handicapped by unfair tonnage dues, were at a disadvantage in the rapidly developing tea trade, where the Americans had a clear lead. In 1851 American clipper owners were asking, and getting, £6 per ton, while the British were hard put to find tea cargoes for half that price. At last, the reform of the tonnage laws in 1854 made possible tea clippers like the *Cutty Sark*.

Thus began, at the end of the American clipper ship period, a wonderful ding-dong competition, producing what are surely the most beautiful ships ever constructed, the British tea clippers that culminated in the *Cutty Sark*. By 1855 the

***Cutty Sark*'s figurehead,** painted white in the clipper tradition, represents the Witch of Robert Burns's poem *Tam O'Shanter*, who wore only a "cutty sark" (short shirt).

Yankee gold rush clippers were getting pushed out of the British tea trade by the ever-growing British fleet.

There are several good reasons for this. Tea clippers, like other ships designed for a certain job, had to have specialized characteristics. The American ships, designed for the New York to California passage by way of Cape Horn, depended on being able to perform in very bad weather, and in the great seas of the southern latitude Fifties. Tea clippers had to be capable of taking on the Roaring Forties of the South Indian Ocean, which though formidable enough are not so devastating as the gales around Cape Horn. They also had to be able to sail at three knots in breezes so light that a candle could be kept burning in the poop. This was because much of their work was done in the reef-strewn South China and Java seas, where a ship that could not sail in light airs had a good chance of either going on a reef or alternatively being captured by marauding pirates.

Another reason for the Americans' downfall was that the American so-called Extreme Clippers were getting old fast. No ship built out of American soft wood could for very long take the beating that clipper racing gave a ship. By 1855, American yards had turned to building larger, easier to handle ships with smaller crews, and safer cargo carriers that could make steady money in the coastal bulk carrying trade, which was an American monopoly. The only economic trade left for clipper ships then was the China trade and, when that was over, the passenger and wool trades to Australia.

Clipper perfection

The monopoly of clipper building reverted to Scotland, where it had begun 16 years before with Hall's *Scottish Maid*. The clipper ships built during the next 15 years were the apogee of sailing ship construction. These were the years of the development of the composite ship: teak planking bolted onto a rigid iron frame (see p.99).

The average tea clipper was small, something under 200ft (60m) long, and able to carry a little more than 1,000 tons of tea. Her lower masts were iron, often painted white or yellow. Decks were almost always teak, and were scrubbed white daily. Below decks, the master's quarters were usually paneled in mahogany, satinwood or bird's-eye maple. Gingerbread work and carving at bow and stern were gilt. Figureheads, remarkably enough, were painted dead white: only coasting vessels decorated their figureheads. All had giant sail plans, and set sails that were amazing even to contemporary 19th century square-rig sailors.*

They were raced like yachts today. It is reported that when two clippers were neck and neck in the Java Sea, all sails set, one crew got the edge by setting their blankets in the rigging! They had sharp bows and little buoyancy forward, and were horribly wet in a head sea. Dismastings were common, and crews were expert at repairing the damage and getting ships going again.

Most clippers lost a few spars on every trip. Many were completely dismasted; crews managed to cut the wreck away, rig jury masts, and get into port. Many went missing with all hands, such as Alexander Hall's beautiful *Caliph* on her maiden voyage in 1869. The reefs of the Java and China seas, many still uncharted, are full of tea clippers.

Mishandled, clippers were terribly dangerous ships. One mistake was enough for the Lutine Bell to ring the only epitaph that 50-odd seamen were likely ever to get. Yet they were built to last for ever, and they did. The ones that were not lost at sea never really wore out. When they were finally scrapped it was usually because there was no longer work for them anywhere.

Cutty Sark, the champion of them all as

to sailing, was built in 1869, and survived as a working ship until 1922. Through typhoons in the China Sea and horrendous gales around Cape Horn, overladen with coal and scrap iron (cargoes she was never designed to handle), dismasted, aground, knocked on her beam ends with hatches in the water and seas breaking right over her, she never leaked a drop. Even at the end, cut down, with perhaps half the sail she was designed to carry, she could still do 16 knots. No wonder that these ships inspired such admiration, and such loyalty from their crews.

It is very fitting that *Cutty Sark*, the ship that best represents the highest development of the clipper, should be the only survivor of that great age. She was launched two weeks before the opening of the Suez Canal, which doomed her and her kind. The last proper tea race took place only four years after *Cutty Sark* was launched, and the last tea cargoes were shipped by clipper in 1878.

Her builder, Hercules Linton, had learnt his trade at Alexander Hall's yard in Aberdeen, so it can truly be said that his beautiful ship descends somehow from *Scottish Maid* and the experiments in the 1830s of William Hall.

A ship's crew at work in heavy weather, photographed as they make fast the mainsail, illustrates the hardship and danger of life on board merchant sailing ships in Victorian and Edwardian times. In addition to the clippers that braved the terrible passage around Cape Horn, bigger ships like the *Inversnaid*, seen above, were frequently in serious difficulties.

Dressed in her full complement of sails, the *Cutty Sark* (left) spread 32,000ft of canvas before the wind, manipulated by 10 miles of rigging. With her mainmast rising 146ft above her deck, and her main yard extending 78ft from tip to tip, she carried more sail for her size than any other clipper ship ever built, and could drive through the water at a top speed of more than 17 knots while carrying a full cargo of 1.3 million pounds of tea.

Elissa: reincarnation of an iron barque

She was called *Christophoros*. As soon as I saw her, I was struck by the large size of her foremast and the old-fashioned quality of the ironwork, with two plates rounded and riveted. Then I saw the rings and spider band with its iron belaying pins, and realized that I was looking at the foremast of what had once been a square-rigged ship. The rings and the iron belaying pin were for the chain sheets of the lower topsail.

It was the fall of 1961, and we were in the little harbor between Piraeus and Perama called Limonadiko. Perama was probably the biggest maritime junkyard in the world. But this ship was not junk, despite her age. She was alive and well and loading a cargo of cement.

The captain was friendly, and ushered me into the battered deckhouse, which had been built right over a teak companionway with circular stairs leading down to a paneled saloon. Attached to the mizzen mast where it passed through the saloon was a bronze plaque:

ALEXANDER HALL
Aberdeen 1877

Alexander Hall had been a famous builder of clipper ships, and I was able to obtain a copy of the ship's original registry certificate. Her first name was *Elissa*, and she had been built originally as a barque (a three-masted vessel with square sails on two of the masts).

The rediscovery of *Elissa*

Christophoros formerly *Elissa* was a familiar sight in the Aegean at that time. Once she must have been a near sister to the little barque *Otago* that Joseph Conrad had commanded and loved. Even with the big ugly wooden deckhouse on her poop, and shorn of her rig, she still had a faded elegance about her; in her shape there was a ghost of the thousands of beautiful little iron ships that had once graced the sea lanes of the world.

I wrote to Lloyd's and received a transcript of her whole history, detailing every voyage. In 1897 she had gone the way of so many of her sisters, smashed up in an Atlantic gale. Sold to the Norwegians, she was then put into the Baltic timber trade. In 1916 they sold her to some Swedes, who cut her rig down to a barquentine. They in turn sold her to the Finns, who cut her down into a schooner and, finally, in the 1950s, reduced her still further to a motorship.

In 1961, the Greeks bought her, but on her first voyage under the Greek flag she was cast away with a cargo of coal in the Baltic. However, the tough old hull

refused to break up, and they put her back to work again.

Collecting *Elissa* lore developed into a hobby, and among those who became interested in the ship was Karl Kortum, director of San Francisco's maritime museum. He made several convincing arguments for saving and restoring her. She was the last restorable vessel of her size and type and, being only 150ft on deck, might be relatively inexpensive and manageable if she could be converted back into a barque. Another reason was that she was a virtual work of art by a famous yard, and the only survivor out of the hundreds of sailing vessels which the yard had built.

In 1967 Kortum got the promise of funding, but the patron did not want to put up the asking price of the ship straightaway. It seemed likely that she would some day be up for scrapping, however, and since I was on hand, I might

The former iron barque *Elissa* awaits reincarnation at the Greek port of Perama, the "biggest maritime junkyard in the world."

be lucky enough to detect the moment when she would be for sale for her scrap value or a little above.

Unfortunately I missed her when she came on sale in 1967, but that fall I saw her in the Adriatic, possibly one of a small fleet of ships in the trade of smuggling cigarettes into Italy. She spent her time hove to 10 miles off the Italian coast, apparently mother ship to a fleet of high-speed motorboats which were illicitly ferrying loads of cigarettes onto hopefully deserted beaches.

The American manager of Citibank in Piraeus, Tom Shortell, now came forward to help me with the project, and we arranged the paperwork for a plan to buy the vessel when she came up for sale again. Of course, if word got out that a museum wanted the vessel, the price would go through the roof, and even a hint of American involvement would spoil

the deal. We had to wait nearly two years before our "front man", Captain Grigori Mentis, discovered that the ship's name had been changed yet again: now she was called *Acheos*.

In the fall of 1970 I was returning from a long hard summer at Pelagos (see p.90). Our little schooner was fairly battered and I made arrangements for the schooner to be hauled out. As we were going down the channel on the way to the shipyard, we spotted *Elissa*, swinging to her moorings, right in front of a scrapyard.

She was deserted. That night I called Kortum in San Francisco and he promised to send me $5,000 to cover immediate expenses. I also warned Shortell. Grigori and our maritime lawyer Elias Eliacopoulos bargained all week with the owners, who were negotiating with another buyer, but eventually decided to give us a chance. It was on a Saturday at noon that they called Grigori to say we had three hours in which to appear with the cash. Shortell had the bank opened specially for us and I walked up to the teller, and handed him the check: "One million drachmas, please."

Reconstruction of the *Elissa*

Grigori and I were now the owners of the oldest ship on the Greek register. I spent most of the next two winters doing research in preparation for the reconstruction of the vessel, when and if we were ever funded.

We never were: in 1972 I sold the ship to Captain David Groos RCN, a Member of Parliament and former Minister in the Canadian parliament. That summer we unloaded 200 tons of sand ballast in *Elissa*'s hold, and stripped the wooden ceiling out of her so that we could survey the framing beneath. The Lloyd's surveyors shook their heads and grumbled, and came to wonder at the condition of the ship after so many years. *Elissa* was the oldest vessel that Lloyd's had ever agreed to reclass.

Doing the work was going to be the simplest part of the job. Writing up the specifications of how the job was done was a nightmare. There were no plans of the ship, but the distinguished Aberdonian ship historian, the late James Henderson, knew all about existing plans for similar vessels.

The problem was not one of designing and making a reasonable replica of a 19th century sailing ship: this job had to be done exactly as it had been done nearly a century before. We knew that we would have to raise a great deal of money. In order to discover how much, we had to know exactly what we were going to do, and get estimates on what it would cost. Every part of the thousands of fittings that would go into *Elissa*'s rigging, for example, would have to be tailor-made. This meant that we would have to find old time blacksmiths who could do hand-forging, and so on.

Halfway through the planning stage of the reconstruction David Groos died tragically, in his mid 50s, after a short illness. *Elissa* was adrift again.

Rescue of the *Elissa*

The research that Lloyd's had done for me so many years ago was the factor that eventually saved her. The ship's record included several trips to Galveston, Texas, and it happened that the Galveston Historical Society wanted a sailing ship. The society's ship person, Michael Creamer, knew all about *Elissa*. In the fall of 1974 the Galveston society bought the ship from David Groos's estate.

Elissa was saved once again, but for how long? She was thousands of miles from Galveston. The oil crisis of 1974 had caused a rampant inflation in Greece, sending shipyard prices soaring, so that they compared in some cases with those of the USA. The Galvestonians were underfunded. Moreover, they spoke no Greek and didn't know their way around the Perama jungle where I had spent so many years.

I was working in Italy and then in the Falkland Islands, and couldn't help much. It took four years to get *Elissa* out of Perama: raising money in Texas for shipyard work on a rusty hulk far away in Greece was almost impossible. However, by the fall of 1978 the hullwork was complete, and it was decided to tow the ship to Galveston from Piraeus. The tow was planned to take place in several stages and over several months, including wintering over in Gibraltar.

It was not till mid 1979 that the rusty hulk arrived in Galveston. Paul Gaido, who had been involved from the beginning in fund-raising for *Elissa*, and David Brink, hired from South Street Seaport museum, did a brilliant public relations job in convincing the press and their financiers that the ugly duckling was about to turn into a swan.

With *Elissa* at Galveston, funding was easier. Walter Ripke, in charge now of the reconstruction, proceeded to finish off the job of rebuilding and rerigging the ship, using hundreds of volunteers. Young craftsmen who wanted a chance at learning almost forgotten trades came from all over the country and pitched in. Three years after her arrival in Galveston, *Elissa* sailed again.

David Brink and Walter Ripke had done a better job of restoration than most shipyards were capable of, with the help of an amateur crew learning as they went along. Their achievement is one of the great success stories in the maritime preservation field.

The reconstruction has also demonstrated that little barques of this type are wonderful ships. The *Elissa*'s handiness and grace as a sailing ship is inspiring the construction of similar little barques. In saving *Elissa* then, we did not just save a ship: we saved a tradition.

Transformed into a barquentine (top), *Elissa* was renamed *Gustav* by her Swedish owners in 1916, who cut down her rig to suit her new role. Her transformation back to barque proceeded erratically. "Before" and "after" pictures of her bow (center) show stages of the metamorphosis, before she could once again sail the seas (above) in her original form. Her reconstruction at Galveston, Texas, is one of the success stories of maritime preservation.

In 1912 the luxury liner *Titanic* struck an iceberg on her maiden voyage and sank with 1,500 passengers to the Atlantic seabed, 12,500ft below. In 1986, millions of viewers watched on television as the undersea craft *Alvin* and *Jason Jr.*, under the direction of marine geologist Robert Ballard, toured the wreckage of the luxury liner, sending back videotapes and photographs in color. "We are now opening up an enormous new era in archaeology," said one observer. "We now have time capsules in the deep oceans."

Modern technology can send a variety of remote-controlled vehicles to the ocean depths. The first and most famous of these submersibles is *Alvin*, designed by Woods Hole oceanographer James Mavor (who has written the chapter on Thera [p.37] for this book). First launched in 1964 as a 23ft craft able to move around the sea floor, to pick up objects with an arm and claw, and to carry three people to a depth of 6,000ft, *Alvin* was among other achievements responsible for locating and helping to recover an H-bomb that fell into the Mediterranean after an air collision. She has since been extended in size and has had her hull strengthened so as to operate at more than 13,000ft.

Remotely operated vehicles (ROVs) can now descend to depths of 20,000ft and are used for a variety of purposes, including the location of mineral deposits and investigation of the planet's shifting tectonic plates. Equipped with mechanical arms, cameras and sonar systems, ROVs provide a comprehensive view of the ocean depths for controllers on the surface. And even more advanced craft are on the way.

Oxygen-free environments

Alvin's cameras sent back immaculate photographs of the *Titanic*, but revealed that most of the ship's woodwork had been devoured by marine creatures, even at a depth of 12,500ft. These voracious organisms are the enemies of marine archaeologists, and it is only in oxygen-free environments, where such creatures cannot survive, that perfectly preserved wrecks will be found in future. Submersibles like *Alvin*, operating in areas where divers cannot go, will aid immeasurably in extending our store of archaeological time capsules, from Bronze Age wrecks in the

Black Sea to 19th century sailers lost in the Canadian Arctic.

High-tech underwater devices, including ROVs, are now becoming available on the open market, to the delight of treasure hunters. This has obvious dangers for our underwater heritage. "This technology is now out of control," Robert Ballard has said. If there is not some slowing down of the treasure-hunting trend, soon there will be little left.

Deepwater salvage technology has made such strides in recent years that detailed studies of wrecks such as the *Titanic*, nearly 13,000ft below the surface, are already within the reach of marine archaeologists. Worldwide patterns of shipwreck distribution, where historic wrecks are sure to be found in future, are controlled by several factors. In the Caribbean (10), the combination of hurricanes, strong currents and numerous reefs and shoals has led to the loss of many ships from the 15th century onwards. Similarly, the typhoon-ridden South China Sea (11) and the Sea of Japan (9) have been equally dangerous,

NORTH AMERICA

ATLANTIC OCEAN

PACIFIC OCEAN

SOUTH AMERICA

Falkland Islands

Cape Horn

South Georgia

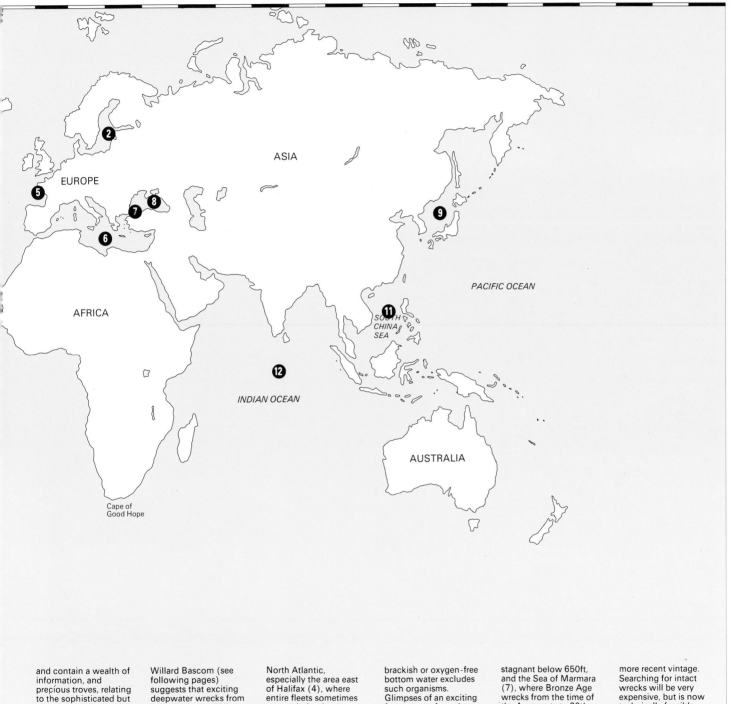

and contain a wealth of information, and precious troves, relating to the sophisticated but little-known Southeast Asian maritime world. The Mediterranean (6) has numerous ship-trapping reefs, like the one at Yassi Ada, which have for the most part been picked clean by sponge divers; but the work of researchers like

Willard Bascom (see following pages) suggests that exciting deepwater wrecks from antiquity may still be found.
Areas like the Bay of Biscay (5), with its infamous gales, or the Indian Ocean (12), with its notorious typhoons, must also hold many deepwater wrecks. This will also be true of the

North Atlantic, especially the area east of Halifax (4), where entire fleets sometimes went missing in wintertime.
Unfortunately, wood-devouring marine organisms survive even in deep waters. The best-preserved wrecks still awaiting discovery will probably be found in areas where fresh,

brackish or oxygen-free bottom water excludes such organisms. Glimpses of an exciting future come from the Baltic (2), with almost intact ships like *Vasa* and *Kronan* (p.102), and the Great Lakes (3) with *Hamilton* and *Scourge* (p.206). Another interesting area could be the Black Sea (8), oxygen-free and

stagnant below 650ft, and the Sea of Marmara (7), where Bronze Age wrecks from the time of the Argonauts to 20th century naval vessels lie intact on the seabed.
In the Western Hemisphere, in addition to the American Great Lakes, the high Arctic (1) and Antarctic (13) are demonstrably depositories for ships of

more recent vintage. Searching for intact wrecks will be very expensive, but is now technically feasible using remotely operated vehicles equipped with side-scanning sonar.

Deepwater salvage and archaeology

From the earliest times to the 20th century, large numbers of ships have sunk in deep water, far beyond the reach of divers. There is good reason to think that many of these vessels have survived in excellent condition. Today we have the technology to locate deepwater wrecks, to examine them carefully, and to raise them or the artifacts they carried. From the Bronze Age to the *Titanic*, deepwater archaeology will throw a powerful searchlight onto the past, using sophisticated salvage techniques.

When a United Airlines Boeing 727 went down in Santa Monica Bay in 1969, an extraordinary coincidence enabled Ocean Science and Engineering's *Oceaneer*, to be at the crash scene. *Oceaneer*, probably the best-equipped deepwater salvage ship on the coast, was looking for – and had already found – another ditched airliner when the news came through on the ship's radio. This made two disasters, both at sea, at an airport that had never before had a serious crash.

Starting at the estimated crash position, *Oceaneer* towed a side-looking sonar through miserable weather in depths of 500–1,200ft (152–366m) twelve hours a day for ten days. Then we found a circular pattern of small objects on the bottom in 950ft (290m) of water. The television cameras went over the side to check, and soon a piece of the 727's tailplane was swung on deck.

We had the spot, which was the hard part. Now we had to rig for salvage. First, to anchor the *Oceaneer* firmly we laid out an equilateral triangle of heavy anchors outside the wreckage, which was about 1,000ft (300m) across. The anchor lines led to large buoys to which *Oceaneer* was moored; then, by adjusting the lines, the ship could be moved to any spot within the triangle.

Once the ship was in place we could rig the J-star cage. This special salvage rig was a cube of steel tubing about 4ft (1m) on a side, containing lights and cameras. J-star's motion, just above the bottom, was rigidly controlled by four steel wires running from the ship down through pulleys on the cage, and thence a few hundred feet to anchors placed north, south, east and west. On the ship's rail were four small winches, one for each of the steel wires.

In order to shift the camera, the operator moved the cage by taking in on one winch while letting out on another. Inside the cage, the TV camera was controlled by a pan and tilt mechanism. Large objects beyond visual range could be spotted with a "searchlight" sonar. The entire J-star device hung from a half-inch cable on the main winch, and beneath it was a double set of tongs so that objects spotted by the TV could be picked up.

Before recovering anything, we mapped all the parts on the bottom, where the TV camera was often able to read the serial numbers of small parts. Then we began to recover the engines, which were 12ft (4m) long and weighed 4,800lb (2,177kg) each. We knew the location of each one within about 10ft (3m), and in one long day we moved the ship over each engine, grasped it with the hydraulic pincers under the J-star, and brought it almost to the surface. Then divers attached slings around each engine, and *Oceaneer's* overside crane and big winch set it on deck.

Next came the tail assembly containing the flight recorder, the wheels, and other large pieces which were "reassembled" on the ground and eventually threw light on the cause of the crash.

That operation was salvage, not archaeology, but it indicates the possibilities between 300 and 1,500ft (90 and 460m). There was no need for delicacy in handling the wreckage or for removing a mud or sand cover from artifacts. But we have no doubt that, with the addition of a "soft" grasper and a ducted blower, similar equipment would be most useful to marine archaeologists.

Shipwrecks by the thousand

Contemporary statistics record that about half the sailing ships operating in the British Isles during the 18th and 19th centuries were eventually lost at sea. More than 20 percent of these sank well out, often in deep water. In the 1860s, 2,537

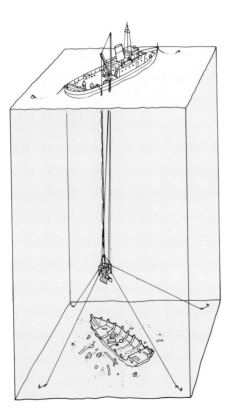

Salvage techniques (left), pioneered by the author, have important implications for deepwater maritime archaeology. The diagram shows how the salvage ship can be maneuvered while a special cage, containing lights, TV cameras, and tongs capable of lifting 5,000lb (2,270kg), is lowered to the wrecksite.

Exploring the *Titanic* (above), the sophisticated robot craft *Jason Jr* is linked to the manned submersible *Alvin* by a 250ft tether. The submersible sits on the boat deck on the starboard side of the ship near the entrance to the grand staircase, while *Jason Jr* sends back pictures and information.

Looking outward from the *Titanic*, the eyes of a remotely operated camera glimpse a piece of ship's ribbing, a railing, and a porthole with a brass rim kept polished by swift currents almost 13,000ft below the surface of the Atlantic. Even at this depth, marine borers have devoured the ship's ornate woodworking.

British ships sank far out to sea, indicating a loss rate of about 250 a year, Lloyds' records show that in the period 1864 to 1869, of the 10,000 sailing ships that were insured, nearly a thousand were lost without trace.*

If these statistics are applied to the number of ships built during the 1st millennium BC, more than 15,000 merchant ships might have gone down in the Mediterranean or Black Sea, probably in deep water. Ships were generally more seaworthy in the 18th and 19th centuries than in ancient times, so that proportion could be higher.

The statistics available on warships in the same period are a little better because of the great number of historical references to sea battles. Large numbers of ships were involved in military operations at sea. At the battle of Ecnomus in 225BC, 250 Roman ships faced 200 Carthaginian ships. Only 16 ships were lost in the battle, but in a storm off Camarina shortly afterwards, 250 of the remaining ships were wrecked.

When Augustus defeated Anthony and Cleopatra at Actium in 37BC, about 100 ships of the 900 involved were lost. Professor Lionel Casson says the Romans lost four ships to the weather for every one lost to enemy action. I estimate that about 5,000 warships were sunk in the course of the 1st millennium BC, many of them in deep water.

Why would ancient ships sink far offshore? Probably the most important reason was "stress of weather". Small ships could easily be overwhelmed by storm winds and waves. The ship could be blown over by brute force, or, running before the wind, it could plow into the steep backside of a wave to be taken in one gulp. A rapid reversal of wind direction at a weather front might blow a ship over backwards. It could be battered to pieces; spars might fall, puncturing the hull, or the mast might go over and its stays pull out the strakes. Repeated waves washing over the deck could rip off the hatch covers.

If the ship flexed too much as wave crests and troughs passed under it, seams between planks would open and uncompartmented hulls weighed with rocky ballast would quickly fill with water and sink. Some ships were not properly built and ballasted; some were sailed by inexperienced or drunken sailors.

Fire was always a danger. At night, below deck, oil lamps were used for light, and blazing oil could be spilled where it was hard to extinguish. Even worse would be an overturned cooking-box filled with glowing coals.

Some ships were sunk by pirates who, after taking what they wanted and enslaving the survivors, poked a hole in the bottom (as Michael Katzev suspected of the Kyrenia ship, p.56). There were many ways for a ship to get into trouble and fall to the bottom of the abyss.

Deepwater preservation

One good reason why ancient ships and their cargoes have not survived well in

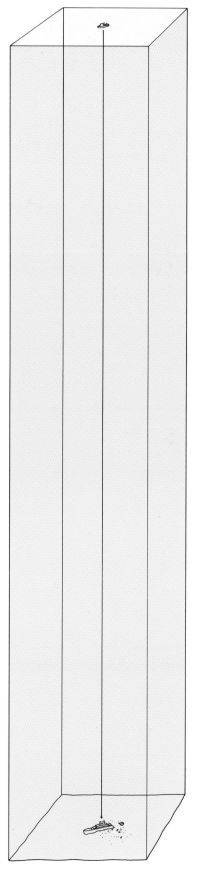

Remotely operated cameras reveal details of *Titanic* for the first time in almost 75 years: two bollards and a railing from the starboard side of the luxury liner's bow. The diagram (right), gives some idea of the final resting place of the *Titanic*, which struck an iceberg on its maiden voyage in 1912, some 400 miles southeast of Newfoundland. As Robert Ballard, leader of the *Titanic* project, writes: "It is quiet and peaceful and a fitting place for the remains of this greatest of sea tragedies to rest. May it forever remain this way and may God bless these now-found souls."

shallow waters is because many of them have for a long time been within the reach of divers. The first important archaeological salvage of modern times, that of the wreck at Antikythera in 1900, was carried out on a wreck lying 200ft (61m) down; most divers today are not prepared to work at so great a depth without using special equipment.

Other advantages of great depths, meaning 1,650–13,000ft (500–4,000m) in the Mediterranean and its nearby seas, include quiet water, a mud cushion, and slow sedimentation rate. The pressure of the surrounding water, although great, has little or no effect on ships or the objects they carried if the latter do not enclose sealed spaces filled with air, such as a partly empty flask which may leak or even collapse.

Low temperatures also help preservation, because every temperature decrease of 10° halves the rate of chemical reaction. But the bottom waters of the Mediterranean and Aegean seas are a relatively warm 55°F (13°C) in comparison with the deep ocean's 39°F (4°C). So Mediterranean bottom conditions are only slightly better for wreck preservation than its shallow waters.

The worst enemies of sunken wrecks are marine borers, organisms that attack and devour the wood of the hull, and sometimes ruin limestone statuary. Most of the metals, ceramics, glassware and stone objects recovered to date have suffered little damage. But wood and soft objects have rarely survived unless they were covered by mud.

The main cause of damage is biological or chemical, and both these factors are dependent on the presence of dissolved oxygen in the water. It is evident therefore that the best preserved wrecks will be in water low in oxygen, where borers and aerobic bacteria cannot live, and chemical reactions are minimal. Unfortunately the deep waters of the Mediterranean are well oxygenated (often one to two parts per million dissolved oxygen) and there is considerable animal life ranging from borers to large fish.

Of the borers, teredos, also called shipworms, are the most destructive. When their tiny larvae touch wood, they quickly bore in, leaving only a pinhole to show the place of entry. Once inside, the organism follows the grain of the wood, growing larger as it goes and leaving behind a tube about 0.3in (8mm) in diameter. US Navy research data suggest that an entire wooden wreck would be devoured within 25–50 years, except where protected by a mud cover that greatly reduces the available oxygen. Thus it is very unlikely that a complete ancient wreck will be found in the Mediterranean or Aegean seas.

Preserved ancient wrecksites

However, two ancient seas that have essentially no available oxygen in their near-bottom waters are the Sea of Marmara and the Black Sea (so called because its bottom is dark with sulfides). An aerobic bacteria dominant in the region, the *microspira*, reduces sulfates to liberate deadly hydrogen sulfide and create a "reducing" or anoxic environment. No animals have lived there for thousands of years, as can be seen from the annually accruing layers of bottom sediments (varves) that would have been disrupted if any invertebrates had been there to plow up the sea floor.

Thus, ships that sank to the floor of the Black Sea are probably completely preserved; any one of these would be a microcosm of the civilization it served: Scythia, Crimea, or Greek ships trading north. Decks, masts and rigging are probably preserved and possibly cloth, fruits and bodies. Finding and recovering such a ship will throw a new kind of searchlight on an ancient civilization. Moreover, a count of the dark and light annual varves, taken from a sample of the sediments on the deck of an ancient ship, would provide an accurate date for the year the ship sank.

The problem is that the Black Sea, averaging an area of 164,000 sq miles (424,760 sq km) and a depth of more than 4,000ft (1,220m), is a huge place to search. The Sea of Marmara is much smaller (3 percent of the area of the Black Sea) and a somewhat shallower place, with similar low oxygen characteristics and a higher density of ships. All the north-south shipping between the Black Sea and the Aegean crossed this inland sea. If the statistics previously mentioned are correct, as many as 4,000 ships, ancient and modern, may have collected on the bottom of the Sea of Marmara over

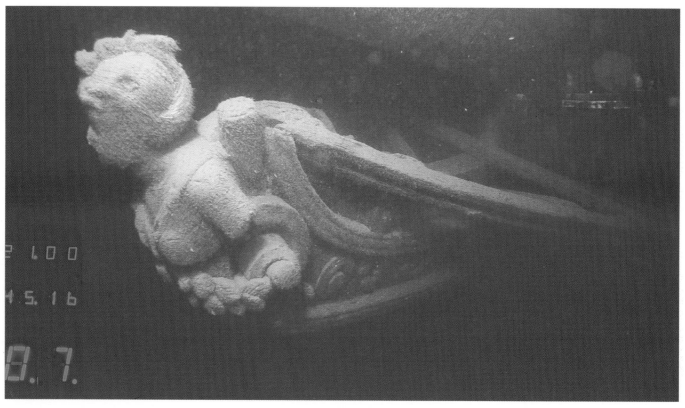

the last 7,000 years of ship traffic – about one per square mile.*

That region is undoubtedly the best target area for the deepwater archaeologist. However, any team would need a special ship to carry out the search, examination, and careful recovery of a deep ship and its artifacts. Such a ship could be similar to the *Alcoa Seaprobe*, which my associates and I designed and built in 1971. This vessel looked like a drilling ship, but was suitable for the location and recovery of ancient wrecks in deep water.

Equipped with several trainable propellers able to produce thrust in any direction, such a ship could use the method of "dynamic positioning" that I devised in 1960 to hold an unanchored drilling ship above a hole in water 12,000ft (3,650m) deep. Then, guided by buoys or sonic transponders, the pilot could constantly adjust the thrust to follow a search pattern or hold the ship in one spot above a wreck in spite of winds and currents. Using a dynamically positioned pipe-handling ship of this kind, deep archaeological work could be carried out, as I proposed in an article in *Science* magazine, October 1971.*

The *Alcoa Seaprobe* had equipment able to handle about 70ft (21m) of pipe at a time, and a derrick which towered above a 13ft × 40ft (4m × 12m) center well and was capable of supporting 400 tons of weight (pipe and load). At the lower end the pipe was weighted with 20 tons of extra heavy pipe to keep the pipe string

nearly vertical while the ship was moving. The main drill pipe was about 3in (76mm) in diameter, and had a breaking strength of 400 tons.

Pipe has a number of virtues for this kind of work in addition to its strength. It has considerable stiffness and does not flex much; it can be used to transmit rotation to the bottom; and water can be pumped down to run turbines at the bottom for power or to "dust off" objects lying on the bottom. A long pin can be extended from its lower tip into a mud bottom so as to steady the instruments and thus make delicate recovery operations possible.

Attached to the bottom of the pipe is a steel framework about 3ft (1m) square and 18ft (5m) long. This "pod" holds and protects an array of instruments including side-looking sonar, floodlights and television cameras, strobe lights and film cameras. A multi-conductor cable, secured by clips to the after side of the pipe, receives information and transmits instructions to these instruments.

After a site of, say, 40 sq miles (104 sq km) is selected, and a precise navigation system is in place (either local sonar transponders or shore-based radio waves), the ship lowers the instrumented pod to, say, 200ft (61m) above the bottom, and begins to search. In water 6,000ft (1,830m) deep, the side-looking sonar can scan a pathway 1,200ft (365m) wide at about 3ft (1m) per second. In such circumstances the ship can examine 1,000 sq ft (93 sq m) each hour and cover

the site in about four days if the weather is good, the bottom reasonably flat, and no objects worth examining are encountered.

If, however, the record of the side-looking sonar shows a dark hump trailed by a white shadow, this could be the hull of a ship. Then the pod would be lowered for a closer scan with the sonar and for a direct examination with television. The question of whether or not the object is a wreck worth further attention can be settled by an hour or so of this near-bottom search, because the pipe can be rapidly raised and lowered by a greater or smaller amount.

Once located, the wreck would be marked with sonar transponders, and the examination of the material would begin, probably with detailed photography and measurements. Then perhaps the sedimentary covering would be gently dusted away and manipulated mechanical arms would move artifacts from the wreck into baskets or other containers.

If recovery of wooden objects showed they had retained much of their original strength, it could then be possible to enclose the wreck and some of the underlying mud in a huge set of tongs, and to raise this almost to the surface where it could be worked on in the usual way.*

Unfortunately the *Alcoa Seaprobe* was scrapped after inexperienced operators dropped the pipe and lost the cable, the pod, and the instruments. Although it no longer exists, *Seaprobe*'s sea tests demonstrated the feasibility of deepwater search and recovery.

Completely intact after more than 150 years on the lake bed 300ft below Lake Ontario (see p.206), the figurehead of the *Hamilton* (left), formerly the *Diana*, is seen in miraculous detail. Her contemporary *Scourge*, which capsized at the same time, is equally well preserved. The hawse-hole at her starboard bow (above) shows wear from the anchor cable, a length of which can be seen. Even the brush strokes are apparent where the ship's hull was painted. Factors responsible for the fine state of preservation include fresh water and a near freezing temperature.

The *Alcoa Seaprobe* at sea (above, right), a center-well, pipe-handling ship capable of lifting 500 tons from 13,000ft (4,000m) of water. Willard Bascom (right), inventor of the deep salvage system, watches the indicator showing the position of the pod relative to the ship while it is searching.

The future underwater

Today's rapidly expanding technology is not only changing our present lives; it also provides increased and fuller access to different environments from the past, as industry uncovers more land and more seabed. And yet, the more these treasures of our past become available, the more we want.

The past, after all, plays an important part in the present. We use the past as an orientation to our own lives. Where did we come from? Why are we here now? The past is also part of the present. We choose to keep or destroy pieces of it, and consequently, we control what part the past plays in our childrens' future.

But values are relative and change over time. What is today a prized antique may have been discarded as trash in the past, and what is discarded as trash today may in the future become a priceless antique.

A cultural resource

"Some people can't seem to tell the difference between something that is old and wet and something that is historic" Gary Kozak, a shipwreck enthusiast, has remarked. How do we distinguish "old wet" wrecks from historic wrecks which have real stories to tell about our nation's great shipping history?

During the 1960s people began to value wrecksites as archaeological sites rather than as sources for commercial salvage. New technologies made oceans and other bodies of water accessible as they had never been before. The SCUBA (Self Contained Underwater Breathing Apparatus) equipment, invented by Jacques Cousteau during World War II, was developed to be inexpensive and safe for sport. SCUBA diving became popular.

At about the same time, shipwrecks were first defined as archaeological sites in the United States when Peter Throckmorton, a marine surveyor working in the Mediterranean, persuaded George Bass, a graduate student at the University of Pennsylvania, to examine pre-Christian era wrecks off the coasts of Turkey and Greece (see p.24). Bass recognized these sites as archaeological treasures.

This impetus and the new accessibility motivated divers to locate and identify shipwreck sites; for example, in Lake Champlain, Revolutionary War ships sunk in Valcour Bay and the British fleet destroyed during the War of 1812 in Plattsburg Bay were listed as national historic landmarks in 1960–61. In 1965, some gold coins washed up on a beach in Florida led to the location of the 1715 Spanish Plate Fleet. As in these examples, most of the shipwrecks off the American coast were engaged in military or commercial enterprises at various stages of the country's growth.

As cultural resources they provide valuable information about the historic changes in vessels and about changes in warfare and commerce. About their place in history, moreover, we learn not only from their cargoes, but also from the utensils and other artifacts of daily life that they carried and that sank with them: plates, glassware, cutlery and clothing for example.

As such, they can be understood as potential museums of behavioral context, preserving a collection of items, and also a narrative segment of history which their routes, logs, and wreckage present to the archaeologist as a unique challenge to preserve. In some cases, they may provide extremely rare evidence. The history of smuggling illustrates, for example, that the excavation of wrecksites may be the only method of gathering information about some types of human activities.

In one of the greatest scientific works of the 19th century, Lyell's *Principles of Geology* (1832), we read:
"It is probable that a greater number of monuments of the skill and industry of man will in the course of ages be collected together in the bed of the oceans, than will exist at any one time on the surface of the Continents."

This is precisely the direction taken by archaeologists who study shipwrecks. Indeed, historic shipwrecks represent an integral part of the total material cultural resource base; social, economic, and technological systems of the past are reflected in the patterned pieces of ship and cargo on the ocean floor.

Industry and archaeology

Historic values are not the only values that must be considered when we look at archaeological sites, especially wrecksites. The bottomlands of our rivers and lakes and our coasts are in high demand.

Ocean dumping, for example, is a habit from the past that we have found hard to break but it is catching up with us and will continue to be a problem for the future. Miners and drillers are recovering sand and gravel, oil and gas, phosphates, sulfur and other minerals. Commercial fishermen demand undisturbed nursery areas for fish and beds for shellfish, as well as areas in which they can drag multi-ton trawls along the bottom, and areas where nets can be pulled unobstructed through the water.

Recreational demands on these bottomlands are very intense. Sport divers tend to have three different and sometimes incompatible interests, namely fishing, photography and wreck-diving. Since shipwrecks act as artificial reefs attracting fish, they are often the best spots for spear fishing, photography and just looking. Photographers and others often prefer undisturbed shipwrecks with artifacts as they were when the ship sank.

Many divers like to collect brass objects or other artifacts. But divers' random collecting can be incompatible with the work of archaeologists. On historic shipwrecks archaeologists need ordered collection to understand the ship's story.

Then there are the treasure hunters. Here the goal is economic; the aim of the treasure salvor is to recover at minimum cost gold, silver or precious artifacts that have a maximum commercial value. The methods used frequently involve wholesale destruction of the wrecksite, where operators require exclusive use to deploy their heavy equipment and to insure security. Gordon Watts, an underwater archaeologist known for his work on the *U.S.S. Monitor*, has written:

Today one of the most important legacies for our seafaring heritage is being destroyed. Shipwrecks, one of our most important sources of information and material associated with our national maritime experience, are rapidly being salvaged with little or no regard for their tremendous historic value and potential public benefit. Free enterprise is not the issue. The real issue is whether we as a nation are willing to see this important and irreplaceable aspect of our past destroyed to satisfy the shortsighted commercial interests of treasure hunters, or whether those resources will be protected and managed to benefit the broadest spectrum of both present and future generations of Americans. What we are looking at is preserving something that not only belongs to the present and the past but also belongs to the future.

In pursuit of their Peter Pan fantasies, treasure hunters have pleaded innocence of environmental destruction in the name of free enterprise. But no one in the USA has ever made a profit from an ancient shipwreck. Only four such wrecks have had any potential commercial value, and those projects all lost millions of dollars.

Meanwhile, the dynamiting of coral reefs, the dredging of endangered turtle nesting beaches, the destruction of shellfish beds and the exclusion of sport divers from favored wrecksites have caused environmental destruction, and conflict between treasure hunters and others.

Myopic economic exploration of the wilderness during the settlement of the New World and the search for gold proved destructive to civilizations, to animals and plants. The equally myopic exploration of the bottomlands will also prove self-destructive. Cries of individual rights, free enterprise and available resources are unconvincing. After all, the creation of national parks and government regulation of clean air and clean water have allowed us all to benefit from the strength and bounty of the natural environment, without diminishing the creation of high-tech industrial economies throughout the world.

An abundance of shipwrecks

Fortunately there are now enough shipwrecks for everyone. But are there enough for the future? That depends on us now. Once a piece of the past is destroyed, it cannot be replaced, it is lost forever. Our management decisions will determine what is left for our children.

The past is a luxury item for a society, and governments can only manage resources hoping to meet as many as possible of the sometimes conflicting uses for the resource or resource area. Interest in mining, fishing, recreation and nature will expand in the future, one activity bumping into and overlapping the area of another. In addition, better technology and the resulting increase in access to the bottomlands will create new demands.

Underwater hotels are already beginning in the Caribbean and may become as popular as the mountain cabin. In order to appease competing interests, zoning of the bottomlands has begun with the designation of underwater parks and marine sanctuaries in several states of the USA, as well as in other countries such as Canada, Egypt and Israel. But we must be careful with our rich underwater treasure. Whether for artifacts on a shipwreck or for the wrecksite, cutting the treasure into little pieces to make it go around would destroy its beauty and its future viability. There must be cooperation as well as compromise.

Technology will make the bottomlands as accessible to us as the New World and its western frontier was to our ancestors. Shipwrecks at a depth of 300ft (100m) or 3 miles (5km) will be as accessible as those at 30ft (10m) now. Archaeologists may be able to "excavate" a shipwreck using only remote sensing equipment, without disturbing the seabed or recovering any artifacts. Archaeology will become a more highly technical, engineering-related discipline demanding highly specialized skills.

On the other hand, vacationers may be able to view a coral reef or a shipwreck by sitting in front of a color screen and pushing computer buttons to guide a video camera as they visually wander over the bottom. In the hotel lobby or nearby museum a freestanding, 3-D holograph of the shipwreck will allow people to walk through and around the site feeling the size, violence and peace that are part of a wrecked ship. However, shipwrecks are part of a larger complex, which includes the seabed, the fish and plants, the currents, water temperature and the depth. Some shipwrecks are best preserved in place so that we can appreciate them as part of a whole – perhaps the *Titanic* is in this category.

In order that we may have shipwrecks for this fascinating future, it is our responsibility now to preserve and manage resources as best we can. Education about the natural and cultural potential of our underwater areas will, it is hoped, provide increased public support for efforts to balance all of our demands on these resources.

Change will be as much or more a part of the future as it is a part of today. With important competing interests using the bottomlands, we will not be able to save all of the wrecksites for historical study. But, by comparing sites, we will be able to choose the shipwrecks with the most complete stories to tell, wrecksites that answer our questions about the past. We can then put our money and energy into detailed study of those truly historic sites.

As the number of known wrecksites increases, the interest in those sites will also increase. As the amount of information about shipwrecks grows, regional, national and international centers will evolve to meet demand. Home computers will be able to access information in a center or institute; information about artifacts and wrecksites from archives will be easily available.

The role of the artifact

Artifacts will make up a significant proportion of the data base. Knowing the origin of carefully excavated artifacts will increase their historical and commercial value. The registration of artifacts to prove authenticity and to discourage theft is becoming an accepted practice. In the future invisible registration marks and a worldwide computer recording of the information will help to distinguish authentic artifacts from fakes and will preserve the information about the artifact that is so important to understanding its story.

In addition, we will have more artifacts to study. Conservation techniques will improve dramatically. Iron cannon fittings and other objects will be preserved at better than the current 50 percent rate. The story and display of the artifacts will have to be considered very carefully, so as not to overload any one building and to distribute the maintenance costs fairly. Just as electronic media have brought us information about many different world cultures, so the sharing of culture through the sharing of artifacts, our arts, will also bring the world in closer touch.

Better conservation and registration systems will make more public and private collections accessible to students of history. The study of these collections and the sites that produced them will allow the past to tell more of its stories.

Archaeologists will perhaps someday be excavating spacecraft, or deserted space station posts on remote planets. Ships have been only a beginning for man's travel beyond the next sea.

Let us hope that the management decisions that we make now reflect the same ingenuity and skill required for the building of a ship. Let us not underestimate the importance of the past in our present or in the future. In carelessly destroying the past we destroy part of our present and part of the future.

Chapter notes and bibliography

Chapter notes and bibliography
Journal abbreviations
BAR British Archaeological Reports
IJNA The International Journal of Nautical Archaeology and Underwater Exploration.
MM The Mariner's Mirror
Nat. Geo. National Geographic Magazine
Trans. Am. Phil. Soc. Transactions of the American Philosophical Society

1 DIVING INTO THE PAST (pp. 8–33)

Introduction

13 The first official British underwater archaeological expedition, under the aegis of the British School at Athens, explored a wrecksite off Emporio, Chios, in 1954. Aqualungs were used. No excavation was attempted, and only a minimum of specimens were brought up from the seabed. See:
GARNETT, R. & BOARDMAN, J. *Annual of the British School at Athens,* 56 (1961) 102–115.

Further general reading

BASS, G. F. (ed) *History of Seafaring, Based on Underwater Archaeology* Walker, New York: Thames & Hudson, London 1972.

GREENHILL, B. *Archaeology of the Boat* Wesleyan University Press, Middletown, Conn: A & C Black, London 1976.

HORNELL, J. *Water Transport; Origins and Early Evolution* University Press, Cambridge 1946.

JOHNSTONE, P. *The Sea-Craft of Prehistory* Routledge & Kegan Paul, London 1980.

LANDSTRÖM, B. *The Ship* Allen & Unwin, London 1961.

McKEE, A. *History Under the Sea* London 1968.

MUCKLEROY, K. *Maritime Archaeology* Macmillan, New York 1979: Cambridge University Press, Cambridge 1978.

TAYLOR, J. du P. (ed) *Marine Archaeology* Crowell, New York 1966: Hutchinson, London 1965.

THROCKMORTON, P. *Shipwrecks and Archaeology* Atlantic Monthly Press, Boston: Gollancz, London, 1970.

International Journal of Nautical Archaeology and Underwater Exploration (IJNA), published quarterly for the Council for Nautical Archaeology by the Academic Press, London and New York. Many of the discoveries described in this book were first described in *IJNA.* .

The road to Gelidonya

Further reading

BASS, G.F. 'Bronze Age shipwreck at Ulu Burun (Kas): 1984 campaign' *Am. J. Archaeology* 90:3 (July 1986), 269–96.

DE SOLLA PRICE, D. 'Gears from the Greeks' *Trans. Am. Phil. Soc.* 64:7 (1974).

THROCKMORTON, P. 'The Antikythera wreck: the beginning of marine archaeology'. Pp. 113–68 in the author's *Shipwrecks and Archaeology* Atlantic Monthly Press, Boston: Gollancz, London, 1970.

WEINBERG, G.D. (ed) 'The Antikythera shipwreck reconsidered' *Trans. Am. Phil. Soc.* 55:3 (1965).

Sailors in the time of Troy

BASS, G.F. 'Cape Gelidonya; a Bronze Age shipwreck' *Trans. Am. Phil. Soc.* 57:8 (1967).

2 THE ANCIENT MEDITERRANEAN (pp. 34–59)

An Aegean Atlantis

37 See Plato's *Critias* and *Timaeus.*

37 GALANOPOULOS, A.G. & BACON E. *Atlantis: The Truth Behind the Legend* Nelson, London 1969.
LUCE, J.V. *The End of Atlantis* Thames & Hudson, London 1969.
MAVOR, J.W. *Voyage to Atlantis* Putnam, New York 1969.

38 COHEN, H.H. *The Drunkenness of Noah* University of Alabama, Alabama 1974.

38 FROST, K.T. 'The Critias and Minoan Crete' *J. Hellenic Studies* 33 (1913) 189 ff.

38 FINLEY, M.I. 'Atlantis or bust' *New York Review of Books* 2 May 1969.
— 'Back to Atlantis' *New York Review of Books* 4 December 1969.
MAVOR, J.W. 'Back to Atlantis again' *New York Review of Books* December 4, 1969.

38 NINKOVICH, D. & HEEZEN, B. 'Santorini tephra' *Colston Papers,* London 1965.

40 HEIKEN, G. & McCOY, F.W. 'Caldera development during the Minoan eruption' *J. Geophysical Research* 89: B10 (1984).

40 FOUQUE, F. *Santorin et Ses Eruptions,* Paris 1874.
MAMET, H. *De Insula Thera* Lille 1874.
VON GÄRTRINGEN, F.H. *Thera* Berlin 1899–1909.

40 DOUMAS, C.G. *Thera, Pompeii of the Ancient Aegean: Excavations at Akrotiri 1967–1979* London 1983.

40 CASSON, L. 'Bronze Age ships. The evidence of the Thera wall paintings' *IJNA* 4:1 (1975) 3–10.
GIESECKE, H.E. 'The Akrotiri ship fresco' *IJNA* 12:2 (1983) 123–43.
GILLMER, T.C. 'The Thera ship' *MM* 61:4 (1975).

40 HEIKEN, G. & McCOY, F.W. *op. cit.*

40 DOWNEY, W.S. & TARLING, D.H. 'Archaeomagnetic dating of Santorini volcanic eruptions and fired destruction levels of late Minoan civilization' *Nature* 309 (1984) 7 June.

40 CYRUS GORDON, on p. 194 of his *Before Columbus,* Crown, New York 1971, argues that Atlantis, to Plato, was America, because he and his Greek-reading public knew about a continent across the Atlantic Ocean.

Archaic and Classical cargoes from the Tyrrhenian Sea

Further reading

BOUND, M. 'A wreck of possible Etruscan origin off Giglio Island' *IJNA* 12:2 (1983) 113–122.
— 'Il relitto arcaico di Giglio Campese. Il recupero', *Archeologia Viva* 5:1 (1986) 48–63.

An Athenian warship recreated

44 *The Constitution of Athens* 1.19–20.

44 HOMER *Odyssey* 9.177–80, 11.640; *Iliad* 1.432–7.

44 HOMER *Odyssey* 5.243–61.

44 AESCHYLUS *Persians* 353–432.

44 EURIPIDES *Iphigeneia at Tauri* 1327–1410.

44 EURIPIDES *Helen* 1530–1614.

44 ARISTOPHANES *Birds* 108.

44 ARISTOPHANES *Knights* 541–4.

44 ARISTOPHANES *Frogs* 207.

44 ARISTOPHANES *Acharnians* 545–54.

44 Compare DEMOSTHENES 51.

44 ARISTOPHANES *Frogs* 1074–5.

44 XENOPHON *Oeconomicus* 8.8.

44 ARISTOTLE *Rhetorica* 1411 and 24.

44 THUCYDIDES 1.45–54. See *AT* 62–8.

45 THUCYDIDES 2.83.3. See *AT* 68–71.

45 THUCYDIDES 2.86–91. See *AT* 72–6.

45 XENOPHON *Anabasis* 6.4.2.

46 THUCYDIDES 3.49.

46 DEMOSTHENES 50.15–6.

46 DEMOSTHENES 50.53–4, 22–3.

46 ARISTOTLE *On the Parts of Animals* 687 b 18.
GALEN *On the Uses of the Parts of the Body* 1.25.

47 PLATO *Republic* 616.

48 MORRISON, J.S. 'The Greek trireme' *MM* 27:1 (1941) 14–44.

49 MORRISON, J.S. 'Notes on certain Greek nautical terms' *Classical Quarterly* 41 (1947) 122–35.

49 MORRISON J.S. & WILLIAMS, R.T. *Greek Oared Ships 900–322BC* University Press, Cambridge 1968.

49 COATES J.F. & McGRAIL S. *The Greek Trireme of the 5th Century BC* University Press, Cambridge 1984.

Further reading

MORRISON, J.S. & COATES, J.F. *The Athenian Trireme* University Press, Cambridge 1986.

FOLEY V. & SOEDEL, W. 'Ancient oared warships' *Scientific American* 244:4 (April 1981) 116–29.

Phoenician explorers

Further reading

CARPENTER, R. 'Pytheas at Massalia'. Ch. 5 in *Beyond the Pillars of Hercules* Delacorte Press, 1966.

HARBISON, P. & LAING, L.R. *Some Iron Age Mediterranean Imports in England* BAR No. 5, Oxford 1974.

HARDEN, D.B. *The Phoenicians* Penguin Books, 1972.

HENCKEN, H. O'N. *The Archaeology of Cornwall and Scilly* Methuen, London 1932, 158–88.

LAING, L.R. 'A Green tin trade with Cornwall?' *Cornish Archaeology* 7 (1968) 15–23.

The Kyrenia ship restored

Further reading

KATZEV, M.L. 'Resurrecting the oldest known Greek ship' *Nat. Geo.* 137:6 (1970) 840–57.
— 'Last harbor for the oldest ship' *Nat. Geo.* 146:5 (1974) 618–25.

STEFFEY, J.R. 'The Kyrenia ship: an interim report on its hull construction' *Am. J. Archaeology* 89:1 (1985) 71–101.

3 FROM ROME TO BYZANTIUM (pp. 60–91)

Introduction

Further reading

CASSON, L. *Ships and Seamanship in the Ancient World* University Press, Princeton 1971.

FROST, H. *Under the Mediterranean* Routledge & Kegan Paul, London 1963.

PARKER, A.J. *Ancient Shipwrecks of the Mediterranean and the Roman Provinces* BAR, Oxford 1987.

TALBERT, R.J.A. (ed) *Atlas of Classical History* Croom Helm, London 1985.

The amphora: jerrycan of antiquity

Further Reading

Amphora wrecksites
LAMBOGLIA, N. 'La campagna 1963 sul relitto di Punta Scaletta' *Rivista di Studi Liguri* 30 (1964) 229–57.
PEACOCK, D.P. & WILLIAMS, D.F. *Amphorae and the Roman Economy* Longman, London 1986.

Grand Congloué wrecksite
BENOIT, F. *L'Épave du Grand Congloué à Marseille,* XIVe supplément à *Gallia* Paris 1961.
— 'Mediterranean trade'. Pp. 24–33 in Taylor, J. du P. (ed) *Marine Archaeology* Hutchinson, London 1965.

Titan wrecksite
TAILLIEZ, P. 'Titan'. Pp. 76–92 in Taylor, J. du P. (ed) *Marine Archaeology* Hutchinson, London 1965.

Madrague de Giens wrecksite
TCHERNIA, M.A. & POMEY, P. *L'Épave Romaine de la Madrague de Giens (Var.)* supplément à *Gallia* 1978.

A million tons of marble

Further reading

GREENE, K.T. *The Archaeology of the Roman Economy* Batsford, London 1986.

Shipwrecks, anchors and St Paul

Further reading

Acts 27

FROST, H. 'Anchors, the potsherds of marine archaeology'. Pp. 397–409 in Blackman, D.J. (ed) *Marine Archaeology* Butterworth, London 1973.

The Galilee boat

Further reading

Manor, D. 'The boat that came up from the sea' *Eretz Magazine* (Winter 1987) 58–67.

Byzantine ships

86 Dr Fred Van Doorninck is professor at George Bass's Institute of Nautical Archaeology at Texas A&M; Avner Raban is professor at Haifa University and director of underwater excavations at Caesarea in Israel; Susan Womer married to Michael Katzev, and together they excavated the Kyrenia ship; Peter Kuniholm and John Clifford are both professors, and Richard Steffy received the prestigious MacArthur Award (USA) for his part in reconstructing the hull. David Switzer, Warren Riess, Sheli Smith and Cemal Pulak, all contributors to this book, were involved with the Yassi Ada wreck.

90 Finds here included a bowl containing chicken-bones, a set of balance-pan weights, several iron swords and a wooden scabbard, and many decorated lead net weights.

Further reading

Historical background
LEWIS, A. *Naval Power and Trade in the Mediterranean AD500–1100* University Press, Princeton 1951.
VRYONIS, S. *Byzantium and Europe* Thames & Hudson, London 1970.

Marzamemi church wreck
KAPITÄN, G. 'The church wreck off Marzamemi' *Archaeology* 21 (1969) 122–33.

Panto Longarini wrecksite
THROCKMORTON, P. & KAPITÄN, G. 'An ancient shipwreck at Pantano Longarini' *Archaeology* 21 (1968) 182–7.

Serçe Limani wrecksite
BASS, G.F. & DOORNINCK, F.H. van 'An 11th century shipwreck at Serçe Limani, Turkey' *IJNA* 7 (1978) 119–132.

7th century ship at Yassi Ada
BASS, G.F. & DOORNINCK, F.H. van *Yassi Ada. Vol. 1, A Seventh-Century Byzantine Shipwreck* Texas A & M University Press 1982.

4 RECONSTRUCTION AND CONSERVATION (pp. 92–105)

The shipwright's art

Further reading

ABELL, W. *The Shipwright's Trade* University Press, Cambridge 1948.

CASSON, L. *Ships and Seamanship in the Ancient World* Princeton University Press, Princeton 1971.

CUTLER, C. *Greyhounds of the Sea* G. P. Putnam's Sons, New York 1930.

GREENHILL, B. *Archaeology of the Boat* Wesleyan University Press, Middletown, Conn: A & C Black, London 1976.

HORNELL, J. *Water Transport: Origins and Early Evolution* University Press, Cambridge 1946.

LANDSTRÖM, B. *Sailing Ships* Allen & Unwin, London 1969.

McGREGOR, D.R. *Fast Sailing Ships: Their Design and Construction, 1775–1875* Heassner Publishing, 1973.

McKAY, R. *Some Famous Sailing Ships and their Builder, Donald McKay* G. P. Putnam's Sons, New York 1928.

Ship stability, ancient and modern

The physics of ship stability were first investigated by Archimedes in the 3rd century BC. For an excellent discussion of the physical factors that guided the design of warships of the time, see:
FOLEY, V. & SOEDEL, W. 'Ancient oared warships' *Scientific American* 244:4 (April 1981) 116–29.

Archaeology and conservation

Further reading

MARX, R.F. 'Preservation of artifacts' Pp. 110–28 in the author's *Shipwrecks in the Americas* Bonanza Books, New York 1983.

5 DARK AGE SEAFARERS (pp. 106–133)

Introduction

Further reading
MARSDEN,P. *A Roman Ship from Blackfriars, London* Guildhall Museum, London 1966.

TAYLOR, J. du P. & CLEERE, H. (eds) *Roman Shipping and Trade: Britain and the Rhine Provinces* Council for British Archaeology Research Report No. 24, London 1978.

Saints and skinboats

108 Surprisingly, the earliest reference to coracles seems to be by Giraldus Cambrensis in his 1188 *Journey through Wales*. He wrote: "The boats which they employ in fishing or in crossing rivers are made of twigs, not oblong or pointed, but almost round or triangular, covered within and without with raw hides."

108 CAESAR, J. *De Bello Civili* 1.4.

110 One enigmatic passage speaks of a coagulated sea which Severin believes may reflect an encounter with forming pack ice where ice in calm water begins, in Severin's words, to "coalesce into lumps which resemble curds floating on the surface of coagulating milk." St Brendan and his companions also seem to have encountered an iceberg surrounded by characteristic broken ice – a phenomenon that they boldly set out to explore, even sailing their fragile curragh into its caverns and attempting to measure its huge girth!

Further reading

DE PAOR, M. & L. *Early Christian Ireland* Thames & Hudson, London 1978.

HORNELL, J. *British Coracles and Irish Curraghs* Society for Nautical Research, London 1938.

SEVERIN, T. *The Brendan Voyage* Hutchinson, London 1978.

The coming of the Anglo-Saxons

112 This was built with a broad flat keel-plank flanked by two wide strakes and fastened by cord threaded tightly through holes drilled along the edges of the planks.

112 The small Halsnoy boat shows a series of claw tholes along the top of the gunwale strake, thorn-shaped pieces of wood cut from selected timber at the junction of the trunk and a small branch.

112 This left pairs of cleats standing proud of the surface to which the cross-frames were lashed, giving the boat lateral strength.

114 Because the keel-plank was still essentially flat, it scarfed horizontally with the stem and stern posts, unlike the fully developed Viking boats, where the deep keel profile demanded a vertical scarf.

Further reading

HILL, D. *An Atlas of Anglo-Saxon England* Blackwell, London 1981.

SHETELIG, H. & JOHANNESSEN, F. 'Das Nydamschiff' *Acta Archaeologica* I (1930).

WILSON, D. *The Anglo-Saxons* Pelican Books, London 1981 (3rd edn).

A kingly burial

121 She was built with a normal clinkered hull with a broad, stubby keel-plank and nine composite strakes a side, and was fastened with iron rivets identical in size to those used in the smaller boat in mound 2 at Sutton Hoo and also in the Snape boat. The hull was braced by 26 close-fitting frames held to the hull with a single iron rivet through the top strake and by treenails elsewhere.

121 The oars were pulled against tholes (natural tree-forks) whose elongated bases formed an almost continuous rail along the top of the expanded upper strake.

121 No evidence for the iron spikes that held the tholes to the top strake was found in the midships area where the burial chamber was built, but it is also possible that the tholes may have been deliberately removed for the burial so that the planks of the burial chamber roof could lie snugly against the hull, preventing sand from filtering into the chamber.

Further reading

BRUCE-MITFORD, R.L.S. *The Sutton Hoo Ship-Burial. Vol. I,* British Museum, London 1978 (3rd edn).

EVANS, A.C. *The Sutton Hoo Ship Burial* British Museum, London 1986.

Swans of the Sea God

Further reading

BRØGGER, A.W. & SHETELIG, H. *The Viking Ships* Arthur Vanous Co., Riveredge, New Jersey: Hurst, London, 1976.

The Viking world

Further reading

CRUMLIN-PEDERSEN, O. 'The Viking ships of Roskilde' *National Maritime Museum Monographs and Reports* I (1970) 7–23.
— 'Viking and Hanseatic merchants: 900–1450'. Pp. 182–204 in Bass, G. (ed) *A History of Seafaring, Based on Underwater Archaeology* Thames & Hudson, London 1972.

JONES, G. *A History of the Vikings* Book Club Associates, London 1973.

OLSEN, O. & CRUMLIN-PEDERSEN, O. 'The Skuldelev Ships (I) and (II)' *Acta Archaeologica* 29 (1958) and 38 (1967).

6 MEDIEVAL WARSHIPS AND TRADERS (pp. 134–151)

North Sea traders

134 Instead of the deep T-shaped keel characteristic of Viking ships she had a much flatter keel-plank, wide amidships and tapered towards the extremities. The straight stern post, too, which raked at a sharp angle from the keel, was quite unlike the curved ends of Scandinavian ships.

134 Long iron nails were driven through previously inserted willow pegs. Small oak wedges set into their inboard ends ensured that the pegs would not be driven out as the nails were driven in, and the fastening holes and plank joints were calked with tar-soaked wool.

136 The hull of the Kalmar boat is reinforced with inserted frames and stringers, and further strengthened by five sets of cross-beams. Each set, or bulkhead, consists of three beams, one above the other, attached to the ship's side with standard knees. The upper two beams of the central three sets project through the planking, with notched ends to lock the whole structure rigidly together.

138 In 1664 Amsterdam's city shipwright, Jan Lucasz Root, was ordered to build 125 large and small mud barges. As each barge was finished the date was inscribed on one of its beams, together with the three vertically set crosses of the city arms. Around the year 1700 one of these barges met with an unfortunate accident which carried it some 22 miles (34km) eastwards across the Zuider Zee, where it sank in shallow water.

In the 1970s this boat, and another almost identical to it, were discovered during the development of Flevoland, an area which had been reclaimed from the southern Zuider Zee a decade earlier. The mud-barges were flat-bottomed craft some 55ft (16m) long by 15ft (4m) wide, with low clinker-built sides and bulkheads fore and aft to contain their semi-liquid cargoes. Three heavy crossbeams connected the sides of the mud hold, and carried gangplanks linked to the decked extremities of the vessel. Badges issued by the mud-mens' guild show that the vessels were normally punted to and from the mud dump (an area known as "Sick Water"). The mud-men, wearing long leather boots, laboriously ladled out the mud with wooden scoops. Two scoops and a pair of mud-boots were found among the barge remains.

138 Various merchant vessels have also come to light. The substantially intact hull of a large trading ship of the mid-17th century is now on display in the Kestelhaven Museum.

Further reading

ELLMERS, D. 'The Cog of Bremen and related boats'. Pp. 1–15 in S. McGrail (ed) *The Archaeology of Medieval Ships and Harbours in Western Europe,* BAR, Oxford 1979.

FENWICK, V. *The Graveney Boat,* BAR, Oxford 1978.

UNGER, R.W. 'Cogs, Hulks and Great Galleys:

1250–1400'. Pp. 161–200 in the author's *The Ship in the Medieval Economy, 600–1600* McGill-Queen's University Press, Montreal: Croom-Helm,London, 1980.

Guns and sails

140 The hull was of a peculiar triple clinker construction, with the inner plank of each composite strake left short to provide a recess for the strake below it to butt into. Tarred moss was used for calking. The ship's stem post, of which the stump survives, scarfed to the forward end of the keel, raked sharply to thrust the fighting castle well forward.

141 *Sovereign*'s sister-ship, *Regent,* carried a total of 225 serpentines. Ten years earlier, in 1485, *Grace Dieu*'s successor of the same name (and also docked in the River Hamble) was recorded with a "feble" armament of 21 guns, 89 chambers, and 140 bows; her better-armed sister-ships, the *Mars, Grosvenor,* and *Martin Garsia,* had 58, 70 and 30 guns and 116, 51 and 40 bows respectively.

141 A clinker hull depended primarily on its shell for strength, but the kind of internal stresses induced by the mounting and operation of large guns required the support of a strong skeleton. This difficulty was overcome by inserting massive internal riders and longitudinal stringers. The transition from clinker to carvel, from shell to skeleton, was now complete.

142 The *Mary Rose*'s establishment is recorded in Anthony Anthony's roll of 1546 – a year after the ship was lost.

144 The bronze barrel, with a bore of 8.6 cm, is enclosed by a wrought-iron breech stirrup which clamps over lugs on the barrel's side. Attached to the rear of the gun is a long aiming shaft, or tiller. A bar welded across the lower part of the stirrup supports the breech-block, which is also made of wrought-iron and has a handle attached. Nine punch-holes in the top of the block match nine similar ones in the stirrup, in much the same way that a modern rifle is matched to its bolt with a serial number; no doubt at least one other breech-block was provided for the gun to speed up reloading. A flared wedge secured to the rear of the breech stirrup with a length of chain ensured a tight fit and provided support against the shock of recoil.

Further reading

MARTIN, C. *Full Fathom Five: The Wrecks of the Spanish Armada* Viking Press, New York: Chatto & Windus, London, 1975.

PRYNNE, M. 'Henry V's *Grace Dieu*' *MM* 54 (1968) 115–28.

RULE, M. *The Mary Rose. The Excavation and Raising of Henry VIII's Flagship* Conway Maritime Press, London 1982.

Ships of the line

148 This indeed happened to one Armada ship, the heavily engaged Portuguese galleon *San Mateo,* which ran aground on the Flemish shoals after she had, in the words of one eye-witness, "pulled herself to pieces with her own artillery".

148 Oak treenails fastened the 10cm thick outer planking to the close-set frames, with strong iron bolts placed where springing stresses were greatest.

150 A streamlined heavy "bomb", fitted with a carpenter's wad punch in its nose, which extracted a sample plug of whatever it hit.

150 A high length-to-breadth ratio, coupled with fine lines, gave her speed and sailing performance. Two continuous gundecks carried a formidable armament of standardized bronze pieces, mounted on compact truck-carriages.

150 In the case of the seamen the choice was not always voluntary, though life aboard a man-o'-war was generally regarded (at least until the latter part of the 18th century) as preferable to the merchant service.

150 After attending the launch of the 1200-ton first-rate *Charles* at Deptford in 1668, Evelyn noted that she was "built by old Shish, a plain honest carpenter, master builder of this dock, but one who can give very little account of his art by discourse, and who is hardly capable of reading, yet of great ability in his calling." Evelyn explains how old Shish's family

had been "ship carpenters in this dock above 300 years."

151 "[Breakfast] is generally cooked in a hook-pot in the galley, where there is a range. Nearly all the crew have one of these pots, a spoon, and a knife; for all these things are indispensable; there are also basons, plates, etc., which are kept in each mess, which generally consists of eight persons, whose berth is between two of the guns on the lower deck, where there is a board placed, which swings with the rolling of the ship, and answers for a table. it sometimes happens that a lurch will dash all the crockery to pieces; they are then obliged to eat out of wooden or tin utensils, until they come into harbour, when they get another supply."

Further reading

FRANZEN, A. *The Warship Vasa* Norestedt & Bonnier, Stockholm 1966.

GLASON, E. 'The raising of the royal Swedish ship *Vasa*' *MM* 48:3 (1962).

KEMP, P.K. *The British Sailor: A Social History of the Lower Deck,* Dent, London 1970.

MARTIN, C. 'The *Dartmouth*, a British frigate wrecked off Mull, 1690. 5. The ship' *IJNA* 7 (1987) 29–58.

7 EASTERN HORIZONS (pp. 152–171)

Introduction

152 South Africa has been the scene of several shipwrecks. One Portuguese (the *Sacramento,* 1647), one English (the *Grosvenor,* 1755) and two Dutch East India Company wrecks (the *Nieuw Rhoon* and the *Merestijn*) have been investigated. See:

ALLEN, G. & ALLEN, D. *The Guns of the Sacramento* London 1978.
— *Clive's Lost Treasure* London 1978.
MARSDEN, P. 'The Meresteyn, wrecked in 1702, near Cape Town, South Africa' *IJNA* 5:3 (1976) 201–19.

In Kenya the *Santo Antonio de Tanna,* which sank off Fort Jesus in Mombasa in 1697, has been investigated by the National Museum of Kenya in conjunction with the Institute of Nautical Archaeology. See:
PIERCY, R.C.M. 'Mombasa Wreck Excavation' *IJNA* 7:4 (1978) 301–19.

The Western Australian Museum has been responsible for the excavation and study of four Dutch East India Company wrecks, including that of the *Batavia.*

154 One of the interesting aspects of the Seychelles site was the discovery of a small section of hull calked with a U-shaped lead strip.

Arab dhows

Further reading

General
LEWIS, B. *The Arabs in History* Hutchinson, London 1975 (5th edn).

The historical Sindbad
FREEMAN-GRENVILLE, G.S.P. (ed) Preface and Introduction to *The Book of the Wonders of India, Mainland, Sea and Islands by Buzurg ibn Shahriyar of Ramhormuz,* East-West Publications, London 1981.

GERHARDT, M.I. 'Sindbad the Sailor'. Pp. 236–63 in the author's *The Art of Story-Telling. A Literary Study of the Thousand and One Nights* E. J. Brill, Leiden 1963.
NASR, S.H. *Islamic Science – an Illustrated Study* World of Islam Festival Co., London 1976, 38–45.

Types of dhow
HORNELL, J. 'A tentative classification of Arab sea-craft' *MM* January 1942.
— 'The development of Arab ship design'. Pp. 229–41 in the author's *Water Transport* University Press, Cambridge 1970.

Early references
HOURANI, G.F. *Arab Seafaring in the Indian Ocean in Ancient and Early Medieval Times* University Press, Princeton 1951.
JOHNSTONE, P. *The Sea-Craft of Pre-History* Routledge & Kegan Paul, London 1980, 177–84.
McGRAIL, S. *The Ship, volume VI: Rafts, Boats and Ships* HMSO, London 1981, 46–8.

The medieval heyday
LEWIS, A. 'Maritime Skills in the Indian Ocean'. Pp. 239–64 in *The Sea and Medieval Civilisations* Variorum Publications, London 1978.

Recent history and likely prospects
HAWKINS, C. *The Dhow: an Illustrated History of the Dhow and Its World* Nautical Publishing Company, Lymington 1977.
MARTIN, E.B. & MARTIN, C.P. *Cargoes of the East: the Ports, Trade and Culture of the Arabian Seas and Western Indian Ocean* Elm Tree Books, London 1978.
VILLIERS, A.J. *Pioneers of the Seven Seas,* Routledge & Kegan Paul, London 1956.

Severin's voyage
SEVERIN, T. *The Sindbad Voyage* Hutchinson, London 1982.
— 'In the Wake of Sindbad', *Nat. Geo.* July 1982.

Chinese ocean-going ships

159 The inner planking is 3 inches (about 80mm) thick, and the first two strakes have carvel joints. The second and third strakes are joined with a rabbeted clinker joint, and this alternating system continues for 16 strakes. The outer planking is 2 inches (about 50mm) thick, carvel-jointed, and irregularly fastened with light nails to the inner planking.

159 Four or five holes on its long side made room for nails attaching it to the bulkhead. The short angle had a single hole through which it was nailed to the hull. All fastenings were sealed.

162 Excavation of the Ko Kradat wrecksite revealed Sawanhalok ceramics in association with Chinese blue and white porcelain, dating back to the reign of Jiajing (1522–66). See:
GREEN, J.N. 'Thailand. The excavation of the Ko Kradat wrecksite, an interim report' *IJNA* 9:2 (1980) 168–72.
GREEN, J.N. & HARPER, R. 'Two seasons of excavation of the Ko Kradat wrecksite, Thailand: conclusions' *IJNA* (in press). Other Thailand wrecksites include the *Rayong*, at a depth of 165 feet (50m), and the Samae Sun site, both briefly investigated by the Thailand Fine Arts Department; and an exceptional site with Chinese export wares of the Wan Li period (1573–1629), investigated in 1983.

162 A number of vessels from the Yangtze River have similar mast sockets, used to locate the tabernacle partners. They are braced against the side of the ship at deck level to prevent lateral movement of the mast. Fore-and-aft movement is restrained by lateral cross-beams and the bulkhead itself. The advantage of this system is that the mast can be lowered or its rake altered from the vertical to take advantage of the wind direction.

Further reading

HUDSON, G.F. *Europe and China: A Survey of their Relations from the Earliest Times to 1800* Arnold, London 1931.

KEITH, D. & BUYS, C. 'New light on medieval Chinese ship construction' *IJNA* 10:2 (1981) 119–32.

NEEDHAM, J. *Science and Civilisation in China. Vol. I.* University Press, Cambridge 1954, 143 ff. and 176–80.

Kublai Khan's invasion of Japan

Further reading

MOZAI, T. 'The lost fleet of Kublai Khan' *Nat. Geo.* (Nov 1982) 635–48.

East Indiamen

168 The clue to the purpose of the facade comes from the journal of Pieter van den Broecke, who sailed to the Indies in 1614 and returned in 1630. A woodcut in his journal shows the town and castle of Batavia with scaffolding and a ladder in the place of an actual gateway. For a historical background to the wreck, see:
DRAKE-BROCKMAN, H. *Voyage to Disaster: the life and times of Francisco Pelsaert* Melbourne 1963.
EDWARDS, H. *Islands of Angry Ghosts* Morrow, New York 1966.

For details of the excavation work, see:
BAKER, P.E. and GREEN, J.N. 'Recording techniques

used during the excavation of the Batavia' *IJNA* 5 (1976) 143–558.

Further reading

GREEN, J. *The Jacht Vergulde Draeck* BAR Supplementary Series, 36, Oxford 1977.

MARSDEN, P. *The Wreck of the Amsterdam* Stein & Day, New York 1975: Hutchinson, London 1974.

Captain Cook in the Pacific

Further reading

BEAGLEHOLE, J.C. (ed) *The Journals of Captain James Cook* Cambridge University Press for The Hakluyt Society, in 4 volumes, Cambridge (1955 onwards).

VILLIERS, A. *Captain Cook, the Seaman's Seaman* Hodder & Stoughton, London 1969.

8 THE AGE OF DISCOVERY (pp. 172–187)

Trade and piracy in the West Indies

Further reading

Spanish seafaring
ANDREWS, K.R. *The Spanish Caribbean. Trade and Plunder 1530–1630* New Haven 1978.
MARX, R.F. *Shipwrecks of the Western Hemisphere, 1492–1825* David McKay, New York 1971.
SMITH, R.C. & KEITH, D.H. 'The archaeology of ships of discovery', *Archaeology* 39:2 (1986) 30–5.
WEDDLE, R.S. *Spanish Sea: the Gulf of Mexico in North American Discovery 1500–1685* College Station, Texas, 1985.
WOOD, P. *The Spanish Main* Alexandra, Va. 1979.

Molasses Reef wreck
KEITH, D.H. & SIMMONS, J.J. 'An analysis of hull remains, ballast and artifact distribution of a 16th century Shipwreck', *J. Field Archaeology* 12:4 (1985) 411–24.

Highborn Cay wreck
SMITH, R.C. & others 'The Highborn Cay wreck' *IJNA* 14:1 (1985) 63–72.

1554 fleet
ARNOLD, J.B. & WEDDLE, R.S. *The Nautical Archaeology of Padre Island. The Spanish Shipwrecks of 1554* Academic Press, New York & London 1978.

Turtle wreck
SMITH, R.C. 'Archaeology of the Cayman Islands' *Archaeology* 36:5 (1983) 16–24.

Port Royal
HAMILTON, D.L. 'Preliminary report on the archaeological investigations of the submerged remains of Port Royal, Jamaica, 1981–1982' IJNA 13:1 (1984) 11–25.
MARX, R.F. *Port Royal Rediscovered* Doubleday, New York 1973: New English Library, London 1973.
PAWSON, M. & BUISSERT, D. *Port Royal, Jamaica* University Press, Oxford 1975.

Spanish treasure fleets

Further reading

The background to the Spanish conquest of the New World
MACKAY, A. *Spain in the Middle Ages: from Frontier to Empire, 1000–1500* Macmillan, London 1977.

The organization of trade
LANG, J. *Conquest and Commerce: Spain and England in the Americas* Academic Press, London 1975.

General texts
ELLIOTT, J.H. *Imperial Spain, 1469–1716* Arnold, London 1977.
PARRY, J.H. *The Spanish Seaborne Empire* Hutchinson, London 1977.

Economic history
HAMILTON, E.J. *American Treasure and the Price Revolution* University Press, Cambridge, Mass. 1934.

see also Elliott's discussion of Hamilton's work, op. cit. 183–8.
VIVES, V. *An Economic History of Spain* University Press, Princeton 1969.

The 1715 and 1733 fleet disasters
PETERSON, M. 'Traders and privateers across the Atlantic: 1492–1733'. Pp. 253–80 in Bass, G.F. (ed) *A History of Seafaring* Thames & Hudson, London 1972.

The ship beneath Manhattan

DEAN, N. & SNOW, R. 'Manhattan's mystery merchant ship' *Wooden Boat* 63 (March/April 1985) 96–104.
RIESS, W. & SMITH, S.O. 'The Ronson Ship finds a good home' *Sea History* 37 (1985) 34–5.

9 MEN-O'-WAR AND PRIVATEERS (pp. 188–209)

The sea remembers Nelson

Further reading

GILLEY, W.O.S. *Narratives of Shipwrecks of the Royal Navy Between 1793 and 1849* Parker, London 1851.

MORRIS, R. *HMS Colossus* Hutchinson, London 1979.

THROCKMORTON, P. 'Ships wrecked in the Aegean Sea' *Archaeology* 17:4 (1964).
— 'Wrecks at Methone' *MM* 51:4 (1965).
—'The wreck of the *Nautilus*' Pp. 76–109 in the author's *Shipwrecks and Archaeology* Atlantic Monthly Press, Noston: Gollancz, London, 1970.

Further reading

COLLEDGE, J.S. *Ships of the Royal Navy: an Historical Index* in 2 volumes, David & Charles, London 1969 and 1970.

HOWARTH, D. *Trafalgar: the Nelson Touch* Collins, Glasgow 1974.

MASEFIELD, J. *Sea-Life in Nelson's Time* Methuen, London 1905.

Privateers, not pirates

194 A license granted by a state to a private citizen to arm a ship and seize merchant vessels of another nation.

Further reading

BOATMER, M.M. *Biographical Dictionary of the American War of Independence,* entries for 'Penobscot' and 'Saltonstall', Cassell, 1973.

CHAPELLE, H. *The Baltimore Clipper* Bonanza Books, New York.

Napoleon's guns

Further reading

WACHSMANN, S. & RAVEH, K. 'Underwater work carried out by the Israeli Department of Antiquities' *IJNA* 9 (1980) 256–64.

Naval wrecks from the Great Lakes

CAIN, E. *Ghost Ships* Beaufort Books, New York and Toronto 1983.

10 THE TWILIGHT OF SAIL (pp. 210–219)

The clipper ship

216 There are perhaps 20 main permutations of how these sails are handled from the deck, the crew needing to know the location of some 15 different ropes and wires, and able to deal with them under any circumstance.

216 Waterman was never again given command of a ship, and became a revivalist minister. There is a famous story of how he boarded a ship in San Francisco, loaded with tracts, to find three *Challenge* veterans among the crew. They threw him overboard and were trying to drown him with poles when the harbor police arrived. Unlike so many of his contemporaries in the clipper trade, Waterman died in his bed, in 1884, at the age of 76.

216 Studding sails outside the regular square sails, water sails under the regular studding sails, passarees boomed outward 30 feet from the ends of the foreyards, and "Jimmy greens" under the bowsprit. Some carried moonsails as well.

Further reading

BATHE, B. & VILLIERS, A. *The Visual Encyclopedia of Nautical Terms Under Sail* Crown, New York: Trewin Copplestone, London, 1978.

CHAPELLE, H.I. *The History of American Sailing Ships* New York 1935.
— *The Search for Speed Under Sail* Allen & Unwin, London 1968: Norton, New York 1967.

CUTLER, C. *Greyhounds of the Sea* Halcyon Press, New York 1930.

FINCH, R. *Coals from Newcastle* Lavenham 1973.

LUBBOCK, B. *The China Clippers* Brown & Ferguson, Glasgow 1946.

MACGREGOR, D.R. *Clipper Ships* Argus Books, Watford 1979.

VILLIERS, A. *The Cutty Sark* Hodder & Stoughton, London 1953.
—*The War with Cape Horn* Hodder & Stoughton, London 1971.

11 THE FUTURE OF THE PAST (pp. 220–227)

Future sites

Global climatic patterns and the Coriolis force cause large areas of oxygen-depleted water to accumulate off the west coasts of South and North America (from Mexico to Alaska), off West Africa, and in the China Sea. See:
DESMAISONS, D.J. & MOORE, G.T. 'Anoxic environments and oil source-bed genesis' *Association of Petroleum Geologists Bulletin* 64:8 (August 1980).

Deepwater salvage and archaeology

223 Gilley's *Shipwrecks of the Royal Navy* reports that between 1793 and 1850, 372 naval ships were lost by "mishap". Of these, 78 foundered at sea, usually with all hands.

225 The Sea of Marmara is of course in Turkish waters, and some arrangement would have to be made with that country before an archaeological project could be considered. A Black Sea search would involve prior negotiations with Turkey, the Soviet Union, Romania and Bulgaria.

225 This scheme was in fact used by the CIA to recover parts of a Soviet submarine from very deep water.

225 Ships or other objects recovered would become the property of the adjacent country for it to display, and perhaps share, by sending artifacts on traveling exhibitions. But the objective of this kind of work is the understanding of ancient civilizations; the examination and analysis of nearly any ancient ship would contribute substantially to that.

Further reading

BALLARD, R.D. & MICHEL, J-L. 'How We Found Titanic' *Nat. Geo.* 168:6 (December 1985).

BASCOM, W. *Deep Water, Ancient Ships.* Doubleday, New York; David & Charles, Newton Abbot, 1976.

Glossary

Nautical terms
(terms marked * are in the index)

aft behind or near the stern of a vessel

after relating to that part of a vessel which lies in or towards the stern

alla sensile rowing with one person on each oar

amidships the middle of the ship lengthwise or crossways

***artemon** a steering sail at the bow of a Greek or Roman ship

athwartships from one side of the ship to the other; at right angles to the keel

a scaloccio rowing with three to five people on each oar

ballast heavy material placed low in a ship's holds to lower her center of gravity and provide greater stability when carrying little or no cargo

beak-head the ship's head forward of the forecastle, forming a small deck over the stem

beam maximum width of a vessel; one of many thick strong timbers stretching across a vessel from side to side, firmly connected to the frames by knees

bilges cavities between a ship's sides and keel where water tends to collect

bitts strong wooden or metal uprights used for securing moorings and other heavy lines

bolt-rope rope sewn round the edge of a sail to prevent the canvas tearing

boom a spar to which is attached the foot of a fore-and-aft sail

bow the forward part of a ship's side, from the point where the planks curve inwards to where they meet at the stem

bowline line attached to the leech rope of a square sail, and used to hold its weather side forward and steady, enabling the ship to sail as close to the wind as possible

bowsprit large spar projecting over the stem and carrying sail forward; also principal support of the foremast

brails small ropes for attaching furled sails to a spar or boom; also used on early ships for shaping sails

***bulkhead** vertical partition between two decks of a ship, running either lengthwise or crossways, dividing the ship into compartments

calk to make the seams between planks watertight by driving fiber into them and covering with pitch or resin

castle a tower or defensive position on the deck of a ship

***carvel-built** said of a vessel whose planks run fore and aft and are laid edge-to-edge

carvel joint joint in which the two members are flush (butt-joint)

cleat piece of wood or metal with two projecting horns around which ropes can be secured

clench to bend over and pound down a bolt or nail

***clinker-built** said of a vessel whose planks run fore and aft, with the lower edge of one plank overlapping the edge of the plank below

clinker-joint joint in which the two members overlap

close to the wind sailing as nearly as possible towards the compass point from which the wind is blowing

counter arched section curving upwards and aft from the wing transom to the bottom of the stern above

cross-beam heavy section of timber running across the bitts in the bows of a vessel

draft or **draught** the depth of water displaced by a vessel

fluke triangular flattened barb at the end of an anchor arm which engages the sea-bottom

fore in the forward part of a vessel; towards the stem

fore and aft running lengthwise from the stem of a vessel to its stern

fore-and-aft sail a sail set on gaffs or stays along the line of the keel

forecastle the forward part of the upper deck, extending from the beak-head to the foremast or just aft of it; the seamen's quarters in merchant ships

foremast the forward mast in a vessel with two or more masts

forward relating to part of ship which lies in or towards the bows and stem

frame one of the curved crossways members of a ship's internal skeleton, branching outward and upward from the keel, determining the shape of the hull, and providing a framework for the side-planking

freeboard the distance between the waterline and the upper deck of a ship

futtock middle section of a frame

gaff spar to which the head of a four-sided fore-and-aft sail is attached

garboard strake the first strake laid along a vessel's bottom next to her keel

gudgeon metal clamp bolted to the stern post

gunwale upper edge of a ship's side

half deck a deck above the main deck which does not continue the whole length of the vessel

head the front or fore part of a vessel, including the bows

helm the apparatus by which the ship is steered, consisting of the rudder, tiller and steering wheel

***hogging** the result of stress on a ship's hull causing her to droop at stem and stern while her middle arches

hogging truss a cable run fore and aft to prevent hogging

jib triangular sail set on a stay before the foremast, extending from the jib-boom or bowsprit

jib-boom a spar extending from the bowsprit and taking a forward stay and the foot of the forward jib

Jimmy green four-sided fore-and-aft sail set under the bowsprit and jib-boom by clippers in light airs

keel the principal and lowest length of timber in a ship, running fore and aft, and attached to the frames

keelson the length of timber fixed above and to the keel

kerling the mast-step in Viking ships

knee an angled member, generally used to connect the beams of a ship with her sides and frames

lapstrake see *clinker-built

***lateen sail** a long triangular sail, typical of Mediterranean and Indian Ocean shipping, attached by its foremost edge to a long yard hoisted at an angle to the mast

leech the side edges of a square sail; the after edge of a fore-and-aft sail

leech rope vertical section of the bolt-rope, usually sewn to the leech

leeward away from the wind; on the side sheltered from the wind

loft to lay out a full-scale working drawing of the lines of a vessel's hull

lower mast bottom part of the mast, erected upon the keel

mainmast principal mast; chief mast in a two-masted vessel; center mast in a three-masted vessel; second mast from forward in others

mast-step a socket or framework, usually mounted on the keelson, which takes the heel (lower end) of the mast

midships see amidships

mizzenmast the mast directly aft of the mainmast

moonsail fineweather sail set above a skysail

orlop deck lowest deck in a warship, laid over the beams of the hold

outrigger a framework extending beyond the ship's sides, used in a trierēs to lend additional support to the oars

passaree rope used to haul out the lower corner of a studding sail along the studding sail spar

pintle vertical bolt at the back of the rudder which lifts into a gudgeon on the stern post to form a hinge

poop, poop-deck highest and aftmost deck of a ship

port left-hand side of a ship, looking forward

prow the pointed stem of a ship

rabbet deep groove or channel cut into a piece of timber to receive the edge of a plank

ribs the curved frames of a ship

rider additional, interior frame mounted inside a ship's hold alongside a main frame and bolted to it

***rigging** the system of ropes and wires used to support the masts and yards (the standing rigging) and to operate the sails (the running rigging)

royal a sail set above the topgallant sail

scantlings square-sectioned pieces of timber; the hull structure of a vessel as a whole

scarf a lapped timber joint; to join the ends of two pieces of timber by tapering or bevelling so that they overlap without any increase in thickness

shank the shaft forming the principal

part of an anchor, connecting the fluke-arms to the stock

skysail a square sail set above the royal

spar a rounded length of timber such as a yard, gaff or boom

square-rigged said of a vessel rigged with square-sails

square-rigger a square-rigged ship

square sail a four-cornered sail set on a yard athwartships

standard knee large angled piece of timber with one arm bolted horizontally to a beam, the other to the ship's side

starboard right-hand side of a ship, looking forward

stays strong ropes supporting the mast

stem upright component uniting the sides of a vessel at its fore end

stem post strong timber forming the foremost part of a ship's frame, rising from the keel; in large ships it is made up of several pieces of wood scarfed together

stern the rear end of a vessel

stern post vertical timber holding rudder mounted on aft end of keel

stock crosspiece fitting at the top of an anchor's shank at right angles to the plane of the arms

strake continuous row of planking running fore and aft along ship's side

stringer longitudinal member of a ship's structure, running fore and aft across the frames

studding sail light auxiliary sail set outboard on spars on either side of a square sail

tabernacle housing in which a mast may be set up and lowered on a deck

thole wooden or metal pin or peg inserted singly or in pairs in a vessel's gunwale to hold and guide an oar

thwarts planks set athwartships in a boat serving as seats for rowers; the ends of the thwarts rest on stringers

tiller wood or iron bar fitted to the head of the rudder in order to move it from side to side and so steer the ship

tingle lead or copper patch

topgallant mast a mast on square-rigger above a topmast; third part of a complete mast

topgallant sail a sail set on a yard of a topgallant mast

topmast mast mounted above lower mast; second part of a complete mast

transom one of the beams fastened across the stern post, strengthening the stern and giving it shape

treenail or **trenail** a cylindrical wooden pin or dowel used to fasten a ship's planks to its frames

wales a number of strong planks extending along the entire length of a ship's side at different heights, reinforcing the decks and forming the distinctive curves of the ship

water sail small fairweather sail sometimes set under the lower studding sail

weather side the side of a vessel towards which the wind is blowing

yard large spar mounted across a mast in order to carry sails

Types of ship

baghla Arabian *dhow with arched transom stern and elongated stem surmounted by plain knob

barque sailing ship of three or more masts having the foremasts rigged square and the aftermast rigged fore-and-aft

barquentine sailing ship of three or more masts rigged square on the foremast and fore-and-aft on the others

boom Arabian or Iranian ocean-going *dhow, sharp-sterned

brig two-masted square-rigger

brigantine two-masted sailing ship, rigged square on the foremast and fore-and-aft with square topsails on the mainmast

caravel two- or three-masted sailing ship with broad beam, high poop-deck, and lateen rig; used by Spanish and Portuguese in 15thC and 16thC

carrack a galleon sailed in the Mediterranean as a merchantman in the 15thC and 16thC

clipper fast sailing ship with concave bow, fine lines and raked masts

cog medieval clinker-built vessel characterized by fore and aft castles; used as warship and cargo-carrier

composite ship ship constructed of timber with iron or steel framing

coracle small roundish boat made of water-proofed hides stretched over a wicker frame

curragh boat with skin-covered frame

dhow lateen-rigged Arab sailing vessel with one or two masts, usually raked

dromon Byzantine war-galley

frigate medium-sized square-rigged warship of 18thC and 19thC

galleon large sailing ship with three or more masts, lateen-rigged on the after masts and square-rigged on the foremast and mainmast; used as a warship or trader from 15thC to 18thC

galley ship propelled by oars or sails used in ancient or medieval times as a warship or trader

gallias three-masted lateen-rigged galley used as a warship in the Mediterranean from 15thC to 18thC

iron ship ship built of iron instead of timber; increasingly common in course of 19thC

junk European name for wide range of one- to three-masted Chinese sailing cargo vessels employed on river and sea, and also in specialized form as warships, pirate and fishing vessels

knarr broad-beamed Scandinavian cargo vessel

lighter small flat-bottomed boat used in port for transporting cargo between ship and quay

longship Viking warship, long and narrow, equipped with oars and often with a sail

merchantman a cargo ship

mtepe East African coastal *dhow (now extinct)

packet vessel transporting goods, passengers or mail over a regular route

pentecontor 50-oared ship

qarib open Arab vessel

schooner sailing vessel with at least two masts, with all lower sails rigged fore-and-aft

square-rigger a square-rigged ship

tesseracontor 40-oared ship

triacontor 30-oared ship

trireme Roman war-galley

trierēs Greek war-galley with three banks of oars on each side

Archaeological terms

amphora storage jar, usually large, plump in shape, and with a narrow mouth and two handles

angon throwing spear

aryballos (plural aryballoi) small jar for oil or perfume, globular in form, with a narrow neck and single handle

beaker pottery drinking vessel deep in comparison with its diameter, normally without a handle

bronze alloy of copper and tin, the optimum proportion being about 9 parts copper to 1 part tin

Bronze Age period between the Stone and Iron Ages (c.4500–1100BC in the Middle East) when tools and weapons were mainly made of bronze

caldron large metal bowl for cooking purposes, usually round, with a flanged rim and three or four handles for supporting it over a fire

dolium large ceramic storage vessel

Dorians a group of people recorded in Greek tradition as invading southern Greece from the north around 1100BC

Helladic period Greek Bronze Age

Hellenistic period from the death of Alexander the Great (323BC) to the defeat of Antony and Cleopatra (30BC)

Iron Age period after the Bronze Age, from about 1100BC to AD40 in Europe, when tools and weapons were made mainly of iron

krater a large open two-handled bowl used for mixing wine

Minoans people of *Bronze Age Crete

Peoples of the Sea a group of peoples of mixed (and highly debated) origin who attempted to overthrow and settle in Egypt in the 13thC–12thC BC

pithos (plural pithoi) large pottery jar for the storage of oil or grain

Saxon Shore a system for defending the coasts of southeast England against raiding Anglo-Saxons; composed of a series of forts placed at strategic sites from the Wash to the Solent

***sgraffito* ware** ceramic objects decorated in such a way that the top layer of glaze is incised with a design to reveal parts of the ground

tessera small square-sectioned block of tile, stone or glass set in cement to form part of a mosaic

Index

Page numbers in *italic* refer to illustrations and captions.

ACKNOWLEDGMENTS

The publishers would like to thank all the archives, agencies and individuals who helped to provide images for this book, including the following: David Collison, Ole Crumlin-Pedersen, Reg Vallintine, Reinder Reinders, Nic Fleming, Honor Frost, Professor T. Save-Soderbergh, Herzog Anton-Museum, S.S. Great Britain Trust, Staff of the National Maritime Museum Greenwich, Staff of the British Museum and British Library.
Credits are keyed as follows: t top; b bottom; c center; l left; r right.

Alinari 148
American Philosophical Society 18
Ancient Art and Architecture Collection 8cl, 17r, 19cb, 39t, 54br
National Archaeological Museum of Athens 37, 41bl
Willard Bascom 225cb, 225br
G Bass 88, 89tc, 89bc, 89br
Bodrum Museum/O Alpozen 23bc
Mensun Bound 42(3), 43(3), 51(2), 64c, 68, 69cl, 69bl, 70(2), 71(2), 80bl
Bridgeman Art Library 201c
British Library 141cr
British Museum 25bl, 31ct, 44cr, 115tr, 116br, 119bl, 120, 121(3), 191cl, 191br
Cutty Sark Trust 216
Museum of Classical Archaeology, Cambridge 47bl
Bill Curtsinger/Nat. Geographic 33(3)
Christopher Daniel 11cl
Danish National Museum 136, 138–9
Nicholas Dean 96t, 98cr, 98br, 133cr, 133bc, 212t, 213cl, 213cr, 213b
D D Denton 175br
C M Dixon 78r, 114, 115tl, 115cl, 120cb
C Doumas 40, 41cl
Field Museum of Natural History, Chicago 92
Hanni Efroni 83c
Angela Evans 113
J A Foex 8bl, 65b
Werner Forman Archive 108, 124, 125, 127br
Greater London Photograph Library 141br
Jeremy Green 154br, 160, 161(3), 162, 163, 164, 165(5), 167(3), 169tl, 169tr, 169bl, 169br
Susan Griggs Agency/Adam Woolfitt 11cr, 12bl, 100br, 103b
Haifa University/E Linder 46

Sonia Halliday 21, 31tr
Hamilton-Scourge Foundation/Ian Morgan 206, 209br, 224, 225cl
Hamilton-Scourge Foundation 207(2), 208, 209
Robert Harding Picture Library 13cr, 149br, 154cl, 154bl
Kim Hart 91tl
Michael Holford 93br, 118bl, 119c, 119br, 127t, 127cl, 132–3
Irish Tourist Board 109br
Israel Dept. Antiquities and Museums 81, 82(3), 83bl, 83br, 203(3), 204(2), 205(3)
Kalmar County Museum/Nils Aukan 151tl
Kalmar County Museum/Lars Einarsson 151tr
Kalmar County Museum/Gösta Sörensen 151bl, 151br
G Kapitän 84, 85cl
S Katzev 55c
M Katzev Cover, 55(3), 57, 58, 59(3)
Louvre/Giraudon 45c
National Archaeological Museum of Madrid 45b
By permission of the Masters and Fellows of Magdalene College Cambridge 142, 147b
Mansell Collection 65cl
The Mariners Museum 185, 186, 187(3)
Colin Martin 133t, 147tr, 149cl, 150(2), 151
Mary Rose Trust 144, 145(3)
J Mayor 38
Nat. Museums and Galleries on Merseyside 112
S Morrison/M Fiennes 47br
Pierpont Morgan Library 126
Estate of Keith Muckelroy 169cr
National Geographic Magazine 12br
National Maritime Museum 11br, 96–7, 100cr, 139t, 171br, 191bl, 202, 217
Nigel O'Gorman 14cr
Univ. Museum of National Antiquities Oslo 122, 123bl
Parks Canada Conserv. Div. 105cr, 105br
Peabody Mus. Salem 99
Planet Earth Pictures/H C Heap 23t
Planet Earth Pictures/Menuhin 16
Planet Earth Pictures/Christian Petron/DIAF 8cr, 9, 67(2), 69br, 80br, 149tl
Planet Earth Pictures/Flip Schulke 181cl
C Pulak 91t, 91c, 91bl, 91br
Reproduced by gracious permission of Her Majesty the Queen 97
Rijksdienst voor de Ijsselmeerpolders 139cr
San Francisco Maritime Museum 215
SCALA 41t, 41cr
Tim Severin 110, 156

Sheffield City Museums 118cr
John Smith 211
K C Smith 177, 180(2), 181br, 182b
R C Smith 184(2)
Snow Squall Project/Nicholas Dern 212t
Sutcliffe Gallery 10
David Switzer 195(3), 198, 199, 200, 201b
Texas Antiquities Committee 176(2), 182l
Peter Throckmorton 14cr, 15(2), 22, 24, 25br, 27(2), 28, 31rcb, 31cl, 36, 66, 74, 75(2), 76(2), 77(3), 80c, 85br, 91cl, 94, 95, 100t, 105bl, 190(2), 212b, 213, 214, 218, 219(3)
Vasa Museum Stockholm 104(2), 149tr
Philip Voss 194
Welsh Folk Museum 109bl
West Stow Anglo-Saxon Village 115br
Woods Hole Oceanographic Institution 13bl, 222, 223(2)
York Archaeological Trust 129(3)